MW00325725

Elin is somewhat older than I am, bu
European history have marked us as
are wartime children, the war and t.
memories. Elin writes about us, but also to us, writes our story, the story of
a childhood partly spent in bomb shelters, fleeing from place to place, finding refuge in houses of friendly strangers. It's a story of helplessness and
despair, but also a story of obstinate determination to survive and to preserve what is perhaps the most valuable—the memory, be it written as
Grandfather's papers or unwritten, as the experiences of a child thrown into
the tragic turbulence of the war and state terror.

Jaan Kaplinski
Estonian poet, philosopher, and culture critic.

A latecomer to modernity and a small country from a boundary region of
Europe which was doomed to become the playground of Europe's powers,
Estonia is much more than merely a statistical unit. Like two other Baltic
States, Latvia and Lithuania, it comes with a rich perspective on modern
history. An imaginative historian or story-teller would always be tempted to
take Estonia as a protagonist when dealing with the history of the twentieth
century which was so unkind to the Baltic region. The emergence of the
Baltic States in 1918 was nothing short of a miracle. The miracle didn't last
long, though. In 1940 the Baltic States were occupied and annexed by the
Soviet Union. In 1941 they were invaded by Nazi Germany, which resulted in
the disastrous and nearly total extermination of Baltic Jews. In 1945 Estonia
and its two sisters in fate and misery were repeatedly occupied and annexed
by the Soviet Union and disappeared from the political map of the world
until the collapse of the Soviet Union. Yet what always remains lost in translation is human grief, loss of childhood, and pain of discontinuity. Then we
can only rely on our powers of memory and the sense of belonging. Elin
Toona Gottschalk's brilliant book comes as the best proof of this simple, albeit frequently forgotten, truth.

Leonidas Donskis
Professor, Member of the European Parliament, a philosopher, political theorist, historian of ideas, social analyst, and political
commentator.

A graphic but serene and compassionate account of the real world. By una-
voidable adult-mediated factors Elin is cast to prioritize her natural wishes
to not relinquish her childhood against the compelling need to prematurely
become an adult. An admirable book about World War II and its invisible
sequelae.

Mai Maddisson.
Psychiatrist, painter, and editor of *When the Noise Had Ended: Geis-
lingen's DP Children Remember.*

A richly detailed, unsentimental memoir of a schoolgirl, torn from home and thrust into the brutal and cynical vortex of World War II, in a time when love, hope, and motherland seemed like childish illusions.

Priit J. Vesilind.
Writer and photographer, formerly a senior writer for the *National Geographic Magazine.*

Elin and I met in America, in 1989. We were two Estonian writers, almost the same age but carrying a past that was formed in diametrically opposed political and cultural environments, in diverse corners of the globe, and we could have remained strangers. We had nothing in common during our formative years or as adults, the same can be said for what our mothers lived through. Exile had hopelessly separated our two worlds. Yet we recognized each other! For that we had to go back two lost generations. Elin was moved to tears while reading my poems dedicated to my grandmother and so was I by her books about her grandmother. It was our grandmothers' Estonian soil which connected us. There were two generations of anchorless exiles scattered worldwide...

Viiu Härm.
Estonian actress, writer and poet.

Elin Toona is an Estonian émigré writer who has the enviable skill of turning her life story into a moving and absorbing book. She has written several in Estonian and this one, in English, is a bumper volume of densely filled pages. But what a life! Elin is an excellent observer and her detailed descriptions are a joy to read. The reader is drawn to the child whose discoveries and perceptions are both matter of fact and fun. Elin Toona's story is fascinating and the reader is bound to find the book interesting.

John Kelday

Elin Toona Gottschalk's book is not just her family's saga. She writes touchingly and intimately about our country Estonia and the fate of its people during a time of difficult and complicated choices. This was a painful period in Europe when people had to flee hostile foreign powers that occupied their homelands. She describes how hard it was for her family to begin a new life far from home with only the knowledge and skills that they had brought with them. They realized that they had to survive these trying times and to maintain their confidence in the future. This family's story is also the story of Europe before the end of the war and the difficult years that followed. A movingly written and empathetic book inspiring hope.

Toomas Hendrick Ilves
President of the Republic of Estonia

INTO EXILE:
a life story
of war and peace

Elin Toona Gottschalk

A shorter version appeared as one of fifteen life stories in the book *Carrying
Linda's Stones: An Anthology of Estonian Women's Life Stories,* Tallinn University Press, Tallinn, Estonia.

This book was previously published by Lakeshore Press and has been updated
and re-released under a new publisher for this printing.

Published by Evershine Press, Inc.
1971 W Lumsden Rd #209
Brandon, FL 33511

Print book ISBN 978-0-9895661-3-1
eBook ISBN 978-0-9895661-4-8

Printed in the United States of America

ACKNOWLEDGEMENTS

My heartfelt thanks to Estonian writer Enn Nõu for his assistance with Estonian history, past and ongoing, as this small country struggles to keep its independence and its fighting spirit alive.

Some names in the book have been changed because there is no need for any shadow to fall upon the descendents of a past generation whose behavior was consistent with the times. Just because "we know better" now, does not mean we would have behaved differently had we been in their shoes.

I dedicate this book
to my mother Liki Toona,
my grandmother Ella Enno,
my husband Don Gottschalk,
my son Tim Gottschalk,
my grandchildren Max and Kemi
and to all the World War II refugees
who were unable to return home after
the war and became lifelong exiles.

TABLE OF CONTENTS

ESTONIA: THE COUNTRY

Estonia is the northern-most of the three Baltic Countries referred to as the Baltic States. The other two are Latvia and Lithuania. Estonia (18,370 sq. miles) is bordered to the north by the Gulf of Finland, to the east by Russia, and to the west by the Baltic Sea. Estonians are ethnically and linguistically closest to Finns. Both belong to the Finno-Ugric peoples who settled the present area around 5000 B.C.

Estonia has always been under siege by its more powerful neighbors Danes, Swedes, Poles, Germans and Russians.

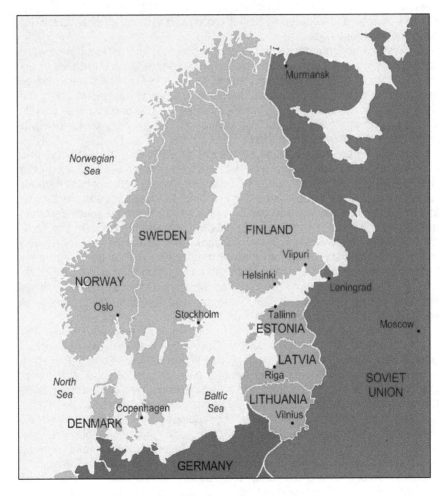

Northern Europe

Following the Russian February Revolution of 1917 Estonian units put together an adequate fighting force and defeated the Bolsheviks in the Estonian War of Liberation. This gave Estonia its first chance at self-government and the independent Republic of Estonia was proclaimed in Tallinn on 24 February 1918.

The first period of Estonian independence was, however, short lived, lasting only until 1940. On 23 August 1939 a non-aggression pact was signed by foreign ministers Ribbentrop of Germany and Molotov of the Soviet Union which contained secret provisions fatal to Estonia. Basically, Hitler and Stalin divided Eastern Europe between them into so-called spheres of influence. Finland, Estonia, Latvia, Lithuania, Romania and eastern parts of Poland were given to the Soviets to do with as they pleased. It was the first step towards complete Soviet occupation. By 17 June 1940, the Republic of Estonia was completely occupied by Soviet troops and had lost all characteristics of an independent state.

Arrests of government leaders and the political and national elite were followed by the murder and deportation of thousands upon thousands of ordinary citizens. In one single night alone, 14 June 1941, 14,890 men women and children were rounded up and deported to Siberia, but this was only the beginning of the national suffering. During three occupations—Soviet, German, and again Soviet—Estonia lost about 20 percent of its pre-war population of just over 1.1 million.

In 1941 when the Germans attacked the USSR they pushed east and north, occupying Estonia from July 1941 until September 1944. Although the Germans also arrested and murdered Estonians, mostly communists and their supporters, they were regarded as "liberators." The Germans and the Estonians had a common enemy and the Germans were able to persuade Estonian men to fight alongside them, albeit, only in German uniforms. All the Estonians wanted to do was keep the Russians from returning to Estonia and thereby to regain their freedom from both oppressors. They had no interest in the German agenda. What the Nazis did on Estonian soil had nothing to do with the Estonian people or the Estonian government because there was no Estonian government, only a German-appointed "quisling" government, as was then common in occupied territories.

The Jews who lived in Estonia before the war had religious freedom and had established roots in the country. They even honored Estonia with a *Golden Book Certificate*, presented by the Jewish National Fund in Palestine in 1927, "in appreciation of the benefit of a unique cultural autonomy, granted by Estonia to its national minorities." During the German occupation the Jews suffered greatly and most were murdered or deported.

With the defeat of Germany, the Soviet occupation resumed its previously interrupted program of Russification. Arrests, shootings, and deportations continued. The Soviet plan was simple. They had already implemented it in Armenia, Georgia, Dagestan, Azerbaijan, Turkestan, Chechnia among others—to clear the country of its ethnic peoples and replace them with Russians—and as quickly as possible, before the rest of the world realized what is happening.

The world should have known as early as 1941, when the hastily retreating Russians left behind photographs of mass graves and documents outlining their long-term agenda. Churchill told Roosevelt about it in a letter dated 7 March 1942 yet the West bought Stalin's lie because it had not yet grasped the magnitude of his secret ambition to keep the countries that had only been ceded to him temporarily during the course of the war.

Before the collapse of the German front in 1944, Estonian units fought a losing battle against the advancing Russians, but their brave resistance gave tens of thousands of Estonians time to flee to the West.

About 80,000 citizens who would otherwise have become victims of the second Soviet occupation were able to flee. My mother, grandmother and I were among them.[1]

---

[1] *Estonia, Story of a Nation,* Published under the patronage of special Commemoration Committees in the United States and Canada, 1974. *The White Book, Losses Inflicted On The Estonian Nation by Occupation Regimes 1940-1991.* Estonian Encyclopedia Publishers, 2005.

INTO EXILE:

a life story
of war and peace

PROLOGUE

THE PROMISED LAND
London 1970

---

91 YEAR OLD ATTACKED IN HER LONDON FLAT

When the victim's daughter came home from work on Wednesday, October 27, she found her 91-year-old mother unconscious and bloody. Her handbag nearby had contained £7. It was empty, but she was still clutching a bloody pound note in her fist. The daughter called the ambulance and the police. It was discovered that the flat next door had also been broken into. The glass door panel was shattered. The next day, after Mrs. Enno recovered from the shock of the beating, the police put together her story and concluded that she had heard a noise in the corridor and had opened her door to investigate. She had thought it was the milkman. When she opened the door she was set upon by a man using his fists. He threw her to the floor and forced his way into the flat. He saw her handbag and emptied it, dropping a pound note on the floor. Mrs. Enno was left dazed and bleeding from her throat and nose. That was how her daughter found her.

The police suggested the robber had been a drug addict looking for ready cash. Mrs. Enno has recovered from the physical injuries, but not yet from the shock. It is hoped that because of her strong will to live and despite her being so far up in years,t the old lady will recover.[2]

"Come quickly!" Mother said over the telephone. "Our Mämmä has recovered physically, but is no longer as she was. There is still time for you two to be together."

I came as soon as I could. I was in the United States, where my husband was ill and my son was in school. I had anticipated and dreaded this summons for years, maybe for most of my adult life. I had seen it coming since Grandmother's handwriting deteriorated into a kind of secret cipher, more like Egyptian hieroglyphics. In her last letter I was barely able to make out the words, "Long live beauty and goodness!"

When Mother opened the door to their London flat on Finborough Road, she seemed like her old self, but I had learned early in life that nothing is, as it seems. People can smile when they are desperate. Mother always had the knack of seizing the moment for all of us. She had led us and dragged us physically through war-torn Germany. She and I had never been as close as

---

[2] Translation from newspaper *Eesti Hääl (Estonian Voice)* October 1970. Ella Enno was actually still a few weeks from her 91st birthday.

Grandmother and I, but I respected her and loved them both. It was only when Mother hugged me that I felt the tension. We were both about to lose a part of ourselves.

For Mothers and Grandmother's generations of Estonian exiles, the dream of a liberated homeland had once been real enough. I grew up beside them sharing their dreams and disappointments and because I was only seven years old when we fled Estonia, I could believe only what I was told and sometimes, things were definitely not as they appeared to be. For instance, "peacetime," a concept I had not experienced since I was two years old, was supposed to make my nightmares end, however when peacetime came, we all found ourselves stranded in it up to our knees—in everybody else's peacetime but our own.

When I married an American and moved to America I promised myself I would not become trapped in what most exiles have come to refer to as the refugee mentality. People who thought the Soviet Union would collapse in our lifetime were living in a dream, and my generation needed to move on. Of course we kept in touch. We honored our elders and recognized that while we still had our own lives, we retained our past and our national identity as Estonians, even while we lived in an English-speaking world where nothing of that past existed.

My husband and son could not speak Estonian. While Mother and Grandmother were alive my identity remained intact, but when they die, everything would die with them that could not be translated into English. One of Grandmother's friends gave me a book on Estonian history. She wrote on the flyleaf, "To dear Elin - don't ever forget your homeland or lose faith in Estonia regaining its independence." That was in the 1960s. The book was like a ball and chain on my conscience, always reminding me that Estonia was not just a country—it was an obligation.

I had been in London for a week, perched awkwardly on a corner of the spare mattress, close to Grandmother's feet, holding her hand and trying to hold on to everything I had ever treasured. Mother was my biological mother, but Grandmother was my life. When the waves broke over the side of the small boat in which we fled Estonia, I kept hold of her coat hem. In the Polish freighter that picked us up at sea she read to me to distract me from the planes shooting at us. During the saturation bombing in Berlin I had only to put my head in her lap to believe no bombs would fall on us. When the British authorities in Leeds separated us I resisted their efforts to train me for domestic service because they called my Grandmother a "bloody foreigner." They refused me an education and put me into a weaving shed at fifteen with other foreigners accused of trying to rise above their station. Exiled doctors became janitors; war heroes and professors were weaving carpets; teachers were scrubbing floors, and established *artistes* like Mother and Grandmother were berated for daring to look their "betters" in the eye. When I finally punched my way out of those postwar conditions and left for London, Grandmother cried as she kissed me, hugged me, and wished me well. I had never been afraid of death—only of losing Grandmother. Now I was panicked.

Grandmother was sitting serenely in her rocking chair, my hand firmly in her grip, but her gaze was constantly shifting away through the window,

2

towards the sky above the wet slate roof of the house across the street. Her physical wounds had healed, but the attack in 1970 had so shocked her system that it had begun to shut down. As Mother said, she was no longer as she was. Her spirit was pulling away in a new direction, towards the "eternities before and after" by which her husband, "dear Erni," the poet, had consoled the Estonian people for their lousy history.

When we left Estonia, Grandmother told me that we were like the Israelites, fleeing to the Promised Land. I had never been sure where that was. Mother thought it might be England. I had come to believe it was in heaven, but mostly it was "in the future," a land even further than dreams. When I was small I used to put my ear close to Grandmother's to hear what she was hearing and my cheek next to hers so I could see what she was seeing. She had always seen further than any of us, as she was now. The expression on her face told me she had found her future and that it was all she had hoped.

That future had always been an elusive goal. Mother with her Tarot cards and our "last-candle-on-Christmas-Eve" tradition, sitting in the darkened room around the Christmas tree, holding our breath, watching the last candle, hoping for a quiet blue flame and getting a red wick, spluttering sparks, and final flare-ups. Of course we never had anything but cheap candles. On a more hopeful note Grandmother would finish the ceremony by reading a prophetic verse from the Bible and finishing with "the light came out of the darkness," sealing our fate for another year.

What we were experiencing now was a last-candle moment. The future had arrived. Mother would remain in England. I had to return to America to a crisis that they did not know about. We had but minutes left.

Mother had already called the taxi.

We were speaking Estonian. Estonian was no longer my language. Every forgotten word I struggled for sounded strange to my ears. My voice was too loud. I was talking too much, chattering like some pesky person in the cinema, while other people were trying to follow events on the screen. I heard myself repeating phrases that were no longer relevant, going over events that had resolved themselves long ago, when the moment actually called for quiet. Time to surrender to silence, to fate, and to God's will.

Mother had gone to sit by the window on her padded *pouffe*. She was smoking as always. Grandmother was wearing her old slippers and "dear Erni's" prayer shawl under which he used to meditate and keep warm. He spent all his income as a school inspector on books and had very little left over for firewood. He died of pneumonia in Estonia when he was fifty-eight years old. Mothers and Grandmother's room in London was also cold. The central heating was acting up. The owners of the buildings could not put old people into the street, but they could freeze them out.

Having spent so much time in one-room rentals, we respected silence. I complied. Besides, I had run out of words. Instead, I was thinking about my own future and what it would mean to lose my Estonian-self forever. Mother would take care of it for a while, but she, too, was not well. I knew I would see Mämmä again in the "eternities" we had established long ago in our conversations, but what about my son? He would never be able to read his grandfather's poetry. Even the best translation is a poor cousin to the original.

3

Everything in this room existed only in our minds. A mindless body in the mirror is deaf and dumb. I would become a prisoner of memories, which would make for a terrible loneliness. Florida was not a land for poetry or Beethoven.

"Come to America," I had pleaded nevertheless.

"America is not for me," Mother always replied. She knew she was breaking my heart, but still shook her head. Washers, dryers, refrigerators, air conditioners. When I first told them I had a dishwasher, we rolled back on the beds laughing. My in-laws visited our flat in London and returned to America, appalled.

"Did you know they live in one room? They don't even have a vacuum cleaner!"

So much for poets and *artistes* from dead countries. America was as different from Mothers and Grandmother's world as the moon is from a pizza!

Not that England had been wonderful in the beginning. Definitely not the Promised Land, but it had made amends. Grandmother's letters were full of praise for the wonders of the welfare state.

"A woman comes once a month to cut my toenails. For nothing! I don't pay a penny. And they still ask if there is anything else I need? Shoes? A new coat? I've already got new reading glasses and new teeth! They even gave me £10 at Christmas to buy presents. Imagine, in this country you get paid for being old and poor!"

Whatever England had taken, it had given back.

Mother could see my turmoil. She got up and shoved the footstool to me so that I would be more comfortable. She went to sit on her bed where she continued to smoke. She had always been with us, but not always close. More often ahead. I had always been exclusively "Mämmä's child" and still was.

Grandmother had started rhythmically stroking my fingers—her way of telling me her journey would be no different from what we had already been through, only this time she was going on ahead instead of Mother. Her face was calm and her eyes the color of quiet waters that had covered the earth since it was created.

We continued to sit in silence until I heard Mother's mattress creak. With her slippered toe she had nudged my suitcase closer to the door. The taxi had stopped at the curb. I saw it, too. Last embraces, as in 1944, then "go with God!"

I believed we really had—gone with God.

4

Chapter 1

YESTERDAY WAS HISTORY
1939

Announcement of the German-Soviet Non-Aggression Pact stupefied the Allies and shattered the rose-colored glasses they had only lately put on.
Robert Leckie

On the shores of the Baltic, summers are brief, often cold and windy. The warm weather barely lasts a few weeks. Grandmother's summers lasted only a few days. When she did let me outside to play, she came to check my hair at intervals, to make sure it was not cold to the touch. Only seldom did she indulge my begging to go outside, even after the lagoon ice melted and the flood waters had receded into the sea. When Aunt Alma went to the wood-shed, I managed to slip out anyway with Grandmother right there after me. She brought me back to the porch where we stood facing the sea, taking deep breaths before the wind, sharp as a knife, cut our cheeks, but it was often long enough for me to smell spring in the air. The smell of Estonian spring grass stayed with me forever.

Grandmother, whom I called Mämmä, was always with me. We did everything together. She was a true artist and lived for her art, the way her sister Alma lived for her music.

Aunt Alma seldom paid attention to me; she was too busy to talk, always moving around the house and garden, chopping wood, hauling water, and tending her vegetable garden. When she worked Grandmother and I tried to help, but when we helped we got in her way. We were better off somewhere else, drawing pictures or painting, making up poems or going for long walks around Haapsalu's many bays and lagoons.

Grandmother and Aunt Alma believed in peace and quiet, and it was Mämmä's job to keep me out of trouble. Aunt Alma worked quickly, impatiently, constantly anxious to get back to her piano. If she was not helping a student go over the scales, she was practicing for her Sunday recitals at the *Kuursaal.*[3] Other times she just played for herself and let music fill the house. We lived quietly and harmoniously to the strains of Chopin, Beethoven, and Bach.

Then there was "dear Erni," Grandfather, who died young because he'd had a "poet's soul." Grandmother was the poet's widow.

Mother and Father were *artistes* - actors. They lived in Tallinn, in the theater, literally in their dressing room. Right after I was birthed by the midwife, Mrs.Takk at the Tallinn clinic, Mrs. Takk took Mother and me home

---

[3] A resort hall, concurrently a concert hall, restaurant, reading room and hotel.

with her where we lived with her and her three daughters until the new theater season began. As Mother could not keep me in the theater dressing room, I was given to Mämmä and Aunt Alma.

Liki Toona, Ella Enno, Elin, and Enn Toona, 1938.

I had no concept of "mothers and fathers," only of people whom I saw every day. At that time in my life relationships were meaningless. A true relationship was a face that on my seeing it, made me happy. A relationship, for me, was a name that upon hearing it, made me glad. When Grandmother first introduced me to her "dear departed Erni," it was in such a way that when I heard his name, I wanted to hear more. She had never lost her husband, but had only lost physical sight of him. He was always included in our activities. When we walked around the town's un-paved paths and narrow streets, my legs short, my Grandmother's old and tired, we always stopped by Grandfather's monument to rest on its base. When we sat down Grandmother never failed to greet her husband or exchange a few words with him. I had the distinct impression that he both heard and understood what she was saying.

When our legs were less tired and the weather was warm, we walked farther, to the cemetery where she tended his grave. We picked up dead leaves, raked the soil, and planted lilies-of-the-valley for Grandfather's birthday. A cherry tree grew over his grave, in accordance with his wishes, "so passers-by can admire the blossoms and birds can enjoy the cherries."

While we weeded I again became privy to their private exchange of pleasantries. It really was as though he were just around the corner or in another room. There did not seem much difference between a person hiding behind a wall, working in a theater in Tallinn, or being in the ground. I had already come to accept that the people I wanted to see most were the ones I was least able to touch, and cemeteries seemed to be where most of Grandmother's friends resided. We always greeted them when we passed their graves. I learned early that everything living lives its own life whether we

6

see it or not, and everyone has a life with me or without me. It seemed that we socialized more with people who were out of sight than with people we could see.

During cold weather, because I was not allowed outside alone, I spent a lot of time in the kitchen, sitting on the kitchen table while Grandmother was nearby, clattering pots and pans, stirring soup, boiling bed sheets, steeping snotty handkerchiefs, or just heating water to wash the dishes. This meant the window was constantly steamed and I had to clear a space on the misted glass to see what was going on outside. My view from the kitchen window was a limitless source of entertainment. As soon as we had finished breakfast, I climbed up on the table and pressed my nose to the glass.

Ernst Enno memorial, Haapsalu Evening Lagoon, 1938

The lagoon side of our house was more interesting than the street side. Besides, I was seldom allowed into the front room. The front room was full of furniture and small porcelain knick-knacks that fell to the floor and broke as soon as I approached them. The piano, too, was off limits. Fingerprints appeared out of nowhere, and when bread with jam fell on the floor it always fell jam side down. Another reason I was kept out of the living room was because the front door had no steps. Aunt Alma used a part of the house money to buy the piano and never got around to finishing the steps. A stool served the purpose nicely. Only the piano students used the front door to avoid coming through the kitchen. Anyone not warned or unaware of the missing steps ended up in the bushes.

Because of the long winters most of my memories are of snow. When the bay was frozen you could, theoretically, have walked right across the horizon to Sweden, but realistically only to the Swedish Estonian settlements joined to Haapsalu by a causeway. In the winter there was a constant flow of traffic across the ice. People pulled sleds and drove horse-drawn sleighs. Truckers used the shortcut until the ice began to melt. Always one truck fell through trying to make one last crossing.

The lagoon also had ice yacht races. Sometimes individual yachts raced each other and ended up crashing into our back fence. When it got dark, daylight only lasting a few hours in the winter, the skaters appeared. Colored lights were strung be-

Elin, 1938.

tween the trees, tinny music was piped in from the *Kuursaal,* and everybody seemed to be having a wonderful time. Kneeling on the kitchen table with my nose pressed against the cold glass, I envied the muffled skaters. I wished we had a Finnish chair sled instead of the ordinary sled Aunt Alma sometimes took me out on. We never went very fast or very far.

When the snow was not yet too deep, I followed Aunt Alma's colorful scarf bobbing between the snow banks, from the house to the woodshed. Our neighbor, Mr. Peterson, of Peterson's Boat Yard, let us use his well in the summer. After it became frozen he brought buckets of snow into the kitchen for us to melt on the stove. Mr. Peterson also shoveled the path to the woodshed and chopped the larger logs. He dropped the logs on the kitchen floor with a clatter and stayed for a hot cup of *chai*. Sometimes they used the word *chaijuhhu*. In our house everybody spoke a mixture of Russian, German, and Estonian, sometimes making up his or her own words. Grandmother said it reflected the unfortunate history of conquered peoples, but when Grandmother and Aunt Alma deliberately started speaking straight Russian or German I paid strict attention. It meant they did not want me to understand what they were saying.

Before Aunt Alma or Mr. Peterson had a chance to spoil the newly fallen snow, my cat Tondu had already left a carefully measured row of paw prints from the house to the roof of the woodshed. He sat there motionless for hours, looking out to sea. Tondu was also a poet and lived for peace and quiet.

Alma Saul

Summers were quite different. Once the new grass had greened, flowers bloomed, and our big trees had come into leaf, the Promenade sprang to life. Visitors began to arrive at Haapsalu's famous mud spa and Haapsalu's other attractions.

→ Haapsalu was a well-known resort at the turn of the century. The mud spa, which used radioactive mud, was founded in 1825. In the 19th century visitors came from all over Europe to seek a cure for their different ailments. The Romanovs arrived in their own private train. Czar Nicholas hoped the radioactive mud would cure the Czarevitch's hemophilia.

→ Another Haapsalu attraction was the "White Lady," whose ghostly image appears in the east window of the Dome Church during the August full moon. She remains there for a time, gazing wistfully across the heads of the spectators before dissolving into the glass. A trick, or a trick of the moonlight, no one has been able to determine although many have tried. Legend has it that when the castle-fortress was a bishop's palace in the 13th century, one of the resident knights fell in love with a local girl. He disguised her as a boy and smuggled her into the castle, but the bishop caught them and had them both immured into the castle walls. During excavations in the 1920s, workmen came across a sealed chamber and found a knight, perfectly preserved, sitting at a table, with his head in his hands. The introduction of air broke the hermetic seal and caused the figure to disintegrate into dust. The lady's remains have never been found, but it's hardly necessary when you can see her in person. She has not missed a date since 1279—over 700 years!

Haapsalu Promenade in the 1970s.

One Midsummer Night Grandmother took me to see the "White Lady." I was all excited until the lady finally appeared. Then I was hugely disappointed. She was just a woman in a long white nightgown, no different from my own Grandmother getting ready for bed.

A third attraction in Haapsalu was Tchaikovsky's Bench which was to the left of our back gate. The bench was dedicated to the composer after he and his twin brothers Anatol and Modest visited Haapsalu in the 1860s. During one of his visits Tchaikovsky completed his Sixth Symphony which includes an Estonian folk song, "Dear Mari." Tchaikovsky also wrote a piece for Haapsalu's "White Lady" and a short piece (Opus 2 No.3) called "Souvenir de Hapsal" (Memories of Haapsalu) dedicated to Vera Davōdov. Notes of the folk song were etched in copper into the backrest of the bench.

The spa clients were completely different from the ordinary people who shuffled purposefully along Haapsalu's unpaved streets—women carrying shopping baskets, wearing shawls, headscarves and muddy shoes, men in rubber boots, fishing nets slung over their shoulders.

The spa clients were also different from the usual summer visitors who rushed about or wobbled on rented bicycles on the way to the beach. The spa visitors never hurried. They were never loaded down with shopping. They promenaded with an open book in one hand or with a small dog trotting alongside on a leash. "The doggy is on a string, so doggy won't fall down," I told Grandmother importantly. She agreed it was so.

Many spa clients were wealthy foreigners who came seasonally or lived in the sumptuous villas around the bay. The Promenade had many names: Tchaikovsky's *allée*, Quiet Lagoon, Back Bay, and Chocolate Promenade—the last, I guessed, was because if you kept your eyes to the ground you could

9

find chocolate wrappers discarded by the visitors. The wrappers smelled delicious! I had never tasted chocolate, but knew I would recognize it by the smell, if I ever got some.

While the Promenade was a never-ending spectacle of unusual sights, there was one that disturbed me greatly.

"Mämmä, Mämmä, come look, a servant!" I called to Grandmother and insisted she come and look.

It was she who answered my questions about everything I wanted to know, and we had reasonings about why and because. I had wanted to know why some people were well-dressed and had shabbier individuals scurrying alongside them, like terriers, fetching and carrying their bags, picking up what they dropped, and sometimes not even getting a "thank you." Why couldn't the well-dressed people pick up their own handerchiefs? The ladies were the worst offenders. They shouted at these others, even when they hadn't done anything wrong.

There were many invalids also well-dressed, but obviously not able to walk. They relied on the people who were pushing their wheelchairs, mostly with great difficulty, the path being sand or mud. Yet the pushers still got yelled at when the chairs got stuck. I had never seen unkind people before. I wanted Grandmother to explain to me why the better-dressed people could not see that their helpers were doing their best.

When Grandmother came to look over my shoulder she sniffed and explained that the unfortunates were the "servants," who were paid to do things for others without being thanked, and anyone who yelled at their servants meant "new money."

After walking around the other bays Grandmother and I returned to ours and sat down for a final rest on Tchaikovsky's bench before turning into our back gate. Grandmother caught her breath or sketched a boat or ducks or something that caught her eye (she always had a pencil and pad in her coat pocket) while I traced my fingers along the composer's copper notes. I had been shown how to pick those notes out on the piano, but they never sounded as good as when Aunt Alma played them.

Alma Saul's house in Haapsalu, 1930s.

One early evening, while sitting on the bench sketching we heard tinny music from one of the villas. It was not as loud as the music from the *Kuursaal* and not piano music either. "What's that?" I asked.

"That's a 'grandmaphone'," Grandmother replied. At least that was what I thought she said.

Liki and Enn with friends on their wedding day, 1934.

Self-awareness came gradually, step by step, from another direction. It met me in the street and greeted me by name. To strangers I was Elin, to Mother and Father I was *Mussa,* and on the farm I was *Kaie.* For those people I also had pet names. *Mämmä* was my constant. The woman I was told was my mother I called *Mimma,* and the man who was an even rarer visitor was referred to as my father, whom I called *Taat.* Aunt Alma was *Tätä,* and "dear Erni," the Ernst Enno etched into the monument below his copper bust, was forever an endearing presence and the silent listener to our occasional joys and daily troubles. His stern gaze never wavered from the eternities about which he wrote. It was in those greetings, in the knowledge of seen and unseen friends and relatives that I, too, became somebody—an individual identified through the eyes of others (and in the mirror) as a member of a family. More importantly I was never alone. When I heard the clatter of dishes in the kitchen, when I was called to the dinner table, when Grandmother or Aunt Alma spoke to me while they went about their business—sometimes it was just a ribbon of light under a closed door where someone was reading, playing the piano, writing, or sketching—it assured me that I would be heard if I called, but what I really liked was when somebody came to sit on my bed. When their soft hands touched me and their gentle voice spoke lovingly, it informed me that I was also someone's beloved child.

Mother and Father were a mysterious couple. They appeared suddenly and departed just as suddenly. Mother was a popular actress specializing in juvenile ingénues; Father was an actor and later a producer. Mother and Father also lived for their art in a more brutal version of that term, refusing to compromise for family, while Grandmother and Aunt Alma compromised for me, for which I'm truly grateful.

Grandmother told me my parents were earning our daily bread. As we usually had a loaf of bread on the table, I made the connection and was grateful. I knew they were family, although they dressed like the people on

11

the Promenade, who came and went along with them from season to season. When they visited us it was "off season" and their presence was like a summer storm blowing through the house.

When Mother and Father's arrival was imminent I knew summer was not far away. Grandmother and Aunt Alma removed the double-glazing, threw the windows wide open, and began to sweep and dust. Doors slammed, curtains billowed, dead flies that had been trapped between the glass littered the floor, and you could smell the sea again, mixed with the smell of Mr. Peterson's newly tarred boats, upturned, drying, and ready for another rental season. Mr. Peterson was there, too, in his big rubber boots, pushing his wheelbarrow between the houses, clearing fallen branches, mending our fence, and stowing away our wooden planks until the next spring flood. He was "family" though he was not even a relative. He was the only real man we knew. The others were actors.

Mother and Father did not have a car, but someone always did. As soon as we heard a car horn Aunt Alma reared up in alarm and began to tear at her scarf and apron. Grandmother also jumped into action, grabbing handfuls of clothing off the backs of chairs, stuffing everything into drawers, under cushions and pillows, even as she moved towards the door. If there were still something on the floor, it was kicked under the bed or sofa. By the time the first high heels clattered onto the porch, Tondu had already leaped out of the nearest window. I would not see my cat again until the final slam of the gate and the last wave "good-bye!"

Elin and Mother in Haapsalu, winter 1943. Mother is wearing the dreaded snapping foxes.

Mother always arrived first. The women followed, skittering unsteadily on heels designed for city streets. The men came up behind, carrying overnight cases and hatboxes. One actress was famous for wearing a cape and monocle. She made large gestures and knocked things off the sideboard. Our house was too small for large gestures.

Mother always rendered me speechless. When she bent to kiss me I became paralyzed with shyness. Her feather boa tickled my nose. When I reached up to kiss her cheek, I was careful not to muss her hair or dislodge her hat, but what I was most scared of, were her silver foxes with their furry snouts full of sharp teeth. The first time I saw one I panicked and started screaming. My screaming must have scared Mother, too, because she never came that close to me again. That incident led to a permanently bad relationship between Mother's furs and me. The feather boas were friendlier because they lacked teeth.

Father also kissed my cheek. He always said, "My, you've grown." Sometimes he lifted me up, twirled me around, and put me down again. I didn't know what to say to him either. He then moved on to kiss Aunt Alma's hand and present her with a bottle. His friends also bowed and kissed Alma's hand,

12

for fun. Some received a playful slap in return. Everybody laughed and re-laxed the way adults always do when they no longer have to be polite.

Father's presence both thrilled and terrified me because he was never the same person twice. Sometimes he had dark hair, at other times his hair was blond. Once he wore a grey wig and said he was Beethoven. Another time he had a moustache, which he tore off with a flourish, causing alarm. I thought he had hurt himself. Another time he arrived wearing glasses, but when I touched them I discovered there were no lenses in them. Everybody laughed. I felt foolish. Grandmother told me later that Father's glasses were a prop, but that Mother's glasses were real. She kept them in her pocket and only took them out when she needed to see something important. She whipped them up to her nose, took a quick look around, and then put them away again. I guessed that was why she couldn't always see me right in front of her and often passed me as though I were not there.

Grandmother assured me my parents loved me—they were just very busy. She described how Father had been so excited to have me born that he was almost run over by a tram on his way to the clinic. Then he must have lost interest in me. I suspected it had to do with my squint. I was two years old when Father and I were in the garden and a neighbor's dog jumped on me from behind. I swiveled so abruptly that my eye muscles overstretched and never returned to normal. All I could remember of that accident was a lot of screaming, most of it my own, and shouting, Mother and Father blam-ing each other, and Grandmother putting me to bed with compresses across my eyes.

I forgot about it until sometime later when Father and I went to get a newspaper. We met a lady in the street who recognized him for the well-known actor he was. She bent down to me and said, "So this is your daugh-ter." She then drew back in shock and exclaimed in German, "*Aber sie schielt*!" I understood perfectly. "She is cross-eyed." The squint changed the way people spoke to me.

Wanting my parents to like me made me over-anxious and clumsy. I was so overwhelmed when they did actually speak to me that my brain got mixed up and I did things that made them angry. Sometimes Mother stopped me in mid-stride and rattled off a row of numbers for me to add up immediately. Snap, snap, she snapped her fingers. I became so scared that I could not even remember what she had said. On one visit she held a perfume bottle out for me to smell. I thought she wanted me to drink it. Another time she was showing off a dress with brown and white patches. "So what do you think?" she asked me. I told her she looked like grandma Tomson's cow, Betti.[4] Mother boxed my ears, but it was true. Betti was a beautiful cow with the same brown and white patches. Then one of the ladies asked me if I liked going to the farm. I told her I did because I liked to chase the cockroaches. Mother's face turned purple and I fled into the kitchen where I found Aunt Alma washing glasses and chopping vegetables.

---

[4] Father's parents were Jaan and Pauline Tomson.

**Elin and Mother in
Haapsalu garden,
summer 1944.**

When we had visitors she prepared dishes from our Danish cookbook. The pages and pictures were greasy and smelled delicious. I was usually given a taste of everything, but no more until the guests had eaten.[5]

The kitchen was a dangerous place when a formal dinner was being prepared. There were sharp knives every-where, pans bubbling and boiling over, wine glasses and breakables on every surface. As soon as Aunt Alma saw me, she ordered me to go pick some dill. She always said that when I was in the way. It meant, "Go find your grandmother."

Finding Mämmä was not difficult. I could hear her muttering on the porch, putting bouquets into vases. While cutting the stems her lips were pursed and her expression stern. Only I knew she didn't like cut flowers. "Leave them alone," she told me during our walks. "Even wildflowers have lives of their own. We have no right to take that from them." Her show of displeasure, mild as it was, eased my own feelings of guilt about my parents and their friends.

The only part of those visits that I enjoyed was the after-dinner music. Although I was not invited to eat with them and sulked over my plate in the kitchen, I kept my ears open for the sound of chairs being scraped back in the Blue Room. At the first surge of louder voices I rushed into the living room and snuggled into one of the big armchairs under the window. The visitors gathered around the piano. Because there were professional singers and pianists among them, they all sang and played, but I still thought Aunt Alma played best. I closed my eyes and leaned back. No "grandmaphones" at our house!

When the curtains began to billow and fill with music I began to weep. I didn't know why. People were dancing, like skaters on the lagoon. It was so beautiful! Grandmother also wept when she read poetry or saw a sunset, but when Mother saw me weeping, quietly she led me from the room and told Grandmother she was worried about my mental health. ⬅

They took me to the doctor. Mother told him they had noticed me making strange noises to music even before I was six months old. The doctor examined me, but found nothing wrong. "She has a vivid imagination," he told them.

Another time one of the actresses brought a huge bouquet of peonies. I fell in love with them. Only Grandmother and I knew that flowers could be unhappy. I promised the peonies that I would not let them die alone. I sat with them every day until they began to lose their petals. When death was

---

[5] In Europe at that time it was not customary for children to eat with adults. They ate in the kitchen or at their own "cat" table, referred to as the *katzentisch*.

14

imminent I became hysterical. After the death of the flowers I was forcefully removed from the living room and put to bed. Grandmother gave me valerian tea. Mother went on and on about my nerves, then suddenly slapped her forehead and had a brilliant idea. She thought they might have overlooked my musical talent.

I was taken to their theater in Tallinn. People made a fuss over me. Someone thumped on a piano and I was asked to repeat the notes. There was disappointment all round when it was discovered that I was tone deaf. I could not reproduce a single note. There was no hope of my becoming another Shirley Temple or of Mother convincing Father she had been right to keep me. (To this day I cannot sing, but I can tell when someone else is off-key.)

Despite their disappointment I spent the night with my parents. It had never happened before and never happened again. Mother slept in the bed, I slept on the couch, and Father stretched out on the floor next to the couch in case I fell off during the night. The next day Mother took me back to Haapsalu. My one opportunity to impress my parents had ended in disgrace.

Mämmä dismissed my tears. She put a big bowl of oatmeal in front of me and told me she could not care less whether I could sing or dance, as long as I could still make up poems and draw pictures. We found the poem I had written before going to Tallinn and spread it on the table so we could look at it critically, going over every word, especially the spelling and handwriting. We discussed proportions and meaning. The poem was about a fly with a thousand eyes, and it could see everything and everywhere at the same time. The drawing that went with it was of a big fly with eyes that resembled small windows. Everything in the room was reflected in each window, including the fly swatter. Grandmother praised my poem and drawing, though the paper was splotched with snot, milk, and oatmeal. After we left the table I looked back and saw Tondu on the table, licking the spilled milk. He was likewise enjoying my poem.

**Elin at Haapsalu,
with Tondu the cat, 1944.**

I was never taken to Tallinn again and for that I was glad. I dared not tell anyone how much I dreaded the arrival of my parents and their friends, but I did tell my "little people" who lived in our horseradish patch. They bore the brunt of my resentment.

15

"Stop that!" I shouted at them, hands on my hips. "Don't touch that!" I screamed at them and marched around the bush to show them that I meant business. "And don't leave your toys around!" I yelled and stamped my foot. I refused to give my "little people" a moment's peace from the first "halloo" of Mother and Father's arrival until the final slam of our front gate that also brought Tondu back in from under the house. Then we were ourselves again— for another season.

Mother called art our "family failing."

The house belonged to Alma. She had built it for her piano, and for Erni's impractical family, "so they would have a roof over the heads in their old age." No one except Aunt Alma had time for mundane concerns such as cooking and household chores. Even caring for me was worked into Grandmother's normal activities so that I did not even notice that I was separate from them until Mother and Father arrived and their different priorities clashed with ours. While my motto was "family and relatives," Mother's was "friendship." She believed friendship was the only relationship that could be relied on not to break one's heart. In the Blue Room there was a photo album of Mother and Father in various productions, and I had fixated on one photo from a play titled "The Snow Queen." Mother did not play the queen; she played a little girl who meets the queen, but in my mind she became the queen, especially when she was annoyed with me.

16

Chapter 2

WHEN THE MUSIC STOPPED
1940-1944

The first shot of the war was fired on a Polish coastal fort near Danzig by an 11-inch gun from the German training ship Schleswig-Holstein on 1 September 1939.

Winston S. Church-ill

Immediately after the signing of the Molotov-Ribbentrop Non-Aggression Pact in August of 1939, Estonia and the other Baltic states falling under the Soviet "sphere of influence" were occupied by Soviet troops. Everything changed.

Mother arrived quietly. I did not even know she was there until I heard someone playing the piano in the front room. The door was locked. Aunt Alma never locked the door when she played. I knew instinctively it was Mother playing. Her music was sad.

Mother came again for my birthday. Again quietly. Father did not come. Grandmother said he was in a production. When we gathered around the table to cut the cake, Mother sparkled, kissed me, and called me "Mussa," but that too was a production. Later when I went to see if she would spend some time with me I found the door locked. Grandmother put her finger to her lips. "Your mother wants to be alone," she told me.

Yet her friends visited her. They came through the front door, the one without steps. There was her friend Marga, the daughter of the midwife who had birthed me, and her two sisters Hilda and Helmi. They spoke in whispers. Every woman we knew had lost a husband. How could they lose husbands I wondered? There was an absence of men, but once in a while we saw Russian soldiers on the Promenade. I realized that the regular promenaders had also vanished.

When Mother was with us she sat perched on the end of the kitchen chair with a book propped over her plate. I stared at the book cover, willing her to notice me. The need for her to notice me had become an obsession. After Mother's plate was empty she went back into the front room and closed the door. I hovered outside. One late afternoon when she was playing the piano in the darkened room, I entered quietly and stood beside her. When she finally noticed me she stopped abruptly with a crash of keys.

"You look just like him," she said bitterly. Then she suddenly screamed, "And you're just like him!" *She meant my father.*

All hell broke loose. I rushed off to find Grandmother.

Grandmother read Tondu and me bedtime stories from "dear Erni's" library. The books were big and heavy and without pictures. Tondu and I did not understand anything, but we liked to hear her voice. "It will all become meaningful when you're older," she assured me. "When you start living your own life."

"I don't want to live my own life," I panicked. "I want to live with you."

She also read us Grandfather's poems. It was like listening to music. Only Grandfather's children's' poems were realistic; the wind talked, the sun smiled, and birds scolded each other, like people. My favorite character was a grasshopper who played the violin and walked about in galoshes, when he wasn't eating.

"Did Grandfather write those poems for me?" I asked.

"Of course, had he lived," Mämmä assured me.

I thought about that for a while.

There was another big book we had been reading when Mother was not at home. It was called the Bible. There were no pictures in that one either. Tondu found it boring. Not to hurt Grandmother's feelings, I kept my eyes closed and pretended to concentrate, but I must have been listening. I remembered the plot and the characters. It was all about old people. The hero was called God. He was born even before the world began, when people still lived in heaven. The other characters were prophets. Really, really old people. That was why it was called the Old Testament. In the New Testament the heroes were younger. God's son was named Jesus. God had created the Earth so everybody in heaven could come down and visit, enjoy the flowers, the animals, the woods, and the fruit trees, but then they didn't want to go back. They were having too much fun on Earth, and before long they were all lost in the woods. God got fed up with them and sent his son Jesus to round them up and bring them back. He was going to make them be reborn, so He and they could start over. The next time they might be more obedient. The New Testament was intended as the road map and instruction manual on how to go back, but it was too late. They wouldn't listen to Jesus either and rebelled, and the next thing they knew, there was the Devil, saying he had an even more fun place for them, called Hell. God was persuading them one way, the Devil the other, but when it was a choice between fun or sermons and lectures, people chose fun. They started ridiculing Jesus and wanted to get rid of him. They nailed him to a cross where Jesus called to his father to come get him, which was as far as we got before Mother turned up again and Grandmother put the Bible into her underwear drawer. Mother didn't like "religious crackpots."

"You will not have my child involved in that nonsense," Mother shouted and reminded Grandmother of the story about her own grandmother, "dear Erni's" mother, and their Baptist relatives. They told Mother our whole family was going to perish in the "Lake of Fire." Artists were going to Hell. Never mind that their own son was a poet.

No more bedtime stories from the Bible, so we turned to the Danish Cookbook, which was my next favorite.

18

A few nights later Grandmother came into my bedroom, put her finger over her lips, closed one eye, and delved into her cardigan pocket. She produced a small book with soft covers titled *The Boyhood of Jesus*. It was about Jesus when he was my age. I hoped he would not become religious.

Mother's presence in the house signaled many things, all-disturbing.

→ I wanted to know why people no longer walked the Promenade. Why did Father no longer visited us? Why did Mother's friends no longer wear high heels, but instead slid through the kitchen like sparrows to join Mother in the front room, where they talked in whispers. No more singing around the piano. No more piano students either.

Aunt Alma was spending most days in the attic. When I tried to follow her up the ladder, Grandmother caught me and turned me back. To keep me from the ladder and stop me hovering by the living room door I was told to "pick dill" until there was no more dill left to pick, so I went to the horseradish patch to berate my "little people" for keeping secrets and not telling me anything. "You're going to die in The Lake of Fire," I told them crossly, then felt foolish. I didn't know where that was, but suspected they did.

One of Mother's friends had a daughter named Vilja. When Vilja's mother disappeared into the front room we were free to play, but sat on the porch steps instead.

I told Vilja I was going back to heaven when I died.

She said she was going to her other grandmother in France.

"Jesus was born in a stable," I told her. "Where were you born?"

"Mother said I was born under a gooseberry bush," said Vilja promptly.

"I was dropped off in Tallinn, at Mrs. Takk's house, and when Mother's theater season started I was brought here, to Haapsalu."

Vilja nodded. It made perfect sense. Our gooseberry bushes were not thriving on account of the annual flooding, and you needed to be born somewhere dry.

I was still hoping to see someone on the Promenade other than the street sweeper or Russian soldiers going to their "base" near the harbor, whatever that was.

I asked Grandmother, "Where are the visitors?"

"They won't be coming anymore," she replied, busying herself by the stove.

"Maybe they'll come tomorrow?" I asked hopefully.

When she did not reply I asked if we could take a walk as far as the villa where I had heard that "grandmaphone" the previous summer.

"The villa people won't be back either," she said tightly.

I guessed it had something to do with this "base" and the soldiers, but she would not take me there either and I didn't ask any more. Something was very wrong.

Mother went back to Tallinn. She did not come for my birthday. No sign of Father at all. Mother sent me a birthday note and added kisses. Grandmother read the note. While she was reading it, I visualized Mother writing it, with her silver foxes hanging over a coat peg behind her, somewhere. Where? I did not even know where she lived.

The grass on the Promenade grew waist high. Mr. Peterson's best boats disappeared. The leaky ones were lying on the grass. The mud barges drifted idly on their moorings, their bottoms coated with cracked mud.

> *In June 1940 Paris fell to the Germans.*
> *On 10 July 1940 the Battle of Britain began.*
> *On 16 July 1940 Hitler began Operation Sea Lion, preparing for the invasion of Great Britain.*
> *By the summer of 1940, the Estonian institutions were dissolving and the leaders were being deported. The government was collapsing.*

Mother's contract with the Workers' Theater ended in the autumn of 1940. She signed a new contract with the combined Workers' and Drama Theater for the 1940/1941 winter season. Father was already in the Drama Theater. He became a producer and spent much of the season touring the provinces. As artists they were not considered political and were not in immediate danger. In fact the Russians found the theater to be a useful tool for spreading propaganda. The theaters came under the aegis of the NKVD or the NKGB and every production had to be rewritten to reflect Communist ideology. The producer was secondary to the party boss who censored the scripts and made sure that every actor attended the daily "red corner" briefings. The re-scripting had to include a patriotic Communist worker or a revolutionary hero. It did not matter what the play was about and period plays became a hoot! Kings had to be re-scripted to look foolish. The original lead character had to be a Communist and if that was impossible, especially in period plays, he had to be depicted as a drunkard or an idiot so that by the end of the play the lowly footman or janitor could rise to great heights and deliver a long monologue on the virtues of the Communist Revolution. Shakespeare's plays were especially difficult. Father's career became a dangerous daily struggle between remaining true to his art and being arrested.

By 1941 the Russian presence in Tallinn was creating conflict. European habits clashed with those of the largely Asiatic occupiers. The soldiers dug up gardens and front yards to use as latrines. Having been told that the Estonians were living in wretched conditions, they were amazed to find us well dressed, our stores full of food, and the farms productive beyond their wildest imagination. At first they thought it was all staged for propaganda purposes, but when they found it was real the officers stripped the stores of everything they could lay their hands on. The locals watched in amazement when the officers' wives turned up at official functions in nightdresses, mistaking them for ball gowns. When the shops were emptied, the officers turned to the townspeople, who were unarmed and already in shock. Nobody was safe from sudden intrusion.

The lagoon was frozen; the snow had not yet started to melt. We were sitting around the kitchen table about to eat our midday meal. Mother had

20

arrived unexpectedly from Tallinn with a ham, from the Tomson farm. Aunt Alma lifted the carving knife to slice the ham and Grandmother was about to serve the boiled potatoes when the kitchen door exploded in a shower of splinters. The kitchen was filled with Russian soldiers in big wet boots and smelly greatcoats, with rifles pointing at us. The lead soldier shouted orders in Russian. "Don't move!"

Then, "Move!"

The rifles pointed this way and that way.

"Stand! Sit down!" Their frosted breath reeked of vodka. As none of us had moved, the orders made no sense. The leader motioned for the men to disperse into the other rooms. They were searching for liquor. We heard them pulling out drawers, opening cupboards, throwing things on the floor. The men who stayed in the kitchen began to search the shelves, opening tins, spilling flour, sugar, salt to crunch underfoot.

We continued to sit. Grandmother remained silent by the stove, a steaming pan of potatoes in her hand. Slowly she lowered the pan back onto the burner and addressed the leader in Russian. His demeanor suggested he was an officer. She spoke quietly and calmly so that the contrast in their voices sounded foolish even to their own ears. They stopped shouting. The officer's cheeks turned red. He lowered his rifle.

I understood enough Russian to follow that they were hungry and thirsty. Tossing aside everything they could not use, they filled their pockets with things they fancied. One of them picked up a music box. He wound the key and it began to play one of Chopin's nocturnes. He put it into his coat pocket, where it continued to tinkle.

Alma remained seated; her scarf low over her forehead, her hands in her lap, while Grandmother answered the officer's questions with a *nyet* a *da* or a *harasho*. She then asked him his name and told him she was from the Peipsi region of Estonia, on the Russian border, which included many Russian villages. This took him back a bit.

Mother's Russian was not so good. She sat with a frozen look on her face, her nostrils slightly distended. I knew the look. She was ready to explode, but dared not.

The other men returned to the kitchen and confirmed we had no liquor. They settled for bread, ham, and potatoes. Grandmother stuffed a dishcloth over the potatoes to keep them warm. This further unsettled the leader. He called her *babushka*, then turned and said to his men *"Poidjom!"* Let's go!

Loaded down with provisions, the soldiers backed out awkwardly, the music box still tinkling, but winding down. It had been a gift from Mother's actress friend, the "monocle."

When they had gone, the stench of vodka and wet wool lingered. Mother got to her feet slowly and began to sweep the floor. Flour, salt, and sugar were mixed among the splintered wood. The sugar was wet and dirty, but she scraped it up anyway. It was precious. No one spoke. When the kitchen floor was clean again and the sugar spread on paper to dry, we all went to the window. The soldiers had not gone far. They were camping beside the lagoon, sitting on the sea wall, passing bottles around, and eating our dinner.

Soon they were even more drunk than before. They chopped a hole into the ice, stripped to their underwear, and began to frolic in the freezing water.

"Disgusting!" said Mother, letting out her breath.

Grandmother took a look over her shoulder and dismissed them with a wave of her hand. "They're just mothers' sons," she said, "far from home."

Alma went to find Mr. Peterson to see if he would repair our door. Mother returned to Tallinn.

Another evening, when it was still light and I could not sleep, I wanted to go to the front room window to see the moon. The door was locked. Thinking Mother had returned again and was in there reading, I knocked. When she did not reply, I knocked louder. Suddenly the door was opened by a stranger, a woman in a nightgown and bedroom slippers. She appeared to be right at home in our house. Grandmother hurried to intercede; she apologized to the woman in Russian. Back in my room Grandmother sat me down on my bed and told me I must never, never go near the front room again. A Russian woman doctor now owned our house. We were only allowed into my room and the kitchen. Grandmother was sleeping in the kitchen chair and Aunt Alma in the attic.

The woman doctor used the front door with the stool. I did not see her again, but I could hear her thumping on the piano, playing tunes that sounded like pots and pans were falling out of the cupboards. One day she came to look for me and beckoned for me to approach her. She held something behind her back. When I reached her she patted my cheek and said I was *krasive*, pretty. She gave me something shaped like a tiny fish wrapped in foil. "You can visit me any time," she said.

Even before I had undone the wrapper I recognized the smell. Chocolate! At last! I was so overwhelmed that I could barely say *spasiba*. The chocolate tasted even better than it smelled. I ate it all, even the wrapper.

The doctor was with us all summer. Then one day she was gone. We got our house back.

Thanks to the Russian doctor who had "owned our house" all summer, we escaped the most tragic period in modern Estonian history, namely the deportation to Siberia of thousands of Estonian men, women, and children on the night of 14 June 1941.

It was an unusually hot night. Only light summer clothes were handy. Roused from a deep sleep and in shock, nobody could think clearly. They arrested the able-bodied men. The women, the sick, the elderly, and mothers with children were taken away in trucks and herded into cattle cars for a journey lasting several months. Some of the pregnant women gave birth en route. Many died. The dead were thrown off the trains at now documented and memorialized stops. Hundreds more died after the first frost.[6]

---

[6] In 2005 The United States Congress declared 14 June "Baltic States Day," a day of mourning for all Estonians, Latvians and Lithuanians who were deported to Siberia and died there.

Just when I thought nobody was going to use the Promenade again, new promenaders appeared. These strollers were also soldiers, but not Russians. They walked in groups of twos and threes, wearing smart grey uniforms with visored caps, what looked like riding britches and shiny leather knee boots. They were very polite, bowing to the ladies and removing their caps when they entered the *Kuursaal*. Sometimes a whole group would go by, laughing and singing in German.

By the end of the summer of 1941 the Germans had occupied Estonia.

Grandmother and I were walking on the Promenade one afternoon when we met four officers coming towards us. Instead of stepping aside one of them shoved Grandmother out of the way. She fell on top of me and we both ended up on the grass.

Mother returned. Apparently she had left the theater and was working at the Haapsalu newspaper as an interpreter. When she came home from work, she ate and then went back into the front room to read. As usual I was "not to disturb her."

One day she had left the living room door open and I sneaked a look inside. She was turning pages. She did not turn many pages. She was not even reading. She heard me and turned her head. I saw that beneath her glasses her eyes were brimming with tears.

The next time I saw Father I was squatting in the garden, "cooking grass soup," when I heard our front gate open and someone come across the porch to the kitchen. A few minutes later I heard Father's voice through the open kitchen window. Normally I would have run inside to greet him, but his voice was so loud and angry that I waited. I heard Grandmother ask him, "So what am I supposed to tell the child?"

"Tell her she no longer has a father and I don't have a daughter." With those words he stormed out of the house, slamming the door and banging the gate. I grabbed a handful of grass and ran into the street after him. When I reached him I stuffed the grass into his jacket pocket.

"What's this?" he asked.

"Nothing," I told him seriously, "But when you next put your hand into your pocket, you will remember that you are my father and that you have a daughter."

The antagonism between the two empires and systems was mortal. Stalin no doubt felt that Hitler would be a less deadly foe to Russia after a year of war with the Western Powers. Hitler followed his method of "one at a time." The fact that such an agreement could be made marks the culminating failure of British and French foreign policy and diplomacy over several years.

Winston S. Churchill

23

The tide of war turned and on 27 January 1944 the siege of Leningrad was lifted.

Küchler[7] had wisely decided that he must pull back or be trapped by the Soviet forces punching through both his flanks. So he conducted an orderly withdrawal all the way back to the Estonian and Latvian borders.

Robert Leckie

In March 1944 the Soviets began bombing Estonia in earnest.

It was spring again. We seemed to live like bears in hibernation until the fence posts stopped exploding from the cold and the white expanse of the bay began to develop a horizon.

Snow was still on the ground, icicles dripped off the roof, and the wooden planks to the woodshed were in place, ready for the thaw. Our cellar was already full of water, and the sun had started showing itself every few days through the sea mist, checking to see if it was safe to come out yet.

It was a morning like any other except that Aunt Alma was coming out of the woodshed, dragging our sled behind her. Grandmother, already fully dressed, was packing clothes into a small trunk. She had already piled kitchen items in a wicker basket nearby. When she saw me she got up and took me back to my bedroom and dressed me in outdoor clothes. I hardly ever got to go out before Easter. It was still March.

The trunk was put on the sled, and we were off, not to the Swedish market or the milk shop, but down the main street, the road out of Haapsalu. Grandmother carried the basket of food and our milk pail. Alma pulled the sled. I sat on the trunk. It was my responsibility to keep it from falling off.

We followed the Haapsalu-Tallinn highway for a while, then turned off onto a side road that eventually became a narrow track between snow banks. Houses were less frequent; we were moving through fields, marshes, and expanses of frozen ground dotted with dead grasses.

There were a lot of dangerous marshes and bottomless bogs around Haapsalu. In the summer the market women talked about how some summer visitor had stepped off the path and got sucked under. The woods too, were dangerous. Only women berry-pickers and mushroomers were safe. It was understood that if a woman saw a bear she had to quickly lift her skirt and show the bear her bare behind. Apparently an old woman's bare bottom scared bears even more than a man with a rifle. This was good to know.

Our progress was slow. The ground was hard-packed snow covered with a layer of ice. A distant farmhouse marked itself with a spire of smoke or a barking dog. All was white. Even the sky was white. The only margins between sky and snow were lines of trees, like pencil markings.

The road was easy to follow at first, but at each junction where the paths converged and the snow became slush, it was clear that we were not the only people going the same way. The snow showed fresh cart tracks, sled

---

[7] General Georg van Küchler was the commander of German Army Group North.

tracks, and horse droppings. Before long we found ourselves trudging through ankle-deep puddles and potholes yellow with horse piss. Our little sled lost traction when the runners hit dirt and stones. I was told to get off and to walk in the icy water. Aunt Alma was muttering to herself. She finally hauled the sled and everything on it over the bank into a field. Here the snow was deep and dry, but the ground was covered with rocks, roots and frozen grasses. I had to walk again. The only smooth places were frozen ponds.

Aunt Alma steered towards the ponds until it got dark. The forest ahead was a black wall, unbroken, but noisy. Was that snow falling off a branch or a bear breaking through the thicket? Was that a wolf howling or a well winch being worked on a distant farm?

Grandmother was humming quietly, as she always did when she was being beset by bad thoughts. "Dear Erni," she told me, would have stamped his foot and shouted "boot!" Aunt Alma did not have any sure way of averting evil, so she just kept muttering and leading the way until we saw a light in the distance. A farmhouse lay low at the edge of a silent moonlit field. A dark island. I wondered if we had in fact crossed over to one of the Swedish islands. As we neared the house dogs began to bark. Voices and sounds carried sharply across the snow. Horses were neighing, snorting, stamping, and jingling their harnesses.

We crossed the road and narrowly missed being run down by a horse pulling a sled piled high with furniture. The driver hadn't seen us in the dark.

The farmhouse was made of logs, with a thatched, pitched roof, familiar from pictures of old Estonia. It had a well. Instead of a chain a long balancing pole lowered the bucket. The pole was easier to use than Mr. Peterson's crank where you had to winch the full bucket up by hand.

The front door was the source of the light. People were moving in and out, unloading the wagons and carrying bundles and bedding into the house. The horses continued stamping and snorting. All around was blackness and silence except when once in a while, a clump of heavy snow slid off a fir boughs and hit the ground with a loud *plop*.

Aunt Alma seemed to know where we were and the people who lived there. She went ahead and came back a few minutes later to tell us we were too late for dinner, too late for a room, but would be comfortable. We followed her into a big central chamber with a dirt floor covered with hand-woven rugs. A long plank table occupied the middle of the floor with benches on both sides. The table was stacked with dirty dishes. A massive dresser with many drawers was set against the far wall. It was the only major piece of furniture.

Alma dragged our trunk to an unoccupied corner between the dresser and a rickety washstand. With a quick hug for Grandmother and a pat on my head she left us, saying she had to go back to the Haapsalu house because she feared looters.

We slept on the floor on a straw-filled sack covered with blankets. No one undressed, for which I was thankful. There were other women and children around us trying to make themselves comfortable. Each little circle was a fort unto itself defended by a pile of personal belongings.

25

I heard bangs during the night and thought it was a thunderstorm, which would have been unusual for that time of year. I had never been afraid of thunderstorms, so I went back to sleep.

It was still dark when I woke to the sound of a cock crowing and quiet whispering around the room which was lighted by a single candle on the central table. The women filed by the washstand to wet their eyes and then disappeared. Grandmother was already up. She gave me a cup of milk and a of slice bread and told me she would be busy all day in the kitchen. When I wanted to go with her she said, "No." I was to stay put.

When it got light enough to see, I went to find Grandmother again, but a woman stopped me and turned me around. "Children are not allowed in the kitchen."

Not knowing where to go, or what to do, I noticed that the central table was covered by a long white tablecloth that almost touched the floor on all sides. Under the table was the perfect place from which to see what was going on. I watched feet go back and forth and got to know their owners by their shoes and slippers before I saw their faces. The other children did not interest me, but one of the toddlers kept crawling over to try to pull the tablecloth off the table. He did not know that I was holding the other end. When he couldn't get it off he started screaming until his mother tied a rope around his waist and tethered him to the leg of the dresser. He continued screaming, but I was safe. All I was interested in was seeing Grandmother's familiar shoes and stockings again so I could ask her why we had to be there. She never told me.

Day followed day. Night followed night. The women seldom left the kitchen. They spent the day cooking soup and baking bread. As I got bolder I crept to the door and watched them. After they had finished kneading the dough they shaped it into long loaves, sprinkled the loaves with water, and put them into the oven using long wooden paddles. After the loaves were taken from the oven they were wrapped into towels and placed on the sideboard. Lined up, they resembled babies in swaddling linens, not far from where two real swaddled newborns slept in the dresser drawers.

Desperate to catch Grandmother's eye, I willed her to stop working. I wanted to be near her. When she did come, she patted my cheek and told me to go "play."

"When can we go home?" I asked her.

"Soon," she promised.

There were no men in the house during the day. The men arrived in the evening. We ate our meal early. A bowl of soup and a slice of bread. When we had eaten, the bowls were washed and the table reset for the men.

We first heard them at the back door, stamping their boots, coughing, and slapping their gloves together. Their deep rumbling voices mingled with the excited chatter of the women half whispering, half laughing, in their gladness to see them, but apparently afraid to sound too loud. The women helped the men remove their coats, wool caps, and scarves. The men entered cautiously, bent over because of the low ceiling or because they were stiff and frozen. They were bearded and rough-looking. The older men had grey beards and grey hair. Most of them wore ragged jackets with pullovers and patched trousers. The younger men's cheeks were unshaven, their eyes sunken. Every face was red raw from the cold. I watched them with interest. The only men I had seen up close were Mr. Peterson and actors. And Father of course, who seldom had a face of his own.

The women served the men until there was no food left. They then sat with them, pulling up extra chairs if the benches were not long enough. As none of the men were familiar to me, I went back to our corner to wait for Grandmother to join me again. The candle had been replaced by oil lamps that cast long shadows on the walls and ceiling. The curtains were closed tightly. Conversations around the table were conducted in whispers. Huddled together, their voices were muted to a continuous drone that faded from my mind as I drifted off to sleep. When I woke up the men had gone and taken the loaves of bread with them.

One day the women were in the kitchen again baking bread when the men came in from the woods in broad daylight carrying pails of birch beer. They were greeted joyfully and everyone began to pass the beer around. I slipped in behind them for some bread and beer.

"Out of here!" someone shouted. I was chased away.

Not used to being spoken to harshly, I went in search of Grandmother. It was a sunny day. The snow was melting. I found a clump of fresh snowdrops under a dome of melting ice. The sun was shining through the filigreed crystals illuminating the fragile white petals, green stems, and black soil with golden light. Cold gold was dripping from the sky. I squatted there for a long time until Grandmother appeared beside me.

"Ah, there you are," she said. "I've been looking for you everywhere."

I was bored. Sometimes women came out of the kitchen, pulled up a stool and looked anxiously through the front windows.

When they had gone back to the kitchen, I also pulled up the stool and hoped to see something interesting, but there was nothing—just the yard and weathered outhouses, a partially collapsed barn, empty sheds, and a sagging wire fence. Beyond that lay the marsh, dotted with black puddles of water and the same clumps of brown grasses we had stumbled over on arrival. There were no animals on the farm, just chickens. Instead of pecking around the yard, they were enclosed into a coop beside the kitchen door. Once in a while one would be taken out in a flurry of feathers and we would have chicken soup. Two dogs were chained to a doghouse by the front entrance. At night I could hear their chains dragging as they paced back and forth.

One evening I watched the men arrive in single file carrying what looked like spades across their shoulders. They had a dog with them, an Alsatian. The men rested their spades against the wall while they scraped their soles free of mud. On closer inspection I saw that the spades were rifles. The dog remained outside the door; it lay quietly and growled every time something moved. We could not see the road, but the dog knew and sat up; the hairs on the back of its neck would raise in a ridge. Remembering the dog that had jumped on me when I was two, I never went near dogs again.

The only place where I felt safe was under the table from whatever everyone seemed to be afraid of, as the long tablecloth was a protective tent, which kept me hidden. I didn't know what it was, but they talked about someone or something that had come before and was coming back. Someone called NKVD. This NKVD had been to a farm somewhere and nailed the family's hands to the kitchen table, placed a jug of milk into the center of the table, and then waited outside for the husband to hear the screams of his wife and children. They expected him to try to rescue them. The mother had broken free to feed her children and had bled to death. At another farm they had taken a baby out of its mother's arms and bashed its head against the wall.

We had three jugs on our table, a blue jug and two white ones. The white one contained milk, the other two fruit juice, and we had those two newborns in the buffet drawer. I hoped when the NKVD came, they would not mistake the babies for loaves of bread and then seeing they were babies, smash them against the wall.

Grandmother reached down intermittently to let me know she was near.

"Remember there are children listening," she warned the person talking, but it made no difference. There was nowhere she could send me, and I would not have gone anywhere anyway, but remained by Grandmother's legs. I missed my Tondu. Despite our frequent differences of opinion he had always been available when I needed a furry pillow under my head. At the farmhouse all I had were Grandmother's slippers.

What the woman had been talking about were the activities of the NKVD, the Destruction Battalions that were set up in 1941 to deal with internal resistance to the Soviet occupiers. Their main targets were men who had fled into the forests to avoid arrest or conscription into the Soviet army. Small and large groups of people lived in the forests and bogs. The men were called "Forest Brothers." Sometimes their women remained on the farms so that they could secretly feed their menfolk. At the farm we were staying at, I believe that was what was happening. This time the men were not avoiding the Soviets, but the retreating Germans who were also rounding up men and forcing young boys into the German Luftwaffe.

We returned to Haapsalu. Now the only people walking along the Promenade were ordinary townspeople taking shortcuts or boys vandalizing the mud barges that had not yet sunk. The spa was closed.

Mother was in Tallinn and sent us desperate letters in which she expressed doubts she would see us again. She told Grandmother she was listening to Finnish radio. The Russians were fighting on the Latvian border. The letters always included a special message for me: "Be a brave girl!" When she was with us I hardly recognized her. She was no longer the Snow Queen, but an ordinary woman in an ordinary dress with a scarf tied around her hair. She paced the floor and smoked dreadful-smelling cigarettes she called *ma-horkas*. She barely spoke to me. She even continued reading while holding her book next to her overflowing ashtray. She ate with one hand and turned pages with the other. It amazed me she knew where to guide the fork. I was told not to disturb her.

"Not disturbing Mother" had been drilled into me for so long that I finally erupted. One afternoon I simply walked into the room. I did not even knock.

→ Mother looked up from her book, startled. Before she could yell at me I put my tongue out at her, turned my back, and flashed her my bare bottom. I expected a beating, but it didn't happen. Mother just closed the book and left the room. The next day she went back to Tallinn.

Mother had left the theater. Through Marga's sister Hilda, she had secured a job as an auditor for a firm affiliated with Philips Electrical. The name of the firm was "Oranje."

→ As soon as Mother had gone, I went to the horseradish patch to my "little people" and reprimanded them for being insolent. They just laughed, so I dumped a bucket of water over them! "There!" They were not even sorry.

→ Mother's and Father's marriage was essentially over. When Marga came for a visit, I overheard her telling Mother that her mother, the midwife, had delivered Father's son, born to a violinist in the theater orchestra. When Father said he no longer had a daughter, it was his way of saying he was no longer a part of our family.

The Russians were returning. No one had forgotten the deportations and terror of 1941, interrupted by the German occupation.

I came into the house and saw the two Anderson sisters from across the street, sitting in our kitchen. They stopped talking as soon as I entered. Aunt Alma looked at me pointedly and said, "Go pick some dill." When I got back with the dill the sisters were saying good-bye. They were going to Sweden and left us their house keys.

→ Mother was living with us again, but still had no time for me. By then I had decided I would not play with her either, even if she begged me.

We had not seen Vilja and her mother for a long time and I missed her. I had another friend, Moonika, but Vilja and I had had more fun. She had been taller than me, and could stand in the shallows by the sea wall without getting her knickers wet. Our goal had been to catch the baby ducks, but the mother ducks always managed to keep them out of reach of our sticks. When I asked Grandmother why Vilja and her mother did not come any more, she made a strange face and changed the subject.

Then another of Mother's friends turned up with a daughter named Salme. Salme had an old aunt, like Aunt Alma. We had met them at the Swedish market. Mother and Salme's mother had become friends.

→ Salme was different from the other children I had known because she had toys. Real toys. I had been quite content to be without toys—drawing pictures, making up poems, floating reed boats, trying to catch ducks, walking with Grandmother, and playing with the spa mud—until Salme brought her toy post office. I had never had store-bought toys before. After that I no longer wanted to play with "natural toys," as Grandmother referred to the sticks and stones I had enjoyed before. I wanted a toy post office like Salme's, which had a counter, a postage scale, play money, postage stamps, envelopes, a rack of rubber stamps, and an inkpad. I was thrilled until Salme insisted on being the postmistress and me the customer, which left me standing in line while Salme banged about with the inkpad.

When Salme had gone I pestered Grandmother to let me up into the attic. The few times I had managed to climb as far as the last rung I had seen a wooden horse and doll furniture.

"Those were your mother's toys," Grandmother told me. She said I was too young for Mother's toys and would break them. She also kept Mother's doll, Marie, under lock and key in the Blue Room cabinet. True. I had poked out its eyes when I was three, but now I was almost seven.

"If I can't have a post office, can I have some doll furniture?" I asked Grandmother. I did not tell her I wanted to take the furniture outside for my "little people."

"I don't know, maybe for your birthday," Grandmother relented. "I'll ask your mother."

On my seventh birthday I got the doll furniture I had asked for.

Mother was still with us and we celebrated according to our family tradition. Mother, Grandmother, and Aunt Alma entering my bedroom with the candle-lit birthday cake awakened me early in the morning. They sang "*Elagu!*" which is the Estonian equivalent of Happy Birthday. ("Live, live, and may you live for another thousand years!")

There was no sign of Father. From the expression on his face at the last meeting I knew we would never see him again. This time Mother was not ignoring me. She watched me open the presents with a sad look on her face.

The doll furniture was beautiful!

As soon as Mother had gone to work I took the furniture outside and set it under the horseradish patch. I covered the table with a handkerchief and told my "little people" they could hide under the table if they got scared, but if you don't behave, I'll send the NKVD to you and they will nail your hands to the table," I warned them. I also scolded them for constantly wanting my attention.

"Can't you see I'm busy?"

Now that I had the furniture, I had no one to show it off to, Salme and her Mother had not come back.

"Why doesn't Salme visit me anymore?" I asked Mother during dinner. I feared it had to do with our fights over the rubber stamps and inkpad.

"They've gone away," replied Mother. She returned to her book.

"To Sweden?"

"I don't know."

"Vilja went to Siberia," I told her.

Mother looked startled. For a moment I thought she might ask me how I knew, but she must have changed her mind.

Another day I had just finished eating and was going to tell my "little people" that I was going to confiscate their house and their front room and would only allow them the use of the kitchen when I heard the front gate latch open and saw Mother running up the path, yelling, "Alma! Memme! They're coming for me. Send the child away!"

Grandmother grabbed the milk pail and shoved it into my hand. "Go get milk," she shouted and pushed me out the door so forcefully that I almost fell down the steps. She had never ever raised her voice to me, and I had never ever gone for milk alone. I had no money. Paralyzed by her unfamiliar behavior, I went around the house and remained under the kitchen window, the only place where I could hear what was going on in the house.

Mother was crying hysterically, throwing things into her suitcase.

Aunt Alma was telling Grandmother to go after me. "Get the child! Go into the forest," she ordered.

I heard Grandmother leave by the front door, calling my name down the street. Mother looked out of the kitchen window and saw me. She was so upset; I thought she was going to jump right through the glass. I dropped the milk pail and ran after Grandmother.

No one came.

When we were all back in the kitchen, Mother took me by the shoulders and shook me so hard my teeth knocked together.

"When I tell you 'run,' you run. When I say 'hide,' you hide. Do you hear me?" she screamed into my face.

Now she wants to play hide and seek, I thought. Well, I was never going to play with her—ever. I went to my room and hid under the bed.

That episode remained a mystery to me until 1997 when I came across an article in a Haapsalu newspaper. "Liki Toona was 'our man in Havana', able to warn us of what the enemy was planning..."[8] Apparently Mother was back at the newspaper as a translator for the Germans, and in that capacity she had access to lists of names of people to be arrested. She was able to warn them to leave home. The day she came running to the house she had seen her own name on the list.

The Germans did not come for her because on that day the front turned and they started retreating.

---

[8] Venda Sõelsepp, *Lääne Elu*, 24 April 1997

Chapter 3

ON THE EVE OF DESTRUCTION
22 September 1944

Hitler and Stalin were mentioned so often that I knew them as two mean men who hated each other and anyone who did not agree with them. They spent their time drawing lines on maps and lobbing countries at each other while secretly hoping to kill each other. Both wanted to own the world, or better yet, each wanted to become King of England.

"Mämmä, come look at the ships! They've got stovepipes on them," I said excitedly, running into the kitchen to tell Grandmother what I had seen from the porch.

Grandmother was not there. She was in the Blue Room frantically sorting through drawers, throwing things on the floor and not putting anything back. Mother and Aunt Alma were huddled over the kitchen table, whispering with their heads together. They ignored me, but Grandmother had noticed me.

"Eat your breakfast," she said, from the other room. Only Grandmother seemed to remember I was still there.

I didn't see any breakfast, so I went into the front room. I had noticed the night before that the sky over the Andersons' rooftop had been orange. Pulling a stool to the window, I now saw black clouds billowing over the same roof. It had started raining dry flakes of ash that settled on the window sill and on the grass. It turned greens grey, covered the pavement, and filled the crevices between the cobblestones with what looked like dirty snow.

The road in front of our house, which was usually boring and barely used, was crowded with people and vehicles moving towards the harbor. The procession included bicycles, open lorries, horse drawn wagons, and pushcarts, all keeping pace with people struggling with heavy suitcases, cardboard boxes, prams, and strollers loaded with bundles. The bundles were made of sheets, tablecloths, blankets, and scarves. Some bundles were too large to carry, some loads too heavy for the people pushing and pulling them. One man was balancing an iron stove on his bicycle; another was carrying a grandfather clock on his back. One man had a suitcase so heavy he had to stop and rest after every few steps. Small children sat on top of the overloaded carts and prams, and the bigger children trotted alongside, with their own little bundles or bags.

"Get away from the window!" shouted Aunt Alma from the kitchen. Amazing how they did not notice me until I had found something interesting!

As the German army was withdrawing from Estonia, the Soviet navy began to bomb harbor facilities. Several bombs fell on Haapsalu.

Mr. Peterson dug a bomb shelter at the bottom of our garden. It was really just a deep hole, half-filled with water. Grandmother took my chamber pot into the shelter with us, but I refused to use it because it kept slithering off the wet planks. I caused such a fuss that we finally traipsed back into the house. A few seconds later a bomb landed near the shelter and toppled one of our trees. The tree fell on the roof and broke an attic window.

Mother had taken to wearing men's trousers and a fisherman's jumper with a hole in one shoulder. Instead of the long cigarette holder she had always used, perfectly poised, she now used a short amber holder, the color of her fingers. The holder was crammed between her teeth in the side of her mouth while she spoke. She was smoking *makhorka* again, the nasty-smelling Russian tobacco that reminded me of the Russian soldiers who had broken into our kitchen. The trousers were too big for her. She was holding them up with a belt that had a pointed copper buckle in the shape of a snake's head. *(I would know that belt again in the spring of 1945.)*

Mother had stopped hiding in the living room and was pacing about the house reading a letter. I wanted to ask her about the ships, the people on the street, and everything else, because I was getting scared, but Grandmother stopped me. She put her finger over her lips.

"Your mother is making an important decision," she said.

I could see that, but I stepped into her path anyway. She looked down at me for a second, puzzled, then moved around me and lit another cigarette.

Marga and the whole Takk family had been by earlier, including Helmi and her newborn baby. I wanted to see the baby, but not her son Rein who was four years old, so I merely listened. They were going to go overland to Holland, pushing the pram. Marga had brought the letter. It was from Father in which he had said he would try to find us.

Aunt Alma had hurt her leg. It thrombosed, she was supposed to lie still. However, she was hobbling around on a crutch fashioned from a broom handle and giving orders to Grandmother who had climbed onto the kitchen table and was hanging blankets to the curtain rail, her mouth was bristling with safety pins.

"How's that?" she called.

"Pull it down on the left, Ella. No! Yes! Now to the right. Not enough. Pull it down some more!" Then, exasperated, "It's too narrow. Get a bigger blanket."

She saw Mother still worrying, the letter in her hand.

"For God's sake, Liki!" Alma snorted in disgust. "He's not here, is he? That should be answer enough. He's not coming."

"Maybe he missed the last train?" Mother's voice was trembly.

"You're making a fool of yourself. You have to go!"

"But he says here ..." She began to read the letter again, but did not seem to find more comforting words. "He would not have sent me a letter if he was not thinking of joining us," Mother reasoned. "I am his legal wife."

Aunt Alma gave another snort. "You have to leave, now! Tallinn has fallen! He is not coming, but the Russians are."

34

So that was it! The smell of Mother's Russian tobacco, explosions, and everybody in a panic again meant that those NKVDs were coming back and our kitchen table was just the right size for us all to fit around it, with our hands nailed to the wood.

I was standing next to it when there was a buzz in my knees and I collapsed on the floor. I couldn't get up. I tried, but my legs had gone numb. Grandmother noticed first. She rushed to me.

"Put her to bed!" shouted Alma from the chair, where she had sat down with her foot on the upturned bucket.

"Yes, she should be in bed," agreed Mother. "Go to bed."

Since I couldn't stand up, I began to crawl along the floor, hoping to pull myself up by Grandmother's skirt. Seven years old and crawling like a baby.

"Nerves," said Mother, with sudden concern. She lifted me and carried me to bed. I was thrilled to be carried by Mother, but I could smell the *mahorka* on her breath. I thought this is my mother, but today she smells like a Russian soldier.

Grandmother undressed me and put a light blanket over me. She lit my bedside candle and stayed beside me. I was afraid to go to sleep. Mother came into the room once or twice and stood at the foot of my bed.

"Not sick, is she? God, that's all we need!"

"Just tired," said Grandmother, stroking my forehead.

I must have dozed off, because when I woke again it was dark. The candle had burned down. Thunder, that I knew was not thunder, rumbled over the rooftops. The door was only partly closed. There was light around the edges and voices in the kitchen. I got out of bed, surprised that I could walk, and crept to the door. Mother, Grandmother, and Aunt Alma were huddled around the kitchen table again, heads together. The window was covered with thick dark blankets, but every time there was a bang and flash the blanket became opaque. I went back to bed and lay with my fingers in my ears. I dared not go to sleep again that night. In the morning we started packing.

Aunt Alma was buttoning my coat, telling me not to whine because I could only bring one doll.

"Hold still," she said, with a safety pin between her teeth. The buttons would not close without the pins. She had already packed my toothbrush, my cup with a picture of bears on the side, and a pair of extra shoes, wrapped into my pink baby blanket.

"This will be your bundle," she said harshly. "Don't drop it." My potty was already in a string bag. I would have to carry that, too.

Grandmother was still in the Blue Room ripping more photographs from albums, pulling books from bookshelves, stuffing documents into envelopes, and throwing them into Grandfather's *suurrätt*, his meditation shawl strewn over the bed, which was to become our "dear Erni" bundle. In another room Mother was filling her suitcase with valuables so she could buy us food and passage. All the cupboard doors in the house were now open and all the drawers were pulled out and up-tipped on the floor; empty photograph frames and piles of clothing lay about or were thrown over chairs. The windows were tightly closed, but the smell of smoke seeped in anyway and shrouded the view across the lagoon. The warships I had seen in the inlet loomed like ghosts beyond the barrier island that lay between the open sea and us. Every once in a while you could hear a distant boom that shook the house and even the ground it stood on. Each time the boom seemed closer.

My fur coat was too tight under the armpits, too hot for September. Stuffed under it were two dresses and three sets of underwear. Then I whined some more when I saw Mother unlock the Blue Room cabinet and remove her own bisque doll Maria. She placed it carefully into the bottom of her suitcase. (*I did not know then that Maria was meant for me, for when I was older. I still have Maria now here in Florida.*)

Then we were ready.

Aunt Alma came to the gate with us, hobbling on her crutch and ignoring the trailing bandages she had no time to adjust. The attack of thrombosis was serious, but her excuse for not coming with us was that she would not leave her piano to the enemy. She held a scarf over her mouth and nose. "Quickly," she said, motioning towards the street. "They won't wait long." The truck had already moved away to pick up a neighbor. Its engine was rumbling loudly. The open back was full of people standing among baggage and shouting for us to hurry. Mother and Grandmother's eyes were watering from the heavy smoke. I had never seen Aunt Alma so agitated. She kissed Grandmother on both cheeks. "Good-bye Sister. Go with God."

She pulled Mother into her arms. "You take care of them, Liki. I'll guard the house. It'll be here when you come back," she promised. She then stooped down to hug me. I thought she would never let me go. This scared me even more than their tears. Aunt Alma had never hugged me, although I knew she loved me. Then, with a quick twist of her hands, she removed her gold and ruby engagement ring, given to her by her "long lost fiancé," who had perished in some Turkish war, and slid it onto my middle finger. It was too loose.

"Keep this for me," she said. "I don't need it anymore." There was no time to ask why, because the truck driver was leaning on his horn impatiently. Something terrible was happening, or maybe even worse than terrible, because Tondu did not come to the gate to say good-bye. My cat must have known that we would never return.

Mother finally crumpled the letter, stuffed it into her pocket, and we set off without Father with our bundles, my potty, and our one suitcase. We joined some of the last refugees still able to leave Estonia on the evening of 23 September 1944.

The truck we boarded took us by ferry to Saaremaa, one of the outer islands off the west coast. The rest of Estonia was already occupied by Soviet troops. As Grandmother could not climb into the back of the truck, despite help, she was allowed to sit in the cab with the driver. I sat on her lap. Mother joined the other refugees in the back.

Mother had forbidden us to look back after we had said our good-byes, but I couldn't help it. Aunt Alma was leaning against the gatepost as though she had become part of it, her hand raised like the crooked branch of a dead tree.

After being let off the truck, we walked to the beach. Mother carried one large bundle and her suitcase. Grandmother held the "dear Erni" bundle and the shopping basket. I had my little bundle and the potty. Usually when we went for a walk Grandmother would let me squat down to examine interesting stones or flowers. Now, walking across the sand dunes and through the sea grasses, I saw all kinds of interesting things and would have bent down to look except Mother was impatient and kept prodding us to keep walking.

"Keep moving!" Grandmother was running into me. The urgency only registered properly when Grandmother pulled my arm and whispered, "Don't upset your mother. Just do as she tells us." She repeated Mother's words. "No looking back."

We arrived on the beach, and Mother left us in the shelter of a thick wall, part of a ruined fortress. She went to find a boat that would have room for three. I knew Grandmother had given Mother the authority to tell us what to do, but I was not used to the pace, the way she had taken charge and how she had started to boss us about. In the baggy trousers, the fisherman's jumper, and with her hair hidden under a man's cap, she not only looked like a real leader, but like one of those women on Russian posters with a hammer in one hand and a sickle in the other. I resented her, but also could not help being proud of her. Instead of teetering around on high heels and in furs with glass eyes and teeth, she had her feet firmly on the ground. I had even seen her cut the head and paws off her silver fox to cushion Maria, before placing her into the suitcase. The horrible beast was now an ordinary collar. Served him right!

It was with pride then that I watched Mother taking large strides across the sand, approaching people purposefully, speaking seriously, and gesturing with her hands. Still the actress, but in a different role.

Mother returned not soon after and said we were ready. She had found a boat that would take us to Sweden and a melon in someone's abandoned garden. There was still time enough to eat it.

"Give me the knife," she asked Grandmother, holding her hand out.

We did not have a knife.

"What? No knife?" Mother looked stunned, and then began to tear at the bundles. "What do you mean no knife?" She pulled the stitched corner of "dear Erni's" bundle open to reveal its contents.

"Paper? I can't believe it! Paper! All you've packed is paper!" She slapped her forehead and started to sob. I had seen my mother cry before, but not like that. She cried and beat her fists into the cloth that was actually her father's prayer shawl. Grandmother tried to comfort her, but Mother would not be consoled. If the stitches had not been so firmly in place, she would have torn the entire bundle apart.

I remembered the packing and "dear Erni's" shawl spread on the bed. The other bundle, our old horse blanket and red crocheted blanket sewn together, was full of clothes and linens (Aunt Alma's unused trousseau.) Everything else was in the large shopping bag we usually carried to market. The

37

bag clonked and clanked because in the center of it was our aluminum cooking pot filled with smaller items: matches, candles, tea towels, and one china cup that we later called our "Dresden." Grandmother had also brought two books for us to read, *The Boyhood of Jesus* and the Danish cookbook. The rest of the books were Grandfather's poems.

Mother's crying upset me. Every time I had seen her cry, something terrible had been about to happen. I was getting ready to jump or hide as she had instructed. Finally Mother lifted her head, removed her glasses (which she had finally taken to wearing every day), wiped her eyes, polished the lenses, and said, "All right! It's done!" She straightened, squared her shoulders, and looked around.

"Ah! And here's the man who said he would take us," she called out, as she went to meet him halfway, smiling as if she had never, ever wept hysterically her whole life.

My last glimpse of Estonia was of piles of furniture, prams, bicycles, handcarts, mattresses, pillows, and open suitcases with their contents spilling over the grass and sand. An old lady was sitting on a mattress, surrounded by pillows, holding a large clock. She had refused to go without the clock and she had been left behind. Just when I thought I had seen enough for that day, I noticed a cat sitting on a small bedside cabinet, washing itself. It was not Tondu, but it might have been.

For years afterwards Mother and Grandmother continued to have words about what had been packed that day. They still argued about it in England. That day on the beach was a turning point in Mother and Grandmother's relationship. With "dear Erni" clutched to her chest, Grandmother insisted her husband's spirit was coming with us, or else she, too, would stay behind.

Ironically, everything in the "dear Erni" bundle became the foundation of Grandfather's biography 56 years later. On that day in 1944 Grandmother had packed for the year 2000.

Chapter 4

PARADISE LOST
23-25 September 1944

The boat was full. The adults were sitting around the sides and the baggage was in the middle. I was among the baggage, at Grandmother's feet, holding on to my bundle with one hand and Grandmother's coattail with the other. Mother was at the front with the men. There were dark storm clouds ahead. We could hear loud booms and explosions behind us. The wind picked up and began spitting plumes of spray that washed over everyone as the boat rose and dipped violently on the huge waves. I prepared myself to grab Grandmother's legs or coat, so we would go overboard together.

It got dark. Soon everybody was soaked. I was sitting on my potty, as a stool. My feet were in water that was cold and sloshing up my legs. Grandmother was sitting grimly, clutching "dear Erni," trusting God as usual, while I was trusting Mother. She was in front, in the bow, her glasses spattered, her hair wet and wild, shouting to be heard over the wind and motor. I hoped she was telling the men to make the boat go faster. I hoped she would box their ears and commandeer us straight to Sweden, because I had wet my pants. I hated Mother when she shook me and yelled at me. "Run when I say run! Hide when I say hide!" With the water lapping at my bottom though, I hoped the men would not dare tangle with an *artiste* who had received five curtain calls.

People were vomiting. The vomit was flying back into their faces. They were leaning over the side, moaning. My own spittle was getting thick and pasty. Strange how Mother had become a "father" since Father had relinquished his role two summers ago. Actors probably never did know who they were when they were out of costume.

Suddenly everybody sat up. There was another noise, another motor nearby. There was a moment of confusion, people yelling, talking, standing up and waving. Others were telling them to sit down. Grandmother began rummaging in her shopping bag for her candles. She tried to light one, but the matches kept going out. People tried to help. Instead of the boat moving up and down it began to rock sideways. I thought we were going to tip over and became so scared that I dared not take my eyes off Grandmother for a second. If we were going to heaven, I was definitely going with her. Mother would find her own way, as she always did.

The candle was lit. It flickered, but held. Nobody fell overboard, but people continued shouting, "Blow out the candle! Are you mad?" Others were standing and waving. "Ahoy! Halloo!" Nobody seemed to agree on what to do, while the boat rocked even more dangerously. The men had taken the oars out of the water and were cursing as they tried to hold the boat steady.

I wondered what the loud rumbling noise on top of us was, turned, and saw that a black wall had appeared beside us. We were going to crash into it. I closed my eyes. No big crash. When I opened my eyes again, we were still close to the wall, almost rocking against it, but the men with the oars were holding the boat away. There was a gap of several feet. The wall was a ship. The ship's hull was darker than the sky around it. There was a small light near the top, beaming down on us. A voice boomed out of the darkness. I imagined God had sounded like that to Moses when Moses found the Ten Commandments, but this was not God. The voice spoke German with a heavy foreign accent. God spoke all languages perfectly or He would not have been able to yell at the men building the Tower of Babel. The Bible stories were still fresh in my mind.

Mother was in the bow of the boat balancing herself, glasses in hand, wiping them furiously while listening to what the voice was saying. A few seconds later a rope ladder came rattling down along the steel side of the ship. It hung against the hull, just out of reach. The ladder had a rope attached to it that was being swung about from above, as though someone were moving it by hand. What happened next made me forget all about my wet clothes, the fear of dying, and even God Himself. When the rope came near the boat again, Mother grabbed it and pulled the ladder forward while the men with the oars fought to maintain the gap long enough for her to jump and swing herself off the boat feet first. I squeezed my eyes shut again. So much for the five curtain calls! Just when I thought I was getting to know her. When I opened my eyes, Mother was climbing up the side of the ship. She was leaving us, going back to Tallinn, to return to a "life of her own." I could not blame her. She had not been happy living with us anyway.

I turned back to Grandmother to see how she was reacting to this latest turn of events, but she was not where I had last seen her. I looked around frantically, trying to find her, and saw a big wooden crate descending down the side of the hull. It came slowly, on creaky ropes, illuminated by the overhead light. The winch brayed and squeaked; the box jerked, swayed, and bumped until it came near and the men caught it. Then the most terrifying moment of all. My own Mämmä with "dear Erni" in her arms was being helped into the box. I had been prepared for anything, but for Grandmother to abandon me. I became hysterical. The constraint of my tight sleeves, the slippery floorboards, the wet bundles, and peoples' hands trying to keep me from following Grandmother, all added to the panic. The box swung clear again and the winch started pulling it up. The underside of the crate tilted this way and that way. Sometimes I caught a quick glimpse of the flower in Grandmother's hat and her hands holding on to the sides of the box.

"Mämmä!" I screamed into the wind and darkness, fighting the strong grips that restrained me. All I knew at that terrible moment was that the only person in my life whom I loved was leaving me and I was going to be taken to Sweden by strangers.

What I did not know was that Grandmother had gone ahead because it had been necessary to test the ropes to see if they held, before sending the box back down for the rest of our baggage and me. I must have been thrown in with the bundles, because I cannot recall anything beyond my Grand-mother disappearing and my crying so hard that I could barely breathe. The next thing I remember was sitting in the hold of the ship, writhing with hiccups and having my wet clothes removed.

The full story, as I heard it later from Mother, was that the Polish freighter's captain had seen our boat, or maybe we had seen them and had lit a candle to warn them of our presence. The freighter had stopped and the captain invited anyone who would brave the rope ladder to come aboard. Mother had climbed and persuaded the captain to take us, too, if they could find a way to pull us up. I don't know if anyone else climbed up and I don't know what happened to the other people in the boat or if they ever made it to Sweden.

Perhaps 30,000 Estonians set off for Sweden in fishing boats large and small. Those who did battled the elements for days before reaching land. No one knows how many boats sank or how many people perished. If we failed to hear from someone by the early 1950's, we had to assume they had died one way or another in Estonia, in Germany, at sea, or in Siberia. We were the lucky ones.

→ *Unfortunately, Mother caught malaria, she thought from mosquitoes trapped in the hold. The ship had recently delivered cattle to Africa. She suffered bouts of high temperature and shaking for the rest of her life.*

We were the only passengers on the Polish freighter. Slime and green animal waste covered the deck, the stairs, and the hold. Straw mixed with manure was ankle deep. The smell was so bad Grandmother made me hold a hand-kerchief over my nose and mouth.

Languages had never been a problem for me, thanks to all the whisper-ings in German and Russian. The ship's crew was Polish and although the sounds were like Russian, I could not understand a word of what the men were saying to us while they helped us down the stairs. One of them asked me in poor German, "Which one is your mother?"

I told him. "Mämmä! The other is our leader." The man looked puzzled.

We kept the door above the stairs open for fresh air and could hear people's footfalls on deck. No one came downstairs, probably because of the smell. After a while we got used to it. We found fresh straw and privacy in a pigpen and hung our wet clothes on the sides of the stall.

Suddenly a loud siren began to wail, so loud I clapped my hands over my ears. More sirens echoed all around us. Other ships? I had thought we were alone.

The lights were turned off. It became black in the hold except for a small patch of sky and stars. When the planes attacked I put my fingers in my ears and hid my face in Grandmother's lap. A crewman appeared at the top of the stairs and tossed something down. "Life vests! Put them on!" he shouted in German. The vests were made out of blocks of cork, held together with string. Grandmother couldn't figure out which string went to what and where to put her arms. Her bosom was too big to close the front. My vest hung loosely to my knees and was uncomfortable over the damp clothes Grandmother forced back on me. The noises above deck were terrifying.

41

Boom! boom! The planes were firing. I had never seen airplanes or heard guns before, but realized I had known about them without having to see them. Everything started going wrong from the day people had stopped walking on the Promenade and had started running, whispering, and disappearing.

Once in a while I turned my head to look up at the stars that twinkled through the skylight between the flashes. The siren continued howling. Heavy things hit the water and made tremendous splashes. The ship rocked. I kept my fingers in my ears and hid my face against Grandmother's cork vest, but did not close my eyes anymore in case I fell asleep and woke up alone. (*This fear of closing my eyes and sleeping continued throughout the war*).

Yet I must have slept. When I opened my eyes again it was daylight above the stairs. No engine sound for the ship had stopped moving and was rolling from side to side. Footsteps were racing on deck. The winch that had brought us on board was braying again loudly, and men were shouting orders in Polish. Wisps of smoke kept drifting over the stair opening. The smell of smoke and a sharper smell (cordite), that I remembered from Haapsalu, burned my nostrils. I wanted to go on deck. Grandmother must have wanted to as well because she didn't protest. She gripped the back of my life vest and led me up the steps. We both held on to the handrail because the steps kept moving away from our feet.

A fierce wind grabbed us as soon as we came out on deck. It was hard to stand. The sea around the ship was a mountainous mass of oily water, sluggishly heaving up and down and littered with the same kind of belongings that I had seen people carrying to the docks and leaving on the roadside. There were suitcases, bundles, toys, pieces of wood, furniture, and a lot of clothing. Some of the clothing was encased in the cork vests. The vests and cloth bundles sloshed together with the debris. The bundles that had their heads up inside the cork collars were swimming and struggling to reach the ropes thrown to them by the crewmen. The still bundles remained unmoving and uncaring.

I became fascinated by the wave patterns pushing the whole mess back and forth, up and down the troughs, out, then in and around again. A boy tied around the armpits was hauled up by the crewmen; he was clinging to his mother's waist. I leaned over the side to see better and was told to get away from the rail. A fishing net was being hauled in. It was hoisted over the side and pushed to a central area. Seawater cascaded out of the bottom as the net was lowered and its contents dumped on deck. A jumble of arms, legs, hair, and tangled wet cloth spilled from where the net separated. The catch was not of fish, but people fighting to free themselves of the netting and each other. They rose to their knees, then to their feet. A few, however, remained in the net and did not move.

One woman got up, looked at her hands, and started screaming. Her hands had no palms, only flaps of white skin. Once out of the water they started bleeding. She had let herself down a metal cable that had stripped away the flesh.

Another woman, crawling on her hands and knees, was dripping wet and confused about which way to go. She had a baby tied to the back of her neck with a belt crossed over her chest. The baby's head was lolling back and forth with her every movement. When she tried to stand I stepped forward to tell her that her baby was dead, but Grandmother noticed my intention and grabbed me by my coat. She forced me back down the stairs.

"Not fair!" I protested. I had only tried to do the right thing, but Mämmä's lips were closed tightly and she refused to listen. I had meant well.

"Let's see where we got to in our story," she said, when we returned to our stall. She pulled our little book out of her coat pocket.

"Moses in the bulrushes," I reminded her.

"That's right." She put on her reading glasses, but then said her eyes were not working properly. "Maybe we should just rest," she suggested, having hardly slept at all during the night.

We had barely put our heads down in the straw when the stairs began to shake. Women and children began to descend the steps to look for a place where they could dry their clothes. Everyone was wet. The few men who had been saved stayed on deck. The women stared Stoney-eyed into the distance. Bigger children were silent. Only the babies and toddlers screamed without ceasing, but no one was being comforted.

Soon the hold was full. Wet clothes hung everywhere. I was glad we had gathered the best straw for ourselves, because the people began to use the animal pens as toilets. The smell of diarrhea soon replaced the smell of manure.

The planes returned the next night. There were no lights on the ship. We were all awake, listening to the drone of the unseen enemy. The planes passed over. Suddenly everyone began to hurry up the steps to the deck. Because there were no lights there was no real darkness, just varying shades of grey and a line of red on the horizon. We were close to land. "Are we there yet?" I asked Grandmother.

She did not hear me.

It was very windy. Distant explosions and flares leaped out of a line of fire that stretched along the entire coastline. Our people gathered at the rail, silently, standing to attention and facing the glowing sky. Beginning slowly, they began to sing the Estonian national anthem. The men removed their caps. Women were weeping. I stayed close to Grandmother, who held me awkwardly against her side because the cork blocks were keeping us apart. She was wiping her nose and eyes with a corner of her scarf. I knew that if she had not sewn "dear Erni's" prayer shawl so securely, she would have pulled it around her shoulders, the way she so often did when we sat on the porch, watching a sunset or sunrise. Now we were watching an entire coastline burning. After the Estonian anthem they sang the Latvian anthem and other anthems I did not recognize, perhaps Lithuanian and Polish.

Flight from Haapsalu to Saaremaa, by boat headed for Sweden and the Polish freighter to Danzig (now Gdansk).

Where was Mother, the Snow Queen? She was standing with the crew, hands to her sides, singing and crying. She became another photograph I had seen in a magazine. It had been the same with Father, probably because I had spent more time looking at their photos than I had seen them in real life, but this was no production.

We were off the coast of Liepäja, Latvia, not far from where the Moero, the largest Lazaretto[9] in the Baltic, had been torpedoed two days earlier on 21 September, despite being protected by the Geneva Convention and having a huge red cross on its side. The Moero carried at least 3,350 people. Of them, 1,200 had been wounded soldiers, below decks, with doctors, nurses, and a crew of 40. The rest were refugees. The ship went down in minutes. Perhaps 360 to 650 survivors were plucked out of the water by other ships. The documented list of Estonians rescued stands at 157.[10]

---

[9] A lazaretto is a quarantine station for maritime travelers. It can be a ship, isolated island, or a mainland building.

[10] The National Archives in Washington has a list of passengers and survivors but that, also, is only an estimate.

44

We arrived in Danzig in the misty early morning of 25 September 1944. From the ship's rail the wharf looked like a cattle market with people pushing and shoving each other in the limited space between the ship and cordoned-off heaps of rubble, some of it smoldering. The docks had recently been bombed. At the end of the wharf was a gate and beyond it a row of temporary buildings pasted with signs. Corrugated tin walls and metal barriers squeezed everybody into a bottleneck where uniformed guards tried to keep order, yelling at anyone who tried to bypass them.

We waited for Mother to tell us where to go, what to do. She had truly become our leader. Every time she reappeared we were relieved to see her even though she handled us roughly and would not tolerate any dawdling. Mämmä and I understood the urgency. We had only to see what happened to people who did not hurry. Unless they had somebody to help them to their feet, if they fell down they were left there.

"We have to get papers before we can continue," said Mother, pushing us into the surging mass that swallowed us as soon as we left the gangplank. Ours was not the only ship in the harbor. A forest of masts—big ships, tug boats, and looming cranes, some of them toppled and twisted—filled the waterfront. A pair of railroad tracks also ended in a pile of twisted metal loops, strewn cobbles, and broken bricks.

"This way!" Mother shouted and shouldered us forcibly into a barred and disused doorway. "Wait here!" She set off alone, moving swiftly through the throng, unencumbered by baggage and us.

She returned not too long afterwards with an envelope between her teeth and her glasses hanging around her neck on a string. She was panting for breath, but smiling and jubilant. She seemed to be enjoying herself at last after all those miserable weeks of burying herself in books, pacing the floor, and weeping secretly in the living room.

"All right! Now we catch a train," she said, grabbing the largest bundle onto her back and striding on ahead.

Mother had registered us with the NSDAP, the German Command which had rubber-stamped us as having arrived from Riga, Latvia. Perhaps that was near where we had been picked up. The other stamps gave us permission to continue to Berlin and the right to claim food rations for three people until 10 October.

The station was in ruins, but there were trains standing at the platforms and every platform was crowded to the edge. People, boosted from behind, were piling into the carriages, despite protests from those already aboard, who were tightly wedged against each other with nowhere to go. Screaming children were pushed through the windows into waiting arms. Mother entered the flow, and we were carried up the steps in a mass of bodies, holding our bundles over our heads. I hung onto a handful of Grandmother's coat, terrified of falling and being trampled on like those others I had seen.

Permit to travel to Berlin.

The compartments and corridors were bursting with people when the doors closed. Every seat was taken and occupied by soldiers. I had not seen any soldiers on our ship, so they must have come from another ship. They wore dirty and torn uniforms with brown-crusted bandages around their heads and limbs. Sometimes the whole face was swathed in a white cocoon except for the eyes, nose, and mouth. The bandages, however, did not hinder the men from dealing the cards with the one good arm or keeping the uncovered eye on the game. Bottles were passed around, cigarettes hung from slack lips. The soldiers were pointedly ignoring the press of bodies jammed against the compartment glass, but one soldier accidentally caught my eye. I put my tongue out at him. He must have thought I was a pig with my nose squashed against the glass. The soldier grinned and said something to the others. Two of them got up and pulled the compartment door open so abruptly that Mother and Grandmother fell through and landed on top of me. All three of us were on the floor, but quickly helped upright. The soldier who had opened the door bowed to Mother and offered her his seat. He had a dirty bandage wrapped around his head and a greatcoat draped like a cape over his bandaged shoulders. He reminded me of the painting Aunt Alma kept over her bed of *A Gallant Hero of the Crimea*, whom she probably likened to her dead fiancé. I remembered the ring. It was still safe.

Mother acknowledged the offer, but hesitated and shifted her gaze pointedly to Grandmother. The soldiers took the hint. Grandmother was also offered a seat. It turned out the soldiers were Latvians, although everybody spoke German. The "gallant hero" took off his greatcoat, moving easily for a wounded man as he tied the coat sleeves and hem corners to both luggage racks, creating a canopy across the compartment. Before I could protest, I was hoisted into this makeshift hammock, so close to the ceiling that I couldn't lift my head without hitting it, but it was wonderful to be free of people's knees, elbows, and suitcase corners. The smoke was thick and made me cough, but I was used to smokers. The only people I knew who did not smoke were Aunt Alma and Grandmother.

The train remained standing at the platform even after there were no more people trying to get on. It was hot; people were uncomfortable. In the corridor they could barely lift an arm without touching someone else's ear or poking them in the eye. I noticed one small boy's face squashed against the compartment glass just like mine had been, and his nose did look like a pig's snout. It occurred to me that if we humans did not wear clothes we really would look more like pigs than any other animal.

When the train finally moved, it was with a jarring scrape of metal and several jerks, which sent my hammock swaying dangerously. I braced myself for a fall but the knots held and the swaying soon became a rhythmic motion that made me realize how tired I was. I had not dared to sleep on the ship, but we seemed to be safe now. The voices below had a comfortable rumble to them, accompanying the steady clickety-clack of the wheels. I had only been on a train once before, to Tallinn, for that unfortunate singing audition.

Since the day when the rain had turned to ash my senses had become alert to any sound of alarm. I understood we were still fleeing this NKVD person or persons, whose terrible behavior had scared everybody at the Saunja Farm. The NKVD was deporting people to Siberia. That was another thing I had heard people whispering about. They did not dare to speak loudly in case they might also get arrested. Thus I heard that Vilja and her mother had been sent to Siberia. They had been turned in by their tenant who wanted their house for himself. I strained my ears for more. One woman who lived near the station said she had heard women and children screaming all night long. I moved closer, but the woman saw me and shut up. Grandmother assured me that we had escaped in time, just like the Israelites. When we reached the Promised Land we would be safe.

Below me the soldiers were still playing cards. Their smoke continued to drift toward the ceiling, although the top of the window was open. Grandmother asked one of the soldiers if he was badly wounded. The question was met with laughter. No more was said. Maybe some of them were not as badly wounded as it appeared.

The words I heard most were "Allies" and "Americans," which prompted more *Posits* and rounds with the bottle. Who were these "Allies" then? I thought there were only Russians and Germans.

In the dark, surrounded by cigarette smoke, unable to see directly below me except by carefully holding on to the luggage rack, I managed to turn onto my stomach and pull aside part of the hammock. There were no lights on in the train, but moonlight illuminated the compartment enough for the card players. The men who had given up their seats were sitting on the floor. The same moonlight showed a passing and swaying jumble of telegraph wires; some were down and snarled, but many were in place. The stations and the villages we passed were dark, but the fields were moonlit and looked covered with snow, when it was actually September. When everything from my hammock looked peaceful, I allowed myself to sleep. In my dream I was climbing the ladder to the attic, anxious to get at Mother's toys. I had to leave all my birthday furniture behind and was allowed only one small cel-luloid doll, while Mother had Maria. The unfairness still rankled. In the dream I had reached the top rung when a sudden jolt and drag of squealing brakes woke me. I raised my head in panic and bumped it on the ceiling. The train had stopped. The drone of planes overhead made me want to get down at once. I called "Mämmä!"

Mother reached up and said, "Shush, it's all right."

It was not all right. I lay frozen and paralyzed on my back as hundreds of planes rolled over us, but they remained high up, higher than the bombers that had attacked us at sea. No shooting, no bombs, the planes passed. Voices outside the carriage window sounded normal. In a few minutes we were moving again. In the natural moonlight I could see other passengers also assuming their former positions. Many had not wakened at all, but lay abandoned in deep sleep. I closed my eyes and joined them.

The next time I looked over the edge of the coat hem, Grandmother was using "dear Erni" as a pillow. Mother had her face turned into the headrest. The soldiers had their feet up, heads back. We were traveling through dark towns, passing silhouettes of houses, churches, and deserted streets. Going through one station, I saw a small illuminated sign on the underside of the stationmaster's office; it appeared to be in Polish. The stationmaster stood on the platform with a raised lantern.

The next time I awoke, the train had stopped again. It was still dark, but there was light on the horizon. Everybody was awake, whispering anx-iously as another sky full of approaching planes began to shake the ground and rattle the windows. It sounded as though the sky would fall on us any minute. Children started crying.

"Amerikaner?" said a voice by the window, in poor German.

"Nein, Engländer. Amis by day, Tommies at night, remember?"

"I say it's the Russkies again, in their sewing machines!" someone joked.

"You're right. Too far for Amis and Tommies." Someone was in the know.

"Whoever they are, they're saving their bombs for Berlin."

The remark was met by silence.

"And guess where we're going," said a small voice, after the pause. He used a rude German word that I had already picked up on the ship, mixing pigs and dogs. Civilians were the pigs, soldiers were the dogs, and the war was destroying every farmyard the world over.

After the planes had passed and we were moving again, there was no more sleep. The bright glow ahead was definitely not the moon or dawn. We were approaching a large city. The track went past overgrown backyards and gardens, tumbledown sheds, windowless factories, and burned out buildings of every kind. Sometimes just walls and blackened chimneys stuck out from a pile of rubble. The train slowed and then just inched along between groups of men leaning on shovels, holding lanterns or just standing, watching us pass. We stopped every few yards, heard hammering, men's voices again, shouting, this time in German. I guessed the Germans were mending the tracks in front of us as we moved along. In the corridor people were opening windows.

We stopped at a station where guards tried to get onto the train. The station sign was in German. The guards were armed and shouting in fluent German, but it was impossible for them to board. Luggage and people jammed the doors. No one would or could make room. The guards tried to pull the luggage out by force, hollering "*Papiere! Papiere!*" Nobody paid attention and they gave up in disgust. They slammed the doors shut and one of them spat on the ground as the train moved on. "*Flüchtlinge! Schweine-hunde!*" shouted one of the guards. Refugees and those pig-hounds again. My German was improving steadily.

We were traveling at a good pace when I felt the urge to go to the toilet. My potty was by Grandmother's feet. Having to go to the toilet had become ⟵ a big problem since leaving Estonia. There was never anywhere private. I held on as long as I could, then wet my pants. Again.

Danzig's population had swelled to over a million by the end of 1944. Most of them were refugees desperate to escape the advancing Russians, but as individuals they fell into many categories and nationalities. There were German soldiers who had been wounded, also Russian deserters and non-German soldiers conscripted into the German army who had managed to escape their battalions. There were Russian soldiers who had been captured by the Germans and were now afraid of their own people who had labeled them deserters. The Soviets could not allow those Russian soldiers back into Russia after they had seen that the Europeans were not poor, starving illiterates, desperately waiting to be rescued by the Communists, but were instead highly educated and prosperous people beyond anything they had known in Russia. It had already happened in Estonia. Having discovered that they had been lied to, the Russian soldiers could not be trusted to keep that knowledge to themselves.

We were not the only refugees. Perhaps 40,000 to 50,000 Estonians escaped during that one week in September—by sea, rail, or on foot. As many or more had escaped from the other two Baltic states.

Chapter 5

INTO THE LIONS' DEN
October 1944

We arrived in Berlin on 27 September 1944. The city was already in ruins.

Mother told me later that she had gone to Berlin because the train had been going there. Like everyone else, she had no clear destination. One survived one day at a time.

We were standing on a crowded platform at the Berlin main train station, unsure which way to go, when we heard a woman's voice calling Mother's name.

"Liki, over here!" The voice was shouting in Estonian.

The caller was Marga. There, just a few feet away was the entire Takk family, still pushing the pram loaded with luggage. Rein was holding onto the handle. I wanted to see the baby, so I looked into the pram while the adults were falling into each other's arms. Only bundles. No baby.

The reunion was joyous and tearful. Between sobbing and lamenting, I learned that they had indeed traveled from Haapsalu on foot, pushing the pram and accepting lifts through Latvia and Lithuania, but the baby had died of starvation. Hilda had a travel permit to report to a job with Philips Electrical in Eindhoven, Holland. She wanted us to come with them, but Mother dithered. It was just not possible to hop on a train without proper permits. We would have to catch up with them in Holland, although they themselves did not know where they were going to be. Mother decided she would stay where she was.

"I speak German," she reasoned. "I might find a job as translator. At least we will eat."

The train was approaching. Hilda pressed a piece of paper into Mother's hand. "Philips, Berlin Office. They might be able to hire you." Then quickly rummaging through her handbag, she produced another slip of paper. "We won't be needing this now. This man helped us bury the baby. He said his wife was a good Christian," she shouted as the train rumbled alongside us in a hiss of steam. The rest of what she said was lost in the noise, as people swarmed towards the doors. The Takks disappeared with their bundles, but they left the pram behind.

Although Mother's permit gave us permission to stay in Berlin only until 10 October, she was not perturbed by the deadline. "Right now we need to find this woman's house in ...", she squinted at the handwriting, "Bernau."

We let ourselves be pulled into the stream of passengers leaving the train and were funnelled with them into the underground. A sign *U-Bahn* hung over the entrance. A wall poster warned: *Der Feind hoert mit.* The enemy listens in. All the station windows were broken, but the glass had been swept into a neat pile next to the stairs.

We barely reached the tunnel before the air raid siren began an urgent wailing. The mass of people behind us started pushing forward. I had never been among so many people in my life. Except when forced to, I had not let go of Grandmother's coat since we got off the train or maybe since we had left Haapsalu. Mother was guiding us along the tunnel, a wide concrete corridor lit by a row of dim light bulbs hanging from a central cable. The tunnel was damp, and the walls lined with cots, mattresses, boxes, bundles, and people sitting or lying down between them or on them. Room-like recesses led off in different directions. Glowing paint indicated the entrances to various sections. In one you could see three-tier bunk beds. One door had a big red cross on it. There were public toilets, but the smell was so awful that Mother pushed us past. I had wet myself so many times already that I did not even think before I let go.

From Berlin to Bernau

Halfway through the tunnel we heard loud explosions. A bombing was in progress above us. After a really loud bang the tunnel vibrated and fine trickles of sand sifted down through cracks in the ceiling. All talking ceased, but we kept moving until we arrived at an open platform and waited for another train. Mother seemed to know where we were going. Grandmother had given up any independent decisions except keeping hold of "dear Erni." Now and then I felt Mother's hand on my shoulder, reassuring me she was still with us.

We arrived in Bernau and found the address on a treelined boulevard not far from the station. It was a big two-story house surrounded by a high stone wall with a pillared gate. Mother raised her eyebrows to show us she was impressed.

The woman was not impressed with us. She was not even pleased to see us. After Mother had explained our situation and because it was already late in the evening, the woman pursed her lips and led us to a room with one small bed. I was given the bed. Mother and Grandmother slept on the floor, using some of the bedding. Alas, when the woman came into the room in the morning to see how we had slept, she discovered we had slept in our clothes. There had been no immediate offer of water and we had been too tired to ask. When she began to pull the sheets off the bed, she became hysterical. My wet underwear had dried unnoticed in the rush and crush of trying to keep moving, but I must have smelled terrible. She started shaking out the white sheets and screaming at us, calling us filthy *Verdammten Flüchtlinge* and *Verfluchte Ausländer*. Damned refugees and pesky foreigners.

Mother's nostrils extended in anger, but she knew her role was crucial in this scene. She bent a bit this way and that way and begged the Frau to let us stay another day, until she returned from Berlin. She was going back to find a job.

"Just one day, please. I can't take them with me," she pleaded so humbly that even Grandmother looked surprised.

The woman relented. She said we could wait in the garden shed.

When the air raid siren sounded, the woman did not invite us to join her and her children in the cellar, so we remained in the shed. There were no windows and we kept the door open.

"At least we're warm and dry," said Grandmother, beating her hat against the door to release the sand, bits of straw, and anything else that had attached itself to us during the journey. Unfortunately there was nowhere to wash or change clothes. So it was just as well the door was open. Grandmother knew I was upset by the things the woman had said about my being dirty and disgusting. I was also frightened by the bombs exploding all around. She sat on a box and pulled me close. I hid my head in her lap and plugged my ears with my fingers. I knew that while I was with Mämmä no bomb would fall on me.

Mother did not return that day or the next. The woman's children must have let word get out that *Verdammte Flüchtlinge* and *Verfluchte Ausländer* were staying with them. Her two boys had looked to be about ten or eleven and wore the *Jungvolk* uniform of the Hitler Youth.[11]

I was playing on the street in the gutter, collecting spent cartridges, ideal for whistles, when a number of *Jungvolk* surrounded me. One of the boys noticed Aunt Alma's ring. He lifted my hand for everyone to see. *Was haben wir hier? Die Braut des Teufels!* What do we have here? The devil's bride. He laughed, took my ring and slid it onto his own finger. They then dragged me to a bomb crater in a neighbor's garden and threw me in. They started pelting me with soil, stones, and bottles, but an air raid saved me.

---

[11] *Hitler Jungend*, Hitler Youth, or H-J, pronounced in German "Ha-Jot," was for older boys. Younger boys, eight to ten years old, were in the *Jungvolk*.

The boys ran away. Grandmother's face appeared above the rim of the hole. She had been looking for me and had heard my screams. She pulled me out. I was so upset that I forgot to tell her about the ring.

Wanting nothing more to do with the *Frau*, we left the shed to find our own water and found a tap several streets away. We were standing in line when the siren began to hoot, but we stayed put, as did everybody else. It was forbidden to stay in the street, but we did anyway, afraid to lose our place in the queue. I had learned to distinguish between the approaching strafers and the duller drone of bombers, but I was keeping a keener ear out for the *Jungvolk*. I had become more afraid of them than of being shot.

Mother returned two days later with a loaf of bread, a sausage, and a bag of sugar beets. She had found Philips Electrical and they had hired her, but she could only work for a few days, helping them pack. Philips was pulling out of Berlin. They had given her a letter of introduction to another branch of Philips in another part of Germany. This provided her with a new travel permit and *Lebensmittelkarten*, ration cards, but we could not leave Berlin until 3 October and had to arrive on the 4th.[12]

The new Philips office she had been assigned to was in a small town called Hausberge, on the River Weser. She felt she had made the right decision to stay in Germany and not go to Holland, because Holland was also essentially "Germany" and occupied by the Nazis.

As Mother could not take us with her to Berlin, she said we would have to "kiss the *Frau's* arse" a little longer. We could hear her at the woman's back door, once more, humbly saying *Gnädige Frau* this, *Gnädige Frau* that, and *Bitte und Danke*—addressing the other woman as though she were the Snow Queen and her garden shed a palace. Mother even persuaded the woman to let Grandmother cook the beets on the *Frau's* stove.

"But you stay only one more night," the woman snapped.

When we were alone, Mother spat on the ground. "We're getting out of here first thing in the morning, even if we have to sleep in the street, but first we cook the beets."

That was what happened. Mother paid the woman with some of our silver, and we returned to Berlin.

While Mother was at work we stayed in the *U-Bahn* (subway). We found a small space and kept it, afraid to leave in case someone else grabbed it. The woman sleeping next to us chatted with Grandmother. She had been bombed out and had nowhere else to go. She did not suspect we were foreigners, because we were all smelly and dirty together, and Mother's and Grandmother's German was that good. I kept my mouth shut around her, remembering Bernau and that Germans did not like foreigners.

Eventually we had to go out for water and a toilet.

Mother had taken her suitcase and the largest bundle to work with her. We carried "dear Erni," the shopping bag, and my bundle and potty everywhere we went. It was especially difficult climbing on rubble or skirting

---

[12] Philips Electrical - Philips Valvo Werke in Berlin was on Kurfürstenstrasse.

54

twisted metal and puddles without a free hand to steady ourselves. Streets were slippery with mud and ash. We trusted our neighbor, but dared not leave anything behind, because every moment could bring another chain of events or we might not find our way back. They did not let you into the shelters once the bombing had started.

When we returned to the *U-Bahn* our neighbor had kept our place. We thanked her by giving her some of our water. It occurred to me that if everybody kept their mouths shut and looked the same, there would be no need for war.

Despite the acidy smell of hot metal and cold concrete and the constant condensation dripping off the ceiling, the tunnel was warm and cozy. The light bulbs had mostly burned out, but those that flickered every time a train passed through added to the flickering of real candles that people had set on ledges, creating a feeling of festive companionship. (*I did not know the candles were used to test air quality.*)

Mother returned that evening and was also in a happy mood. The workers had been told to help themselves to anything they wanted before the office doors were locked. Mother had acquired a rucksack, something she had wanted. She up tipped it. Out tumbled paperclips, pencils, pads, office forms, rubber bands, even scissors. Lastly she pulled out a pair of men's boots, a man's jacket, and a pair of wool socks for Grandmother. Mother was having a life of her own again, which was the way she liked it when she was at her best. Grandmother examined the socks with a strange expression.

"Don't worry, nobody died in them," Mother assured her.

The air raids continued.

When the explosions became too loud and sounded too close, Mother made us lie down in an established order: me on the bottom, Grandmother on top of me, and Mother herself spread above us. "That way," she said, "we will all go together."

I thought of the *U-Bahn* as home. I had come to like crowded places and lots of people around me. Hearing normal conversations meant we were safe and I could close my eyes. Mother was lying on one side of me, Grandmother on the other. I might have been asleep already when there was a terrible explosion. The entire tunnel rocked and all the lights went out, including the candles. A mixture of sand and water began to rain down from the ceiling. Everyone jumped up. There was panic. People were saying that the station had received a direct hit down the line and that we had to get out quickly.

On the way out, in the dark, in a mass of people and baggage heading for the steps and in the faint glow of a hand-held lantern, Mother held my coat collar and Grandmother's arm. Our bundles rode the tide. The flow was hugging the wall; everyone was afraid of falling off the edge of the platform. The guard at the exit was shouting out the address of a public shelter. We followed everyone else, but when we got to the shelter, it was full. We were given yet another address. It was dark without streetlights and this time there were not enough people to follow. We did not know where to go. It was also past curfew.

The sirens howled again, but Mother said to heck with it. We climbed a broken garden wall into a ruined building that had two upright walls.

"We'll be safe here," she said. There were no streetlights, but the sky always glowed at night because of the burning buildings. We ate some bread, sausage, a few beets, and then wedged ourselves into a corner of what looked like a ruined kitchen. Mother's last words were, "I hope it doesn't rain."

When the planes arrived they brought rain, but it was not the rain Mother had feared. In the tunnel we had been aware of the bombers and felt the explosions, but in the roofless ruin we were also seeing the planes and the explosions all around us. The noise was deafening. The siren, the rattle of anti-aircraft guns, and the explosions were the same as usual, but now we could also see the underbellies of the bombers. Wave after wave of them, illuminated by flares, searchlights, and tracers. The planes formed a droning, moving canopy, surrounded by smoke and a steady stream of dark objects falling vertically. Once in a while a larger object burst into flames and spiraled down along with them. Everything that hit the ground exploded.

Holding my fingers in my ears did not help. Hiding my face in Grandmother's lap so I would not see the flashes did not help much either. There were more planes, more bombs, more of everything than there had been at sea or on the train journey from Danzig, and everything looked like it was going to fall on us. Some bombs exploded in red and yellow fire while others flared into white fireballs, bright as daylight that caused a hot wind to rise and sweep down the street. It tore at the trees. Mother shouted for us to press into the ground. We were buttressed into a crevice between the ground and the wall. Squeezed against Grandmother's chest with my eyes closed and my fingers plugged nearly into my eardrums, I could see flares and flames through my eyelids. Tree branches flew past us along with all other kinds of rubbish. Mother was on top again, holding us both down. I wanted to cry, but could not get enough breath. Instead I began to shake violently, thrashing my head from side to side. Grandmother squashed me tighter still, right into her bosoms. I could feel her heart beating through her clothes. Mother's hand gripped the back of my head, her other arm went around Grandmother's neck and her face was against my back. I could hear Grandmother praying, not just talking to "dear Erni", but speaking to God himself. She needed more spiritual comfort. The danger was not earthly, but coming from heaven; she was appealing to a higher authority than that of a well-known poet.

Until that night I had thought of myself as Grandmother's child, but seeing my Mother as frightened as I was, also clinging to Grandmother, made me realize that she, too, was Grandmother's child. The relationships I had struggled to understand finally fell into place. Grandmother and Mother were both mothers, Mother and I were both Mämmä's children.

The bombing seemed to last for hours, but might have only lasted minutes. I did not find my voice until the all clear sounded and even then I could only hiccup, as the trembling became less. We remained where we were and did not move until the wind turned cold. It was morning.

Mother got up shakily and said it was her fault. She had made a bad choice of shelters. Mother and Grandmother were covered with a white dust.

Mother's face was a white mask. Grandmother's face was muddy, with leaves and twigs in her hair where her hat had slipped. I could not see my face. I touched it and found it was wet.

Mother followed the rusty sink fixture of the former kitchen to a broken water pipe and a puddle beneath it. This supplied enough water to wash our faces and hands, but we dared not drink it.

Grandmother said we needed to find that air raid shelter or a cellar before the next air raid. There were plenty of cellars, but they were usually occupied by the people who owned the ruins above, or the cellars had been claimed a long time ago, but Mother was thinking again. She was furiously cleaning her glasses, holding them up, making sure they had not cracked.

"That's it!" she said suddenly, having made another decision. "Not another night in Berlin, but we can't leave until tomorrow. The people at Philips told me there's an old cemetery outside the city, a kind of refugee village among the graves. Nothing left out there to bomb. The planes just fly over it. It will be a long walk."

To prepare for the journey we needed to repack. Towels, extra shoes, one set of extra clothes she stuffed into her new rucksack. "We don't want to be rummaging in our bundles among strangers," she warned. "People have been living there for months. We can expect it to be crowded." She then reached for the "dear Erni" bundle, but Grandmother pulled it close. The message was clear. She had elected to bring it and she was going to carry it, no matter how heavy or cumbersome it had become.

We set off after dawn and walked until noon. We spent the first air raid of the day in a *U-Bahn* station, but the trains were not going where we wanted to go. Mother had directions.

We were not able to walk fast. People in the streets were walking faster and with purpose. Many of them were going to work. I had already discovered where all the missing men were—they were all in uniform. Russian soldiers in Estonia. German soldiers in Germany. War seemed to be something only the men enjoyed until they were caught and made prisoners.

At that time of day and after the night air raids the streets were full of debris. Some streets were blocked off, closed to pedestrians where men in chains were mending tram tracks and clearing rubble from burning buildings, surrounded by guards with vicious dogs. Some prisoners wore ragged Russian greatcoats and *ushankas*, fur hats with dangling ear shields, while others wore striped pajamas with letters on their backs. Nobody was allowed near these workers, and the guards never gave them a minute's peace.

We took a tram, but it did not go far enough. The tracks were too damaged. If a street was completely blocked we had to go around it and find the same street again farther along.

The big buildings were nearly all damaged. Sometimes we came upon a block of flats still standing, but missing a front wall. The rooms were exposed as in a doll's house. There were beds, tables, chairs, and washstands. Pictures and mirrors hung on the walls. It looked like one could live there just by pulling a blanket across the open part, but there also were chains across the doors and plywood fences to keep people out. Guards and soldiers were everywhere, wearing armbands and different kinds of uniforms. Women and children did not seem to have a role or a function in war except to be scared to death and to stay out of the way.

Every time we saw an *S-Bahn* or *U-Bahn* station, I called to Mother, "Can't we go by train?" I was getting tired.

"Won't be long now," Mother promised cheerily. "The tracks have been destroyed. We need to stay away from stations and train tracks." When Mother started using her bright stage voice, it meant she, too, was tiring. We were ready to sit or lie down in the nearest garden. Grandmother was having trouble keeping up. The "dear Erni" bundle was heavy, but she could also be a Snow Queen if she wanted to.

When it appeared Mämmä could not take another step, Mother pointed to a thickly wooded park surrounded by a moss-covered wall. The wall was in pieces, but it had been built magnificently out of colored bricks. The gate had an ornate topping.

"We've arrived. This is it. The cemetery." Mother spread her arms to embrace the victory not just for herself, but also for the three of us. She appeared to have accepted that she was now Act One in a family of three.

For me cemeteries were friendly places. They were where our friends and relatives resided and the only places where people stayed put. You always knew where to find them. They did not go away for "the summer" and there were no "on" or "off" seasons. They listened to your complaints and did not tell you to go pick dill or find something to do. They did not even mind if you sat on them or stepped on them by accident.

In the cemetery, the central walk was bordered by a canopy of trees so dense that light could barely break through the foliage. It was an *allée*. Grandmother often used such words as *allée* and *triste*. Some things, she said, sounded better in French. Grandmother spoke five languages. Grandmother's governess, Lise, had taught Alma and Grandmother French. Most Estonians spoke Russian and German and Grandmother also spoke Finnish. She now wished she had learned English instead. Mother had told us that, if the Allies won, English was going to be the next world language.

The cemetery had an old section and a new section. In the old section the grass was high and the gravestones leaned all over the place. The church that had belonged to the cemetery was in ruins. In the new section there was little grass, just weeds, gravel and plain markers. In the old section the graves were very elaborate. Stone cherubs and weeping angels were everywhere. Blankets and canvas had been thrown over tree limbs; pieces of cardboard had been propped against grave markers as supports for crude tents. Every space was taken by someone's belongings or feet sticking out onto the path.

"Look there." I pointed to a tiny house surrounded by a fence. It had steps leading down to a padlocked door and looked unoccupied. I had seen similar houses and was ready to go down the steps and look through the tiny grill set into the door to check if the house was empty. Mother laughed and held me back. "Those are mausoleums. They're only for the dead."

"The whole house? Maybe they'll share?"

58

Mother thought I was being funny. We were not used to talking to each other.

"Actually it's a family tomb," Mother explained.

"The padlock is rusted. If they're all dead, it wouldn't matter."

"You don't understand. It's a crypt."

"So how much room do these dead people need?"

Grandmother could see me starting one of my "reasoning's." She reminded us that we were supposed to be looking for the best possible grave. "Off the ground, sheltered. And make sure the area is dry," she advised.

Grandmother was always patient with me, but Mother had only lately become "family" and had begun to sound annoyed. Grandmother nudged me past the mausoleum. So unfair, I thought—whole houses for dead families when live ones were sleeping outside in the open. The grave slabs were beds with people curled up on them like fallen angels, wrapped in dirty sheets and blankets. In the shelters, too, people had slept during the day because the nights were so noisy.

Mother had been right. The cemetery was crowded. All the better graves had been taken.

Finally Mother spotted an unoccupied slab in a dark corner of the old cemetery. It was surrounded by weeds and nettles. The grave was of the raised kind, marker less with a pedestal. The slab cover had been moved off on one side and was broken. Mother made a face to indicate that it was not ideal, but it would have to do. She and Grandmother began to pull weeds and clear nettles around the slab. An overhanging oak tree was as good as a roof—a lot better than a dripping concrete ceiling.

While we were clearing the area, the air raid siren sounded. A few minutes later a mass of bombers rumbled in. The planes flew high and amazingly did not drop anything. Mother had been right again, nothing here to bomb, but trees and an already blackened church spire.

Everyone ignored the planes. Some sleepers sat up, blinked at the sky, and lay down again. A few people walked by us. They nodded a greeting. Mothers shepherded their children into the bushes. I could see why the area around had not been taken.

With nowhere to wash except the cemetery tap, Mother told me to go get some water, but I refused to go without Grandmother. Before Mother could become annoyed again, Grandmother took my hand and we went together. We joined a line of women and children. Grandmother started talking to a woman in front of her. The children all seemed to know each other and cast curious glances at us. Friendly glances. Our dirty appearance again made us indistinguishable from homeless Germans, but my fear of German children and of being marked a *Verfluchter Ausländer* had become a constant worry. The *Jungvolk* in Bernau had not hurt me, but they had taken something from me, along with Aunt Alma's ring. I turned my back and made sure my hand touched Grandmother's coat.

When we returned to our slab, Mother was searching through her rucksack. Grandmother leaned up against a tree and fell asleep with "dear Erni" in her arms. I sat on the edge of the slab and mustered enough courage to look down the hole under the slab. I wondered whether I would see bones or worse, Death himself.

The smell that emanated from the hole was of cold pits, flooded cellars, ruined houses, newly dug graves, and open coffin funerals. When the pastor was talking and the coffin was being lowered, I could always visualize the person inside the casket: with painted cheeks and crossed hands, giving a sigh of relief under the closed lid. The next step would be the resurrection. In between, the dead person could look forward to *Hingedeöö* (All Souls' Night) when an extra plate would be set for them at the dinner table. Dead souls liked to eat. Estonian traditions paid a lot of attention to dead souls. Grandmother and I had always celebrated them at Haapsalu cemetery where the entire cemetery became blanketed with flickering candles, a field of fallen stars, extinguishing and dying in the snow. That was when I first became interested in life and death.

I looked down the hole and thought I heard a groan. Mother heard me gasp. "Not afraid of ghosts, are you?" Mother came and looked down the hole with me, then patted my knee. "Right now it's the living we need to worry about, not the dead," she said lightly, trying to sound reassuring.

Ah, but she was not talking about old death. She was talking about new death. New death was messier. The newly dead just lay in the streets until someone removed them. Or they were run over by a truck. I had seen that, too, after an air raid. Sometimes it happened so quickly they probably did not even know they had died.

Mother saw I was still apprehensive and solved the problem by placing her rucksack over the hole. She went through the pockets and produced more boiled beets and half a squashed loaf of bread wrapped in a towel. When she turned away I dropped a boiled beet down the hole, just in case.

Grandmother had not been napping deeply; she sat up as soon as Mother mentioned bread. Grandmother volunteered to get more water. Left alone with Mother, I watched her rummage some more until she found her amber cigarette holder and a small metal gadget with rollers. Using the scissors she had confiscated from the office, she cut an order form into small squares, inserted a bit of paper into the rollers, filled the gap with dried leaves, licked the edge of the paper, and began to roll the gadget until she produced a "cigarette." She tried to light it, but after two tries with our precious matches, she gave up. "Damn!" she said, actually using the Estonian word *kurat* (devil). I was fascinated. Mother's life had been such a mystery to me. Now, suddenly here she was, brave and beautiful, grumpy and annoyed, but even with her face dirty and her hair bundled under the beret, she still had the lead role and would never miss a cue. She had told us once that she had acted right through scarlet fever because the show had to go on. Then I noticed that her hand was trembling. I remembered how scared she had been when we had stayed in the ruins. I wanted to comfort her and tell her that I, too, had been scared, but she was still too much of a stranger. So all I did was move a bit closer. Mother wasted another match and then swore again when it started to rain.

The tree kept off the worst of the rain, but retained water, and the branches were dripping long after it had stopped raining elsewhere. More water dripped off the tree than off the *U-Bahn* ceiling. Grandmother took me under her coat. Mother put a towel over her head and went to speak to a small knot of people huddled around a flickering candle in one of the plywood shelters. They were listening to a crackling box.

When Mother returned she said, "The British have pulled out of Arnheim after severe losses. The Russians have reached Yugoslavia and are in Latvia." She then lowered her voice and said with some excitement, "The Allies have captured thousands of Germans in Calais."

Allies again. She called the crackling box a "radio" and "BBC." Seeing that I was listening, she turned her back and lowered her voice, but I heard her. "Something, something...Polish uprising...Warsaw... terrible, terrible." She mimed the rest with raised eyebrows and facial expressions...another catastrophe that I was not supposed to know about. She was good at miming. It meant I had to start keeping my eyes open as well as my ears.

Chapter 6

IN THE LIONS' DEN
1944 - 1945

On 1 August 1944 at five o'clock in the afternoon thousands of windows flashed as they were thrown open in the sun and a hail of bullets riddled German soldiers on the streets below. Within fifteen minutes an entire city of about a million inhabitants was engulfed in battle. Nearly a quarter of a million Poles perished in the Warsaw Uprising, and when the Red Army's formations at last crossed the Vistula, they entered a ruined city whose streets were littered with the reeking, rotten corpses of the unburied dead.

Robert Leckie

From Bernau to Hausberge

We arrived in Hausberge on 4 October 1944. Hausberge is part of the town of Porta-Westphalica, thus named by Julius Caesar's Roman legions when they occupied this double-mountain location during the Gallic Wars of 51-58 B.C. The River Weser flows between the two mountains. Houses built on steep streets rise up the mountainsides, and on the Porta side, to a massive monument to Kaiser Wilhelm I, which the Allies tried to blow up in April 1945, but failed even to budge.

A man sweeping the floor at Hausberge Station gave us the address of a woman he said was taking in refugees. The man had a strong foreign accent, but did not tell us where he was from. Following his directions we crossed an open square with a shuttered church on the right and an uphill fork on the left, leading to the first tier of houses above the main street. We were looking for a big brick three-story house covered with ivy. We found it immediately. It sat sideways to the street with two large wrought iron gates over a crumbling tiled walkway leading to the front door. The entire building was thickly covered with ivy except for two ornamental turrets at each corner of the house. Two dormers and a round central dome in the roof proclaimed it to be a house and not a clever green box. Grandmother said the house was a parsonage, the dome was a skylight, and the lady we were going to speak to was a parson's widow—"a good woman," the man had said. I remembered the "good woman" in Bernau and stayed back.

After Mother's prolonged knocking, the door was opened by a reed-thin old lady dressed in a long black gown with a white collar and white cuffs. Small black-buttoned boots with pointed toes peeped from under the dress hem. Buttons on the boots matched her eyes. The woman's grey hair was piled upon her head in the style of a loaf of farm bread.

While Mother talked, the woman kept her lips pursed, nodding often to show that she was listening. When Mother finally stopped for breath, the woman laced her hands and said *ja,* but shook her head *nein.* The house was already full of *Flüchtlinge,* refugees, she explained. All she could offer us was a closet in the attic in which she kept the church furniture.

Mother assured her we would be most *dankbar,* thankful.

"*Ja. Gut. Bitte.*" She stepped back.

The entrance hall was very big with panelled walls and a tiled floor, lit by a skylight, which explained the dome in the roof.

"Who is it?" a voice called from inside one of the many doors that opened into the hall. The door was ajar.

"Refugees," the woman called back. "My daughter," she explained to us, "from Breslau." The daughter seemed satisfied and did not make an appearance. The woman then told us to follow her up the ornate staircase. It had several landings. The woodwork was exquisite.

Frau Qwirll and daughter Gerda, Hausberge, 1961.

Grandmother went first, then Mother. I trailed behind, wanting to see what was in the other rooms, but the doors were closed.

The woman kept up a brisk narration about her dead husband, the pastor of the abandoned church we had passed. She explained that she and her daughter were both widows. Other relatives were in the house, from Silesia.[13]

"These are difficult times," she explained, but it was her Christian duty to take in unfortunates. Her husband would have done the same.

Grandmother, who was a good listener, bent her head, but Mother had moved on. She wanted to see what we were getting into. I remembered she did not care for religious people, which explained why she did not take part in the conversation. I also knew she would normally have objected to us being referred to as "unfortunates," but after Berlin she was definitely less the Snow Queen and more like someone who also needed to be comforted once in a while.

Frau Qwirll took us into a large attic filled with furniture. The closet she had mentioned really was only a small enclosure heaped with pew cushions, a pulpit, and a small table. We were welcome to use the cushions to sleep on and could use any other furniture we could fit inside. The house rules, she mentioned rather apologetically, were that we could use her downstairs hall toilet and her kitchen stove once a day, but we had to supply our own cooking pot and get our own water from the public tap. Her well was not working properly and we had to add to the supply of firewood, if possible. We were not to enter any of the doors on the first and second floors or go into the garden.

"*Danke.*" She crossed her hands over her stomach and left us alone.

Mother looked stunned, having expected a repeat of Bernau, but Grandmother was not surprised by the woman's kindness. She handed me our cooking pot and told me to go find this public tap. It could not be far. She was going to boil potatoes. I didn't even know we had potatoes.

The tap was at the beginning of the street. We had passed it and I had noted its ornamental shell-shaped bowl and horse's head tap. It was a horse trough. Before I filled the pot I wanted to know where the water was coming from. I climbed up the stone chute to discover it was fed by a mountain spring farther up the slope.

I had never seen mountains, never lived near a river or explored woods like these so close to the house. I looked forward to wading in the river and climbing to the top of the mountain, so that I could look down on the town. I had noticed cable cars crossing the river from one summit to the other. The cable car station was beyond the bridge where the railroad tracks continued along the foot of the mountain. Access was cut off by iron gates, barriers, and sentry boxes patrolled by the same kinds of armed guards with dogs that we had seen in Berlin. Now and then, a blast of steam would issue out of the mountainside. No one was allowed past the bridge and certainly nowhere near the gate or beyond it.

Grandmother went to heat the water. Mother set out to find the Philips office she was supposed to report to, "I'll be back soon," she said and left.

---

[13] A historical region in central Europe, located mostly in modern Poland, with smaller parts in the Czech Republic and Germany.

The closet to be "our room" was actually one of the turrets. From the narrow floor-to-ceiling window we had a clear view of the entire valley. Autumn foliage was in full color. The river was a flat and sparkling ribbon of green and brown reflections. A broad meadow dotted with wildflowers sloped from the road to the riverbank. The wildflowers reminded me of midsummer nights in Haapsalu, where children were called upon to make flower crowns for the dancers. The only time Grandmother did not scold me for willfully plucking flowers, but instead praised my crown. Estonians believed that trees and flowers were sacred entities, and many believed that the oak tree was a kind of god. Midsummer Night celebrations, with food, singing, dancing, and bonfires, was another tradition from the old times. Near the end of the festivities young couples in folk costume held hands, jumped over the bonfire to cheers and toasts, and continued on into the forest to look for a rare fern that only bloomed one night a year—on Midsummer Night. I asked Grandmother whether she had seen the fern. She said she had not, but that those who found it got married and had a baby the following March.

I was standing in the window overlooking the peaceful scene below, when the valley was ripped apart by the wail of the air raid siren. I had not been prepared. I had even forgotten that we were still in a war. Grandmother ran to the door to call Mother, but she was not back yet.

Village of Hausberge in the 1960s.

At the same time Frau Qwirll came running upstairs.

"*Schnell!*" Hurry. We had to come with her to the cellar, but in the future, and if there were time, we would have to go into the town shelter inside the mountain. She sounded apologetic. Her cellar was small, only for family. And *ja*, she would show us the shelter. It was not far. I had a feeling those were not her house rules, but complaints voiced by her relatives from Silesia, not happy to be sharing the house with *Ausländer*.

It was still daylight, so the bombers had to be Americans. I recognized the smooth droning of their approach. A steady thunder filled the valley and dimmed the daylight, as though a cloud had come between us and the sun.

66

Mother turned up breathless. She had located her office, but could not tell us more at the moment.

The planes continued in a steady stream. No bombing of any kind. Nobody seemed worried although the anti-aircraft fire was deafening and spitting orange.

Frau Qwirll had begun to introduce us to the people already gathered on the benches. There was the sweeper from the station, still in his guard's uniform. He touched his hat when he saw us. Next, Frau Qwirll introduced us to her daughter, a big robust woman, three times the size of her mother. She appeared friendly, but worn out. Women were definitely more worn out by this war than men.

Then we met Frau Qwirll's Silesian relatives, an older woman and a younger one. They gave us their disapproving glares and barely acknowledged the introductions. They had a daughter named Grete, younger than me and beautifully dressed in white knee socks and sporting a *Dolle*, a kind of French roll hairstyle that I had seen on almost every German girl in Berlin. She was sucking on some kind of white confection, smacking her lips and letting me know how good it tasted. When Frau Qwirll told her my name, she, too, turned away from me. The adults must have been discussing us unfavorably and she was siding with her mother. All this while the cellar shook and vibrated.

A young Latvian woman was yelling over the noise, telling Mother she had been a school teacher in Riga. She introduced us to her *mutter*, her mother, who sat at her side staring into space. I had seen those vacant stares in the *U-Bahn* stations. At least she was sitting upright and not curled up on the floor.

Another woman who had a daughter about my age also latched on to Mother's hand and didn't let go. She introduced herself as Frau Schneider, speaking loudly and clearly with a regional accent I could not place. The daughter's name was Ursula. Their room was at the top of the stairs next to the attic.

"We're neighbors," she told us, falling into rapid German.

Mother had found a new friend. They both smoked and neither had had a real cigarette for months or a cup of decent coffee. "Ah, for real coffee, not that awful *Ersatz*." Frau Schneider rolled her eyes. They further discovered they were both *artistes*—performers. Frau Schneider had been in cabaret. "Ah!" She turned pink at the thought of better days.

I watched her with resentment. The woman could sing and dance, even though she looked like a horse. She might have been a great *artiste*, but it must have been before all the fat had drained out of her body, leaving her skin empty and hanging. Her underarms jiggled and her neck hung loose. When she gestured and turned her head, or worse, laughed out loud, she really did look like a horse in profile. Her side teeth were missing and her hair was a strange orange. It looked burned. Grandmother caught me staring and nudged me to remind me that it was rude to stare at people who had met with misfortune.

Ursula was a smaller, undamaged version of her mother. Her hair was also short, probably cut with a knife, but it was real hair. They must not have had scissors. We could lend them our scissors if they would let us borrow their knife. Meanwhile we were using a small axe that worked as well, except for peeling potatoes.

Ursula smiled shyly and got to her feet when we were told to shake hands. She remained standing politely, as did I, until we were told we could sit. While we were standing, I noticed Ursula twisting her knees in a pose I recognized and related to daily. There was nowhere to go to the toilet in all of Germany except behind walls and into bushes; in houses you had to hold it. The toilet on the first floor was constantly in use.

I knew Ursula and I would become friends. She was not a *Jungvolk*. She seemed to understand my German and although she wore nice clothes, she had not once wrinkled her nose at me because I was an *Ausländer*.

The sweeper from the railroad station was the only man in the cellar and probably the only man in the house. He and Grandmother moved to a corner, sat on a wooden crate and began to converse quietly in Russian. She told us later the man was a White Russian. How you could tell a White Russian from a Red Russian was a mystery to me.[14]

Going back upstairs to our attic, slowly this time, with Frau Schneider and Mother leading the way, we passed a big window on the second floor landing. I had passed it before, but not when the sun was on it. It was a church window with colored glass moldings, part of a big pane that depicted the biblical scene of the Crucifixion. I had only seen church windows from the outside, never from the inside. With the light shining through, it was absolutely beautiful! The side panels had white lilies and green vines entwined from the bottom to the top into a central arch. Angels perched on fluffy clouds and peered down from between the clouds at the goings-on in the central panel. Here was the part of the Bible where we had been forced to stop because it upset Mother. Obviously God was going to rescue his son from the people who hated him for being too good and too perfect. The son was certainly ready to go and was looking up at the sky waiting for his father to lower the gangplank and take him aboard. The saints, having been roused out of bed, were also there in their bathrobes. Only the angels seemed to know what was going to happen next, but they had been told to stay clear.

It was a wonderful window. I could not wait to start reading our little book again. Gradmother and I were up to the part where Jesus runs off to the temple without telling his mother. His mother must have been frantic with worry wondering what had happened to him. Jesus should have told his mother where he was going. He probably got a spanking for running off without permission.

Before we parted at the top of the stairs, I asked Ursula why nobody bothered about the bombers.

"Because the Americans are going to Berlin and Hannover."

"So why bother with the ack-ack?"

"They have to stop as many planes reaching the big cities as they can."

---

[14] White Russians were identified as those Russians opposed to the Bolshevik takeover during the 1917 revolution. White Russians are also, literally, "Belarus," or people from Belarus.

"But if they don't bomb, why do we need to take shelter?"

"Sometimes they still drop bombs. And they nearly always strafe if the dive bombers see someone running. Mother said men do that on purpose, like hunting. Also, when the planes are shot down, nobody knows where they will land."

That was not good news. I wished I had not asked.

Despite the beautiful valley, the wooded mountainsides, and the silver river running between them, the night raids in Hausberge became even more frightning than anything in Berlin, even worse than in that roofless kitchen.

There was hardly time to get my shoes on before the flak started barking and searchlights began to rake the sky. In the kitchen in Berlin we had been at ground level, partly protected by the ruins. Now in the turret, on the side of the mountain, we were closer to the bombers and could see and hear everything brightly illuminated, as on a stage. The ack-ack guns rattled continuously, while searchlights picked out individual planes that left the formation in a puff of smoke, burst into flames, and spiralled towards houses below. There was also something else I had not seen in Berlin—tinfoil streamers by the thousands, raining from the sky like strands of Christmas tree tinsel. They glittered, shimmered, and shivered gold and silver, depending on whether they reflected the searchlights or the gunfire. Some came so close to our window that I thought I could open the casement and catch them in my hand. The worst was when the searchlights aimed their beams on our hillside. I had visions of pilots becoming blinded and flying straight into our room.

The former Hausberge air raid shelter, in 1961.

After the first night we started sleeping in our clothes again and headed downstairs as soon as the sirens sounded. If we had time we ran to the air raid shelter in the side of the mountain. We had to get there before the planes arrived and the night show began. Not getting there in time was everyone's fear.

My fear was something altogether different. It had to do with the church window on the second floor landing, so beautiful in daylight, but the focal point of new nightmares that made me afraid to close my eyes after dark. When the searchlights backlit the Crucifixion scene, the biblical sky turned white, and when a shell exploded, it turned red. When there was smoke as well, it looked as if the entire cast of characters gathered around the cross was being blasted into hell instead of heaven, and that was what I had been afraid of all along. The scene disturbed me so badly that I would no longer sleep in the room. I pleaded to be allowed to sleep in the hall on the bottom step of the staircase. If Grandmother was distracted, I hurried down by myself and curled up on the step as soon as it got dark. All the same I always woke up in the air raid shelter or back in our room. I suspected someone from the house carried me—probably the White Russian. Mother said my nerves were acting up again. I didn't care.

Soon there was no way to escape my nightmares. In Berlin I had nightmares about returning to Haapsalu, climbing into the attic to get at Mother's toys, and being blasted off the ladder. In my dreams in Hausberge I merely passed the window when it exploded. To control the dreams I taught myself to blink rapidly, shake my head, and shout, "Wake up!" Sometimes it worked, but not on the double dreams, where I thought I was awake until the turret exploded again, and then I had to wake up a second time. Sometimes I woke up and didn't know where I was. That, too, was a double dream, but the worst dream of all was of flying like an angel, then suddenly losing altitude over a city of smoldering ruins and landing on the pavement, where people in grey shrouds were crawling on their hands and knees in mud. The mud became thicker, slimier, and deeper until it rose above my head and I drowned. I couldn't breathe and woke up with Grandmother holding me.

I still have that dream, sometimes I'm in London looking for the 31 bus to Finborough Road. Or I'm sitting on a hillside overlooking a valley with no idea what country I'm in. There have been so many valleys. Occasionally the dream ends with me opening my arms and launching myself into the wind, flying across towns, villages, woods, fields, churches and farmhouses, lakes and rivers, vaguely aware that I have lived in all those places, either in dreams or in reality.

It became impossible for me to sleep without Grandmother sitting beside me holding my hand. When there was an air raid, she woke me by shaking me gently, saying, "It's time." She always said, "It's time." Time to go to the shelter. I could hear the sirens. The shelter was across the railroad tracks in a cave that was actually a tunnel that extended into the mountain. We used only the front part. A gate closed off the rest of the tunnel. Beyond the gate it was the same as in the *U-Bahn* stations in Berlin, but without train tracks to fall down onto.

It was a relief when we got to the shelter. Wires and cables bracketed the tunnel's walls and ceiling and continued deeper into the mountain. The cables were new and the light bulbs worked. Wooden planks covered the wet floor. We were so close to the river that the bottom of the cave was flooded, just as our shelter had been in Haapsalu. The planks were muddy and slippery, but I no longer complained. I dragged at Grandmother's hand to run faster, to get there sooner. Once we were inside, Grandmother found space for us on a bench, and I curled up beside her, put my head into her lap, and closed my eyes. Only then could I sleep without nightmares.

It was on such a night that Grandmother noticed that I was no longer wearing Aunt Alma's ring. She lifted my hand for a closer look, held it for about three seconds, sighed, then lifted my finger to her lips. I held my breath, then relaxed. Mother would have been furious. How could I have been so careless? Did I not know how valuable the ring had been? A real ruby, for heaven's sake!

"Bride of the devil," those *Jungvolk* boys had called me.

Mother came and went. The job at Philips was easy, mostly typing and filling out order forms. We had ration cards and she was getting a wage. We did not see her for days. At one point for weeks. When we saw her again she said she had been ill with malaria. She was staying with her Polish friends and co-workers where she had more room than in our attic. When she did turn up, her rucksack bulged with foodstuffs she and her friends had salvaged or "liberated" from neglected fields, abandoned gardens, and bombed factories, often still in flames when the villagers swarmed over them. She brought us rotten pears and over-ripe cherries from local orchards, or moldy potatoes from abandoned fields. Her greatest triumph was a huge sack of wheat flour. Grandmother began to make flour gruel, uncooked if she could not get to the stove. She cooked when she could, adding rotten fruit to give the gruel flavor. She cut off the rotten bits, but I could still taste the mold. Our main food was boiled potatoes dipped in salt. The salt was from Frau Qwirll, who came upstairs almost daily with something we could use.

Mother's absences had never surprised us in the past, and I was not surprised when, one day, she told us she was going to live with her new friends for good. She said she needed a "life of her own." That way she had always been happier.

I did not know the full story of Philips Electrical's secret radio installation until later in life. Mother's closest friend and co-worker at the Philips office was a Polish woman whose husband and several electrical engineering students had been arrested by the Germans during the Warsaw Uprising. Instead of being sent to a prison camp, they had been brought to Hausberge to build radio transmitters with parts brought in from Eindhoven. (Holland was occupied by the Nazis.) Nothing of the factory was visible from the outside, but the mountain concealed an eleven-story factory. The offices were on the tenth level. Seven levels used male political prisoners from Russia and Poland. The eighth level was closed to everybody, but the SS. Laborers in that sector were Hungarian female Jews and gypsies from the Theresienstadt Concentration Camp. The factory went under the name of Hammerwerke Gmbh, a code name designed to disguise its actual function.

After the engineers had been taken away from Warsaw, Mother's friend found out where her husband was being sent and followed him to Hausberge. To be near him, she had applied for the office job. Her husband and the other Polish engineers were somewhere inside the mountain.

Although Mother's office dealt only with orders, she had learned what was going on and had become privy to dangerous information. She had distanced herself from us on purpose to protect us should she and her friend be arrested.

Since I had started having nightmares about the Crucifixion, I had been pestering Grandmother with the question, "Does Jesus' father rescue him or not?" She said "yes", but because the subject was upsetting me she put away our little book of Bible stories, and we returned to our regular standby, the

Danish cookbook. Cakes and desserts had less disturbing plots, but left me hungry.

Mother sometimes stayed with us over weekends. Instead of reading all day, she had started playing solitaire or consulting her fortune. When Grandmother was too tired to play with me during the day, after having held my hand all night, Mother and I played cards. We played Black Peter and a French game called Marriage.

Ursula and I had become good friends, but there was not much adventure in her because her mother terrified us both. Every time her mother yelled "Ursula!" through the open window Ursula leaped as though a bomb had gone off in her knickers. I did not leap, but I dared not disobey either. She not only looked terrifying with her burned hair and missing teeth, but she also acted as though some disaster were constantly imminent and she needed to know where we were and what we were doing. When Mother was not with us, she appointed Frau Schneider to watch over me, too. I was to heed the Frau's rules, which were rigid and frightening. The rules were that Ursula and I had to remain together at all times and never, never lose sight of each other when we were away from the house. The last she emphasized with a terrifying clutch on our shoulders and a wild look in her eyes that scared me even more than whatever she envisioned might happen to us. I had already guessed something terrible must have happened to her, but I had seen people looking worse in Berlin, where Grandmother had ordered me not to stare or ask questions. At the end of the lecture she made us repeat, "I will not leave my friend's side. If something happens to one, the other will run home immediately." We nodded. We understood.

Because the back garden was off limits we had nowhere to play. Ready for another air raid, we sat on the front steps with our chin in our hands. Then we discovered that the two iron gates cleared the ground sufficiently to swing out and give us a nice long ride. We enjoyed that until Frau Qwirll saw the deep trough we had worn into the sand and scolded us for breaking her gate. We had not broken her gate. The gate was already broken like everything in Germany.

One night I woke up to go to the potty and saw Grandmother reading a Bible, a big one without pictures. She was holding it, clasping it to her chest, but not really reading. Her head was bowed. She was praying again.

"Frau Qwirll gave it to me," she said, seeing I was awake. "You know her husband was a preacher."

"Did he become a martyr?" I asked.

"I hope so," she replied.

"Does God hear everybody's prayers?"

"Yes, if your prayers are sincere."

"Is God waiting for us when we get to the Promised Land?"

"He is and He will be glad to see us."

"So when are we going to get there?"

"Soon," she assured me.

I nodded, but I was starting to wonder about that.

One night, on the way to the shelter I dropped my doll. Someone stepped on its head and left a dent in the celluloid. Another casualty of war. Grandmother pasted some of her own hair over the dent, which made my doll look like Frau Schneider. I bandaged her up completely. She was "war-wounded", but had been a good soldier. The same seemed to have happened to the men we saw around town. Any man who was not in uniform looked like he had been stepped on or had been rejected. It had to be difficult to be a man during wartime and be without a regiment. The man we bought milk from had a part of his face missing and only one good eye. He looked lost among so many women. The White Russian was Frau Qwirll's handyman and sweeper at Hausberge Station and he also tried to be invisible. He only spoke to Mämmä. He wore the same rubber boots and carried a clanking bucket whereever he went, closing doors and latching the back gate overly carefully. We guessed he lived in the garden shed and that Frau Qwirll was keeping chickens and rabbits and a pig in the padlocked garage.

One day Ursula and I heard the pig grunting, snuffling, and rubbing its sides against the door. The Russian was talking to it soothingly. Ursula and I looked at each other and agreed the pig was being lied to, tested to see if it was ready to be slaughtered. Animals were too honest to understand the treachery of human beings.

We had not met many nice people since coming to Germany. When Grandmother and I shopped in the town square, we were often glared at by other shoppers, mostly women with children, women who had that "Bernau look" of proud victors whose husbands and fathers were fighting the rest of the world and it was their responsibility at home to make sure everyone around them was equally respectful of the *Führer*.

One day Grandmother came up from Frau Qwirll's kitchen upset about something. She told me to listen carefully to what she had to say. "Frau Qwirll's neighbors have noticed that we do not respond to their greetings. In future if someone says '*Heil Hitler!*' we need to make a show of raising our arm, at least for Frau Qwirll's sake. She has taken us in out of the goodness of her heart, and we don't want her to be punished for her kindness to foreigners."

"All right," I agreed, and then I forgot about it.

Ursula and I were sitting on the front steps when a woman came and asked for Mother. I took her to Grandmother. She had come to take me to school. I had never been to school. We left Estonia before I could enter first grade. Although I could read and write in Estonian, I did not know all my German letters. There was no time to learn. She was coming back for me the next morning.

Grandmother washed my dress and let down the hem. The hem extension was uneven and darker than the rest of the dress. My coat had shrunk even more. She moved the buttons, but the coat had been wet so many times it looked like a dead animal.

Ursula was not going to school.

"Why is Ursula not going to school?" I asked Frau Schneider.

It seemed like a simple question, but the woman became so agitated that she began to grind her teeth, and there were not many left to grind.

When Mother came that evening, the Frau must have mentioned my question, because Mother spoke sternly. "Frau Schneider is not on the list and she wants it that way. Don't mention her to anyone. Do you hear me?" I promised, but noticed that Mother had become nervous again, same as in Haapsalu. She seldom laughed any more.

Grandmother and I went over the German letters together. "If you can read and write Estonian, you can read and write German," she assured me. We practiced the long "s" that looks like "f" and capital letters that look like elaborate drawings of landscapes. The "ph" combination, pronounced "fau," was completely new to me. When to use a "fau" and when to use an "f" was not clear. We never finished the lesson because a bombing raid cut us short.

I was already sitting on the front step when the woman arrived to take me to school. My altered dress was longer than my coat. When I got up to greet her, I noticed that the hem had become muddy from sitting on the step. The shoes I had worn from Estonia had become too small. I was wearing someone else's with padding. To keep them on I had to clench my toes or the shoes slipped off.

The woman looked me up and down and sniffed. She seemed about to say something, but thought better of it. Her frown told me there was nothing about me that pleased her.

We walked quickly. The woman held her head high and her back straight. She did not speak to me and I did not speak to her, although I spoke good German, thanks to Ursula.

The schoolhouse was near the station. The building backed onto a ledge overlooking the river, with a steep drop behind it to the meadow that I admired from our turret. Upper-storey windows of the school were covered with plywood. The first-floor windows were clean and clear. A Nazi flag hung over the doorway.

The front yard was a grassless patch of dirt, surrounded by weeds. A narrow path had been worn through the weeds to a row of outside toilets perched on the same overhang as the schoolhouse. The flood plain gleamed wet below, bordered by willows along the riverbank.

The woman showed me the toilets and a key on a nail beside the door. Having done her duty, she said *also*, a German word that fills in for "so much for that," and we approached the front steps of the school.

"You will be in Herr Koch's combined class," she announced. "There is a shortage of teachers. They are all at the front," she added proudly. "And the older boys, the *Junge*, are in the *Volkssturm* fighting for den *Führer und das Vaterland.*"

I nodded.

"*Gut.* Follow the others after the bell," she informed me and hurried into the building. I was left on the steps.

When we entered the gate, the schoolyard had been full of children running, playing tag, jumping rope, or standing about in groups talking. As soon as we appeared the activities ceased and the staring began. Although I had never been to school, I recognized that I had again entered a world where children made their own rules and friendships. In Germany the rules were set by adults. The adults did not like refugees and foreigners, and the children had already noticed my appearance, which shouted *Ausländer*. In Berlin, in the chaos of constant bombing, we had blended in with the rest of the population, but in Bernau and now in the small town of Hausberge people took great pride in remaining clean and *putzig*. The *Jungvolk* boys wore ironed shirts, shorts, and neckerchiefs; the girls had sparkling white knee socks, heavy wool D*irndl* skirts, white blouses, and had their hair rolled into a D*olle* or braided into a crown. Grandmother tried the *dolle*, but lacked the proper comb; my hair was not long enough for a braided crown. I just hoped I did not look like Frau Schneider.

Mercifully the bell rang almost immediately after the woman disappeared into the building. I slipped in after her. There was only one open door to my right. A man stood in the doorway and beckoned for me to step into his classroom.

Herr Koch must have known I was coming and had recognized me. "Stand there," he said and pointed to a spot beside his desk.

I did as I was told.

The children came in shortly afterwards and filed in around me and past me. Each child stopped in front of the teacher, raised an arm and gave an enthusiastic "*Heil Hitler!*" in a loud, clear voice before sitting down.

When everyone was in place, Herr Koch perched himself on the corner of one of the front desks, thus revealing an artificial leg with a real shoe at the end of it.

"So where do you come from?" he asked me, bending a ruler between his fingers.

I told him, "*Estland.*"

The children were looking at me with various expressions of curiosity and something else—anticipation. They ranged in age from my seven years to early teens. The dreaded *Jungvolk* boys in uniform sat at the back of the class. I had come to fear them worse than bombs.

The classroom was cold. Luckily I had not been asked to remove my coat. The Frau in Bernau had called us filthy. Even Ursula had mentioned that I smelled of wet washcloths. Ursula's room had a sink bigger than our cooking pot and her mother let us wash our hair from time to time with water heated in the downstairs kitchen. It was a big job for Grandmother to keep the water hot between potfuls. If my hair was not dry when the siren sounded, I would have to go to the shelter with wet hair and risk catching a cold. It was November already.

"So, *Estland*, eh?" The teacher looked around the class for confirmation that everyone knew where Estonia was and that it was not in Germany.

"So what do you think of our glorious leader, Adolf Hitler?" he asked unexpectedly.

I understood the question. Hitler was wonderful according to the woman who had brought me to school, but I had also heard terrible things about him in fearful whispers. It was best not to respond.

The teacher waited, then smiled at the floor, musing to himself as he bent the ruler back and forth. Finally he raised his head and smiled again, but the expression on his face was one I had seen before. He got to his feet slowly.

"First, I think you forgot something important when you entered the classroom, *Estnisches Fräulein*." Estonian Miss. He looked to the class. "Did we hear a *Gruss* for our *Führer*?"

Nobody replied, but there were a few titters at the back of the room. I knew what he meant and what I had forgotten.

"*Heil Hitler!*" I said quickly and raised my arm.

Herr Koch banged the ruler on the edge of the desk and addressed the room directly this time. "I think we need to teach our *Ausländer* from *Estland* the proper *Gruss* and respect for *den Führer*. How shall we go about it?"

Nobody answered, but some of the big boys in the back began to smirk and whisper. One even raised his hand, but was ignored. Herr Koch apparently had his own ideas. He said something in rapid German, too fast for me to catch. Something about the *Witwe Qwirll und ihre Flüchtlinge,* the widow Qwirll and her refugees. He knew where I lived then. The word *Russen* (Russians) also entered the flow. When he finished speaking the girls all stood up and came forward to form a line behind me. There were eleven of them.

"No, not the boys." He waved them back. "Girls only."

When they were in line he handed the first girl his pencil and told her to step forward and poke me with the point. She stabbed me in the shoulder. When the pencil touched me I had to raise my arm and shouted "*Heil Hitler!*

The pencil was passed down in turn. The girls were not allowed to stab my face, but anywhere else was fine. The point broke immediately. I had thick clothes on. Still I felt the pricks on my arms through the sleeves. It was worse having to keep shouting "*Heil Hitler!*" every time the pencil landed. If I was not loud enough or respectful enough, the girl was allowed another stab. Once or twice Herr Koch leaned forward himself, as if to strike me, but I shouted louder, I saluted better, I copied the *Jungvolk* boys the way I had first seen them enter the room. When the last girl was back at her desk, Herr Koch seemed satisfied. He nodded.

"Your first German lesson," he said. "You have learned well." He then showed me to a desk, gave me a slate and a piece of chalk, and instructed me to start copying the German alphabet as though nothing had happened.

I kept my head down. The letters were all there, the "f" that was an "s," the "ph" that was a "fau," but they were all swimming in water. I couldn't see anything for tears, and my heart was pounding so loudly I thought everyone could hear it. I willed my chalk to write and myself not to cry and shame myself further, when suddenly the air raid siren began to howl. Everybody jumped to their feet, grabbed their slates and satchels, and headed for the door.

To the shelter? Into the cellar? I didn't know where to go.

"*Mach schnell!*" shouted Herr Koch. Quickly!

I followed everyone else leaving the school, running towards the gate. Apparently the school had no cellar. We were supposed to go home.

When I got to the outside toilets, I noticed the *Jungvolk* boys around the entrance shuffling their feet, hands in pockets, waiting for me. *They're going to beat me up*, I thought. I looked around frantically for another exit, but there was only the one gate.

Two boys grabbed my arms. Together they dragged me into the toilets where, with help from the others, they stripped me and stuffed my clothes down the four bowls as far as they would go. They then locked the door from the outside and left me. Their laughter mingled with the siren and the first sound of approaching bombers. It was a huge joke to them. Naked, crying, and shivering with cold and fright, I fished my clothes out of the toilets, put them on, and crawled out through one of the air vents next to the waste outlet. My clothes were wet, stained brown, and smelled of *kaka*.

Nobody was in the school yard when I emerged from the back of the building. The street, too, was empty of people. Bombers were overhead, droning along steadily. Anti-aircraft guns were barking back at them from the mountainside. There was only one place for me to go and that was home. I crossed the cobbled square towards the parsonage. At one of the shops a woman grabbed my arm and tried to pull me into the doorway, but I struggled free. She meant well, but I had to get to Grandmother. Almost home now, running down the middle of the street, I heard a plane suddenly behind me, flying low, followed by the ping-ping of machine gun bullets hitting cobblestones, kicking up small chips of stone and dirt. Strafers! Ursula had warned me, but I was so intent on getting back to Grandmother that the bullets might as well have been peas. My mind was on another track altogether. Night after night I heard Grandmother asking God to deliver us, so why could I not ask God to drop a bomb on the schoolhouse and deliver me, too, from Herr Koch and the *Jungvolk*?

"Bomb the schoolhouse!" I shouted at the bombers above the noise of the ack-ack, in a rhythm of retaliation and revenge. My ears were ringing and my body was hot with rage. I had never dared raise my voice before, even when I had been angry at Mother for reading her stupid books and ignoring me. "Bomb the schoolhouse!" I yelled as I zig-zagged along the deserted street. The strafer had long gone, to Hannover, to Berlin; it no longer mattered. It had become clear that we needed a deliverer. We needed to be rescued.

The ivy-covered house had never looked more welcoming. I ran up the stairs to the attic and burst through the door. Grandmother was sitting in her chair. She had not gone to the shelter without me. When she saw me she turned ashen. Nobody was supposed to be out in the street in the middle of a bombing raid. She had thought I was still in school. When she saw the state of my clothes, she burst into tears. Held in her arms, I told her what had happened.

Alas, I had to go back to school the next day. It was the law. Mother came by and confirmed it. In fact, she said I must go back and do whatever Herr Koch wanted me to do.

"Pretend if necessary. Do you hear me?"

I heard.

I returned to school in great fear, but nobody touched me again, at least not physically. Instead the children continued to call me names and the girls danced around me holding their noses, even though I no longer smelled bad. Ursula's mother had allowed us into their room so that Grandmother could wash me at their sink. Frau Schneider also gave me a wool *tracht* (folk costume) that Ursula had grown out of, one that German children often wore for best. It included a jacket with wooden, buttons and frog buttonholes, white knee socks, and a fairly clean shirt.

Herr Koch continued to smirk at me during the salutation to the *Führer* and the flag, but he had made his point. I performed perfectly. Every time I shouted *"Heil Hitler!"* I was defying him, refusing to give him another opportunity to correct me, but his smile said he could punish me anyway, any time he wanted to.

Grandmother and I were reading the little book again and had reached the story of "Daniel in the Lions' Den." I always held my breath at the end. Would Daniel escape? Would God rescue him? He always did. When the "all clear" sounded and we were walking back to our attic, Grandmother always said, "Thank God, it's over." Now all I needed was for God to hear my prayers about the schoolhouse.

Being rescued had become my latest obsession, as Mother put it. She and I were not getting along too well. My fear of the Crucifixion window had definitely convinced her there was something wrong with me.

The people in Hausberge did not like us any better than the people we had met in Bernau. On the way back and forth from school I had to pass a milliner's shop owned by Ilse's mother. Ilse was a girl in my class who was especially nasty. Her mother was worse. Their shop was on the corner of the main street, opposite the turn-off to the parsonage. The front door was usually open. Ilse made sure she arrived home first so she could wait for me. As soon as they saw me, her mother made a show of testing the hot iron with her finger, then shoving it at Ilse and shouting, "Go, iron the girl's clothes!" Clapping her hands, she urged her daughter to *"Mach schnell!"* Quickly, quickly!

With Ilse behind me I charged up the slope to the Qwirlls' gate to laughter and encouragement from below. *Verdammte Russen!* Damned Russians! I always reached the gate, and Ilse stopped, too. I knew it was a game, but I was scared in case she caught me and I would be forced to take the iron from her and burn her.

"They think we're Russians," I told Grandmother.

Grandmother put her hand to her mouth. Someone must have heard her speaking to the White Russian.

The word in town was that we were Russians.

My list of grievances to God was getting so long and complicated that I had a hard time keeping track. Bomb the school. Bomb the milliner's shop. Bomb Herr Koch and the *Jungvolk*. Bomb Ilse and her mother. Before long I was praying hellfire, brimstone, and heavenly hordes upon everyone in town except Frau Qwirll and a few others who had been nice to us. The Latvian woman and her mother were exempted. Also the White Russian, but not Grete and the Silesians.

78

Winter was upon us. Frau Qwirll was running out of firewood. The tap over the horse trough froze. Frau Qwirll began to allow us a potful of hot water once a day. There was something wrong with the water pipes. The Russian had wrapped the cellar pipes with rags. We could hear hollow hammering from time to time and gurgling from Frau Schneider's room taps. The horse trough had been our only reliable source of water. We had to have water for the flour gruel and to boil potatoes. It was very cold.

One morning after an air raid near Bielefeld, Mother surprised us with a bucket of molasses. A molasses factory had been bombed. Grandmother mixed the molasses into the gruel. It was tasty, but not as sweet as the artificial honey we received with our rations. Another afternoon Mother stumbled up the stairs with a soot-stained quilt. Grandmother eyed it with suspicion until one of the corners began to release feathers. Real feathers. Grandmother examined a handful. "Original German *Federbett* feathers. Real goose down!" she exclaimed in surprise and approval.

I threw myself onto the quilt so that more feathers blew out. We chased feathers around the room, laughing and saying, "It's snowing already!"

Finally it snowed.

The entire valley turned white except for the dark smudges of the railway station and the steaming, forbidden area around the end of the tracks. As for the River Weser it, too, was half frozen, leaving a narrow black pencil line in the middle of the white landscape, marking off the west bank from the right bank and one mountain from the other.

In the shops there was talk of Christmas. In school too, but I was not part of anything there and was glad.

Grandmother leafed through her cookbook to see what she could prepare with just two ingredients—flour and molasses. Mother was going to stay with us over Christmas.

One evening we were all together, ignoring the air raid siren because we could barely see outside and did not expect the Tommies to do any better. In fact they were flying so high we could barely hear them. Even the ack-ack was muffled. The searchlights only helped to define heavy snowflakes swirling in their beams.

Grandmother was reading. Mother was sitting on an extra chair she got from the attic and was mending her rucksack straps. I was lying on the new quilt and watching her. Watching Mother was still a novelty. She was not used to sewing and kept pricking her finger. I had never seen her cook anything, not even to heat water, but she knew where the planes were coming from and going. We had started guessing together.

"Hamburg," she lifted her head towards the ceiling and bit the thread with her teeth.

I agreed. To Bielefeld, they would have been lower. To Minden a little higher.

Suddenly there was a knock on our door.

"Someone downstairs asking for you," shouted Frau Qwirll. "It's a man," she added. "Says he's a relative of yours," she sniffed audibly. You could always tell from a knock or announcement how people felt about the news they were about to bring you.

Father?

Mother threw the sewing aside and hurried down the stairs at a run.

We waited. I wondered would he recognize me. Would I recognize him? Maybe he had come to wish us Merry Christmas.

A few minutes later a deep male voice could be heard coming up the stairs and talking to Mother. The man was wearing heavy boots and sounded drunk. It was not Father.

Mother and the visitor reached the attic. Mother stepped aside and the man's bulk filled the doorway. He was stooping slightly so that all I could see was the *ushanka*. A Russian soldier. I froze in fear, but his greeting was in Estonian.

"Ah, Ella!" he boomed, letting his knapsack slide to the floor as he opened his arms wide. "My little sister-in-law!"

"Paul!" Grandmother threw herself into his embrace.

I hadn't known we had any relatives other than dead ones and Aunt Alma. The man unwound a big woolen scarf from around his neck, removed the fur hat, and made a bow to Mother and me. His head did not have a single hair on it. It was as bald as a boiled egg. In his smile I counted four gold teeth, two of them in the front. They twinkled in the candlelight.

"Your Great Uncle Paul," said Mother in her Snow Queen voice, which I had not heard for some time. She sat down again and continued sewing while she introduced him to me. Or rather me to him, which was the proper way. Always lady to gentleman.

"Your grand-niece, my daughter," she said, biting the thread off a second time and spitting it out.

I knew my manners and curtsied.

"*Mademoiselle!*" He kissed my hand. "I spent months looking for you."

"Ran out of money," said Mother under her breath. One of her famous asides. I knew then that they had met before and perhaps not always under the best circumstances.

"So, how did you find us?" asked Mother, directly.

"Ah," he said, putting a finger alongside his red nose. "I followed my lucky star and here I am." He winked at me.

I loved him immediately.

Paul Enno was Ernst Enno's youngest brother—younger by seventeen years. He started drinking at an early age and was the black sheep in the family. After the poet's death, Paul joined the French Foreign Legion as a flautist. He was also a remittance man. The family paid his debts and sent him money in the hope he would stay away.

Yet here he was, straight from North Africa. He was traveling on a French passport with legitimate discharge papers from the French Foreign Legion. He had been on his way to Estonia when the war broke out.

Paul Enno spoke eight languages and had managed to stay out of both the German and Russian armies by walking backwards through Europe. He

persuaded everyone that he was on his way home to join up with whichever
side they were on when he had been picked up by convoys and patrols. He
waved a red handkerchief for the Russians and sang German Lieder for the
Germans. When they gave him a lift, he accepted it gratefully, and after
they dropped him off, he doubled back to resume his original journey.
Through the "bar and bottle" network he arrived in Hausberge and found us
living with the widow Qwirll.

Frau Qwirll said he could not stay, this man who looked like a Russian soldier
and a drinker and she did not trust his papers. He was not welcome in her
house. Absolutely "*nein!*"

Uncle Paul nodded. He said he understood. "Of course, *Gnädige Frau,*"
gracious lady. Then he winked at me again over her head. I knew we would
see him again soon.

We did. He turned up at least twice a week, after dark, sometimes letting himself in during an air raid. He always brought food or something useful
that he pulled along behind him on a small sled. One day, for Frau Qwirll,
he brought firewood hidden under a pile of rags. She who had protested
"*nein*" was persuaded to light a little fire in her kitchen stove. Maybe heat
some water for a cup of tea.

"Tea? Who has tea?"

"You do." He produced a little bundle wrapped in burlap. "Chinese tea."

It was "*ja*" after that. We all got a little sip from our one cup that Grandmother had christened our "Dresden."

Uncle Paul was the best thing that had happened. We did not know
where he lived, probably in one of the abandoned houses in the area. We
were not allowed into the woods around the cable car fixtures or anywhere
near the mountain except to use the shelter. We knew Unki's twigs came
from there. I started calling him Unki. I often woke up in his arms after an
air raid, when he had found me asleep on the bottom steps. He carried me
upstairs and then disappeared again. Grandmother no longer stopped me
from sleeping on the stairs. She even put a cushion under my head, knowing
Unki would bring me up later.

Ponds and meadows around the river froze solid. Neither Ursula nor I
had skates, but we went anyway and slid alongside the German children. We
remembered to stay together. Frau Schneider could not see the valley from
her window, but I was sure she came to check on us, looking for Ursula's
green scarf and Grandmother's Fair Isle cardigan, which Grandmother sometimes put over my coat for extra warmth. It reached to my knees.

Germans had also started looking like bundles of rags because of the
cold, the lack of firewood, and frozen water taps. The bombing raids had
stepped up, too, and everyone was sleeping in their clothes or at least looked
like it. Ilse had dropped out of school. The milliner's blinds were drawn, the
door closed. I didn't know if they still lived there. A lot of people were leaving town. No one bothered with "*Heil Hitler!*" anymore either, except in the
presence of men in uniform. Only Herr Koch kept up the momentum. Ours
was the only class in the school; he seemed to be the only teacher left. The

Jungvolk boys remained eager, but the girls were dwindling, especially the younger ones. It was very cold.

The owner of the dairy, who had always insisted on the proper salute, now only mumbled the words. Mother told us his wife and daughter had been killed in an air raid. One day we entered the shop and found him clearing his shelves and washing the counter. "No more milk or bread," he told us, "But I have something else for you." He disappeared behind the curtain into his living quarters and came back with a brown parcel tied with string. "For you and the child. I have no use for them anymore." I think the parcel of clothes might have belonged to his wife and daughter.

Sometimes three or four squadrons of planes appeared in one day, with short intervals between, and twice as many squadrons at night. It was still Amis in daylight and Tommies in the dark. Still the ack-ack and searchlights raking our window with all that other stuff falling from the sky tinsel, fireballs and flaming smoke.

I refused even to lie down unless Grandmother was sitting in the chair next to me holding my hand. It was too cold on the stairs. She had promised not to fall asleep, but sometimes she did. I would wake up and find her hand hanging down beside the chair.

One night I woke up. Bombers were already in the valley; searchlights were lighting the room with what Mother called our "Christmas trees for this year." Mother had gone somewhere. Grandmother was asleep. She had let go of my hand. Panicked, I was about to shake her awake when our door opened and Jesus walked into the room. At last! I had been waiting for him, hoping to see him. He looked the same as in the storybook—long hair to his shoulders, a short beard, a white bathrobe, and he was carrying a jug of milk. I remembered the jugs of milk in the farmhouse, but this was not NKVD; this was Jesus! I had so many questions for him, but first I had to wake Grandmother. I thought she might want to say hello to him.

When Jesus saw that I was going to wake Mämmä, he shook his head. "No, don't." He smiled and put a finger across his lips. "Shush." Without speaking he placed the jug of milk in the center of our table. With another gesture he told me it was all right. Everything was going to be all right. "Go back to sleep."

In the morning the first thing I saw was the jug of milk in the middle of the table.

"Jesus brought that," I told Grandmother, importantly.

Mother came in at that moment and heard me.

"What nonsense. The child was dreaming," she laughed. "Frau Qwirll must have brought the milk." Frau Qwirll had started bringing us hot water and boiled eggs from time to time in return for Unki bringing her firewood.

"But this was Jesus," I persisted.

Mother's cheeks got red, as they always did when she and I got into arguments. I waited until Mother left and then again insisted that Jesus had visited us and brought us the milk.

"It was Jesus. I know it was. He told me not to wake you." I kept repeating until Grandmother took me onto her lap to calm me.

82

"If you say it was Jesus, then it must have been Jesus," she said, patting my cheek.

"He came to tell me he would rescue us, just like He rescued Daniel."

"Just like Daniel," Grandmother agreed. She went to see if Frau Qwirll could make me a cup of warm tea. We did not have any valerian tea, but we had Chinese, sweetened with molasses.

On Christmas Eve Frau Qwirll, her daughter Gerda, the Latvian teacher with her mother, Frau Schneider, Ursula, and the White Russian came into the attic to wish us a Merry Christmas and to hear me recite my Christmas rhyme. It was customary for every child to recite a verse before receiving a present. Ursula had already recited hers and was clutching a rag doll. The adults were waiting. My verse was in French and German. Unki had taught it to me.

> Le boeuf, der Ochs',
> La vache, die Kuh,
> Fermez la porte, die Tür mach zu.

The ox, the ox, the cow, the cow, close the door, close the door. First in French, then in German.

Everybody applauded. Frau Qwirll handed me a piece of something wrapped in greaseproof paper. It was that same white stuff that Grete sucked on in the cellar.

"Nougat," said Grandmother, in French. "Made from egg whites."

The White Russian gave me a small wooden box he had made for my treasures. It was just what I needed. It would make a good coffin for my doll, should I decide she had to die and I had to bury her. She was not looking any better.

Grandmother received a bag of dried apples. She was good with dried apples. Our room looked nice. There was a lighted candle in the center of the table and a fir branch stuck into a jam jar next to it. The Danish cookbook had produced molasses cookies. They were passed around. Mother was happy with a rare cigarette from the Philips office party she had been to. No sign of Unki, he had started keeping out of Mother's way.

We were handing out more presents when the siren began to hoot. No time for *Heilige Nacht*, we scrambled for the stairs and into the cellar. I ran behind Frau Qwirll and was amazed at how quickly she could move when she wanted to. The bombers flew over in such numbers that the house shook and plaster fell off the ceiling onto Mother's back. Fearing the ceiling would collapse, Mother had ordered us down into our Berlin formation: me on the bottom, Grandmother over me, and Mother on top. Having had only one bite, I managed to keep a grip on the white *nougat* confection. I did not want it to touch the dirty floor.

Chapter 7

END OF THE WAR
1945

On 4 January 1945 General Montgomery joined Patton's advance from the south; the two American corps, with the British on their western flank, pressed down upon the enemy. The British and Americans met at Houffalize, Belgium, on 16 January 1945.

Another snowy afternoon. After the "all clear" Unki said we were going sledding in the woods. He put me on his sled and pulled me to the base of the mountain where the road wound up between the trees. A guard stopped us, but Unki said, "Surely, with the child." The guard waved us past. When we were out of sight of the road, Unki instructed me to lie down by a fallen tree branch. Making sure no one could see us, he began to whittle at the branch with his penknife. In no time we were lying next to a nice pile of firewood, which he wrapped in a blanket. He put me on the sled on top of the bundle, sat behind me, and we "'swhooshed" down the slope. Unki called out a greeting to the guard, who waved back. The momentum took us as far as the square. From there he pulled me to Frau Qwirll's. She was already waiting for the firewood. The garbage pit in the front yard was almost full. Everybody had a garbage pit, but few had any garbage.

Another day in January or February, after the start of the new year, which mother said was unlucky to celebrate, Unki and I were walking by the railroad tracks when he said it was time for me to eat protein. When I asked what that meant, he said "Meat." We joined a queue outside the station. A couple were ladling food out of a big pot. When it was our turn, a woman handed us each a bowl of brown liquid called "stew." She told us to eat there and return the bowl.

We carried our bowl to the front steps; having no spoon, we sipped from the side. There were bits of vegetables in the stew and brown cubes that Unki said were meat. The cubes were tough to chew, so I spit them out, but the liquid was hot and tasted wonderful. I licked the bowl clean.

When we got home I told grandmother about the stew.

"Stew?" Grandmother stopped rummaging in her bundles.

"What's this about stew?" Mother came in from the attic, where she had been pounding frozen clothes taken off the clothesline.

Unki began to explain, but only got a few words out before Mother told Grandmother to take me downstairs. Mother's voice became so loud that there was no point in going downstairs; we could hear her all over the house. We stopped on the top landing. The words I picked out were "eating rats".

and "My God! Have you no sense?" and "You haven't changed a bit. You'd better leave."

Unki left, but I had a feeling we would see him again, like the last time he had been told not to return.

The bombing raids were more and more frequent. They pounded Minden, only a few miles upriver, and Bielefeld, as never before. We could see the explosions. There was barely time to get to the shelter between the sirens; the first squadron was already approaching, like a voracious thundercloud.

"Unki"-Paul¶

→ School continued, but classes were constantly interrupted by air raids. Every time the bombers came I reminded God of my prayers to bomb the schoolhouse and end my daily fear of Herr Koch. Herr Koch still monitored my crisp salute, but he was beginning to lose interest. Instead he focused his attention on the older children and the *Jungvolk*, with whom he had been following the progress of the war on a large wall map with Nazi flag pushpins. I noticed that the pushpins were rapidly dwindling. Most of the girls who had tormented me had also disappeared. Something was going on. The stores around the market square were closing and not because of the bombing. People were leaving town, loading up trucks with furniture and belongings. It looked like Haapsalu all over again, except this panic was more orderly.

After another terrible night in the Qwirlls' cellar and another bowl of cold flour gruel, it was back to school. School was the law. The smell of smoke from the night's air raid hung in the air, heavier than usual. Had it not been the law to go to school, had there not been the possibility of Mother finding out, and had it not been raining, I would have hidden in the woods above the water trough until the next siren, but I did not want to lie to Grandmother. Not wanting to lie to Mämmä was a burden; it kept me from doing a lot of things I would have done normally. I had no trouble lying to people I did not like.

Practically sleepwalking, not thinking at all, just putting one foot in front of the other, I passed the shuttered church and rounded the corner into the market square, where the smell of smoke became stronger. There were more people about than usual. I crossed the square by the war memorial. It occurred to me that someone must have lit an oil drum near the station. That was a popular way to keep warm. People gathered around it to talk while waiting for trains.

I could see flames, but they appeared to be beyond the station. It was not an oil drum fire, but a pile of smoldering rubble spread across the ground. It took me a few seconds to register what I was seeing. I stopped dead and my heart leaped with shock. The school building had disappeared.

A crowd of townspeople stood around what was left of half of the first floor, mainly the steps and front door. The rest was smoking bricks and smoldering rubbish. The schoolhouse had received a direct hit. The bulk of the building had slid over the ledge into the meadow below. It took me a moment to understand. Then the implications of the event hit me. I gasped in horror, turned and ran back home in torment. What had I done? I ran straight up the stairs to Grandmother and fell upon her, sobbing and confessing. "It was my fault! I'm sorry! I'm sorry!" I cried, clutching her waist, hanging on her, almost pulling her down with me. The worst thing was that I had stopped praying about the schoolhouse. I had practically forgotten my vengeance list since Ilse and her mother had left town and Herr Koch had stopped picking on me, but God had not forgotten.

"God destroyed the schoolhouse at my request," I blurted out and repeated, in tears, "It was my fault."

Grandmother disengaged herself and looked stern. She made me catch my breath and sit down so that we could discuss the situation calmly.

I told her everything: how, since my first day in class, I had been praying for the schoolhouse to be bombed and for other things that I could no longer remember. I told her that I had wanted Ilse to disappear as well. And she had.

"Let's see now," Grandmother considered me for a moment. "When you prayed, did you kneel down?" she asked.

"Not really," I admitted.

"Did you put your hands together?"

"No." There had been no time with that plane strafing the street behind me or while staying ahead of Ilse with her hot iron. "But I did close my eyes sometimes."

Grandmother thought that over, too. "We know God hears prayers, but in the end it's His decision, not ours. Do you think God might have wanted to destroy the schoolhouse?"

"I hope so!"

"Then it was God's decision. You just happened to think of it as well."

"And Ilse?"

"God might have told them to move, maybe to another town?"

"Did I think like God?"

"No, but maybe God decided to think like you. Maybe He didn't like that school either or the way Ilse and her mother were treating you."

That made sense. It also explained how God was "our father," not an actor, but more like a "real man in the family."

No more school! Ursula and I played together every day between air raids and while getting water from the horse trough. Because there was always a long line, we made the line longer with just a small white lie. We climbed up the hill into the garden of an abandoned house where other children played hide-and-seek around several sheds. The children recognized me, but without Herr Koch to tell them what to do, they accepted Ursula and me as locals, although they had not yet asked us to join their games.

One day the owner of the abandoned house turned up. Ursula and I were concealed by the bushes, so he didn't know we were watching. He had come in a van and was taking armloads of boxes from the van and dumping them on the grass. The boxes opened when they fell; they contained books, photographs, reels of film, and German uniforms. We had seen other people burning things up and down the hillside and had found all kinds of interesting things in the ashes. We hung around, waiting for him to light the fire, but we must have made a noise, because he saw us and lunged at us, shaking his fist. We ran away, but crept back. The bonfire burned with lots of black smoke. The reels of film always flared up highest. The man stood beside it with a bucket of water; he looked pleased until he saw us again.

"Schweinhunde!" he yelled and emptied the bucket in our direction.

We went back the next day. Ursula found a German Military Cross. I found half a photograph of several soldiers standing around a naked man. Our best find was Ursula's, it was a sooty and charred helmet. Frau Schneider took it to use as a mixing bowl. Luckily she did not ask where we had found it.

When we were sure the man had gone for good, we ventured into the house. There was nothing left inside except, in the kitchen, a ginger cat sitting by the sink. It must have heard us and was waiting to be fed.

By late February the pace of the Allied armies had quickened. On the 21st of that month the whole western transportation system of Germany was shattered by a gigantic bombing from no fewer than 7,000 airplanes. The next night the Allies crossed the Roer River, last water barrier before the Rhine. The big jump came on 24 March when four armies hurdled the Rhine and two paratroop divisions were dropped five miles inland at Wesel. With six armies now across the Rhine, the crust of German resistance was broken. Now only 250 miles separated the Allied armies in the west from the Red Army in the east.

Henry Steele Commager

By April the Germans north of Cologne had begun to feel the heat of the approaching Allies. Porta-Westfalica was just north of Cologne, and the organizers of the Philips factory decided to pull out. It took them three days to evacuate the prisoners from all the different factory levels to Hamburg. The concentration camp prisoners disappeared the day before the final evacuation. Another similar camp was emptied that same day. The Allies arrived a couple of days later, around 5 or 6 April 1945.

One day Mother turned up with some Polish engineers who, with help from a guard who had befriended them, had been able to slip away during the evacuation of the secret factory inside the mountain. The older men were grim and distracted, the younger students polite and respectful, until they all began to argue among themselves about retaliation, naming names of townspeople who had been guards and had mistreated them. I did not understand what they were talking about until I heard a familiar name. It was that of our milkman, the one who had given us the bundle of clothes. Grandmother heard it, too, and intervened.

"No! He's a good man," she protested and stepped forward to explain her point, but she never got a chance to make it, because one of the men pulled a gun out of his pocket and pointed it at her.

I was lifted out of the room. Before the door closed I saw Mother fall on her knees beside Grandmother and grasp her legs. "Nein!"

There was no bang. A few minutes later they all left, speaking the hated German language, the only language foreigners had in common.

At Yalta the Soviets were handed all of Eastern Europe except Greece. Estonia, Latvia, and Lithuania would become Soviet republics. In Estonia deportations continued. Sentences of "10 plus 5" (10 years slave labor and another 5 years forced resettlement) became the norm for those not shot. The systematic destruction of the Estonian people that had started in 1940 raged on, unabated.

Although we were still not allowed to play in Frau Qwirll's garden, I found that by climbing on top of the attic furniture I could look down through one of the dormers. At the very back of the garden were several sheds surrounded by chicken wire. No chickens, but I did see elevated rabbit hutches, and there was definitely a pig in the garage.

One day I arrived in the front yard just in time to see the White Russian holding the pig between his legs. It squealed and wriggled until the man was about to stick a knife between its ears. Even before the knife found its target, the pig stopped struggling. The knife went in. Blood spurted out of the pig's head, a red fountain that spattered the walls of the shed, the man's clothes, his arms, and his face. What amazed me was that once the man had the pig immobilized, it stopped protesting. It just stood there waiting for the knife.

On 27 April 1945 the Russians in Estonia rounded up another 1,200 Estonian men and 30 women and put them into closed cattle cars (30 men to a car.) Their destination was Magadan-Kolõma in Siberia.

In March 1949 another 20,072 persons, mostly women, children, and grandparents of farmers' families whose menfolk had already been repressed, were deported to Siberia. In all, 32,536 persons, including 10,331 not deported, lost their homes and lived under the constant persecution of the NKVD or NKGB. (The NKVD became the KGB in 1952.)
The White Book,Estonian State Commission on Examination of the Policies of Repression

Spring arrived. It ignored war and politics. Grass grew over the ruins and in the abandoned gardens, apple trees burst into bloom. Songbirds chirped in Frau Qwirll's birdbath. Water flowed down the mountainside and overflowed the lip of the horse trough.

Grandmother was shaking me. "It's time," she whispered. I thought she meant there was another air raid, but instead she was packing our bundles.

It was dark outside. Our candle was lit, flickering in the cup on the table, throwing shadows against the window glass.

I was waking up when mother came in and saw me still rubbing my eyes. "Hurry!" she said. "We have to leave the village. At once! And put your shoes on." She raised her voice to a level she had not used since Danzig.

I started to put my shoes on, but we were not ready when Frau Qwirll put her head inside the door. She was dressed in a long black coat and carried a huge cloth handbag.

"Now!" she said. "Immediately!" For the first time since she had taken us in, her hair was not in a perfect bun. Wisps were escaping the pins, and her little buttoned boots were muddy. She, too, must have been sleeping heavily, finally, after months of constant air raids.

The urgency was obvious, though I did not know why. We left our bundles half packed and hurried after the woman who had given shelter to foreigners, in a country where *Verfluchte Ausländer* were scorned and mistreated daily.

It was just before dawn. The smell of morning greeted us as soon as we stepped outside. The air was cold and crisp, no falling ash, no smoldering ruins or rubble dust from collapsed buildings or the acrid, sharp smell of cordite. Despite the dark, the main street was full of people coming from all directions and moving towards the main square.

We followed the river along a wide tree-lined boulevard that led out of town. There were no streetlights. It was pitch black. Mother was working her hand-generated flashlight. We followed its narrow beam. Other people had the same kind of torches. The torches hummed all around us like crickets on a warm summer night.

"Where are we going?" I asked. It was a pointless question as usual, because Mother was ahead and Grandmother behind me; we had no time to turn and fall behind. I tried to keep pace. From snatches of conversation I learned that the Allies were coming. They were just miles away. People were frightened.

When the morning light touched the trees, we were clear of the valley. Husberge lay behind us, between the two dark mountain slopes with the River Weser glittering between them. It was going to be a beautiful day. The ground evened out and the road continued between untilled fields. Birds, looking for early worms, flitted between the stubble.

We lost track of Frau Qwirll. She might have gone another way while it was dark. The people hurrying alongside us were strangers. I had never been this far outside the town or out of the valley.

We passed several ruined farmhouses. Grandmother was having difficulty keeping up and was wanting to rest, but Mother urged us on. She said we had to get clear of the town, when suddenly two planes approached, flying low. We knew what that meant. Everyone scattered. Some dived into the ditch. We ran to one of the bombed farmhouses and down a flight of stairs into the cellar. Others followed us. Mother pushed us to the floor in the usual formation. I covered my ears. The planes passed over us with a loud swoosh. A few seconds later we heard an explosion. A bomb had been dropped somewhere in the valley. We kept our heads down, expecting more, but nothing happened.

We returned to the road. Suddenly a terrible and distant rumble started up ahead of us further along the highway. Soon the ground was shaking. A giant was approaching! The rumble became louder and louder. The concrete was vibrating. I looked at the sky to see if there were bombers, but no, this noisy thing was on the road, moving slowly and steadily in our direction.

"Tanks." Mother pulled us into a ditch, pushing my face into the grass. I had already seen tanks in Berlin. My nose was pressed into the ground. The ground was vibrating, but the tanks had not yet appeared.

When the rumble seemed to be right over us, I lifted my head above the rim of the ditch and saw a khaki green wall of metal rolling closer, filling the entire highway, two tanks abreast with their long gun turrets sweeping right and left. In front of the tanks were jeeps. The vehicles all had a white star on the hood. Two soldiers sat in the back of each jeep, and a gunner stood next to the driver, his hand on the machine gun. He, too, was moving the gun barrel back and forth.

There was panic in the ditch. People scrambled upright and began to run across the fields, but Mother's expression had changed. She sat up, and suddenly, something I had not seen for weeks, for months—Mother smiled. She stood up and began to wave. She pulled a white handkerchief from her pocket and waved it furiously, practically jumping up and down with joy, except she was crying.

"Get up and take a look at this!" she shouted to Grandmother and me. "You'll remember this sight for the rest of your lives."

In the lead jeep the soldiers had risen to their feet. The gunners were holding their guns loosely now, acknowledging the people who were waving, like mother, grinning from ear to ear. The soldiers were even pushing back their helmets to see better. They pointed at the people running across the fields and laughed out loud.

The column continued. It was an endless steel monster breathing heat from its flanks, rolling itself along tread-by-tread, heaving one grinding hot wheel upon the other. There must have been hundreds of them. Or maybe forty? We sat down on the grass verge not knowing what to say or think. Mother reached out and held both our hands, still with tears in her eyes, her glasses spattered with mud. We were watching the liberators of World War II, but in the joy of the moment we forgot that in their eyes we were all Germans.

Back at Frau Qwirll's house above the main road, the tanks passed below us in single file due to the narrow twisty street they had to negotiate. The tank hatches were open, and the gun turrets were level with our wall. We could see the soldiers close up. Frau Qwirll had hung a white bed sheet out of one of her windows, but it became obvious no harm would come to the towns-people. The one bomb that was dropped while we were in the cellar had landed harmlessly.

It was a thrill to finally see the Allies I had heard so much about, but I was a bit disappointed to see that they were also soldiers—cleaner than Russians and more casual than the Germans, but still men in uniform. The soldiers standing in the open hatches were looking at us with huge grins on their faces. If we waved, they waved back.

All along the route the German townspeople stood silently, mostly women and children, forming a fence of grim faces between the road and the boarded church, the charred ruins and the closed shops, remnants of a *Vaterland* that had few fathers left in it.

Then I saw a black man. I rushed upstairs to tell Grandmother. "He has totally black skin," I told her excitedly. "I'm not telling a lie. Only his eyeballs and his teeth are white."

Grandmother said he was from Africa. I said no, he was from America. "They're speaking American."

Grandmother said they were speaking English. I disagreed. If they were Americans, why would they be speaking English? Russians spoke Russian, Estonians spoke Estonian.

"It's all English, silly!" said Ursula. She and her mother had been watching through the landing window. "They all speak English, even the Africans."

I remained silent, as I always did when I learned something new, something I should have known and would be sure to announce with authority the next time the subject came up.

My first word in the Allies' language was "candy." The soldiers were throwing it to us by the handfuls, also something called "chewing gum." It appeared to be good for the teeth. The black soldiers had beautiful teeth. The black soldiers were also nicer. They did not just throw the candy, but made sure we caught it or sometimes handed it to us personally with their big brown hands that had soft white palms. I told Grandmother they were really white people who had been in the sun too long. Grandmother agreed. I, too, wanted to have nice white teeth. I chewed this gum until all that was left in my mouth was a sticky goo.

The procession lasted a long time. After the tanks came the big guns, then smaller guns, then canvas-covered trucks, then motorbikes, and in the rear more jeeps, until it was all over. Lying on my pew cushion that night in the attic, I was thinking how strange it was that the same soldiers who were giving us candy had been trying to kill us for months. Maybe the candy was a reward for having stayed alive.

A few days later a new procession arrived. This one had different markings on their jeeps, tanks, and trucks. Different uniforms, too. These soldiers also smiled and spoke English. They called candy "sweets." We filled our pockets and socks, even our underwear, because we feared they, too, were only passing through, but they stayed.

"Those are the real English," Ursula told me by way of her mother.

"Those are the real English," I told Grandmother.

"Maybe we should start learning English?"

I told her I already spoke English and reeled off some words I knew: "svits," "soklit," "tenkju," "kudbai."

Before long the soldiers were all over town, walking the streets, sitting by the river. Boys had started following the soldiers for the cigarette butts they dropped. No more *Jungvolk* uniforms.

Ursula and I decided to do the same. We collected enough tobacco for my mother so she could roll a real cigarette instead of tree leaves. As long as we stayed together we were allowed to venture further from the house. We went down to the riverbank to wade in the cold water. Grandmother told me not to sit on cold stones because that could lead to a bladder infection. Ursula's mother spanked Ursula every time she came home with wet shoes. I had never been spanked in my life except for a clout across the bottom from mother for defying her. Mother was living with her Polish friends again. When she came she had even more food for us than before. Sometimes we had cooked eggs and bread.

One day Ursula and I were playing hide-and-seek with the children in the abandoned garden. It was a warm day. I was wearing one of the dresses the dairyman had given us. It was a nuisance that Ursula and I had to hide together, but we managed and were enjoying ourselves when a soldier came up the hill to watch us. He was bareheaded and was carrying a rifle over his shoulder. We noticed at once that he was eating a bar of chocolate. Could he play with us, he mimed?

Not needing any language, we shrugged and let him become part of the game. He joined right in. When it was Ursula's and my turn to hide, he followed us. We were going to hide in the denser bushes by the wall. I saw Ursula fall behind. Perhaps she thought she should not come with us. *(In hindsight I don't know what she thought.)*

The soldier and I reached the bushes and threw ourselves on the ground, but instead of lying beside me, the soldier dumped his rifle and lay on top of me. I pushed him off, but he began to tear at my underwear. I realized he wanted to urinate between my legs. We all knew that men urinated anywhere they wanted to. We saw them do it every day, but I was not going to be a tree or a wall for this one. I started to fight him. I bit his hand and kicked him, but he hardly noticed. Hot and sweaty, he held me down and hurt me. He wet me, too, the filthy beast! When he rolled away, I pulled up my pants and started to run, but there was the bar of chocolate on the grass. I picked it up automatically while fleeing to the hole in the wall that Ursula and I used as a shortcut.

I was going home to tell Grandmother that a soldier had peed on me and hurt me. Ursula was already waiting by the wall and ran alongside me. She had stayed nearby, as her mother had instructed. She had seen me pick up the chocolate and wanted some.

"I'm going home," I told her. I was about to give her one small piece, but she wanted half. We started to argue. In the argument I got sidetracked from the pain, the soldier, and from going home and telling Grandmother what had happened. Instead Ursula and I fought and wrestled for the chocolate bar. Being bigger, I won.

Ursula was a sore loser.

"I'm going to tell my mother," she said and continued down the hill. I thought she was going to tell her mother that I would not give her half my chocolate. When she was out of sight, I felt the pain again and remembered the nasty soldier. There was wet running down my legs and some blood near my knees where I must have cut myself on the twigs.

The chocolate tasted good. Now that I was away and alone, I remembered worse things that had happened to me, like when those boys had tried to bury me in Bernau, and the humiliation of Herr Koch's class, then being stripped in the school toilets. Yet not forgetting Ilse with her mother's iron, none of those things were happening any more. The soldier, too, had disappeared. What was left to tell Grandmother? That I had been peed on. Everybody said men had no restraint. Mother said so constantly, and Grandmother simply said, "Pay no attention." Women at least waited until they could find a wall to squat behind. When I arrived in the yard, I sat on the step and finished the chocolate without going upstairs.

That evening sitting on my potty I felt a terrible pain. The pain was so sharp I cried out and kept crying all the way through while Grandmother held my hand. Grandmother saw blood in the potty and said I must have caught a bladder infection. "I told you not to sit on the cold ground," she admonished.

I began to dread going to the toilet. Walking, too, was painful. Frau Qwirll filled a bottle with hot water, wrapped it into a towel, and placed it between my legs. It eased the pain so that I was able to sleep. I healed and thought no more about it.

Several days later, Mother turned up with a full rucksack. I was excited to see her. When she called me through the window, I thought it was to give me some American candy or English sweets. I hurried upstairs in anticipation.

When I got inside the room, she closed the door and stood against it. Grandmother was by the window, white in the face and crying. She kept reaching out with one hand, saying "Don't!" and "Please don't!"

Slowly, without a word, Mother undid her belt, the one with the sharp brass buckle I had noticed in Haapsalu. She doubled it into her fist so the buckle hung loose.

"Take off your underpants and bend over," she ordered.

What was she going to do? I had never seen Mother with that wild look on her face. Her nostrils were distended and her jaw was so rigid she could barely speak.

I did as I was told. I bent over the cushions, thinking maybe she wanted to know why it had hurt so when I urinated. She took a step backwards and raised her arm. From then on, any nightmare I had experienced was only a mild annoyance compared to the beating Mother gave me, for reasons I did not understand until I was an adult.

Every time the belt came down it pushed my face into the cushions, and when the belt lifted, the sting of the buckle seemed to pull my flesh with it. Blood spattered the wall, the cushions. Maybe she hit me five times, maybe ten times. I had no idea, but every time the belt came down, she said these words, "Never, never go near a man again!"

I was seven years old. I didn't know if Mother was beating me because I had let the soldier urinate on me or because I didn't share my chocolate with Ursula. I didn't even know that sex existed. The boys in Bernau, Herr Koch's

94

class, even Ilse, had all been strangers. They had meant nothing to me. I had never wanted them to love me, as I had wanted Mother to love me. The beating confirmed she would never never love me. Ursula cannot have known what happened to me either. She probably told her mother she had seen me fighting with a soldier. Frau Scneider's adult version to my mother had to have been extreme for Mother to react the way she did. Much later, when I was fourteen and in the British orphanage, I found out how babies were made. That information did not help either. I thought then that Mother had beaten me because she didn't want me to have a baby, which would have given her another mouth to feed.

Finally Grandmother could not stand it any longer; she threw herself upon Mother and tried to wrest the belt from her hands. Mother pushed her aside, but Grandmother grasped me into her arms and received the last blows on her own back. When Mother realized she was now beating her own mother, she threw the belt aside and left the room. We did not see her again for days.

Grandmother lay me down on my stomach and began to mop up the blood with my panties. The wiping hurt even worse than the beating. I was screaming so loudly that Frau Qwirll came up to see what was wrong. She brought hot water from the kitchen. They washed me and whispered together in low tones, using single words and head nods. I stopped screaming mainly to find out what they were saying, but as usual I missed the most important information of all—the real reason for the beating.

For several days and nights I remained on my stomach on the cushions with Grandmother bathing my buttocks and placing warm compresses on me, winding them around my legs like diapers. Frau Qwirll brought a jar of pork fat to smear on my wounds and tore old sheets into bandages. I wore the bandages until I healed.

When I felt a bit better, I went to see if Ursula was home. I felt guilty that I had not shared the chocolate as fairly as I should have. I had been greedy. Ursula opened the door to my knock, but just a fraction. She shook her head and before I could find out why, her mother came up behind her and slammed the door in my face. "Don't come here again!" she shouted through the panel. I vowed I would never eat chocolate again without sharing it.

Because rape was rare among the Allies, what happened to me was an exception by an individual who might have been a pedophile all along. This might also be the place to explain that although my relationship with my mother was rocky, it was finally resolved when I was eighteen years old. We had a major blowup during a holiday in Munich. We fought all night, but by morning we had cleared the air and became best of friends forever after.

Chapter 8

DISPLACED
1945-1946

Hitler committed suicide on 30 April 1945. On 2 May 1945 Berlin surrendered. On 4 May 1945 Montgomery received the surrender of German forces in northwest Germany.

Robert Leckie

In the months after the war's end, all of Europe was crawling with disoriented people, moving in all directions, most of them crossing in and out of Central Europe. In a continent overrun with armies, the face of war did not belong to the soldier, but to the refugee.

Displaced persons (DPs)...numbered about 13 million in the summer of 1945. Among these were 10 million foreign workers who had been shipped into Germany from all across Europe to provide slave labor for the German war machine. Millions of prisoners of war and concentration camp survivors joined the flood. The bulk of these people passed through massive refugee camps established by the United Nations Relief and Rehabilitation Administration (UNRRA.) This organization provided relief, albeit very limited, to an astonishing array of nationalities: Russians, Poles, Balts, Yugoslavs, and Central European Jews.

Life in the UNRRA camps was terribly hard. Every sort of accommodation was used for housing people, including barracks, concentration camps, schools, factories, barns, stables, and tents. The DPs interned in such facilities were looked after by a skeletal team of Allied soldiers, doctors, and orderlies who attempted to establish at least some basic order. German POWs were used to dig latrines and build shelters. Supplies were requisitioned from the local German population, though the Germans themselves were already in bad shape. DPs were provided with meager rations of potatoes and soup and were lucky to receive fifteen hundred calories a day-barely enough to survive.

William I. Hitchcock

After the war Germany was divided into four zones. Hausberge was in the British zone, and the nearest displaced persons camp was in Meerbeck, near Hannover. Mother left Philips Hammerwerke on 30 April 1945 and went ahead to see if she could get us into the camp. She came back and said all was well, we would be accepted. We set off from Hausberge on the morning of 25 June.

Mother had become a Member of the Estonian Committee by permission of the Military Government in Detmold, Lippe, Germany, British Zone.

The day was hot and sunny.

"We are approaching the camp," said Grandmother. "I thought you would want to see."

We had become "displaced persons," which sounded a bit better than *Ausländer*. I licked my lips—they were dry and cracked—and sat up straight in the jeep. The word "camps" had always meant Siberia and people freezing to death, but it was warm and we were going to start a new life in peacetime. Peacetime meant no more air raids, no more bombs.

We left Hausberge at dawn after spending the night packing. It was nearly noon. The sun was directly overhead. The English soldier driving the jeep was laughing and talking to Mother, who was sitting in the front with him smoking American Camels, cigarettes worth dying for, according to everyone. No more tree leaves or that awful Russian *makhorka* for her.

After that painful experience with the English soldier and the beating from Mother, I steered clear of her and she of me. Grandmother kept patting my hand and saying, "Don't worry, it will blow over."

At least Mother was happy again, laughing with the Allies. This one was obviously a war hero, a real Englishman, with a long face, red hair, and blue eyes. The jeep had a red, white, and blue circle on the hood instead of the white star of the Americans. They both spoke English. So how was one to tell the English from the American? "Look at their teeth," I heard someone say. The Americans had the whiter teeth. It had to be the chewing gum.

Grandmother and I were sitting in the back of the jeep surrounded by our bundles. We were marveling at Mother speaking English, although I was not sure the man understood anything she was saying or she everything he said. It was enough that they had a conversation.

Listening to people's conversations was always informative. I often learned things no one told me, but sometimes what I heard puzzled me and it took me a long time to work it all out. I overheard some Germans saying that the Russians were also the Allies. If that were true, then why had we fled Estonia? I puzzled over that for a long time and finally came to the conclusion that the Soviets had only pretended to be Allies; they had not meant to liberate anyone. They had just wanted to take over other countries. The Germans had also wanted countries, but first they had needed to help Hitler become King of England. As incentive, the Germans had been given smart uniforms, highly polished boots, and medals. It was harder to understand why the English had gone to war, unless they had simply hated Hitler and had not wanted another German king. Now that the war was over, only the Allies could wear their medals in public. The Germans were forced to learn English if they wanted Camels and American stockings called "nailons."

I was sitting on top of our biggest bundle, holding my pink blanket bundle, and we had another bundle, a thick UNRRA quilt the soldier had given us. Grandmother was still holding on to "dear Erni," who had been rearranged, resewn, and tied with string, so that the parcel looked more like a cloth suitcase than a bundle.

Germany was definitely in ruins. Half the towns we passed through were mounds of rubble. Work crews were busy clearing the streets. In the villages men were pushing wheelbarrows, planting seeds, and putting in potatoes. The fields remained untouched. The current harvest was metal—overturned jeeps, blackened military trucks, and ambulances on their backs like dead beetles. Some of the wrecks bore the American star, others the British tricolor. Large stretches of road were unpaved. Here workmen were applying fresh asphalt, digging ditches, and laying pipes. I expected that in a short time everything would be back to how it had been before the war. The war had been a waste of time.

"When are we going home?" I asked Grandmother.

"I don't know," she replied.

Going home seemed like the next step. There was nothing left to fight for—just clean up and repair. That's what the Germans were doing. I couldn't wait to see Tondu again.

"Hannover." Grandmother pointed to a sign on the *autobahn*. She had a line of suffering across her forehead, between the tightly wrapped scarf over her mouth and the dusty hat pulled down to her eyebrows. There was dust in my teeth. I must have napped with my mouth open.

Suddenly the driver pointed to a field on the right. He mimed a plane zooming down and crashing. He then mimed a pitchfork and vicious jabbing. Mother turned and translated for Grandmother. A pilot had crashed in the field, and the villagers had killed him with their pitchforks. As punishment the British had turned the village into a DP camp. And that was where we were going. Mother pointed to a second sign, battered and smaller, at the side of the road. I read "Meerbeck." The sign had fallen off its pole and was propped against it.

I was going to be eight years old soon. I hoped we would be home for my birthday

The jeep kept stopping at train barriers to let trains go by. The trains were festooned with flowers and tree branches. When the people saw us at the barrier, they waved and threw kisses to the English soldier and his jeep. "Going home!" they shouted happily in German and Polish.

"The Poles are going home," said Mother, turning to explain to Mämmä. Mother did not look happy for them and changed the subject.

The trains we saw actually went directly to forced labor camps in Poland where the people were incarcerated because they committed the crime of leaving Poland for the West. The Allies had not yet realized how Stalin was going to betray them and take advantage of their naiveté.

We turned off the *autobahn* onto a narrower road that had lost all its asphalt to bomb blasts. The jeep bounced, lifted, and landed with bone-jarring jolts. Our bundles rolled this way and that way. We were flung along with them. Grandmother clutched the back of my dress. She must have sensed my apprehension, but also my desire to stand up and take a look at this warm-weather camp where we were going to eat white bread. She had described the texture as something between *kringle* and cake.

Suddenly I heard a noise I knew intimately.

"Sit still," Grandmother warned me, through her scarf.

But I couldn't. It was an airplane flying low. I leaped onto my feet in panic. The jeep bucked. I stumbled, ready to fling myself over the side, but Grandmother's grasp on my dress pressed me back down to my knees. The plane passed over. Nothing happened. No strafing.

I had forgotten. It was this new peacetime. We watched the plane until it became a silver dot glinting in the sunlight; its steady sweet droning grew weaker and weaker. I had never known that a plane could be a beautiful sight. Peacetime was a definite improvement on the way things had been, but it was hard to get used to.

From Hausberge to Meerbeck

"The camp," said Mother and pointed straight ahead to roofs and houses, a windmill, and even a church spire beyond the untilled fields. Another village. I don't know what I had expected.

The road divided. We took the left fork. The farmhouse on the fork had a large white, runny number *1* painted on its side. The next two farmhouses were daubed *2* and *3* in crude whitewashed lettering. Number *3* had an additional hand-lettered sign nailed to a tree. It said *kõrts*, the Estonian for pub.

The boarded-up windmill with broken shafts was numbered *4*.

Untilled fields on either side of the road supported the story that Mother had translated about the villagers having been evicted for killing the English pilot. People like us were now living in their houses. I bet they were not happy about it.

The village itself was small: a main street, a dozen houses, a church that I had already spotted, a tall brick building that I identified as the

100

schoolhouse, and a few other larger buildings before the road opened up again and disappeared between more fields and ruined barns.

The jeep stopped outside house number 9, an ordinary two-story farmhouse with a large ground-floor entrance. An old hay wagon stood inside it, surrounded by doors and a staircase to the second floor.

Our driver jumped out, both feet together. Mother eased herself off the seat slowly, rubbing her hips and tugging at her skirt. It was her only skirt and had a matching jacket with padded shoulders. She had not worn the suit since Estonia. Her hair was done up in a twist. She was a woman again.

"Let's see what we have here." She threw away her cigarette and disappeared into the house. The driver lifted me down first, then offered Grandmother his elbow. She tripped and almost fell. He caught her deftly and said something that sounded like "upsedeisi!"

Grandmother was embarrassed and began to fix her hat pin. A knot of people had come out of the house. They stood around the wagon entrance and watched us. Children were in the crowd—not a comforting sight in Germany.

Suddenly a big woman stepped out of the group. She had her sleeves rolled up to the elbows. Without a word she hoisted our UNRRA quilt bundle off the jeep and flung it over her shoulder.

"Here, let me help," she said in Estonian. "You've probably come a long way and are tired. My name is Lepatree." Mrs. Lepatree carried the first and biggest of our bundles into the house. As if on cue, arms reached out for the other bundles. Soon everybody was helping us move in. A woman bent down and asked me my name. I was unable to speak. I was so surprised to find myself among Estonians again. We were shown to our room.

"This, our room?" asked Mother, raising her voice. It was even smaller than the attic closet we had in Hausberge. The only furniture was a small table. An argument sprang up between Mother and the house superintendent. It ended with both of them and the driver getting back into the jeep and driving off to headquarters. Grandmother and I were left on our bundles which stuck halfway out into the hall. We could not close the door.

"All right," said Grandmother firmly. "Let's get to work." She removed her coat and banged her hat against the wall. It released a cloud of dust. Then she put it back on again. Grandmother refused to be seen in public without her hat. She said a lady always keeps her hat on in the company of strangers, also when her hair is a mess. She handed me a pair of scissors and told me to unravel the bundles, starting with my pink blanket bundle. "And be careful not to cut the cloth." Grandmother was humming under her breath. I would have hummed, too, but I had refrained from singing a note since being told I was tone deaf. Instead I cut into the blanket.

Every one of the girls standing around was wearing an identical dress with tiny white flowers on a blue background, and here I was, in Ursula's woolen Dirndl. Now patched, darned, and let out beyond recognition. It had been all right in Hausberge, but was all wrong in this Meerbeck. I was going to be different again and knew what that meant. I shook Grandmother's sleeve urgently and whispered that I had to have a dress like that. I pointed

101

to the dress. Grandmother turned to see what I was pointing to and noticed the hole I had cut into the blanket. She took away the scissors.

"See if Mother is coming yet," she suggested.

There was no need to look. Mother's return would have been noticed.

As people lost interest and returned to their rooms I sat down on the biggest bundle and started thinking about the dress. Mother had connections. I wished I could speak to Mother normally. She had started scaring me again.

"Don't fall asleep out there," called Grandmother. She was hunting for her candles and matches. There was still light outside, but the tiny window was not letting in more than a little of it. She stuck the candle into our Dresden and placed the cup on the windowsill. With the bundles unravelled there was more room to move about. We had been given three grey army blankets and three burlap sacks. We were supposed to fill the sacks with straw from the hay wagon in the middle of the hall.

There was a strong smell of food. Real food. And there was a kitchen nearby. I could hear a pump. People were going back and forth with pots and pans. I was hungry. Grandmother must have had the same thought. She paused in her sewing and handed me a crust of rye bread. It was rock hard, but I had good teeth.

As the hall began to get darker, the sky became lighter. That always happened when the sun reflected on the edges of the clouds on a summer night. I had not seen a clear sky for a long time. The pump eventually became silent. A hall lamp was lit on the upstairs landing. There was electric light.

Mother finally returned. She and the superintendent had settled their differences and were talking theater. He was saying he had seen Mother in various roles. He had seen her in *The Snow Queen* and was describing the scenes in detail. I saw Mother stifle a yawn and discreetly look at her watch. She began to take the combs out of her hair when he wasn't looking. She was tired. "And we'll get you a bigger room as soon as one becomes available," the superintendent promised.

"That's fine," said Mother and stumbled over me in the dark.

"We had to go all the way to Stadthagen," she grumbled, when she had closed the door. She removed her jacket. Grandmother motioned for me to do the same. It was still a novelty to undress at night. I wore one of Grandmother's old summer dresses to sleep in.

Mother placed my straw sleeping sack under the table. The fresh straw rustled and bit through the sheets. A gift from Frau Qwirll. Grandmother was sighing and turning. Mother got up and opened the window to let in fresh air. Faint moonlight gave the room back its shapes and angles. A cool evening breeze brushed my face and neck. I could smell the garden, hear the crickets and village noises far off, when suddenly the peaceful night was shattered by loud singing.

A ragged chorus of drunks was staggering up the village street and approaching our house. There were three voices, but I knew Unki's right away. Unki had caught up with us again. I knew he would. Just as he had found us in Hausberge, he had found us in the camp. He must have stopped at house number 3 first, for a quick snort. Closer and closer came the singers.

102

First in Estonian: "Mari's white knickers are a sight to behold!" Then Unki alone with *La Marseillaise* in French. His friends cheered him on.

Grandmother's mattress became quiet.

"My God, that's Paul!" Mother sat up and went white as a sheet, even in the dark.

Other angry voices could be heard in the hall. A door slammed. The hall light went on. The village dogs started barking. Windows were opened. The singers paid no heed, but turned into our drive. "Mari's white knickers" rang out again loud and clear. My heart stopped for Unki and his friends. At the same moment Mother jumped to her feet, grabbed Mämmä's coat, and left the room.

Grandmother's straw remained quiet. I, too, had stopped breathing. We heard the words "decent people" and "damned drunks" and "we don't care whose brother you are!" The singing had stopped on a half-note. Mother was explaining, using her best voice. The superintendent was saying, "Is that so?" He didn't believe a word of it. The commotion ceased eventually. The hall light went off again. People returned to their rooms.

Unki came into our room. Mother threw the coat aside and without another word climbed back onto her sack. Grandmother had thoughtfully vacated her mattress and moved over to share mine, leaving hers for Unki, who sat down on the vacant sack of straw and stayed sitting there, head in his hands. He did not even take his coat off.

I could see him clearly. My eyes had adjusted again to the light through the little window. I had started breathing normally, but I dared not go to him yet. There were so many things I wanted to tell Unki and to ask him. If anybody could find out about the dead English pilot, it would be Unki.

A long time later, when the straw had stopped rustling, I saw Unki lie down, but not to sleep. He was staring at the ceiling. I wanted to take his hand. I had missed him and his stories about jungles, snakes, and crocodiles—how he had wrestled a lion once and ridden a camel in Egypt. Unki always felt bad after a drinking scene with Mother. Grandmother blamed their quarrels on their Enno blood.

It was a long time later when Grandmother started snoring and Mother's mattress became still. Unki had been waiting and listening for the same thing. He sat up, folded his coat into a pillow, and began to unwind his feet. He did not have socks and wore rags wound around his feet the way they did in the Legion.

When Unki began to rub his corns, I knew the time was right. I slipped off my sack, quiet as a mouse, and took his hand. "I knew you'd come back," I whispered happily. "I never stopped waiting for you."

Unki's gold teeth flashed brilliantly. He hugged me close.

The resettlement process began the next day, 26 June 1945, with the screening of all DPs in the camp by the United Nations Relief and Rehabilitation Administreation, UNRRA.

When we got up Unki had disappeared. Apparently he had drunk away his French passport and documents, and a man without documents in post-war

103

Germany could be arrested on sight. He definitely could not be screened. Mother was beside herself, but she was not going to betray him. She had told him to get lost and not come back until she had found a solution for him. He was, after all, her father's younger brother.

Screening tables were set up in the assembly hall in the village schoolhouse. Everyone lined up to be questioned. Mother had already been screened and said she would help us. She was anxious to make sure Grandmother filled in the questionnaire the way she wanted her to. No one asked me anything.

Halfway through, Mother discovered that Grandmother had put her desired destination as Canada. It was too late to change it. "We're in the British Zone. We want to go to England." When Grandmother started to argue, Mother slapped her forehead in frustration and said, "Let's get this over with."

We were approved for resettlement by UNRRA team No. 158 out of Detmold-Lippe.

Because the room was too small for us, we were moved to house number *15* on the perimeter of the village, where the Germans had retained their properties. Houses *16, 17, 18,* and *19* bordered a potato field across from the Germans. Our house was directly next to a large working farm that even had a new greenhouse. We shared a dirt track with the German farmer, a track that led to some nearby woods.

Our number *15* farmhouse had the same layout as number *9,* but there was no hay wagon in the hall. Our room was the last one on the upstairs landing, next to the attic. After moving in, Grandmother discovered a door concealed behind the wallpaper. This led to a tiny chamber with a small window, masked from the outside by a curtain of ivy. It was a storage room of some kind. Mother came in and nodded. "It will be ideal for Paul."

"Is that where they hid the dead pilot?" I asked.

Mother gave me a stern look and pushed the table and chairs in front of the door to further conceal it. She told us to always do the same if official-looking people came into the house to look around.

Unki turned up a few nights later, quietly, looking a bit sheepish. He was our secret, but by the second night everyone knew he was there because they heard him stumbling up the stairs in the middle of the night, missing steps, cursing in French and Russian. Unki became everybody's secret.

"Just don't show yourself during the day," Mother warned him.

"At least we have a man in the family," said Grandmother.

Uncle Paul built us a stove by knocking a hole into the wall for the stovepipe. Mother went berserk, but later admitted, "Paul has his uses." Yet she still did not like him.

I loved Unki. I was glad he hadn't lost his gold teeth along with his passport. When I came in from playing he was usually sitting at the table, head in hands, but even when he was hung over, he always grinned and acknowledged me.

104

The new stove smoked and sparked. The floor around it became charred and pitted, but Grandmother was happy. She could heat water and cook soup. Unki himself could roast onions to put on his corns. Grandmother also baked on the stove, using empty sardine tins, which she stacked one on top of another. The best tins still had parts of the tops attached, which could be twisted into handles. Sometimes the stacks fell over or the labels caught fire, but it saved Grandmother from having to share the kitchen with other women.

Unki was whittling a ladle for Grandmother so she could mete out larger portions of soup than with a sardine can. Unki also let Grandmother use his penknife to trim her toenails after she had seen him trim his. The knife had something to pick your teeth with, three blades and a corkscrew. Unki had already seen me coveting his penknife and promised to leave it to me in his Will.

"Tell me about the world," I asked him.

"We're all animals," he began. "When you're eye to eye with a tiger, at least the tiger is doing what comes naturally, but human animals should know better. They enjoy your pain. If you're taken prisoner, your first duty is to escape," he instructed me.

"I'll remember," I promised.

We saw very little of Mother.

When my eighth birthday came around, Mother woke me. Grandmother carried the tiny cake with half a burned candle on it. Unki was getting us eggs from the German farms. It was a "three-sardine-tin" birthday cake.

Mother also had a gift for me. She had made me a trouser suit out of one of the grey army blankets, and I was issued a pair of UNRRA camp clogs with wooden soles and canvas uppers. The clogs were plain wood, unfinished. Mud built up under the soles. I developed blisters. Unki promised to wind rags around my feet the way they did in the Legion, but he kept forgetting or was hung over again. Grandmother saw the problem and cut the sleeves off one of her cardigans. She made me cardigan socks. I didn't want socks; I wanted rags like Unki's.

The village schoolhouse was in the Latvian sector. Estonians had to set up their own classrooms in house number *10*. The teachers were people who had been teachers in Estonia. Instead of a German school I was now going to an Estonian school.

The direct route to number *10* was across the German fields. Germans no longer scared me. Mother had told me we were protected by the authorities—the same authorities Unki tried to avoid, the ones who drove around in jeeps, had the letters MP on their armbands, and made sure nobody was keeping pigs.

Ration card, for three days, 4, 5 and 6 August 1946.

The food truck came once a week, but the food ration was meager and people were still hungry.

The three-day bread ration for everyone over 18 was 448 grams (about one pound.) Other rations were: vegetables, 210 grams; potatoes, 960 grams; sausage, 58 grams; butter, 42 grams; biscuits and peas, 170 grams; meat, 56 grams; sugar, 84 grams; powdered milk and soup powder, 60 grams each; canned fish, 8 oz.; oatmeal for infants, invalids, and pregnant women, 4 oz.; soap, 4 oz.; sweets for the children and 6 eggs for the sick.

However, of real value were the ten American cigarettes for each person and 20 for those who worked. Cigarettes were the currency in the surrounding villages. Although Paul was not on the list, he already had connections and traded ours. Grandmother also went to Stadthagen Station once a week to barter for such things as salt and pepper, needles, and thread.

Not long after we had settled down at number *15*, I met Cat. She was a dignified black and white. The last thing I needed was a pet. I had vowed I would never get involved with another animal as long as I lived, no more heartaches. I didn't ask her to follow me, but she did anyway.

Grandmother was unraveling another cardigan when Cat and I walked into the room. She didn't even look up. "No!" she said.

"But Mämmä!"

"I said no, no, no!"

"She could lick out the sardine cans."

"No! Besides she's female," said Grandmother, taking a closer look. "That could mean trouble."

However, Grandmother was still my Grandmother, and half an hour later Cat was lapping condensed milk beside the stove.

"Be sure the superintendent doesn't see her," she warned. "He doesn't like cats."

I repeated this to Cat and she nodded. I put my cheek next to hers and said, "Hello, Cat," in Estonian, knowing that animals speak every language on earth as long as it's spoken lovingly and with a promise of food.

"And she'll have to catch her own food," Grandmother continued, having read my mind.

Cat said that was all right, too. She agreed to everything. "She has an old soul," said Grandmother.

Mrs. Vallas, our teacher, looked like Mother, with the same hairdo and jackets with padded shoulders. As I could read and write, there was no need to give me special instruction. I concentrated on composition, sums, and Estonian history. While we worked, Mrs. Vallas sat on a chair by the stove and knitted, but every once in a while she used her knitting needle to scratch for lice or bedbugs that got into the hems of our clothes. We all had lice and bedbugs.

Unki had taught me a song about lice in Siberia that was sung around the brewery, a song about how men married women so they could have milk in their coffee. Unki put his finger to the side of his nose, the signal not to repeat the song in front of Mother or Grandmother.

Estonian Girl Scouts ("Hellakesed") at the Meerbeck
DP Camp, 1946. Elin is second from right.

107

No pigs were allowed in the DP camp, but ours were already snorting happily and scratching themselves in the pigsty next to the kitchen. Like Unki, the pigs were also an open secret. They were going to be slaughtered for Christmas, and everybody was going to get some meat. I remembered the Qwirlls' pig in Hausberge. Another trusting soul.

Elin, on the left, and friends at the Meerbeck DP Camp, 1946.

The weather got colder by the day. When it was really miserable outside, Mrs. Vallas opened the stove door and sat with her feet on a stool until her legs turned red. I also got the benefit of the heat; I sat in front of the class because I could not see the blackboard from further back. My blanket suit was always wet and steaming. The girl next to me said I smelled like a dog. I told her she looked like a dog.

Camp life was making me feel bold again. Crossing the barren UNRRA-held fields back to house 15, I marveled at this peacetime. I took my time—jumping rain puddles, riding the wind, and squatting outside animal burrows, waiting for earthworms and moles to pop out of the soil. The crows were right there, too, waiting for their next meal. The sound of the crows was a constant dirge of discontent. They hopped and cawed about the barren fields like distracted pastors at a funeral, their feathers unkempt and their song joyless. Sometimes Cat came to meet me halfway. I worried about our relationship. Memories of Tondu were still deep and painful. Cats could break your heart and walk away.

Christmas arrived suddenly. Unki brought a tree from the nearby woods, but we never got to put it up because I became ill. Grandmother burned the Christmas candles so she could see to heat water and wind compresses around my chest. The room became distorted. The walls pulled together, and then drew apart. The ceiling came down, and then shot up out of sight.

The compresses were uncomfortable. They were just woolen rags soaked in hot water and wound so tightly around my chest that I could barely move. There was no doctor, but Grandmother held a cold spoon to my forehead and fed me sour cooking apples. We prayed for Jesus to protect me:

Take me under your wing, oh Jesus.
Let this little bird be safe.
If the Devil is flying near,
Let your angels interfere.
This child shall sleep in peace. Amen.

Mother chopped up the Christmas tree and added it to the wet logs.

When my temperature came down and the room's dimensions returned to normal, Grandmother would not let me go out to play for ten days. Ten days! No other children were in the house, so I went down to the pigsty to scratch the Angoroffs' pig's tummy with the kitchen broom. He was the fattest and ugliest pig of the three. He loved it when I scratched his hide. He rolled over and grunted with pleasure.

"Stupid pigs," I told them all. "Nobody likes you. They tickle your tummies and feed you, they click their tongues and fondle your sides, feeling if you're fat enough yet for hams and sausages. If you knew all that, you wouldn't lie down and grunt with pleasure; you'd try to escape." I then whacked the Mölders' pig with the broom, but it, too, lay down immediately, closed its eyes, and rolled over. "Grunt," it said.

"Something is going on," I confided to them. All those whisperings again. "You wait and see."

Sure enough. Mother announced at the dinner table that a new program had been put together that would allow the DPs to go to different countries around the world and that our camp was recruiting single women for England. Her friend, Hilda Takk, now employed by Philips Electrical in Eindhoven, had promised to try to get Mother a job in Holland, but Mother thought England would be a better choice.

"England is the country of Thomas Hardy, Shakespeare and most of the great institutions of civilization. If Hilda does not reply soon, I'm going to England with the Swans," she told us.

"A swan?" I looked up from my potato soup.

"That's what they call the program, 'The Swans'." Mother was excited.

Then she remembered something. She took me by the hand and led me to Unki's chamber. Unki was out. I had seen him trudging up the road earlier, to the brewery, hunched into his greatcoat, head down against the driving rain.

His chamber exuded a cold musty smell of wet dogs, dried apples, and the smell of an animal. Mother encouraged me to go ahead. There was a definite animal smell, and it was not a dog. I went down the step and there it was—a little black rabbit, black all over except for a pink nose that twitched and wriggled.

"Pick her up," Mother said. "She won't bite."

Of course she didn't bite. She was bewildered, wondering where her next meal was coming from. Pigs, birds, all animals had but two things on their minds: food and a place to sleep. Just like people during wartime.

"She needs a carrot," said Grandmother, standing behind us and then went to fetch one.

I named the rabbit Muki. I recognized that she was a peace offering from Mother, but also another good-bye. I hoped she was not leaving us because of Unki.

A lot of people didn't like Unki. "Imagine having someone like that in the family," I heard one woman comment to Grandmother after Unki had staggered past, looking like he had spent the night in a barn.

"He provides," Grandmother answered curtly.

Mother left early the next morning. I felt her kiss me good-bye. As soon as she was out the door, I rushed to the window. She was standing in a truck with Mrs. Mölder and a few other women from our house. They were all waving. Grandmother was standing in the road blowing her nose.

To make sure Muki wouldn't run away, Unki built her a sturdy cage. I cleaned the cage every day, fed her dried apples, and wrinkled carrots. When spring arrived I picked fresh grass and dandelion leaves.

One day I came home from school and found Grandmother lying down on her cot. Her breathing was short and labored. "A touch of asthma," she explained. She said she had inherited the huffing and puffing from her father, who also had huffed and puffed for no reason. She still had difficulty breathing the next morning.

Chapter 9

"BALTIC SWANS"
1947

Nineteen forty-seven was a difficult year for the DPs [Displaced Persons.] Resettlement was negligible and there seemed little hope of their finding new homes and opportunities. Everything possible in a disrupted economy was being done to help them.

General Lucious D. Clay

The British Government was the first to open its doors to Baltic DPs. Initially the only openings for women were with the "Baltic Swans" scheme, although Polish men had already been brought into British coal mines. The British government was negotiating with the labor unions on the number of textile workers that could be brought into the mills without threatening the jobs of English weavers.

Only single women were accepted in the "Swans" program. A thousand Baltic women signed labor agreements of up to five years. After five years they could obtain British citizenship. Mother signed up for five years. Her primary goal was to get us out of the camps and out of Germany. She arrived in the UK on 21 January 1947 and was assigned to Leeds Hospital for Women, Coventry Place.

About three weeks after Mother had left Germany, the following letter arrived for her from Holland, written on 6 February 1947:

We herewith declare that the Estonian citizen, Liki Toona, born in 1910 in Estonia, at present staying in a Displaced Persons Camp in Meerbeck, Stadthagen, 135 DP Assembly Center, English zone, will be engaged by our Company as an employee for our Accountancy Department in Eindhoven, Netherlands.

Hilda Takk, our friend from Haapsalu, had come through for her again, but it was too late. Mother was already in England. Hilda had become a Director of Philips Electrical, Polish Division, a rich and powerful woman.

Leeds Hospital for Women was a small hospital.

Mother's letters from England were cheerful. She said the work was not too demanding for someone who had never used a broom or a duster in her life. She was scrubbing floors on her hands and knees for 48 hours a week, but had made friends with one of the sisters who had promised to try to find her something easier.

"Eating grapes, cake, drinking real coffee...," Grandmother read the letters aloud and marveled over every word. The camp rations were still meager, although Unki was helping out by bringing eggs from the villages.

I didn't know at the time that Grandmother was giving her rations to me. In England, too, food was rationed.

Mother's packages from England contained butter, peanut butter, English cereal, raisins, flour and macaroni. Inside the bigger packages there were usually small parcels for me. I thanked her and told her what I was doing.

> *Dear Mimma! I got your parcel. Thank you for the chocolate and sweets. The school is still closed. It's so cold. We are being fed in the clubroom. The doll I got from Tante Friida got burned. She lost her legs. Mämmä was able to stamp out the flames, but they burned anyway. A man came around selling colored pencils. He did not come to our room. I went to Katrin's birthday party. We had bread and butter and wine.*
> *Your Elin*

Sitting on the well cover, tickling Cat's tummy the way she liked me to, I told Cat how Mother had been our leader and was leading us again. In the kitchen the women had been saying that God was an Englishman.

"England must be the Promised Land. They speak English in the Promised Land," I told Cat. We were also learning English in school.

While speaking to Cat I noticed a convoy of trucks cruising down the main road from Stadthagen. Three of them turned into our fork, while the others continued on into the village. "Extra rations," I told Cat.

People had come out of the house, probably hoping the same.

The trucks came to a stop between our house and number 16. Not rations, but people. The drivers jumped down and opened the back flaps. The usual jumble of refugees with their bundles, boxes, and battered suitcases tumbled out—only three men, the rest women and five children. One was a boy, sitting on his mother's suitcase. His mother hobbled around him like a stork in high heels. She reminded me of Ursula's mother, only younger and less used. Other children were running about. They did not interest me. I had gone right off children since coming to Germany. All the same I couldn't help noticing a girl of about four or five parading up and down in front of the crowd of onlookers with a stick under her arm, army fashion. She was shouting, "One, two, three. Hup! Two, three," as she paraded along the line. Her voice was rough and gravelly like a soldier's.

"Hup, two, three!" Those who did not move their feet away fast enough got a tap on the toes. When she turned back for another round, a man broke through the knot of new arrivals and shouted, "Inge, stop that!" He scooped the girl up in his arms and gave her a whack on the bottom. He threw the stick into the bushes, but this Inge didn't even flinch. She picked herself up, used a word Unki dared not use in Grandmother's presence, and went to retrieve the stick. With the stick back in her possession she looked around aggressively, saw Cat on the rain barrel, and without hesitation rushed over and grabbed her by the back legs.

"You stop messing with my cat!" I yelled. Cat didn't like it anyway. With a hiss she streaked up the pear tree, Inge right behind her. What a girl! My anger turned to admiration. She would have made a marvelous friend, were she older.

When Cat returned I scooped her up for myself. Grandmother was standing near me and Unki was there, too, picking his teeth with a safety pin.

Among the people and bundles was another girl. This one was my age. Their bundles looked like ours. A woman busying herself with the knots and ties was a Mämmä-type grandmother, except that this one wore a scarf. My grandmother only wore her scarf to bed because of straw getting into her hair. This girl I wanted to befriend. They just *had* to move into the empty room on our landing.

"Unki, Unki!" I shook his hand to ask him to help me, but he wasn't listening. His grin was focused on a man who looked like himself, except this man had wild greying hair and no gold teeth, but their noses were similar, red and knobbly. "Drinkers," Mother would have said. The man also wore an army greatcoat, but it had a dirty sheepskin lining.

"Hei, Juhan!" Unki dropped my hand and jumped across the ditch. The man stopped what he was doing and threw up his arms; the two men embraced like two trees falling into each other's branches. They hopped, punched, and slapped each other.

The girl's mother looked up and smiled. She was a square hard-working type and shouted something to the girl. The girl jumped off the bundles and started helping the old lady. I understood the man was a member of their family.

Unki and sheepskin coat moved away to sit on the grass verge for a re-union. Unki had a bottle. He took a slug, and then wiped the lip. His friend did the same, but not before sneaking a quick glance at his women. The signal was "not now." The bottle disappeared as quickly as it had appeared.

Unki motioned for us to join them. Introductions were made. Unki told the man that my name was Rin-Tin-Tin. The man's name was Juhan.

"Call me Uncle Juhan," he said and motioned for his family to come and be introduced. To my great dismay it turned out the family did not share a common language. Uncle Juhan spoke Estonian, Russian, and German. His wife spoke Estonian, Russian, Finnish, and German, all at the same time. The old lady, Mrs. Grigorjev, spoke Finnish, Russian, and French. They were Ingrians, from Ingria, a small country south of Finland.

When it was my turn to speak to the girl, I said in Estonian, "This is Cat." The girl continued to look at me.

"My Leena," said the mother finally, "does not speak Estonian. She speaks Russian and German."

Leena's limp hand barely brushed my fingers. Her grandmother wrapped her arms around the girl from behind. It was a protective gesture I understood.

"*Meine Katze,*" I ventured in German and waved my hand towards the defecting cat who had taken off again.

Leena smiled. At least we could speak German.

The superintendent called for attention and started reading names off a long list. As each name was called, the owners climbed back into the truck. The first full load was going to number *18*.

I heard him call out the names Elmer and Grigorjev. They were assigned to number *16* across the road from ours, overlooking the German fields.

When we were back in our room Unki explained how he and Juhan had been in the same Legion Post, the only Estonians there. They had last seen each other in Cambodia. Unki had been surprised to find Juhan a married man. He told us how it had come about. Juhan had been standing in line in Hannover, waiting to register for the camps. The woman in front of him was trying to explain to the UNRRA official that they were not Russians. The English official had never heard of Ingria and was going to send them into the Russian zone. Juhan had seen a tragedy unfolding because of ignorance and had stepped forward to help. To cut a long story short, Juhan had solved the problem by marrying the woman, and here they all were—Estonians! Unki beamed at us proudly, as though it had been his doing.

"The old lady is a fine cook, like you, Ella. And she mends his clothes," Unki continued happily.

"No life is wasted," was Grandmother's reply.

From then on Mrs. Grigorjev was in our room every day, talking. Speaking Russian. *Da! Da! Nyet! Nyet!* Grandmother had been lonely for a friend to replace her sister Alma. While all this *da, da* and *nyet, nyet* was going on, I was left to sit and pick bed bugs out of my dress hem.

It was another one of those cold school mornings. The logs were sizzling, the pine resin was popping, smoke filled the room, and the gruel was burned. Grandmother was shaking the clock and saying it had stopped. I was going to be late. Suddenly there was a loud knock on the door.

"Who can that be so early?" Grandmother gasped and panicked. She reached for a hundred things at once and shoved them under the bed.

"Just a minute," she called out. She flung her coat over her nightdress, smoothed her hair, and went to open the door a crack. It was Leena and Mrs. Grigorjev, or *Babushka*[15]. That much Russian I already knew and more, but they spoke so quickly that I could not distinguish one word from the other.

Leena was pushed into the room reluctantly, fighting her grandmother's grip. She was all dressed up and ready for school. Her hair was tightly braided and her face shiny from soap. Babushka flopped down on Grandmother's bed exhausted, wiped her brow, and burst into a flood of Russian. I didn't know

[15] Babushka is Russian for grandmother. It is also the name of a headscarf worn by most older Eastern European women.

114

what they were saying, but Leena did not like it and kept shouting "*Nyet, Nyet!*" She did not want to go to school. "*Nyet, babushka!*" she screamed, stamping her feet. Babushka flung her arms about in despair. Grandmother nodded in sympathy. I knew exactly how Leena felt. I remembered my own first school day here and how Grandmother had dragged me across the field. Maybe Leena, too, had had a teacher like Herr Koch somewhere in Germany.

Grandmother turned to me finally and asked if I was ready. I pushed my bowl of gruel aside and said I was.

"You're taking Leena to school with you this morning. Take her straight to Mrs. Kuimets."

I said, "Will do!"

Secretly I was very excited. This was what I had been waiting for. I grabbed my schoolbag and was ready. A bit of luck, too, being able to leave without finishing the gruel and not having to think up an excuse for being late.

Babushka said to me, "*Da, da,* the German, she speaks good."

Leena began to cry.

Babushka was patting and hugging her. Both grandmothers were exhausted when we finally left and they could now make themselves a glass of *chai*.

Leena and I did not speak, but hurried side by side across the field path. I knew Leena spoke German, but I respected her silence. I, too, would have vowed never to speak to another living soul until my dying day. Promises like that gave one the strength to face a tiger, Unki had explained.

The front yard of number *10* was small compared to the yards of other farmhouses around it. The classes had not yet filed in. Leena was immediately spotted as new, and the ritual began. The girls inspected Leena's dress and schoolbag. Nice! The bag was made of leather, not out of potato sacking like mine. I was wearing my blanket suit. Leena had on the grey UNRRA issue winter dress. I had one also, but Grandmother was soaking it in Unki's spirits to kill the bed bugs. Unki had laughed and said that they were the happiest bedbugs in Germany.

The boys did not pay attention to Leena at first. She was just another girl after all.

"So what's your name?" someone asked. "I like your schoolbag."

As Leena did not answer there was a pause, then an overall silence. "Or don't you have a name?" a voice called from the back.

"They want to know what your name is," I translated into German.

This brought the boys alongside. Silence had descended over the schoolyard.

"German girl," a voice jeered.

The cry was taken up immediately. "German girl! German girl!" They all started shouting at once.

"No, no! She's not German," I tried to explain. "Listen, she's not German. She's Russian."

"Russian?" The shouting stopped abruptly.

"Russian, dirty Russian!" Hoots rippled through the bystanders. There was no stopping them now. "Russian! Dirty Russian!"

Mrs. Kuimets came running from the house to see what was going on. Leena was led inside, weeping.

Everyone gathered around me wanting to know why I had brought a Russian girl to school. Why was a Russian even in the camp?

I told them Leena's grandmother and my grandmother were having tea together in our room. "Does that make my grandmother Russian?"

I was close to tears myself. I had forgotten Ingria, a country I had never heard of. I had inadvertently done to Leena what had been done to me in Hausberge.

Leena and I became sort-of friends, because Babushka and Grandmother were the real friends and we could not avoid each other. Babushka was as much in our room as I was in theirs, speaking non-stop Russian. I had promised to teach Leena Estonian, but Leena would not speak German in anyone's hearing, and it was impossible to teach her if I could not translate as we went along. To make things worse, Grandmother and Mrs. Grigorjev spoke French when they did not want Leena and me to understand them.

When Leena and I were alone we spoke German. I learned that Babushka's husband, a writer, had been killed by the Bolševiks. Leena's real father was dead. Babushka's home language had been French. All the better Russians had spoken French, Grandmother explained.

When Grandmother went to Stadthagen Station to sell our ration of Camels, Babushka invited me to their room to eat. While sitting at the table, I was forced to speak Russian whether I could or not. Babushka just took it for granted that I knew what she was saying. Not to let her down, I memorized what I could. I said, "*Spasiba babushka, kuusnaja sup.*" I enjoyed the soup, *kapusta* soup. Cabbage soup. To this Babushka replied, "*Vasmiitje jesh cho.*" Have some more. I always did.

The girl Inge and her parents moved into the empty room on our landing. After that I did not have a day's peace. Inge was everywhere. While I was in school she found all my secret nests. She bothered Cat and tried to come into our room after she heard I had a rabbit. Now I had two friends. One couldn't speak Estonian and the other wouldn't leave me alone. In my next letter to Mother I complained about Inge: *First thing in the morning I hear this awful screaming. "Inge wants into Elin's r-o-o-o-m!"*

Mother's letters were mostly about her new job. She had left Leeds Hospital for Women and had gone to work in a larger hospital named Ida, on the edge of the Yorkshire Moors. She was no longer an orderly, but the matron's maid. She wore black dresses, white aprons, and little white starched caps, which she had to fold for herself every morning. She wrote to us:

> *Being a maid is demeaning, but I feel I have raised myself and can't grumble. I can handle it. I don't see if I don't want to, I don't hear if I don't want to, and I don't feel if it interferes with the goals I have set*

for myself. I can clench my teeth quite nicely, too, if I have to, as long as my health stays good and my head is clear. My only desire is to get you two over here.

The summer of 1947 was hot in Germany and in England. I was outside all day, enjoying every minute of this wonderful peacetime, but the nights were an ordeal because of the bedbugs. Unki's spirits did not kill them, and he said he hated to see us waste good liquor.

Exterminators were brought in and we were told to get out of the house. We sat in the garden. Everybody had their suitcases and took out things they had saved when they fled. There were stiff white tablecloths yellowing along the creases. There were tiny silver shoes that no longer fit the owner's swollen feet, but the shoes were a reminder of her partner and the dancing that had lasted until dawn. Felt hats were punched into shape again, donned and posed at jaunty angles. Furs reminded me of Mother's beady-eyed foxes. White gloves were put away quickly. They would never be white again, or worn again. Nothing was really white anymore, but a mixture of old grey or older yellow. Inadequate washing had paled even the brightest colors. When a young woman turned up in a fresh white garment, it meant she had a boyfriend. Was he German? Was he English?

Mrs. Mölder and Liki, " Baltic Swans," at Leeds Hospital for Women, 1947.

When the talk turned to men, Grandmother heaved herself off the grass and said we were going for a walk in the woods.

My squint was still with me, but no one seemed to care. One of the boys in school said I had one eye on heaven and the other on hell. To that I replied, "And you have both of yours up your...!" I used a word I had learned from Inge.

My ninth birthday had been lost in the chaos of screening and moving into the camp. For my tenth birthday Mother wrote me a long letter from England:

My own little love! You turned ten years old today. Be strong and courageous on your new year, study well in school, but most importantly, help your Mämmä to the best of your ability. Be her little helper. Today begins a new decade in your life. You have become a big girl. This is what I want you to do today. Go and thank your grandmother for having raised you and

117

> *taken care of you better than a mother—thank her for her devotion and love. Love her for her loving you, for always being with you and for having sacrificed everything for you.*

I went to Grandmother and gave her a big, big hug, but forgot to mention the sacrifices.

When school started again, Leena's mother and Uncle Juhan also left for England. Juhan went to a farm camp and Leena's mother into an asbestos factory. Babushka and Leena remained behind as part of the "B" group waiting for their summons.

The "B" group consisted of children and dependents. We did not know that Mother had signed up as a single person, and in order to get Grandmother over more quickly, and despite Grandmother being sixty-nine years old, she had changed her status from "dependent" to "potential worker." Mother meant well, but it was a serious tactical error.

Mother's next letter informed us that she had found Grandmother a job at the same hospital, in the sewing room, mending sheets.

One dry Sunday between a lot of wet ones Unki reached for his greatcoat, took his knapsack off the peg, and said, "Come on, Rin-Tin-Tin, we're going mushrooming."

Cat came, too. As she was under strict orders not to love me, we only talked formally. I had made it clear to her there would be no more loving and leaving—not in this family.

The woods around Meerbeck were full of wild mushrooms. Unki had taught me how to smell the difference between an edible mushroom and a poisonous toadstool. "If the smell is sweet or a little bird has taken a bite, it's good." But I liked the pretty red ones, so I picked mine and he picked ours.

Halfway through the picking we had refreshments. Grandmother had packed rye bread into a piece of cloth. Cat and I drank from a stream while Unki drank from his flask. I asked him to give me a little sip. He did. It tasted awful! It was the same spirits we used on bedbugs and on my knee scrapes.

"I'm glad you don't like it," he said. "When you grow up and become a young lady and you drink this, it will look bad." He jammed the cork back in.

After Unki's knapsack was full, he took us on his rounds. I was not happy to be going into the German village, but Unki was confident and strode ahead. He said he knew several widows who needed their lamps fixed and were waiting for him.

Dogs started barking as soon as we approached the first gate. I picked up Cat, whose fur was rising. Unki barely lifted the latch before the farmhouse door opened and the *Frau* came out like a boat in full sail, aprons and skirts flying, wearing *Tracht* with masses of lace and frills at the neck and cuffs. That was the Sunday version of the folk costume for the area. It was

118

clear that she had been waiting. She and Unki hugged, and when she tried to nibble his ear, Unki remembered me and Cat. He introduced us.

The *Frau* invited us into the kitchen. What a kitchen! There were so many cupboards you could not see the walls. There was an iron range like ours in Haapsalu and a kitchen table in the center of the room with four chairs. The view through the window was of the forest.

Unki and the *Frau* forgot us again. Unki began to chase the woman around the kitchen table. She kept pushing him away with an 'oih' and an 'aih' and a *Lass mal, das Kind sieht doch!* Not in front of the child! While all the time she was pushing him away she was really getting closer to him. Reaching across Unki to get some plates from a cupboard, she again nipped his earlobe, this time so hard that he slapped her behind, but cheerfully, so that she had difficulty getting the platter of ham, a loaf of bread, and a pitcher of milk to the table without dropping everything.

"For the child," she said in German, indicating for me to sit down.

"Sit," said Unki with a wink. Then with a sudden "*Uih*" he pinched her quite hard and let her steer him off to another room. "To fix her bedroom lamp," he explained as he kicked the door shut.

As soon as the bedroom door closed, Cat and I dove into the food. It was delicious! Cat had not had real milk for years. We shared the cup.

I told Cat about the olden days and pointed to the grandfather clock and the two heavy brass pendulums, when suddenly the clock began to boom. I put my head down on my arms to feel the vibrations in the floor. Unki had told me vibrations moved mountains in Tibet. The only things that had moved anything in Germany had been bombs. Cat also felt the vibrations and leaped into my lap. A few minutes later the sound of giggling from the bedroom proved that whatever had moved mountains in Tibet had also fixed the German widow's lamp.

The *Frau* stuffed Unki's knapsack with food. When we reached the gate, she handed me six eggs wrapped into a real table napkin. The eggs were still warm and so was the chicken *kaka* that was smeared on them.

At the next farm the widow gave us a piece of bacon and a jar of butter. There was no lamp to fix, they decided, with a look that passed between them, marking me and Cat.

"Another time," they mouthed.

At the gate the woman reminded Unki of his promise to send her coffee beans from Brazil.

"How are you going to get coffee beans, and where is Brazil?" I asked.

Unki laughed and pinched my cheek. *"Mit Speck fängt man Mäuse,"* he winked. "To catch a mouse, you have to first bait the trap!"

It turned cold. The berries dried up, the mushrooms disappeared, and the dried apples that had been hung from Unki's ceiling were eaten. Unki's supplies ended. The Germans were also starving.

At night the German perimeter fields swarmed with dark shapes bumping into each other in the dark as they dug through the soil for leftover potatoes. On the side of the road, humped figures bent over, filling buckets and sacks with the spoils. Unki was in the field, and Grandmother was waiting by the well with one of her underskirts tied at the bottom to form a sack. I wanted to help, but she ordered me back to bed.

When school started again, only half the class turned up. We huddled in the front row, close to the stove, until there was no more coal and we were sent home.

Everybody's coal ration had been cut in half. The bread ration, too. The cooking oil tasted so bad that Grandmother used it to soften the scabs on her cold sores. I became ill and stayed in bed.

People were coughing throughout the house. Grandmother's compresses were on constant loan. Unki still brought in firewood, but it was wet and smoked so fiercely that we had to keep the window open. Bunches of dried herbs hung from Unki's chamber ceiling, replacing the dried apples. Because of smoke from the stove and rising steam from the simmering teas, our room became shrouded in mist like a toxic bog.

Leena was also sick. Babushka had her own herbs, and we shared ours. Everybody wanted camomile or the Lindenblüten, lime blossoms, because they did not smell as bad as some of the other herbs. Grandmother forced small sips on me to ease my cough and bring my temperature down. When I slept, I was not hungry. "You need vitamins and meat," she said.

People were getting thinner, but the pigs were getting fatter. The talk in the house was not about coughs and chest rubs, but about smoked pork and hams for Christmas.

Muki, my little rabbit, did not look well. She huddled in a corner of her cage, shivering, and even refused dried carrots.

"Why won't she eat?" I asked Unki.

"She's lonely for other rabbits," he said. "She needs to get married."

Unki took her around to House 16 where they also had rabbits. He was going to find Muki a husband before she got any thinner.

"The fatter the bride, the softer the ri... ," he stopped and snapped his mouth shut on seeing Grandmother's expression.

"Muki is on her honeymoon," I told Inge.

The school remained closed because we had no proper shoes or warm clothes. We still had to make that trip every morning because UNRRA was serving the children oatmeal and a sweet brown liquid called cocoa. It was liquid chocolate. Chocolate had become a dangerous drink, so I made sure everyone had some before I touched mine. It was so delicious we all licked our bowls and held them up for more. There was seldom more to go around. When school started again, we continued to get the oatmeal and cocoa, but Grandmother still worried that I was not having enough meat.

A few days later, I stepped into our room and immediately noticed a delicious smell. Our pot was bubbling on the stove; it was not just full of water and vegetables, but also brown stuff.

"What's to eat?" I asked as usual. Grandmother was strangely quiet.

"Sit down," she said and ladled me a bowlful. She was keeping her back to me.

"I have to feed Muki first." Then I remembered that Muki was still on her honeymoon.

120

I ate the soup. It tasted good.

"That's meat," said Grandmother, watching me. "Fresh meat. You must have meat to stay healthy." I remembered the fresh meat called rat stew that Unki and I had eaten in Hausberge, after which Mother had told Unki to clear out.

Grandmother sat opposite me while I ate and watched me. She was wiping her eyes and blowing her nose. Maybe she was crying.

"What is it, Mämmä?" I asked.

"Stew," she said. She misunderstood my question. At least not rat stew. To please her I finished the plateful.

When I had finished, Grandmother led me to the bed and took my hand. "About meat," she began. "You know God created fish and animals so we could eat and thrive," she said.

"Like pigs?"

"Yes, pigs, too. Also rabbits."

She did not need to continue. I tore loose of Grandmother's hand and rushed into Unki's chamber. Muki's cage had disappeared. Grandmother tried to console me. She explained that Muki would not have lived anyway.

I had eaten my best friend.

In my next letter to Mother I explained to her that Muki had gone to get married so she could have babies, but that her husband had bit her leg. A rabbit with a bad leg could not have healthy babies.

I vowed never to eat meat again.

When I arrived at the pigsty, Inge was already there. It had been too much trouble to chase her away, so I decided we could become friends, despite her age. And she had turned out to be a better friend than Leena. Leena did not like to get wet. Inge and I were always wet. The ditches were flooded to road level. We found an old oil drum and rolled it in the water, balancing ourselves to see who would fall off first. Inge never cried if she fell first and got soaked. She never complained and never told on me.

When my blanket suit became stiff, Grandmother placed me in front of the stove and scraped the ice off with a spoon. She then found something else for me to wear. Because I had grown out of everything except the blanket suit, Grandmother often dressed me in her old dresses and cardigans, cut to size and shortened.

As soon as I saw Inge I told her that I had eaten my best friend. "Her bridegroom attacked her." I repeated the story.

"Not unusual," said Inge. "Men and women fight all the time, especially when they are married."

I told her I didn't know many husbands, only soldiers.

"People are all the same. They live in constant fear of each other," she nodded sagely.

"Maybe, but animals only fear being eaten. At least human beings don't eat each other."

"But they hurt each other and shoot each other," Inge said in disgust, kicking her toe against the pigsty.

"My grandmother said animals don't know death. They only know the moment."

"I suppose." Inge gave the nearest pig a sharp dig with her stick.
I felt bad about the pigs, grunting happily, wanting to be scratched.
"Pork chops and ham by Christmas," I said in disgust.
"Sausage and smoked bacon," Inge agreed, throwing away the stick.
I wanted to say "and stew", but could not. I hoped we were both wrong about men and women, but I could not think of a single happy couple to contradict her. As for death, it did not seem to matter how you died, as long as it didn't hurt.

When I returned to the room, Grandmother was by the window. She was watching for Unki.

"They are brewing Christmas ale," she told me. I knew she was worried about Unki, who had not come home the night before. Some of Unki's friends had burned to death in a barn on the other side of the camp. They had been drinking and smoking and had fallen asleep in the straw. We knew Unki had not been one of the dead, but he had been in the barn earlier. He had friends, but also enemies. I feared he might have got into a fight. Men were still fighting, even in peacetime. "It's their nature," Grandmother had told me.

After dark she was still waiting. I could not sleep either. When Unki did finally come home, he was drunk and woke everybody in the house with his shouting and cursing.

"All liars and cheats!" he shouted. He said he was going to kill himself right away. He opened his penknife and waved it around the room. "Liars and cheats!" He yelled and cursed in Russian, not caring who was listening, using the French word *merde* which he had told me not to repeat in Grandmother's hearing. He staggered into his chamber. Grandmother went after him and sat down next to him on the cot.

"I'll kill myself," I heard Unki say.

"All right, Paul," said Mämmä. "But why don't you rest a bit first? Then you'll have more strength. That knife of yours looks so blunt it wouldn't cut butter."

Unki agreed. He grunted. Then he saw me watching from my straw mattress. He came over, lifted me in his arms, and held me close to his chest. "They're all liars and cheats except you, Rin-Tin-Tin!" He kissed me. His chin scratched and he smelled of the brewery, but he was the second most wonderful person I had ever known.

Grandmother came and perched on the bed next to us. "Tomorrow you'll feel much better, Paul," she soothed.

"I think I need to settle down," said Unki. He put his head in his hands. "I need to get married, like Juhan, but what woman will have me?"

"Get rid of the bottle," suggested Grandmother.

"I can't," he said. "It won't let go."

"Then find a woman who will put up with you."

"Do you think there is such a person?"

"If you believe in saints."

"You're the only saint I've ever known," Unki laughed harshly and staggered back to his chamber. On the way I saw him remove another bottle from his pocket.

122

"Married to his bottle," said Grandmother, clearing the table. Seeing the door was still open, she kicked it shut.

Grandmother's birthday was in December. Mother sent her a card.

> *I would be nothing without you. You are my reliable mother and true comrade. Even in your weakness you can work miracles. I pray I will get a chance to repay you with a quiet and peaceful worry-free future. Please stay with us a lot longer and be our strength until we return home again. I love you very much, my own Memmeke.*
> *Your daughter, Liki.*

And then it was Christmas.

On Christmas Eve I joined my *sepik* uncle, an old gentleman who drove a horse and cart around the camp selling lemonade and *sepik* or wheat bread. Sometimes he let me ride with him. Sometimes he gave me a piece of bread or a sip from his bottle of lemonade. The agreement was that I could ride with him as long as I did not talk too much. Not talking was all right with me. Grandmother and Unki were the only adults who had ever talked to me. I found out a lot more anyway by watching and listening.

We sat together on the buckboard, swaying side to side over the jarring ruts. *Sepik* uncle kept the reins in his hands and watched for deep holes in the hard packed snow. I was holding on to the wooden seat and moving to the rhythm of the jolts, the steady plodding of the horse's hooves, the creaking of harness, and the lemonade bottles chiming merrily in their crates.

Because it was Christmas Eve, the load was twice as big as usual. It included a dozen stars made out of silver paper to hang on Christmas trees. I was keeping count of the stars, wishing I could buy one for Grandmother, but I had no money.

It was getting dark; I knew I should go home soon. Grandmother would be waiting. At number 6, Mrs. Roog, one of Grandmother's friends, looked at me questioningly and asked, "Shouldn't you be home?" At another house I heard one of the women say to another, "That grandmother of hers has no control over her."

I heard that! It pricked my conscience. Before I could change my mind, I jumped off the cart, but *sepik* uncle grabbed my sleeve.

"Merry Christmas!" he said.

"And a Merry Christmas to you, too," I replied quickly and did a polite curtsy. "I must go home," I told him. "Thank you for the ride."

"Take this to your Grandmother with my compliments." He reached under the seat for a warm *sepik*. His fingers moved onto the box. "And this is for you." It was one of the silver stars.

My wish had come true! I made another curtsy and gave the uncle a big kiss on his frozen whiskers. As I did not have pockets, I tucked the bread into my jacket, the star into my trouser leg, and set off across the fields to our

123

house. The star was going to be my Christmas present for Grandmother. At school I had been forced to make her a pincushion; that did not count.

As soon as I stepped off the road, I sank into the ditch up to my waist. It was not a good choice of route. While I was punching my way through waist deep snow, it started sleeting. Our roof disapeared behind a white curtain of snowflakes, and when I reached the other side of the field, I saw that I had veered off course. My legs were tired and I wanted to sit down in the snow to rest, but a friend of Unki's who had done that had frozen to death. He had been drunk, of course, and didn't feel a thing. I had also heard that the Devil met people at crossroads and took them down to hell.

The bread inside my jacket began to fall apart. With trembling frozen fingers I lifted my trouser leg. The star was safe! Finally at house *16* I recognized Leena's red curtains in an upstairs window, actually Babushka's underskirt. From there on it was easy.

I burst into our room. The room was dark except for the light from the stove. Grandmother was sitting by the window. I ran to her and put my head in her lap. I was home!

"I was going to look for you, but I knew you would come sooner or later." Grandmother stroked my wet hair.

"I came as quickly as I could," I told her.

She sighed. "You didn't see your Uncle Paul in the village, did you?"

Just then the door opened and Unki staggered in. He put his palms up and said, "I'm not drunk. Just a little on the nose." A Christmas tree stand was under his arm. That was why Grandmother had been waiting. She could not put up the tree without the stand. Unki went to his chamber to get a hammer and nails. The tree was downstairs in the pigsty, in a bucket of water.

With us all home, Grandmother got busy. She switched on the electric light bulb, another of Unki's many provisions. The candles had already been cut, six small ones from two big ones. While Unki hammered and sawed, Grandmother undressed me. She dried my hair first. When I took off my jacket, a big handful of bread crumbs fell on the floor like dirty sawdust. As Grandmother did not ask what it was, there seemed no point in explaining something that no longer existed. Grandmother draped my trouser suit across the stovepipe to dry.

With "dear Erni's" prayer shawl around me, I ate supper. I had already noticed that Grandmother's blanket was pulled way down in front of her cot. As we had no cupboards, everything not kept in Unki's chamber was put under the cots.

Unki set up the tree. It was a good-sized tree with firm branches and only a slight bald spot, which Unki turned to the wall.

Being the "man of the house" now that Mother was gone, Unki lit the candles. I closed my eyes and said a quick prayer to Jesus, thanking him for bringing me home safely and for not making Grandmother angry with me because I was late and wet, and for keeping me safe from the Devil on the crossroads. Unki, too. Amen.

"You can look now," said Grandmother.

I opened my eyes. The candles were lit. Mämmä switched off the light bulb. I went to sit next to her on the bed. The tree was a beautiful sight reflected against the black window, making it look like we had two trees instead of one.

Grandmother had already pinned the family photographs to the wallpaper. Mother's picture was among them. "They are thinking of us, as we are thinking of them," said Grandmother. "Although they cannot be here in the flesh, they are here in spirit."

Suddenly I remembered the star. Panicked, I grabbed for my steaming trousers on the stove pipe and groped inside the leg. It was there. The corners were a bit wilted and it was soft, but otherwise all right.

I pressed the star into Grandmother's palm, put my arms around her neck, and kissed her. "Merry Christmas, Mämmä!"

Grandmother called to Unki. Unki lifted me up and let me fasten the star to the tip of the tree. The silver paper caught the candlelight and was reflected in the window pane. We now had two trees and two stars.

Grandmother then began the ceremony that she said had been part of her childhood and her grandmother's childhood, maybe even before that, because it was a tradition. Unki sat at the table with his arms hanging heavy by his side. He had a headache.

We looked at the candles in silence, as we had in Haapsalu and Hausberge. "The light came out of the darkness," said Grandmother. She began singing "Silent Night" with her eyes closed and her voice thin and trembly. I dared not sing at all, always mindful of being tone deaf, but Unki rumbled right along in tune. Grandmother reached for her Bible and read the first lines that opened to her hand: "*He brought me also out of the horrible pit, out of the mire and clay, and set my feet upon the rock, and ordered my goings. Amen.*"

"I find that prophetic," she added, pleased.

After that we talked about the family, remembering our nearest and dearest, always the same names except that she now included Mother, in England. When she got to the end of the list she said, "Amen."

Unki had been shifting uncomfortably throughout. He got up off the bench, mumbled something about being chilly, and went into his chamber. Grandmother got on her hands and knees and started pulling packages from under her bed.

"Merry Christmas!" She kissed my hair and perched on a corner of her mattress to watch me open them. She kept dabbing her eyes with a corner of her apron and was moved, as she always was on special occasions.

Unki had opened his door, but was stuck in the doorway with a bulky object that refused to come through. Grandmother went to help by holding the door wider. The object was pulled into the middle of the room. A sled! So that was what Unki had been hammering in there.

"Merry Christmas, Rin-Tin-Tin," he grinned. "And don't break your neck."

"Oh, Unki!" I hugged him until he pleaded for mercy.

From Grandmother: woollen stockings, a drawing block, and a box of watercolors. From Mother in England: a rubber ball, English books, and a flashlight. Grandmother and I both got warm gloves. One parcel contained raisins and an orange. We passed the orange around, smelled it, patted it, felt its texture. I put it under my pillow.

One package was left. This one had arrived some time ago. It was from Mother, addressed to Grandmother, but with my name under hers. Unki came to help me undo the strings, but the knots were too tight and he cut them with his penknife. Grandmother shook her head. "You'll never make a good husband," she wagged her finger at him. "Cutting the string is a sign of impatience."

The parcel contained a pair of boy's boots with hooks and metal cleats. It was Grandmother's and Unki's turn to smell and admire. They passed the boots back and forth. "Good and watertight," said Grandmother, tapping the soles.

"Expensive leather," said Unki, smelling them. "Much better than mine." Grandmother gathered up my wooden clogs and stuffed them into the stove.

I suddenly remembered my presents to them. I groped inside my mattress for the pincushion and Unki's scarf, both class projects. Mrs. Kuimets said the scarf was too narrow and too short, but Unki liked it. He said it was just what he wanted. I wrapped it around his neck, and he kept it on. Grandmother eyed the pincushion, noting the blood stains, and pronounced it very artistic. She stuck a pin in it right away for safekeeping.

We watched the candles until they burned lower and lower. Cat stirred in her sleep, her whiskers twitching now and then. Her fur was probably getting hot from the burning clogs, or perhaps she was dreaming she was a young kitten again. Grandmother often said she dreamed that she was a young girl again, aged sixteen, running down a hill until she reached the old woman she had become, at the bottom, and woke up.

The last candle went out in a wisp of smoke.

"It will be an eventful year," noted Grandmother.

Watching the last candle was Mother's thing. She had also started doing predictions with cards. When Mother began to shuffle the cards, Grandmother usually moved away, picked up her pencil, and began to sketch. "The future is in God's hands," she would say. "It will come in His time." But the last candle was different. It was important to Mother and she would want to know how it ended.

We were spooning up the last of our Christmas dinner of cabbage soup when a group of drunks passed below the window, singing off-key. Unki pretended not to hear them, yawned, stretched, mumbled something about tomorrow's light, and disappeared into his chamber.

Grandmother began to hum "Lo, how a rose e'er blooming," her favorite.

"Why can't we go back to Haapsalu now?" I asked. "I thought the war was over."

"It's a long story," said Grandmother. I assured her that I liked long stories, but she said this one was too complicated. "It will have to wait until you're older."

Juhan's marriage had emboldened Uncle Paul to begin thinking seriously about his future. The camps were closing. A major destination for men without proper papers was Brazil.

126

I was doing sums when Mrs. Kuimets appeared at the door of the classroom. "Your uncle is outside," she told me.

Unki? I dashed outside. A big army truck was idling by the gate. The back was full of men. Unki was among them. "Here, Rin-Tin-Tin," he whistled.

"What are you doing up there?" I asked him. "Where are you going?" I knew, his knapsack was over his shoulder. He had my Christmas scarf around his neck. The other men made room so that he could lift me up.

"He's taking his little bride with him," they joked.

"I'm going to Brazil," said Unki seriously.

"Brazil?" Yes, of course. To his coffee mountains and the ten pounds of coffee he had promised all the widows across the countryside. He held me close for a long time. "Look after Mämmä," he said, into my hair. "And grow up to become a beautiful lady." He pressed something warm into my hand— his penknife—before he lowered me back onto the tarmac. This time I knew I would never see him again.

Like all the others.

"Unki ..." I tried to climb back up, but he shook his head. The motor had gone into first gear, and the truck started pulling forward. Unki's gold teeth flashed the way they always had.

"But Unki ...!" I cried, hoping he might change his mind, but adults never did. Unki was keeping his balance, hand raised. The other men waved, too, some with white handkerchiefs, but all I saw was Unki. I started running, but the truck picked up speed and I got left farther and farther behind. The truck reached the bend by the mill and was gone, yet I kept on running anyway, as in dreams, hoping to wake up in a better place.

Unki's chamber became mine, which was no consolation. Without Unki's smell it was just another room.

After Uncle Paul left we had no more firewood; the coal ration was cut in half again.

UNRRA was pulling out of Germany. The DP Camps were being phased out. Uncle Paul departed for San Paulo in February 1948. He promised to leave me his gold watch and gold teeth in his Will. He left his greatcoat for Grandmother to cut up into something warm to wear.

Grandmother wrote to Mother to explain our situation.

20 February 1948.

Mrs. Grigorjev had been told to pack and be ready to leave several times, but something always comes up. She is still here. It's too cold to travel. We received a shipment of good coal this week and some firewood. What luck! Amazing how thankful people have become. My dear child, I'm glad you have some time to yourself now your Madame has gone on holiday. Elin is working on fractions and decimals. She missed the initial lesson when she was ill and has to catch up. I told her to ask you to help with some of the more complicated assignments, but she said no, I don't want Mother to think I can't manage. The next time you go into town please see if you can get me a zipper. I am making myself a pinafore dress out of Paul's coat. The material is very sturdy and will last for many years. I haven't had time to study English. There is so much else that needs doing—the long trips to Stadthagen to sell cigarettes, collecting firewood, mending and patching our clothes. The firewood came to us through the generosity of two English nurses. When the sun melts the ice on the window at mid-day and we can light the stove again, I feel hopeful. Mrs. Grigorjev and I have enjoyed sitting together and talking— she has been so good to me—she is the only person in Meerbeck with whom I have had anything in common. If she leaves I will still have Mrs. Andrejev, so I won't be alone. The last time they delivered coal everybody rushed out to get it, leaving me behind, but Mrs. Andrejev came to help me. We worked in pairs. God always looks after old people.

Mrs. T. went to Canada, to be a housemaid. Conditions were so bad she changed jobs, only to be a maid again. It's the same all over—it doesn't matter how well educated you are. What a terrible state this world is in.

Mother wrote to us about English life. She told us about bathrooms with hot and cold-water taps and toilets that flushed. You pulled a string and water cascaded down from a water tank under the ceiling. I could not imagine anything like that, and the bathtubs; she said, were so big and deep you could lie full-length in them with hot water up to your neck. All I had ever known was a tin tub in the kitchen and a bowl and a washcloth. Mother's letters usually included something English, like cornflakes or cocoa at the bottom of the envelope.

The summons came unexpectedly. I was in class. Mrs. Kuimets appeared at the classroom door. My heart stopped. Who was it this time? There was only one person left. I dashed for the door, but Mrs. Vallas stopped me.

"Take your things with you," she said. I stuffed my notebook and pencils into my school bag. "The ink, too. And your hat."

I didn't want anything, but Mrs. Vallas insisted, and Mrs. Kuimets waited until I closed the bag. "Now run home as fast as you can."

I did not need urging. Fear and questions spurred me on. The field path had never been so long. I hardly noticed that it was raining. The goose at Number 16 ran forward to attack me, and then changed its mind because of my new boots. An army truck was standing in our yard, just like the ones Mother and Unki had left in.

"Mämmä!" I screamed in terror and jumped up to look inside. It was empty. The hall was full of people in various states of excitement.

"Here she is," someone called out, when I appeared.

Grandmother had her hat and coat on. All our bundles were on the floor: the red knitted blanket bundle, my pink blanket bundle, the "dear Erni" bundle, and the UNRRA quilt bundle, as well as a bundle made of what was left of Unki's greatcoat.

"Where are we going?" I asked.

"To England," said Grandmother.

Mrs. Andrejev came into the hall to say the driver was ready, but I had one more important thing to do. Inge's mother was standing and watching us from her doorway. I ran up the stairs and asked if I could see Inge.

"Not now. Inge is taking a nap."

"But I want to say goodbye."

Inge's mother saw I was getting frantic and agreed to let me in. "But don't wake her. It will be best that way."

Inge was fast asleep. I stood over the bed. "I'll write to you," I promised, whispering as loud as I dared. "I'll tell you what England is like." Inge remained sleeping, thumb in her mouth, looking more peaceful than I had ever seen her when she was awake.

"I'll tell her," said Inge's mother at my shoulder, anxious to lead me out of the room again. Now I knew that Inge had loved me; otherwise she would have been allowed to say goodbye. Inge's mother's actions were meant to spare Inge the way adults always spared us when our loved ones were leaving. What a terrible thing it had become to love.

While our belongings were loaded onto the truck, I took a last look at our room. The door was open. Only the furniture was there, and the stove and soup kettle, which Grandmother had forgotten or could not carry because they were hot.

Suddenly Mrs. Ott appeared behind me and grabbed the soup kettle. We went downstairs together where everyone was wishing Grandmother a safe journey. There was Babushka racing across the road, her skirts flying, as if she had just found out we were leaving. She and Grandmother fell into each other's arms. Mrs. Ott had already handed Grandmother the soup kettle, so that Mämmä and Babushka embraced with the soup kettle between them. Babushka then stroked my cheeks and called me *kushla*, a Russian dialect version of *kukolka*, little doll.

I could not say goodbye to Leena because she was at school.

The two grandmothers kissed each other on both cheeks, as was the French and Russian custom. More handshakes until the driver threw away his cigarette and hopped into the cab. We were helped up beside him when Grandmother realized she was still holding the soup kettle. She thrust it against Babushka's chest. "The soup is warm," she told her.

My last glimpse of house number 15 was of Babushka standing in the yard, wiping her eyes with a corner of her headscarf and our soup kettle clutched to her chest.

The first transit camp was Poggenhagen. We arrived there at the end of February 1948. Poggenhagen had been a concentration camp. The woods around the camp were full of decomposing corpses of German soldiers. I found some interesting buttons attached to uniform jackets, but after tugging at the jackets, I discovered that the jackets were still occupied.

The second transit camp was really the Münster military barracks, several rows of four-story concrete buildings. Grandmother and I became separated on the train platform when she went to get me a drink of water, and I got pushed into a train window while she was away. I spent the first night alone, terrified that I would never see her again. The English guards took care of me, letting me sleep in one of their bunks. A soldier helped me look for Grandmother the next day. We toured every building.

I was in one of the fancy bathrooms Mother had told us about, with porcelain bowls and hot water, sitting in one of the cubicles, when I heard Grandmother's voice. With my pants around my knees I ran out of the cubicle crying "Mämmä, Mämmä!" I threw myself into her waiting arms.

"Where did you get to, where did you go?" she asked.

"Where were you?" I demanded and started to cry.

A woman with her shook me roughly by the collar and wagged a finger in my face. "Your Grandmother has been worried to death about you. Aren't you ashamed?"

I ignored the woman.

Chapter 10

GOD IS AN ENGLISHMAN
1948

England had been the first choice for many displaced persons (DPs) because of its cultural reputation. Many believed they were going to "Hardy country." This vision included thatched cottages, village greens, duck ponds, and, of course, London. What they got instead was William Blake's "Satanic Mills," the filth and squalor of the Industrial North. Nor were they prepared for England's rigid class structure, which rivaled India's caste system in the exploitation of their own lower classes and the xenophobia directed at "bloody foreigners." The highly educated DPs, most of them professionals (or they would not have had to flee Communism) were treated like illiterates and discouraged from "rising above their station," even after refugees in the rest of the world were returning to normal lives. The British expression "Wogs begin at Calais!" was supposed to be a bit of a joke, but was actually a strongly held philosophy that prevailed at least through the 1950s without censure or apology.

The Channel crossing to England began in Hoek van Holland. There were about thirty of us in the group. Our Red Cross escorts treated us to our first traditional English meal of roast beef, gravy, Brussels sprouts, and mashed potatoes, followed by Christmas pudding and custard. I sat next to Grandmother at the long table, but did not recognize any of the food except the mashed potatoes and the tiniest cabbages I had ever seen. The roast beef looked like shoe leather. Grandmother cautioned me to eat carefully. She said it was the best food in the world, but too rich for my stomach. Grandmother also warned me not to eat the sardine sandwiches. I ate them anyway and began to vomit as soon as the ship left the harbor. With each rolling wave I deposited another load of the small cabbages, Christmas pudding, and sardines into the magnificent toilet bowl I was kneeling over; it was like vomiting into a huge Dresden china cup.

"I'm never going to eat English food again," I told Grandmother between heaves. I was losing track of all the things I had vowed never to do or touch again since leaving Haapsalu, but this time I meant it.

"When we get to England, everything will be all right," Grandmother promised, wiping my face periodically with a wet cloth. "Our lives will return to normal, and the last four years will be like a bad dream. You were too young to remember peacetime, but you will get used to it. She nodded and gave a little chuckle. "I always wanted to see England. It's a very famous country."

"Will we live in a palace?"

"No, but we will live like human beings again. You read your Mother's letters. I can't wait to sleep in a real bed with clean sheets, maybe with a feather pillow. We'll learn English."

We stayed in the toilet all night. When we heard the engine dragging we knew we were arriving in England; Grandmother suggested we go on deck. "We don't want to miss a first glimpse of our new country," she said, giving my face a last wipe.

"Is this the Promised Land?" I asked cautiously.

"Let's hope so." Grandmother started buttoning her coat against the rain.

"Will God be here?"

"I hope so." Grandmother looked happy. "But more important, we'll be back together as a family and that's all that matters at the moment."

It was bitterly cold on deck. The wind nearly knocked us over. The harbor was shrouded in mist. Unlike in Danzig, there was no panic. Passengers were leaning against the rails. Everyone seemed eager to see England, having heard so much about it. Mother had said England was the most civilized country in the world.

I recalled the rhyme we had chanted in Meerbeck:

A small white dove of peace
Flew to England with its pleas.
But England was bespoken,
The key to it was broken.
How many locksmiths would it take to fix it?

We landed at Harwich on 21 March 1948. The Red Cross escort took us to London, to a small hotel in Hans Place, next to Harrods. After settling us into a room, she took us for a walk along Knightsbridge. Harrods was the first department store I had ever seen. I saw more food there than I had in my entire lifetime.

A Red Cross woman accompanied us to the King's Cross train station. She was going to deliver us to Mother in person. Lots of people were in the station, but again there was no panic here either. The glass in the roof was broken, but there were no other signs that London had been bombed.

I sat by the train window and kept my eyes on the passing landscape, waiting to see something wonderful. Nothing new appeared. After London the landscape became bleak and ordinary—grey fields, clumps of trees, solitary farmhouses. Looping telegraph wires dipped, climbed and raced beside us. We whizzed past brick buildings with slate roofs, wet streets bordered with similar looking houses. Many had garages or sheds. This meant we were passing through a small town or village. Larger towns had multi-storey houses. Abandoned-looking factories and shops meant bigger towns. We might as well have been back in Germany. The only difference was that there were no ruins and the peeling posters on the brick walls were in English.

The train itself, however, was another matter. What a train! It had red velvet seats as soft as couches, and the windows had curtains. Our escort took us into the restaurant car and bought me an ice cream. I had never heard of ice cream and thought it was butter, so I waited for the knife to spread it on the two wafers to make a sandwich. The woman finally realized what I was waiting for and mimed for me to use my fingers. I still thought it was butter until I tasted it. It was even better than chocolate! Grandmother whispered that she had eaten ice cream in St. Petersburg, before the Russian Revolution. She had warmed it for Mother, who had been seven years old, so that it would not be too cold for her throat. Mother had drunk it dutifully and wondered what the fuss was about.

The magnificent surroundings kept me from licking my fingers in full enjoyment. I feared even to breathe in case I stained the white tablecloth. Grandmother was also nervous. There were mirrors over each seat. We had already compared ourselves to the other passengers. Everybody had suitcases. Nobody had bundles. In the dining car we were being watched discreetly by the other diners who looked as if they were dressed for a wedding or a funeral. Nobody looked as if they had slept in their clothes, to make things worse; the Red Cross woman had tied a nametag around my neck.

Ever since we had started this journey, I had been embarrassed by my appearance and it was happening again. Grandmother was also embarrassed. The Red Cross lady was embarrassed because we were embarrassed. I wanted to tell her it was nice of her to be embarrassed for us, but as English people did not seem to have a third language to fall back on, all I could do was smile. We were all smiling and kept on smiling.

We arrived at Leeds Central Station in a cloud of steam that momentarily obscured the end of the platform. When it cleared we could see people waiting behind a barrier gate. I began to jump up and down in hope of seeing Mother.

"There!" said Grandmother, pointing.

I had already discovered in the camp school that I was not seeing as well as other people. I guessed it had to do with my squint or maybe I had bad eyesight like Mother, but Grandmother had better eyesight than anyone and had already spotted Mother pressed against the metal gate. The steam cleared and I, too, recognized her shape, but only just. She was smaller, thinner, so different from the woman who had left us over a year ago that I wondered if I had ever really known her. I drew closer to Grandmother and took her hand for reassurance. Only Grandmother had not changed with our circumstances, for which I was glad.

Mother had pushed herself to the front of the crowd and was waving at us. I wanted to run over to her, but the Red Cross woman took my arm and led us to a side office instead. The usual sheaf of papers was waiting, officials smiling, nodding, shaking Grandmother's hand, and saying things we did not understand.

The outer door opened and Mother came in. She had been brought around to translate. Embraces had to wait. We made glad eye contact instead. Mother's glasses were blurry and teary. She managed to fill the paperwork without taking her eyes off us, and she spoke English so that everybody understood her.

As soon as we were outside the office, we fell into each other's arms. Mother and Grandmother were crying outright. Tears of joy! I relaxed. Finally nobody was leaving; instead we were arriving. Not another ending, but a new beginning. Peacetime was finally upon us and we were going to become a family again, with real mattresses, clean sheets, and blankets.

Mother was definitely thinner. As we huddled, I could feel her bones through her coat. I also noticed that I had grown taller. I was almost four months from my eleventh birthday.

While we hugged, I looked over Mother's shoulder and noticed a man standing nearby watching us and smiling. He was dressed all in white. When we broke apart, Mother wiped her eyes and turned to him. She introduced us.

"This is (I missed the name) the Polish chef at the hospital." The chef made a slight bow to me and kissed Grandmother's hand. I curtsied. We spoke German, not having any other language in common.

The chef carried our bundles out of the station entrance to his car. It was still raining, the raindrops pelting down in sheets, bouncing off the pitted concrete pavement of a grimy station square surrounded by dirty buildings, under a scowling wartime sky. At first glance we appeared to be back in Berlin again, without the rubble and ruins. There were even tram tracks and two-story trams clattering along in a mass of traffic that shimmered under flickering gas streetlights. I had hoped to see the red double-decker buses that we had seen in London, but did not see a one. It was early afternoon and already getting dark.

I didn't know what I had expected, but this was not it.

In front of the station was a small square park surrounded by street intersections with office buildings on the corners. The station square itself was dominated by a large bronze statue of a horse and rider. He looked ready for battle, but it was doubtful he had plans to go anywhere. White bird *kaka* had humbled his victory charge a long time ago and his dignity was further diminished by rain-soaked pigeons huddled on his shoulders and among his armor, heads tucked down into their feathers. "That's the Black Prince," said Mother, noting my interest.

Ah, yes, the Kings and Queens. "But why is he green?"

"The statue is very old," said Mother. "It's made of copper."

Why couldn't they paint him black? I wanted to ask, but I was not going to argue with Mother on our first day together.

The chef held his umbrella over Grandmother while the rest of us scrambled into the car. Mother sat in front. Grandmother and I got into the back, with the smaller bundles. The large bundles were crammed into the trunk.

Grandmother and I exchanged glances. I knew she was thinking the same as me and also wondering what the terrible smell was.

We set off, driving on the wrong side of the road. The chef was hunched over the wheel, trying to see through the windshield. Only one wiper blade was working and that was on Mother's side. I had seen a lot of cars in my life, but had never been inside one. For Mother's sake I did my best to be impressed by England, but the awful smell was making my eyes water.

Leeds in Yorkshire

"Gas", said Mother. She had caught Grandmother motioning for me to hold my hanky over my nose and mouth. "Those are the gasworks over there." She pointed to a pair of giant metal domes behind the station, wreathed in a billowing white cloud. "Don't worry, the smell won't harm you," she smiled reassuringly. After she had turned away, Grandmother signaled for me to keep the hanky in place.

Any minute I expected Mother to ask me how I liked England or London, where we had spent an entire day with our Red Cross escort. I vowed from now on to please Mother. To turn a new page on our past misunderstandings and to not upset her by giving stupid answers. When the question came I was ready.

"So how do you like England?" she asked.

"It's nice," I told her.

"And did you see anything interesting in London?"

"Yes, Fyffes."

"Bananas," the chef corrected.

So much for the new page! The yellow fruit we had seen at a shop called Harrods had been clearly marked "Fyffes."[16]

Afraid to say any more, I turned to the window and concentrated on the sights and sounds of England. I willed the sun to shine. Even Berlin had looked cheerful with a bit of sun for people to look up at, instead of down at their shoes.

"That's the Leeds Town Hall." Mother interrupted my thoughts again and pointed to a huge black edifice with stained black pillars, a clock tower and a pair of equally stained stone lions resting on pedestals on each side of the wide steps.

"And that's the Civil Hall." Mother waved to a blur of grey down a side street.

---

[16] Fyffes is a major importer of tropical fruit in the UK.

135

"Leeds University", said Mother, as another dirty grey building slid past. I suspected the last two buildings had originally been white.

We left the town center and entered an area of factories and warehouses. A heavy yellow cloud hung over the entire area, below the rain clouds and above the factories and smoking chimneys. Taller smokestacks were issuing green smoke that drifted downwards and created a kind of haze. I caught a quick glimpse of a canal glinting black and silver between more factories and factory yards bordering the main road. From the main road long cobbled streets fanned uphill, regular as furrows in a field. Rows and rows of identical back-to-back terraces. The terraces were built in blocks that shared a common roof. Each house had its own front step, front door, a window upstairs, a window downstairs, and a shared central chimney, also smoking. A smaller brick building at the end of each block appeared to be an outside toilet. Lines of washing hung across the streets despite the rain.

What had really caught my eye, and Grandmother's also, were the prams left outside many of the steps. The pram tops were up. Some were covered by a bit of muslin. If there were babies in the prams, surely they would be feeling the cold and damp, smelling the gas and breathing the same smoke that was penetrating the car despite the closed windows.

"Where are the mothers?" asked Grandmother, looking concerned.

"At work," Mother replied and turned to see what we were looking at. "Oh, that's a tradition," she said.

"Letting the babies catch cold?" Grandmother did not hide her shock.

"No. The decorated steps."

It was then that I noticed how each front step had been carefully edged a vivid beige. The beige was in stark contrast to the dirt.

"I'm talking about the babies, Liki. Don't the mothers know it's raining?" Grandmother was stabbing the glass.

"Oh, that." Mother and the chef exchanged glances. "That's another tradition. Babies are put outside soon after they're born to acclimatize them to the weather."

"But the cold, the rain, the ...," Grandmother waved her arms.

"In England, cold is 'bracing'," said Mother, now speaking German to include the chef. "Cold is healthy. Cold bedrooms, open windows. Wanting to be warm is a character flaw for the working class, while a more privileged class enjoys fireplaces, lots of coal, and plenty of servants who keep the fires going. They put up with that kind of moral weakness very nicely, thank you." Mother gave a brittle laugh. The chef looked at her funny, as if they had just shared a joke.

"Ridiculous," said Grandmother and settled back in her seat. Luckily we were on a new stretch of road, rising uphill and nearing a park.

"Hyde Park," Mother gestured. The trees and grass were black.

"Spring must be late this year," Grandmother murmured.

"It's the soot and coal dust. It covers everything." Mother reached back and patted Grandmother's knee. "At least we're together again."

The car chugged on, bouncing on ruts and tram tracks. As we began to emerge from the cauldron of mist and smoke, the sky got lighter. When we reached the top of the hill, it stopped raining. I looked back through the car's rear window and saw that the entire city had sunk below the clouds, into the bottom of a kettle of gray soup. Only the Town Hall dome and clock were still visible, drowning among yellow and green smoke stacks.

What we were seeing for the first time and what shocked every foreign worker who had signed up to work in Great Britain was the reality of this "other England"—no "demy-Paradise," but a mucky, money-making machine of the Industrial Revolution. The 'two up and two down' terraces had been built for factory workers. There was a water tap in each kitchen, but no inside toilet. In many cases the toilet was at the end of the street. The lighting was mostly by gas with electricity available for some.

> Gradually the advent of cheap wallpaper and linoleum added some feeling of domestic comfort to the bleak interiors. Sometimes workers lived in flats called 'model dwellings,' though wherever they lived it had to be within walking distance of their place of work. (...) Much of the work people were involved in was noisy, dangerous, monotonous and arduous. There was no lack either of accidents, from pit disasters to maiming by machinery.
>
> **Sir Roy Strong**

Past the point where the tram tracks ended, the chef opened the car windows and we were able to breathe clean air, still cold and damp, but without chemicals and gas smells. We had left the town behind us and had arrived in an area of high walls and large gates that obscured the houses beyond. This was where rich people lived. After the last big house, there were no more buildings of any kind, just moorland as far as the eye could see. The wind had picked up, too, and was literally sweeping rain clouds across the sky, pushing them over the curve of the earth.

"The Yorkshire Moors," said Mother, pointing right. We turned left and began to follow a private road bordered by chestnut trees and another high wall. We passed a gatehouse and continued along a sharp ridge towards a large old-fashioned building with a pitched roof and ornamental trimmings.

"The hospital," said Mother, extinguishing her cigarette and picking up her handbag. We had arrived. The car crunched to a halt by the front steps.

We were on the edge of a steep valley. The back of the hospital was densely forested. The view was breathtaking. No more rain clouds, no green and yellow smoke or any kind of smoke. It had looked like evening around the station, but here the sky was still light and covered with the naturally multicolored clouds that precede sunset. Some white clouds looked like giant sheep racing each other to the fold before night could catch up with them.

Mother and the chef jumped out of the car and began to unload our bundles. Mother helped Grandmother out, but when I started to follow, she stopped me.

"No, you stay here. The chef will show you where you have to go."

Dear Inge!

Here I am, in England. On the train I drew some pictures for you of what England looks like and will send them to you as soon as Grandmother can get me a stamp, but to have a stamp she has to go to the post office, and as Mother's only time off right now is on Sunday, when the post office is closed, you might not get this letter for a long time, but I'm going to write it anyway. Living in peacetime in civilization is a lot more complicated than we imagined. To do anything at all of your own you have to wait for your time off, because you are not allowed a personal life. Mother and Grandmother no longer have a personal life. ←

Inside the train I knew we were in a country that has kings and queens, but since arriving in Leeds, I don't think we are close to any royalty. It's very dirty. The hospital is outside the town, on the edge of the Yorkshire Moors. Mother says the Yorkshire Moors are very famous. Everything in England is famous. That's why the English are so proud and why foreigners are servants. The Red Cross woman took us to a famous food store in London to show us how well they had fought the war—they even had food left over.

Mother and Grandmother live in the hospital. They have a room on the top floor, but are only allowed into their room after their shift ends, and on Saturdays and Sundays.

It was wonderful to see Mother again. I hardly recognized her in her maid's uniform. She looks very tired, not at all like her real self, but I've never really known her real self. I had hoped we would get to know each other better, but now it looks like we will hardly see each other at all. Apparently I'm not supposed to be here, not in the hospital and maybe not even in England. No one is allowed to live in the hospital except the people who work there and definitely no children! So you can see Mother and Grandmother have personal problems they are not allowed to worry about except during their time off. By which time it's dark already and they are too tired to do anything about it, and that is why I'm writing to you from the hospital woods.

I like England and I like the hospital woods where I have my own little house. It's a fine house, with a roof, a door, and a window. The house used to be a boiler or some kind of storage tank and the window looks like an oven door, but it can be opened and closed so that dogs can't get in and pee on the rug (an old rag really, but even English rags are better quality.) I've always liked the woods, and English woods are very old, overgrown with bracken and littered with giant boulders that Grandmother says have been here since the Ice Age—I think at least as long as England has been here and before foreigners came to disturb them.

English people don't like foreigners any more than the Germans did, but they are more polite about it. You have to be their servant before they can slap you. I'm really better off than Mother and Grandmother because I can come and go as I please. Mother says we are still "displaced." I don't think she's happy that she signed this "denture" with the Government to serve the matron and her dog. Mother calls the matron Madame. This Madame treats Mother terribly and the dog poops on the floor. Mother has to curtsy, and then scoop up the poop. The dog bites her if she doesn't serve it properly. I think the English are scared of all the foreigners coming in from the displaced persons camps and not knowing how to serve afternoon tea. The first thing they taught Mother to do was to serve tea, to keep her eyes down, and to speak only when spoken to. She was slapped for stepping on the dog's tail while picking white dog hairs off the navy blue carpet. She swears that if there is an afterlife, she's coming back as an English dog. She did not tell us about those things in her letters because she was afraid we might not come if we had known, but she still thinks England was a good choice. She says I will get a good education and become "civilized," although I can't go to school yet. To go to school you have to have an address.

I wish you were here with me. We could climb the boulders and explore the woods together. Writing to you is not the same as being with you. Even writing is difficult because to write, you need paper. Grandmother used to bring me used envelopes until one of the Sisters saw her going through the wastepaper baskets. In England you can't just pick things up as you go along, the way we used to. Finally one of the cleaners gave me this notebook, but I have trouble keeping it dry. I have nowhere to store my valuables. There is no security. My pockets are full. Grandmother's pockets are full. Everything is at the mercy of wild animals, dogs, and hospital staff. Someday I hope to live in a country where it never rains, like Egypt, but Unki explained that in those countries, instead of rain you get sand in your clothes and scorpions in your shoes.

While this house is my home, I don't sleep here. I sleep at the Bollers across the valley, in a bed as big as a lifeboat, with real sheets and pillows. When I snuggle under the covers I'm a "happy bedbug," as Unki used to say when he had a bottle of "white" in his back pocket and an American Camel hanging from his lip. You remember Unki, don't you? I hope he got to Brazil where the "nights are hot and women tropical" or maybe it was the other way around? Nothing like that here in England, just workers and people like the Bollers, who work as hard as any foreigners do, although they are English. It's the "class system," Mother explained. Nothing to do with being rich or poor, but what family you were born into, and you have to be English born to even enter the class. That's why Mother is no longer the daughter of a poet, but Madame's maid and why Grandmother has to hide "dear Erni's" bundle in the unused fireplace. You're not allowed to have "clutter." She was told to get rid of our bundles. Clutter is against hospital rules. She can't even place her toothbrush on the sink; it has to be in a glass. Everything has to be in its place or out of sight. Even her shoes have to be put under the bed just so. Mother learned all those things when she first arrived. When Grandmother laughed and said she was nearly seventy years old and knew how to line up her shoes, Mother took her by the arm and sat her on the bed.

"If you think this is a joke, it isn't. You can't even leave a cardigan on the back of the chair. Clothes have to be neatly folded. They even check the drawers," said Mother grimly. "You have no idea!" Grandmother sobered, but stared again in disbelief when Mother reopened the window she had just closed.

"But it's cold!"

"I know, but the window has to stay open," said Mother. "Hospital rules. And you're not supposed to sit on the bed during the day," Mother warned, "unless it's your day off or you're sick."

While Mother was teaching Grandmother English life, I was making my own discoveries. There were the sink taps with hot and cold water as Mother had told us. I turned them on and off for fun. "So where am I going to sleep?" I asked Mother, after she told me not to do that. That's when she stopped talking and looked at me as though she had only just realized I was there. "Oh my God!" she groaned and put her head in her hands. It was that bad.

Grandmother is getting along nicely. The sewing women are friendly because, she says, they're "low class" with kind hearts. Although they pile all the big jobs on her table while they sit around and gossip, they know they are doing wrong. They feel guilty and try to make it up to her by bringing her tea and biscuits. They call her "Eno," (after some famous salts.) I think Grandmother would also be a happy bedbug if it were not for the hospital rules and me not being allowed to live with them or visit them. Even on weekends when they are supposed to be free Mother is often called back to work because Madame wants a backrub. Grandmother is in shock. In the train she kept saying how wonderful it was to be back in "civilization." Now she is not so sure, like I said, I sleep at the Bollers. Mrs. Boller hates working and she especially hates Monday mornings. She looks ready to murder anyone who says "Good morning", so I remain silent, while she digs into her handbag for her keys. I don't want to leave until she sees me leave. English people think all foreigners are thieves, and Mrs. Boller locks her doors and windows because she has a lot of valuables. Also some furniture. I don't want her to think I will be coming back to climb through her windows. I tried to help by offering to hold her handbag while she fiddled with the keys, but she thought I was going to steal it. Now I just step back and wait until she has checked the last padlock. Then with the bag clasped to her stomach she is ready to descend the steps to the main road. The steps are very steep. She starts with both feet together, stops, pauses, takes another step, then a deep breath, and so on. When I can no longer hear her gasping and wheezing, I look over the wall and watch her sprint across the road towards the factory, which towers over the end of the valley like a haunted castle with chimneys instead of turrets. In the morning black smoke billows against the first light and reminds me of dawns after an air raid. I've seen the sun twice since we arrived.

After Mrs. Boller leaves, I remain leaning over the wall and follow her progress, marked by her swinging handbag, as she joins a steady stream of similar dark figures converging from all sides upon the open

140

factory gate that receives them into its gaping jaws, like a lion devouring the wildebeests. You remember Unki's stories; there is a light pole at each side of the gate. Rain puddles reflect the lights and windows, and from my high point, watching workers streaming into the gate is like watching an overflowing gutter rushing into a drain. Once past the gate, the waters divide and spread in different directions until they finally ebb away between the sheds. At precisely that time, a shrill whistle breaks the morning silence, and the gate closes. The castle has accepted ← its tribute and no one is left on the streets except me and the village dogs. The village dogs used to bark at me. Now they just amble alongside, sniffing their way in the same direction as I'm going, making for the hospital trash bins.

While I'm writing this letter, I'm waiting for Grandmother. I used to wait by the hospital gate, but the Sisters usually come out that way, and I'm afraid they'll see me. The Sisters are the ones we have to watch out for because they monitor the hospital rules. It's their job to see that the windows stay open. They check for food. You're not supposed to bring food to your room. Foreigners have been caught with wursts and jars of pickled herring under the mattresses. One of the Czech porters rigged a teakettle to the electric light bulb and was dismissed, probably sent back to the camps. Although it's peacetime there are still enemies all around. I have to be very careful not to be caught "without papers," taken off the train and shot, like in Germany. Mother says it's not that bad, but I must not be discovered. Before Mother rented the bed, I had to hide in the wardrobe or fireplace alcove at the top of the back stairs leading down to Madame's private suite. After the Manor house was converted into a hospital the alcove and closed-off fireplace were no longer used. Luckily they've probably even forgotten the fireplace exists. When I was still hiding in the room, before Mother was able to rent the bed, only the foreign maids knew I was there. When they cleaned the room, they left sweets on the beds. Sometimes they called "psst, psst!" knowing I was hiding nearby, but they never found me. Like a mouse, I never came out while strangers were near. I was every maid's secret and even the chef sent me treats from the kitchen. Now Grandmother brings me food from the hospital canteen where they all eat during their dinner hour.

Mother rents the bed from the Bollers and we're safe as long as she can afford to pay them one pound a week and I stay out of sight. I also must not climb on the roof or try to get back into the house between seven in the morning and six at night, when the Bollers are at work. It would be easy to clamber from the Bollers' roof up the hillside and keep going across the moors, but Mother gets agitated when I mention anything at all other than promising to do what she tells me to do. I remember she started laughing again in the camp, but doesn't laugh any more. I don't think servants are allowed to laugh, at least not when they're on duty. Nothing is allowed during the shift. You can only act normal when it's your time off, as I said before, and by that time nothing normal makes any sense any more. The only other place I am supposed to be normal is in the Bollers' coalhole and the outside toilet. I don't like either, so now you know why I'm happy in my house in the woods. When I open the window and look out across the valley, I have the whole world at my feet. I can see people walking along the path, I can watch for Grandmother, and in the evening I can see the Bollers coming home from work around six.

Did I tell you that when we were on the boat train to England, the Red Cross lady put a tag around my neck with my name on it? Grandmother took it off before we got to Leeds. "Not dog!" she said, wagging a finger in the lady's face. Grandmother and I are learning English words, one at a time. It's like learning the dictionary. It will take years to even get past the A's!

When I came to your room to say "Good-bye" you were asleep. Your mother wouldn't let me wake you. That's all for now.

Love,

Elin

I tucked the notebook into my waistband and crawled out the opening so I could meet Grandmother halfway and watch for her from behind a tree. I had to be sure it was she and not one of the Sisters.

It was she! The collapsed umbrella around her head. The rain cape forming a tent around her middle. She was not happy to know I was living on a rubbish dump, but I reassured her it was the ideal camouflage, considering we were still at war. In this case, at war with Sisters and hospital rules. Grandmother said the Sisters were merely doing their job and the hospital rules have a purpose, "in the big picture" to which Grandmother often referred, when she could not think of a better explanation.

When Grandmother saw me, she straightened, waved and hurried forward. Never mind the rain! I threw myself at her as usual, glad that she still smelled of food—no longer the fried onions of her own cooking, but of hospital canteen dinners.

"Mämmä!" I hugged her, careful not to squash the potatoes and gravy in her pockets. Grandmother had no trouble bringing potatoes wrapped in wax paper, but it was hard to bring gravy. Besides, the gravy clinging to the potatoes wasn't real gravy.

"English gravy smells of mothballs," I told her, recognizing the flavor of camphor.

"That's because it's made of chemicals. You'll have to get used to it."

I did not. "Why can't you cook your own gravy?" I asked. "The hospital kitchen is big enough for twenty people to use the stove."

"Nobody is allowed to cook in the hospital except the cook. And nobody is allowed to eat anywhere except in the canteen," she explained. Getting the food out to me was risky. Nobody was allowed to have food outside the canteen. She explained her routine to me. She filled her plate, ate first, then, when no one was looking, she filled her pockets with what was left on the plate and announced to anyone who asked that she was going for a walk.

"In the rain? Every day?" People had noticed.

"Yes lof"[17] was Grandmother's reply, to which she added "ta, ta!" Those few words of Yorkshire had made her popular among the English workers. It was the best answer to everything, she explained. "I smile even when I don't understand the question, and they smile back, thinking I'm deaf or daft. It's useful being a foreigner in England. They don't expect you to know anything about anything."

We ate under an overhanging crag. Grandmother unloaded the potatoes and gravy into my lap. There was usually a bun from Mother, from Madame's table. Mindful of my request not to bring meat, she only brought small amounts. "Just to taste," she insisted. I had vowed never to eat meat again after eating my friend Muki.

"You have to eat meat," Grandmother said. "Everybody eats meat in peacetime." It was true. Meat was everywhere. Now we were eating pigs, cows and sheep. Grandmother wrote down everything we were eating so we could learn English together. How could anyone mistake a chicken leg for a "drum stick"?

On wet days there was no chance of anyone coming this far into the woods, but on dry days some of the Sisters took longer walks to the edge of the valley. I had to keep a constant ear out for sounds of approaching footsteps.

"I could get my own food," I volunteered. In Germany there had never been enough food, but now I was seeing the kitchen staff throwing away piles and piles of it, sometimes entire loaves of bread still in their wrappers. The village dogs and birds scavenged around the trash bins all day. I was sure I could find something that had not yet been chewed on.

Now it was Grandmother's turn to become agitated. Mother had forbidden me to go anywhere near the hospital trash bins. I was to stay out of sight of the windows and not touch anything lying in the woods, especially clothing. "This hospital is for infectious diseases and worse," she warned. "You could get sick."

So much for my curtains and rugs, but I had washed them in the creek and could not see anything wrong with them. I was "living my own life" now and needed rugs and curtains.

Dear Inge,

It's another day. I'm waiting for Grandmother as usual and as usual, it's raining again. The rain is drumming onto the metal roof and the ground around me thumps back on a lower note. I like the rain. It makes music for different seasons. This is April and today's rain is for spring, for trees to bud and ferns to unfurl. As I can hardly see across the valley, it doesn't matter what country I'm in, in April there will always be flowers. There will also be vegetables in a month or so, because I saw them

---

[17] "Yes, love," a standard Yorkshire response to almost all questions.

being planted not far from here, in a big farm near Hull. I didn't tell you about Hull.

The day after we arrived, Mother put me on a bus to Hull. Hull is by the sea and I was going to live with a family in a farm camp that allows children. You remember Ollie. Ollie's parents had one room and one bed for the four of us. Ollie's father is not happy to be in England. He kept shouting at Ollie's mother, "You're the one who wanted to come to Hardy country!" While Ollie's parents worked in the fields, Ollie and I played around the barracks. We ate at the canteen and then went to bed. Ollie's parents are not used to all that bending and picking. They fell asleep immediately. The bed was small. As soon as Ollie's father started snoring and his mother began throwing her arms about, I got pushed to the floor. To save the sudden jolt of falling and waking under the bed, I removed myself to the rug as soon as the snoring, tossing, and turning began. I slept well, but alas, Ollie's mother woke up one night and found me on the floor. "You can't sleep on the floor," she said. "It's not civilized to sleep on the floor."

The end result was that they put me on the bus back to Leeds, but I got off at the wrong stop. I thought it was the end stop, but the driver and conductor had only gone into the pub for a pint. By the time I realized it was not the right stop, the bus had left. Luckily I remembered where the other blue bus station was and the number of the bus to the hospital from our first trip into Leeds. I found the right bus station, the right bus, marked "Cookridge," and sat down next to a lady. The conductor thought I was with her. The lady thought I was with someone else. I arrived at the hospital without a word of English spoken and sneaked through the kitchen and up the back stairs, thinking Mother and Grandmother would be proud and pleased to see me. The opposite happened. Mother had notified the police. They had been searching for me all evening. Mother was so relieved to see me that she boxed my ears, started to cry, then fainted.

The Bollers are also civilized, but in a more modest way. I think the idea of renting the bed must have been Mrs. Boller's alone. Mr. Boller never addresses me directly, but keeps his eyes on his newspaper. I'm glad because I don't know what to say to him either. You would like the Bollers' cottage. It's very old with a sod roof and a dirt floor; low ceiling beams, and has a feeling of nests and burrows. We live the life of moles, badgers, and hedgehogs. The cottage is held in place by the roots of a cherry tree that has spread across our roof, and the root fingers keep us from tumbling down the hillside. Someday I expect the cottage, the cherry tree, and the entire hillside to collapse into the road, but not for years yet because the roots are strong. All things English have deep roots, Grandmother said, and all we foreigners have are our bare backsides.

Another thing about the Bollers' cottage that makes it so much nicer than the hospital is that there are no white walls or scrubbed floors, no starched sheets, metal beds, stiff uniforms, and disinfectant. I find a bit of warm dirt comforting. There is only one big room downstairs. Worn hand-knitted rugs cover the floor, and a big stone fireplace takes up an entire wall. When it's not lit, it smells of cold soot, burned peat, and dried moss. When it is lit, it fills the entire room with a warm orange glow. When the wind howls down the chimney it makes the flames leap, the peat spark, and the logs crackle in the grate. The firelight shifts and throws shadows against the ceiling as though the room were on fire. It might have been once. The ceiling beams are so black with soot they look charred, and they're so low that Mr. Boller has to walk with a stoop. Just as well since he's a coal miner. Mr. Boller's face is black until Friday night, when he goes to the Bath House in the village. When he returns, his face is the shiny pink of a newborn baby and I barely recognize him. It's the only time I see him smile. "I'm off to't pub," he says cheerfully, and goes, waving "ta-ta!"

There are only two small windows in the Bollers' downstairs room, one on either side of the door. Under one window is a flat stone sink with a pump. You rest the buckets and bowls on the flat surface while you pump them full of water. A drainage hole in the middle of the sink allows the excess water to be pushed away. There is no slope to the sink, so the water doesn't drain naturally. When Mrs. Boller works the pump, the sound is so loud you think there are a hundred donkeys braying together. Sometimes it reminds me of the winch that pulled us up the side of that cargo ship that brought us to Danzig. That's why I said the bed is as big as a ship. Grandmother is praying to God again to "deliver" us once more; England doesn't appear to be the Promised Land she had hoped for, there are more "dos and "don'ts" than in the Bible!

The hospital rules don't apply to me, but Mother's rules do for when I'm at the Bollers. She says that because they don't trust me, I have to be extra careful. I must not try to enter the house when they are away. I must not touch anything. I must not eat anything, unless specifically invited. I must not spread my things around the house, but keep everything in my little suitcase, and I must not knock on their door until I've seen through the window that they've finished eating. Grandmother explained a long time ago that you must never enter a stranger's house during a meal. It makes them feel obligated to invite you to join them, even if they don't want to. I'm not a stranger, but I'm also not a guest.

One Saturday morning Mrs. Boller invited me to have breakfast with them. After watching me eating, she came up behind me to show me how to use a knife and fork properly. "Always knife over fork", she said, but she turned the fork the wrong way around, putting the curved part on top. She showed me that you are supposed to balance the food on the back of the fork not the front. It's impossible! I tried and I'm still trying. One day she put peas on my plate. I was supposed to catch the peas before they fell on the floor. Mr. Boller watches us over the top of his newspaper and shakes his head. He doesn't eat like that. He just shovels the food into his mouth, but Mrs. Boller must have learned differently. I've concluded that the flaw is in the fork's design. The forks need to be flattened with a stone. I told Mother about this and she became hysterical

After Mrs. Boller has washed the dishes and we are sitting together in front of the fire, there begins the hardest part of the bed rental arrangement. Mr. Boller keeps his newspaper in front of him, but Mrs. Boller and I don't have anything to hide behind. We sit and make faces; we smile every time our eyes meet. We listen to the fireplace logs, the clock ticking, the rain beating on the windows. We even count the times the cherry tree branches tap against the upstairs casements and pray our stomachs won't rumble. What we are waiting for is for Mr. Boller to get up and start winding the mantelpiece clock. To keep us from grinning like idiots for two hours. Mrs. Boller has started to brush my hair. The sound of the hairbrush puts us all at ease and Mrs. Boller does it very gently, with soft strokes. It's nice, but what I really want to do is to run upstairs, throw myself into that big soft bed and let my dreams come early. Now that I've stopped having nightmares I can't wait to get to sleep. My dreams are my bedtime stories. I'm recalling all the books Grandmother used to read to me in Estonia. We've had to put aside the Danish cookbook and the book about Jesus. They're in the alcove with the rest of our things, safe and dry until we can be together again.

But speaking of eating, I think I'd better sign off because I heard the gate hinges creak and need to see if it's Grandmother coming to feed me. Mother gave me a watch so I would know when to start listening for her. As it's raining, Grandmother will have borrowed the Polish cook's umbrella again. After she leaves the hospital path she looks around carefully before ducking into the trees. She doesn't want people to think she's going into the woods to pee. I'll write again soon, if the village dogs don't eat my notebook.

Love,
Elin

Not everyone in England lived like Mother, Grandmother, and me—or the Bollers. Madame's dog, for example, had a good life. Mother said the dog is a "cork," a Corgi—a famous breed. King George had Corgis.

I had nothing against dogs, but I was still wary of Alsatians. I didn't like this "cork" because Mother had to serve it. I didn't think people should serve animals. They should care for them out of love. The Bollers had no pets. Mrs. Boller took good care of Mr. Boller.

Mother's treats from Madame's table were becoming scarce. Madame had started counting her buns and biscuits. Mother was bringing me what Madame had put aside for the dog, but I had a feeling the "cork" knew he was sharing his treats with me and was being short-changed. I thought he was pooping on the floor deliberately to let Mother know he was on to her.

The "cork" didn't like rain. If it was wet outside he dug himself into the nearest patch of grass and refused to budge until he was wearing his own rain cape and boots. I had never seen a dog in a rain cape and boots. No wonder Mother wanted to become an English dog.

When Mother did turn up, bobbing along behind the "cork," we went to the quarry and sat down to talk. The quarry was in the center of the woods.

It was from there that the original house had been built a long time ago. We usually sat down and Mother talked, always seriously, giving me instructions on how not to get us into trouble. I listened carefully, mindful of how important it was to obey her. She said I must not draw attention to myself by doing something stupid, because she could not help me anymore. I remembered her telling me the same in Hausberge. It was my job to "read between the lines," as Unki used to say, when people talked too much. Clearly drawing attention to myself would bring on dire disasters. Yet Mother still believed she had made a good choice by choosing England over Holland.

"English law, English literature, English education, English achievements, and English institutions are the backbone of the 20th century," she emphasized, wasting cigarettes, crushing them out after only a few puffs. "Even America belonged to England once. That's why they still speak English." Mother often spoke her "inner monologues" aloud without realizing it. I called them her "muttering monologues." Grandmother said it was God telling her right from wrong. It was also a change from talking to the dog, but I saw that she was having second thoughts and persuading herself that it was not so, and doing her best to persuade me also. She told me how the British had got to own most of the world.

"Many of the early explorers came from right here. They were Yorkshire men, like Mr. Boller...."

I knew the story by heart. It was my favorite. While she talked I had already sent Mr. Boller off to Africa, wearing his pit boots and helmet with the built-in light so he could see his way through the jungle at night. My version was a mixture of Unki's exploits in Africa and "dear Erni's" library books, plus the world at large. I followed the images like the newsreel film we had been shown at the DP camp called "war footage." After five minutes of flashing numbers, most of them upside down, and a lot of cursing by the film operator, we had seen soldiers being blown to bits, after which Grandmother took me by the collar and shunted me outside, but I got the idea. Those "muttering monologues" had been on film. Mothers were in person. They were supposed to teach you to ignore what was right there before your eyes.

"The British colonized most of Africa, India, China, and countries in the Far East." Puffing away at her cigarette, Mother warmed to her subject, while the "cork" sat on its haunches glaring at us, puzzled by the sound of a foreign language.

"It was the British East India Company in the 17th century that monopolized trade with India. In the 19th century John Speke discovered Lake Victoria in Africa by following the Nile from Egypt to its source. Then together with another man, Grant I think his name was, they found the exit and named it Ripon Falls. Ripon is right close to here," said Mother.

"How could they discover something the Africans already knew was there?"

Mother ignored me.

"There was another Englishman, Richard Burton in the Middle East ...."

From the light and faraway look in Mother's eyes I could see why she was hating the life she had at present. She had been at her best striding through

147

perilous times in army boots with a rucksack on her back. She would rather be risking the Gestapo than Madame and the Sisters. Leaping tigers would be an improvement on curtsying to a lap dog and its nasty owner. I wished I could comfort her, but that was not possible, because most of her troubles had started by my being born.

As she continued, warming to the subject of bringing civilization to India and China, I found myself siding with people who might not want to line their shoes just so or eat peas off the back of a fork. It seemed like too many people had been used, sold, and cheated to create the famous institutions Mother admired.

I preferred to imagine "Mr. Boller, The Explorer" (or rather his great-grandfather) sitting in front of the same fireplace, in their cottage a hundred years ago, except there was no fire. He had run out of peat. There was no coal. The wind was beating at the walls. The room was cold, the snow was piling against the outhouse, the pump was frozen, the thatched roof was leaking...

"Are you listening?" asked Mother, stopping to glance at me suspiciously.

"Of course I'm listening," I told her. "Honestly."

Anyway ... the roof was leaking and Mrs. Boller was in bed with her head under the covers. "Damnation!" shouted Mr. Boller, the elder, and jumped off the couch. "I'm sick of supervisors, cold bedrooms, frozen pipes, and ice-covered toilet seats. I'm going to look for a country where I can be warm and boss people about", and off he went. His wife stayed in bed, but followed soon afterwards, because Mr. Boller had found a world full of foreigners, all potential servants. Some could even be turned into servants in their own countries. What luck! They had discovered that thousands of people in the world were all eager to serve the British. Of course they could not use them all, so they sold the leftovers (especially the black Africans) to America, who also used them as maids and servants, farm hands and slaves, and that's why nearly all maids and servants are foreigners. They come to England willingly to work in hospitals and factories so that they, too, can become British.

"And here we are," I said aloud.

"Yes, we are here," said Mother, not noticing that I had not said that very nicely. She was still savoring her own vision, taking a deep satisfied puff to fill her lungs, and reflecting on clever Mr. Clive, famous Mr. Livingstone, and even Mr. Burton's wife, who had burned all her husband's discoveries on a backyard bonfire. Mrs. Boller was itching to burn all of Mr. Boller's newspapers piling up in a corner of the room, but he had told her "not until I drop dead." I, too, was forbidden to touch them. I had never read a newspaper, but had seen people hold them up to avoid talking.

"Once you've learned English, you'll understand the advantages that await you," Mother continued, patting my hand. "Once we're out of this hospital *põrgu*," she used the Estonian word for hell, "there will be no looking back.

Saturdays were our favorite days. Mother either had the day off, or Madame was away in the country with her dog. We usually went to Leeds City.

148

On our first Saturday together Mother used all her clothing coupons to make Grandmother and me look like normal people instead of refugees. The change took place in a big department store called Lewis's that had appropriately named "changing rooms." We went in and changed. We left our old selves behind the curtains. When we were walking away, I looked over my shoulder and saw the sales lady dump our camp clothes into the waste bin.

From the department store we went to a portrait studio where Mother had a picture taken of the three of us. She called it "The Three Doves", but upon reflection changed her mind and renamed it "The Three Pigeons." In the picture Mother is wearing new glasses and Grandmother has assumed her photograph face, with pursed lips. She explained that in her young days it was important to impress on the prospective in-laws that the new bride had a small mouth and would not eat too much. In the camp it had been enough to put on eyebrows and a smile. In peacetime even the smile had to be painted on with lipstick.

"The Three Pigeons," Liki Toona, Elin, and Ella Enno, 1948.

Before setting off, Mother and Grandmother dressed with care. Grandmother wrestled with several elastics she called holders. She had a holder for her stomach, a holder for her breasts and a holder for her stockings. She even had a varicose veins holder under her stockings. I was surprised that, with all those things holding her up, she could still keep two feet on the ground. When she was finally dressed, she looked like the Queen Mother. She looked nice, but not comfortable, and I was careful not to hug her too hard and set all those elastics popping.

Mother, too, looked smart. She was getting used to wearing high heels again. She was no longer the Snow Queen or queen of anything, not even Madame's dog, but when she got out of her uniform, her spirits perked and she assumed a happier stride. Anyone seeing us walking along the lane could have sworn we were English, except for the chain of safety pins around Grandmother's neck—in case one of her elastics popped.

149

We traveled to Leeds by bus. We climbed upstairs so I could see where we were in relation to the hospital, the moors, and the rest of England.

"I'll buy you an atlas," Mother promised, "so you can see where we are and where we've been." She did and I got the shock of my life. There was no Estonia in the atlas. The entire area had become the Soviet Union.

On Saturdays Grandmother washed my hair, bathed me, and changed my clothes. She prepared the way by taking the shampoo, soap, and towels to the bathtub, made sure the corridor was clear before I could make my dash to join her. There were a dozen doors on the corridor. Anyone could have opened at any time and I would have been caught. It was worse on the way back when I had a towel over my hair. I could not say I had just stopped in for a cup of tea. Because it was too cold to go to the Bollers with wet hair, I stayed the night. In the morning I slipped down the back stairs again so that I could come back early on Sunday morning, when it was officially all right for me to visit them. If the receptionist was suspicious, she did not show it.

Sundays Grandmother and I walked in the woods or on the moors. The moors were my favorite walk because we soon lost sight of the hospital. The wind was a wild gale, off the North Sea, blowing into our faces, trying to shove us off the path. The clouds never remained still; they were a living, swirling ceiling of swiftly moving light. There were grey clouds, turquoise clouds, even pink ones. Occasionally a black cloud would come creeping along like a stalking black cat, dragging its shadow along the ground, ready to pounce down with rain and thunder. When the sun did appear, it was as if God had turned on the light, but only for a minute. Night came from the east. It covered the entire sky, the way people cover birdcages so the birds can sleep, and then it was time to return to the hospital.

"Will there be another war?" I asked Grandmother.

"I hope not, but there probably will be. There will always be wars because men need to fight the way rats need to gnaw, to keep their teeth from growing into their brains," she replied heavily.

On the way back to the hospital we passed a ledge jutting out from the path. Grandmother liked to walk to the end so that she could see the entire valley and part of the way we had come. The wind caught her coat and scarf as soon as we got into the clear. The path rose uphill and Grandmother positioned herself on the very edge with her hands in the pockets of her coat, facing north. I stood beside her. She was going to speak to her loved ones, by way of the wind. I moved away to give her privacy, but watched her. To Alma first—then Grandmother spoke determinedly and gestured with her hands. When she closed her eyes and started murmuring, she was speaking to "dear Erni." When her lips barely moved, she was praying to God.

Since coming to England it had become obvious to me that God had turned a deaf ear to our prayers. Not to upset Grandmother, I remained silent, but could have told her she was waiting in the wrong places, for the wrong rescuers. From overheard conversations I knew our deliverance would not come from "providence", but from the Town Hall and Home Office and the Ministry of Labor. They were the ones who had our papers. The solitary figure standing at the edge of the bluff made me angry. Everlasting hope and inevitable fate were rolling over us like Russian tanks.

150

One Sunday we were sitting in the hospital room looking through our family photos when the Polish chef came to the door with a large tray. He had come up the back stairs and was breathless. "Sorry I'm late!" He raised his eyebrows at Mother, who must have known he was coming.

"Merry Christmas and next birthday!" he said to me in German, kissing the top of my head while still managing to keep the tray aloft.

I was totally confused. It was April, not anyone's birthday or Christmas.

"Surprise!" said Mother, leaping off the bed. She pulled some canteen plates from under her bedclothes. The explanation was simple. We had missed last Christmas and both Mother's and Grandmother's birthdays.

The chef had brought us a cake so we could catch up.

A cake? On the tray was a white concrete slab with the name "DAVID" written on it in blue. It looked like a grave marker. I tapped the sides. Tombstones for sure, but with gifts you were not supposed to ask questions; just say "thank you" and "how nice."

Mother and the chef exchanged glances. Grandmother inspected the mysterious slab politely and appreciatively. She grunted and went to get our axe from the concealed fireplace. The axe had doubled as a knife throughout the war and now seemed appropriate.

The chef must have noticed our puzzlement. He bent to Mother's ear, and Mother exclaimed, "Oh no!" and began to laugh.

"That's Royal Icing," Mother explained. The concrete-looking stuff was a special English cake covering, very expensive. She told Grandmother to go ahead and cut the cake.

The axe was the perfect tool because the cake was still frozen solid from the hospital freezer. The chef explained that it had been intended for a soldier in the private wing, but the soldier had died before he could eat it. Instead of destroying it, he had brought it to us. I had been right. It was a grave marker.

Grandmother chopped the cake into pieces. The chef popped a piece into his mouth, licked his fingers, and said it was good. He gave me a little hug, kissed Grandmother's hand, wished us a happy everything, and went back to work.

The inside of the cake was soft and sweet. After tasting a sliver of the concrete, I discovered that it, too, was sweet. Grandmother ate only the soft part. She was afraid the concrete would break her teeth. I ate everything until I could eat no more.

A few minutes later we heard steps in the corridor. We froze. Three Estonian orderlies appeared at the door, brooms and buckets at the ready in case a Sister saw them. "Hallo! Hallo! Is this the party?" they asked.

"Come in! Come in!"

A little later one of the Italian maids appeared. I recognized her as one of two who left sweets for me when they made the beds.

"It is gude dei," she said, trying to speak English. She gave me a comb wrapped in an embroidered handkerchief, kissed both my cheeks, and accepted a piece of cake. She dared not stay long. "Vork! Alves de vork," she laughed, rolled her eyes, and shook a duster in the air. "Gude bai."

More tapping in the corridor. Mother's Latvian friend Sigrida, a former opera singer known as the "Valkyrie," made her entrance. She smoothed her chest, cleared her throat, and let go with a high C, executing a perfect pitch before stepping across the threshold. She worked in a coat factory. Very chic on her day off, she wore a black suit with a skirt so tight that she walked bent over. She threw her arms up in greeting. "You slaves still here?" she asked, tottering on high heels toward Mother's bed. Grandmother wafted her hand in front of her face to dispel the perfume and surreptitiously opened the window a bit wider.

I recognized stolen time when I saw it. The orderlies kept checking their watches while they ate. Only the Latvian looked relaxed. She said she was living the good life. She was renting a room and had her own bed and furniture. She cooked on her own gas ring. I bet she even had her own knives and forks. Everybody was impressed. If not actually jealous, the others at least were wistfully quiet, feeling the weight of their five-year sentences pulling them to their knees.

When Mother was with her friends they never stopped talking. It had upset me when I was younger because I had thought she was ignoring me. I had since learned that women talked incessantly because only other women would listen to them. Men hated to hear women talk too much.

One of the orderlies had been singled out by a male patient, an older man.

"He's looking for a wife," said one.

"Not a wife, dear, a nurse and cleaner," said another scornfully.

"Better to be nursing your own and scrubbing your own floors," the speaker retorted. Everyone agreed.

Another woman had received a proposal of marriage from one of the private wing patients, a pilot who had lost both legs. She wondered if he would still want to marry her once he recovered.

"Englishmen don't marry out of their class," Mother warned her.

"My father was in the government."

"What government? Here you're a maid." They all laughed.

"Marry an Estonian. At least he'll appreciate your family," said the first.

"I've heard Englishmen wash dishes and change diapers," said another. They had heard that, too.

"So what's the answer?"

"America." They all nodded.

"You have to pass the screening. No TB."

"I'm looking for a rich man," chipped in Sigrida, the opera diva.

"Aren't we all?" However, they agreed that what they needed was a good breadwinner.

Mother did not contribute much because she was still married.

"What about love?" asked one of the orderlies. "If he loves me...?" She trailed off.

"Love!" Mother lit a cigarette and dragged a deep puff, then picked loose tobacco off her tongue. "God help us!"

Nobody left before Mother had read their cards. Now they all wanted a man who was tall, dark, and handsome but when the cards had been read, the cake eaten, and they were studying their red work-worn hands, they all agreed that what they really wanted was a man who would pass the screening to America.

Suddenly one of the kitchen orderlies glanced at her watch and shrieked, "My God, look at the time!" They all hurried away, buckets clonking.

Another Saturday. I only touched the doorknob before Grandmother caught me.

"Close your eyes," she instructed solemnly, before letting me into the room.

I covered my eyes with my hands and heard something heavy being dragged from under the bed, followed by the lifting of a squeaky lid and the cranking of a handle.

"It's a sewing machine?" I guessed, part of the game. Mother had mentioned putting a deposit down on one on hire/purchase.

"No, but don't look yet." There was more cranking.

"A meat grinder?" I guessed again. I remembered one from Haapsalu.

"No." The winding was followed by a sharp screech. The screech startled me to open my eyes and clamp my hands over my ears.

"All right now." Grandmother moved back from a box on the floor.

"A gramophone!" she announced happily and sat on the bed beside me. Of course! Haapsalu again! The music from the summer villa. Screeching and scratching continued. Grandmother said it was Handel's *Largo*.

"The man in the market didn't have Tchaikovsky," she apologized, "but he is keeping an eye open. I also got a Beethoven."

I said it was lovely, but the awful noise from the machine sounded like one of the floor polishers the orderlies pushed around the wards.

Mother came in a few minutes later and suggested we put on the Beethoven. "It's less cracked."

She told me how, when they had first played the Beethoven, they had heard a sound outside their door. Thinking somebody was discovering our bundles, Mother had gone to investigate and found Madame sitting on the back stairs in the dark, listening to our music. She had risen immediately and returned to her apartment, but had later commented to Mother that it was the first time she had known of servants listening to Beethoven.

Grandmother walked me back to the Bollers on Sunday night. She came as far as the bridge, then remained standing to watch me complete the rest of the way alone until I stood above the road by the wall and waved to her. Then it was my turn to watch her return to the hospital. When she reached the hospital gate, she turned and waved back.

The days in the hospital woods were long and boring. Mother had forbidden me to go into the village. One day I ended up near a small house that looked like a doll's house, but was also part of the hospital complex. It was separated from me by a low stonewall and a thicket of brambles, bracken, and waist high nettles. The house had black wooden beams in the walls, an overhanging second floor window, and covered terrace-like extensions on both sides. These extensions were furnished with lounge chairs and side tables so

153

that patients could sit outside and enjoy fresh air without being rained on. This had to be the private wing that people talked about, the little house looked like it had been one of the original buildings, older even than the hospital, from before the estate had been converted into an institution.

After I first discovered it I began to go there every day, although my stockings were torn and my legs on fire from the nettles long before I reached the wall. The terrace reminded me of the Promenade in Haapsalu and many other disturbing things I had forgotten.

My focus was on the Sisters and patients, the way they interacted. I knew the Sisters were not servants and could never have been classed as maids or attendants. In the main hospital wards they ignored even the patients; everyone knew better than to speak to them without being spoken to first. The nurses deferred to them and it was a miracle to catch them smiling or talking normally while on duty. Yet here they smiled and even laughed. I watched them bend down to adjust cushions, plump pillows, fetch lap robes, and even help patients to their feet. They chatted with patients, especially the men, and sometimes perched on the armrest of a chair, but they also attended to women, bringing them their glasses or a book. While not actually bowing, scurrying, or bobbing curtsies, they showed a deference to their patients that was totally absent in the main hospital. I wondered whether they were being paid extra to be nice.

The entire atmosphere around the little house was relaxed, and completely different from what I had seen of English life, not that I had seen a lot—just offices, shops, and places around the main hospital. I was thinking about the way people always held themselves rigid, observed protocol, and only gave orders, speaking downwards instead of upwards. Doctors were at the top, with Madame, the matron. Only they could speak to the Sisters. The Sisters then gave orders to the nurses, who in turn told the orderlies and porters what to do and to hurry.

In the little house, however, everyone seemed more relaxed. There was no one yelling "Nurse!" because the nurses were right there, nearby, bending over them. There was no clatter of bedpans and no moaning, although the windows were open. Even the air that wafted through the windows was different. No smells of Dettol disinfectant, bleach, carbolic soap, mentholated spirits, or the chemical odors of English gravy. Instead I could smell the flowers in the planters, and occasionally I caught a whiff of perfume or a blend of nutty pipe tobacco that would drift to me where I was hiding behind the trees. Music, too. A radio was usually playing somewhere inside the house. I had not yet seen a radio, but Mother said it would be our next purchase after the gramophone was paid off.

Perhaps the biggest draw for me was the clothing the patients wore, as opposed to backless hospital gowns and faded cotton robes worn by patients in the wards. These patients wore frilly nightdresses, satin pajamas, silk robes, and quilted bed jackets. I had last seen such nightclothes on Mother and her friends in Haapsalu when they had stayed over and gathered on the porch in the mornings to smoke or drink coffee. I also remembered the flowers and music, the perfume and even the smell of nutty pipe tobacco and

154

had thought it had all been props and costumes like Father's lenseless spectacles and his Beethoven wig—all theatre. Yet these patients were not actors, which meant that I had been wrong about my parents and their friends. They had been actors, but I had also been watching real people in real life, wearing real clothes, enjoying themselves, and behaving in ways I had not seen since the Promenade had emptied and the music had stopped. This then had to be the real peacetime everybody had talked about, I was seeing it at last.

There was one-woman patient I came to watch especially. She wore the most beautiful nightdress I had ever seen, under a blue silk robe tied with a sash. When she came out she usually walked to the edge of the terrace, lifted her dark head, closed her eyes, and took deep breaths through both nostrils, the way a horse scents a stranger's presence. I stayed back in case the woman was smelling my muddy, damp clothes, and me but I continued to watch her. I was thrilled. She even looked a bit like Mother had looked in Estonia. She had the same dark hair and a bit of a Snow Queen profile. I was seeing happiness. I was not scared of death, only of unhappiness and despair, and I could see what Mother had lost when she had started wearing a maid's uniform.

"I'm Madame's maid," she had told us in her letters. I had assumed her job was to serve tea and walk the "cork", but it was more. Like those servants on the Promenade, she no longer had a right to a life and lived in constant fear of being discovered having one. Mother always looked terrified when she heard Madame's bell summoning her back to work on her day off. One day she had come back to the room in tears, holding her cheek and hiding what looked like fingerprints. Mother had become a servant!

I knew how it had happened. It had happened to us, too, that first Saturday in Leeds, when Mämmä and I had gone into that changing room at Lewis's department store, stepped out of our camp rags, put on English clothes, and had become strangers even to ourselves. When I saw the sales lady throwing our old selves into the trash bin, I should have run back and stopped her. Now it was too late. We would never again be the people we had been again.

I could not take my eyes off the woman in the blue silk robe. Everything fell into place, like the tumbling of a lock when the key turns and the door opens—Mother's grumpiness, her cards, her saying that if she came back in the afterlife, she wanted to be an English dog.

Then something terrible happened and I never went back to that private wing again.

I was hiding behind the tree and thinking how beautiful the woman was and how lucky she was, when suddenly a huge tear rolled down her cheek and she began to sob uncontrollably, the way Mother had sobbed on the beach in Kuressaare. I pulled back, terrified that I had seen too much. Here was someone who had everything—money, beauty, nice clothes, and yet she was still unhappy. I had believed there really was a world like the one I was seeing on the terrace, where people treated each other nicely, did not yell at strangers, did not call them dirty *Ausländer* and filthy foreigners. I had thought that was where we were going. Grandmother had taught me to believe in beauty and goodness and that everything we had endured since Estonia was caused by people who had been scarred by misfortune, like Frau Schneider. I had thought beauty and goodness meant being rich and having everything we lacked. The woman on the terrace turned that world upside down with her tears.

Another Saturday. We had just returned from town, when Madame called Mother back into her flat to serve tea to an important visitor. We were used to Mother being called back to work when she was supposed to be with us. When she returned an hour later, she threw herself on the bed and burst into tears. The story came out between sobs. She had served tea to Lady someone, a real Lady, who had just opened a new hospital wing. When Mother had put the tray down, the Lady had asked her, "Where are you from? How do you like England?"

Mother had answered, "Estonia" and added, "We are all very grateful that England has accepted us."

The Lady had then asked Mother if she had received any schooling. Mother told her she had graduated from university and had started medical school, but had cut short her studies to marry an actor. She had been a successful actress. The Lady had been shocked.

"How is that possible?" she had asked.

When it transpired that the university had not been in England, that she had not been an actress in London, the woman had snorted and said to Madame, as though Mother were deaf, "Such rubbish! These DP's are all the same. All liars."

The Lady had tipped Mother ten shillings and dismissed her. After the woman left, Madame had come into the kitchen and berated Mother angrily, "Did you know who you were speaking to? What impertinence! All you needed to say was, 'Yes, Mum! Thank you Mum!' A servant's place is not to enter into conversations with their betters."

Grandmother took Mother's hand. "This, too, shall pass," she said. "But Madame is right. Tell them nothing. They are only temporarily in our lives."

I remained silent by the sink and watched through the mirror. I had been right about that woman on the terrace being like Mother. There was no shield against unhappiness and despair—not in beauty, not in riches. No one was safe. I looked at Mother despairing on the bed and hoped that when it was Mother's turn to die; she would not die as a servant in a maid's uniform.

Because England had never been occupied by a foreign power, and despite being threatened and bombed during the war, the average English person knew nothing of the conditions the DPs experienced. Because of their own rigid class structure, they never experienced an educated servant. When a foreign servant attempted to explain a non-servile past and a superior education, the story was received with skepticism. It was even worse when someone attempted to describe the horrors of the NKVD breaking down their door at two o'clock in the morning to deport them to Siberia. The common reaction was demeaning: "Why didn't you call the police?"

156

Grandmother was learning English. You had to stay clear when she got her tongue between her teeth and did the "th's" and "ough" sounds, or you got spit on.

Spring had not fully arrived yet, but I was looking out for it, and what better place to do so than in the deepest part of the hospital woods. Grandmother and I discovered a clearing full of huge boulders embedded deeply into the ground, surrounded by bracken. The exposed sides of these behemoths were covered with moss and lichen. Grandmother called them traveling stones, left behind in the Ice Age. I looked at the stones carefully. It did not look like they had made much progress since, but Grandmother was excited and made up a poem about them:

> Are the stones tired of lying still,
> Sleeping through eternity,
> Or maybe longer still?
> Do they know of night and day,
> Or are they only waiting
> For us to go away?

We pretended to go away and hid in the bushes to see if any of the stones moved. Not a one traveled while we were there.

"They're in metamorphosis," said Grandmother, teaching me a new word. "In transition, constantly changing. Have you ever seen grass grow? When did you last see a flower burst into bloom or a caterpillar change into a butterfly? Yet it happens all the time." She had a point.

When together, we talked like that and laughed a lot, but I noticed that Grandmother's laughter was not as wholehearted as usual. I feared the hospital was beginning to change her, too, as it had changed Mother.

"Are you also in metamorphosis?" I asked.

"Everything has a destiny, be it long or short," she replied, and again her eyes strayed to the path. She was clearly fearing change.

Change was also visible from the hospital ridge. Earth-moving equipment had been parked at the edge of the moor. It looked like they were going to build a new road through the valley, straight into Cookridge. A large part of the area had already been cleared. Steamrollers, concrete mixers, and portable toilets lined the main road to the hospital turn-off. Across from the bus stop, on what had been moorland, a grid of foundations was being laid down for an entire housing estate. Leeds was moving closer to the hospital. Only we were standing still.

With brisk efficiency and a notable lack of political acrimony, the government launched a massive project for the renovation of Britain.

William I. Hitchcock

The demand for houses inevitably accelerated the rape of the countryside, begun in the thirties, when already 60,000 acres of land a year

157

were being swallowed up for building. The New Towns Act of 1946 created fourteen new towns between 1947 and 1950. These were formed by taking people out of the congested inner city areas of London and Glasgow and re-housing them. The government gave power to local authorities to designate development areas in the countryside and countered its spoliation by the creation of national parks, embracing Dartmoor, the Peak District, Snowdonia, the Lake District, and the North Yorkshire moors.

Sir Roy Strong

One morning I arrived in the woods to find it entirely carpeted with blue flowers. I gathered an armful for Mrs. Boller.

"Bluebells," she said, putting them into a bucket of water.

"Blue bells," I repeated.

That evening Mrs. Boller made me a cup of hot cocoa as usual, and as Mr. Boller declined his share, I had a second cup. The second cup was to be my undoing.

The Bollers had no inside toilet. The potty in the Bollers' bedroom was under their bed. At night, if I had to go, I had been told to use the Bollers' potty, but who would use a stranger's potty? This one was under their bed and Mrs. Boller was a light sleeper. She was liable to wake up if she heard me pass wind.

As soon as Mr. Boller began to wind the clock and Mrs. Boller was gathering the chains and padlocks for the night, it was the signal for me to go to the outhouse at the end of the street. The outhouse was in the shape of a sentry box with a Turkish moon carved into the door. The toilet was for the whole street, and the hole in the door was not just to let out the smell, but also to allow people to see your head and not barge in.

That night I used the outhouse as usual before Mrs. Boller locked the door. I went to bed happy and full of cocoa. The Bollers had begun to feel like family. It was nice to have a man about the house, an expression most woman seemed to appreciate. Until Unki had moved in with us at the DP camp, I had never heard a man snoring, coughing, or grunting in his sleep. Mr. Boller always yawned and scratched his tummy in the morning before he shuffled downstairs in his bedroom slippers. He sat on the bottom step to put on his pit boots, undid the door locks, and left. A little while later Mrs. Boller got up. She shuffled around briskly, thumping pillows and grumbling to herself. When she passed the bottom of my bed, I could smell the urine in the chamber pot and I was glad it was not mine. Shortly afterwards I heard her go to the outhouse to empty the potty. That was when I got up and dressed so she wouldn't have to call me. I wanted to do everything right, the way Mother had instructed. I did not want to let us down, but I did.

That night of the second cup of cocoa I woke up desperate to go to the toilet. The Bollers' bedroom door was ajar. A night candle was burning on their dresser and the chamber pot was visible under the bed. The Bollers were fast asleep, snoring lustily, but I dared not go in there; I had to get to the outside toilet.

158

The stairs creaked. I stepped on the corners and made it downstairs to the front door. It was padlocked. There were no keys in sight. I dared not search for them in Mrs. Bollers' handbag, so I tried the window fastenings. Everything was tightly closed. Nothing yielded. The windows had been fitted with bolts. I worked on them, pushing and pulling, but I think they had been screwed in extra firmly since my arrival. Through the glass I could see the outhouse grinning at me. With my bladder close to bursting and rather than wetting myself, I climbed onto the stone sink and urinated under the pump. The urine should have gone down the hole, but instead it just spread and stayed put. I looked around for water to swill it down. There was only the pump. After barely touching the pump handle. I realized that pumping was going to be too noisy. I pushed as much of the urine down the drain as I could and sneaked back to bed. It was impossible to sleep. I knew the Bollers would discover what I had done as soon as they went down, which is exactly what happened.

Mr. Boller noticed nothing, but Mrs. Boller gave a loud shriek just a few seconds after going downstairs. She flew back up, yanked me out of bed and pulled me to the pump. It did not require much English to know she was furious and no interpretation of the crime was necessary. The stone slab bore a yellow stain at its center. Mrs. Boller sprinkled something on it called Vim and pumped so vigorously it sounded like an entire herd of donkeys was stampeding through the house. The slab came clean, but my good times at the Bollers' ended that morning.

Mrs. Boller did not even go to work. Instead she packed my little suitcase and marched me up the hill to the hospital. We had to wait in Admissions for Mother to come down from Madame's flat. Mrs. Boller told her what had happened, shouting and gesturing all the while. She called us "derti foriners" at least ten times, and then stalked off before Mother could say a word.

Instead of slapping me or shouting at me, as she would have done in the past, Mother just looked grim and pushed me ahead of her up to their room. "Wait here, until Mämmä gets off her shift." She herself had to go back to work.

When Grandmother came into the room, she was shocked to see me step out of the wardrobe with my suitcase. I need not have bothered to hide, but it was a habit. I told her about the Bollers' potty, the locked doors and windows. As usual, she understood. She said she would have done the same and she let me bury my face in her lap, something I had not done since the bombing stopped. We waited for Mother. Grandmother smoothed my hair and sighed. "We knew the situation would not last, but things will get better, you'll see."

Instead things got worse.

In the morning Madame herself came to our room and discovered me formally in front of witnesses (the assistant matron). She said she had turned a blind eye, but now the situation was out of her hands.

I hoped she would send us back to Germany. English life was not for us, and peacetime was a major disaster. All my life I had heard adults say, "Wait until we can live the way we used to live before the war." Well, I had seen my share by now, and while I did not know exactly how they had lived before the war, I could see what was happening before my eyes, no wonder peace-time never lasted long.

Two women in uniform came at noon, shuffling important papers. They said I had to be put into an orphanage. In peacetime children could not live in the woods. It was not civilized and against the law. Just as dogs had to be on leashes, children had to be in school and under supervision. Grandmother started to cry. Mother put an arm around my shoulders and said it would be all right, that Madame had pulled strings and had arranged for me to be put into a Quaker orphanage where my hair would not be cut off, as was the rule in state-run homes. She said I would receive excellent discipline, to which Grandmother added that I would attend church and be given religious instruction. I had no idea what that meant, but the word "religious" warned me to be wary.

When Mother spoke again, she caught her breath. I expected the worst. "You will not be allowed to see us for a time to be determined by the people in charge." She looked around, clearly not sure who those people were. I knew who they were; they were the authorities everybody feared—they controlled the planet.

"But you will learn English," said Mother.

Chapter 11

SUFFER LITTLE CHILDREN
1948

Headingley Orphan Homes was founded in 1865 by Anna Rebecca Whiting and closed in 1959. It was a Quaker institution run by well-meaning people and certified by the local Government Board for the Reception of Destitute Orphan Children from any part of England and Wales. Although founded by Quakers the Home did not use a Meeting House, but attended a local Anglican church for services and Bible study. The children attended local schools. The goals and achievements had been drawn up in 1912 and were still in effect in 1948.

The girls are trained for domestic service (...) These little orphans are commanded to the continued kind care and notice of Friends, believing that, having been rescued from much evil and destitution, they are now preparing to become useful members of society, special endeavor being made to lead them to Him who said, 'Suffer little children to come unto me.'

Annual Report of Headingley Orphan Homes, 1912.

On 1 May 1948 I became one of those little orphans.

Mother's eyes were red-rimmed. Grandmother ran after the taxi, waving her white handkerchief. She had already called me a "poor orphan." Mother told her not to exaggerate, but as the taxi turned the corner and Grandmother got left behind, I felt the first pangs of panic. Just where was I being taken? I knew I had peed into the Bollers' sink, but I hadn't broken anything, no one had been hurt. So why was I being arrested?

"I told you, you are not being arrested," said Mother impatiently; I kept asking the same questions, forcing her to be short with me. "You have to live somewhere. We're lucky. They don't usually take children at such short notice, but Madame knows one of the women on the committee."

I did not feel lucky despite wearing new clothes. Mother wanted to impress on the people that we were not just ragged refugees, but knew how to dress properly. She had used all our clothes coupons to buy me a camel hair coat, a green velvet dress with a white lace collar, a green felt hat to match the dress, and new shoes and stockings. The shoes were black patent leather pumps so shiny I could see my face in them. The saleslady had suggested a "liberty bodice," a cross between bindings that keep hospital patients in their wheelchairs and the elastics Grandmother wore for her varicose veins. Mother drew the line. The stockings were kept up by suspenders attached to my panties.

Mother was no help. She was sitting next to me, stiff as a board, deaf, dumb, in shock, and powerless to help me. I forced myself to look out of the window to keep my bottom lip from wobbling. I didn't want Mother to think I was crying. To remove the lump in my throat, I began to memorize the route along which we were traveling. The main road to Leeds was familiar. After Hyde Park we had turned left. Mother noticed my interest in street signs and warned me.

"No bright ideas."

"I just want to see where we're going," I told her, but Mother was right. I was getting bright ideas.

"Even if you run away and find your way back to the hospital, you can't stay," she warned me in a wooden voice. "We can't keep you. You will be taken back."

"Maybe Mrs. Boller will forgive me?"

"This has nothing to do with Mrs. Boller."

We lapsed back into silence, but I kept an eye on road and shop signs anyway and on plaques on some gates we passed. There was a "Royal something Society" and a "something Hall." One brass plaque was marked "Surgery." I was not surprised. Doctors were the most important people in ← England, just below royalty. Maids and orderlies were forbidden to look a doctor in the eye; if a doctor could not be avoided, they had to step aside or face the wall.

We turned into a tree-lined street, where the taxi lurched to the curb. I saw an open gate in front of a two-storied brick building in the same style as other houses, except this one had been stripped naked of all moldings, gables, and roof trim. From the façade alone I knew it was a government building, a hospital or a prison, made ugly on purpose. They did not want people to want to return.

We got out. Mother handed me her suitcase, which had now become mine. The suitcase contained the gabardine, a hairbrush, a toothbrush, and also the flannel nightie that Mother had bought for me for sleeping at the Bollers' house. I had hoped for a silk nightie like those I had seen on private patients, and Grandmother had promised me something with rosebuds, but the coupons had only extended to the camel coat outfit.

The Home had two front entrances. Two identical bay windows at each end of the building held window boxes containing limp grasses. The front of the house was spread with gravel and had a divided path. A small lawn under the ground floor windows was staked with a sign: KEEP OFF THE GRASS. A brown tortoise with a string through its shell was struggling in the center of the lawn, trying to reach one of the denuded rhododendron bushes. Its back leg was extended, but the string was only long enough for it to reach its food dish, not the bush. I made a silent promise to the tortoise that if I escaped I ← would take it with me.

Mother checked a piece of paper and turned to the left. I glanced at my watch. The drive had taken less than half an hour. When I raised my head I saw a long chin appear in the left bay window just before the curtain fell back. Our arrival had been marked.

162

In the privacy of the small portico Mother adjusted her hat, and before ringing the doorbell she did something she had not done in years—she licked her hanky and ran it over the corners of my mouth. Mother's hankies had always smelled of cigarette tobacco, and they still did. I could tell she was nervous. Her hand trembled. Mother's nervousness made me clutch the suitcase to my chest the way Mrs. Boller had shielded herself against me and all "filthy foreigners." No matter how nicely you treated "foreigners," they still peed into your sink.

We heard the doorbell jangle inside the house. A few seconds later the heavy door was opened by a girl about my own age, hanging onto the doorknob. She was blonde, blue-eyed, and looked a bit like Inge. She was wrapped into a black apron that reached to her ankles. Keeping her head down she asked us to step inside, for a brief second her blue eyes had caught mine. We both looked away quickly. At least she had all her hair. In the camps, if you got lice, your head was shaved. Grandmother had assured me she had already rid me of lice in the Poggenhagen Transit Camp.

The hall was so dark it looked like a black tunnel. As my eyes adjusted I could make out a coat rack with a mirror next to a closed door. On the left a recessed alcove was lined with numbered pegs. A navy gabardine like mine hung on each peg. I wondered how Mother had known what to buy. She had to have already been here.

Because of the darkness my eyes were drawn to the only area at the end of the passage that was receiving light from several sources. A room directly ahead of us had large curtain-less windows and a large fireplace that contained a blazing fire. Long tables with benches lined the length of the room. A circular table stood next to the hearth, and a solid sideboard ran along one wall, suggesting it was the dining room.

The house smelled of lemons and disinfectant, hospital smells, but had enough wood paneling so your eyes did not bounce off stark white walls. The hall floor was red brick. I also noticed a long black church pew next to the dining room door. Frau Qwrill had had one like it in her attic.

It would be wrong to say I was interested in the furniture. The truth was that I kept my eyes on it to avoid making eye contact with a bogus work crew of girls in long black aprons. They pretended to scrub, sweep, dust, and polish, but actually they must have known we were coming and wanted to see what we looked like. They stared at us outright. Some were kneeling, standing on chairs, on step stools or hanging onto the outside of the banisters like monkeys, their dusters idle, but their eyes busy.

We realized that we were being kept waiting on purpose, to let us know we were there at the pleasure of the management, and not ours. It was a tactic Mother's Madame used when Mother had first introduced us to her. She had let us stand a full minute while she pretended to finish looking through some papers. Mother's cheeks had turned red with embarrassment, as they did now, while we waited painfully for official acknowledgement.

The slight was not lost on anyone in the hall. Two of the biggest girls began to smirk and whisper. One of them was big-boned with whitewashed blonde hair, raw knuckles, and yellow fingers. Her thin lips curled; her pale eyes fixed on me deliberately, as though she knew me already. I had never seen her before, but I knew the type. Her friend was fat with short dark hair, cut too high above her ears. Her cheeks bulged out and were covered with bloody pimples. Those two would shortly be breathing on me. That knowledge, coupled with bad memories of Bernau and Herr Koch's class, made my mouth go dry. In their black aprons they reminded me of a flock of crows on an unplowed field, ready to peck at any bird not matching their feathers.

Headingley Orphan Homes building, after it had become the Methodist International House, 1960s.

Finally a recessed side door opened and a chin thrust out as though expecting to be chalenged. The chin belonged to a thin, hatchet-faced person of undetermined sex, whose tight smile never reached the eyes. Only the heavy tweed skirt suggested it was a woman, not a man.

Looking down her nose through the bottom of her glasses, she introduced herself as the matron of this establishment, no handshake. In the briefest flash of time it takes to determine those things, I knew I did not like her, nor she me.

It was an unfortunate first meeting. Although she refused Mother's hand, I grabbed for hers and made my curtsey, as Mother had instructed. Big mistake! Sniggers and titters confirmed that English children did not curtsey. It was my turn to flame with embarrassment.

The sniggers brought additional observers into the hall from another side door. These girls seemed a bit younger than the ones already watching us.

164

They were holding plates, cups, cutlery, and tea towels; we had interrupted their washing-up.

Matron began to talk to Mother in English. Mother was answering nervously with hesitant and unsure pauses between words. I was so nervous I did not even hear Matron's question directed at me. Sudden silence in the hall signaled that it was my turn to speak.

Had she asked me my name or was I supposed to say "Hallo"? I ran my tongue across my dry lips to come up with the English words I had rehearsed: "Madame do you how? You how do?" The sequence escaped me, but there was no need to continue. The woman jerked upright, her face turned red, and her chin hairs quivered alarmingly.

Mother grabbed my arm and spun me into a corner. "How could you? Have you no shame?" I had no idea what she was talking about. "I can't believe you stuck your tongue out at her!" she hissed.

I did? Impossible! I had wet my lips to speak, but she must have seen the tip of my tongue. Not liking us, she had reached the wrong conclusion. Grandmother had told me that if someone was determined to dislike you, it did not matter what you said you had already offended them.

"I didn't stick my tongue out at her," I told Mother in Estonian. It was the truth. Speaking a foreign language made the situation worse. Another woman emerged from the kitchen to see what was going on. She was young with thick red curls and a face so full of freckles it looked orange. She was clearly an adult because of her ample breasts, but she appeared not much older than the girls on the stairs. She wore a cotton dress and a white apron, which meant she was an employee, but her manner was not that of a servant. She leaned against the doorjamb, arms folded, ankles crossed; her green eyes looked right at me. With a lopsided grin she was taking in the scene, the atmosphere, the mood and all, but reading my mind. Her unspoken message to me was, "Don't believe any of this. It's complete rubbish."

Mother was also receiving a message, that it was time to go. I dreaded a scene in front of these English crows and was relieved when she merely gripped my shoulder, lightly this time, and whispered "courage." Then before anyone could open the door for her, she turned the doorknob and let herself out.

After my suitcase was taken from me, Matron led me upstairs to a bathroom and handed me over to a woman kneeling and scouring the bathtub. The woman wiped her hands on her wet apron and motioned for me to follow her. She took me to a big bedroom with rows of identical beds and told me to undress and change into clothes that were already waiting for me at the foot of one of the beds. I could not understand what she was saying, but her gestures and expressions were clear. The camel coat outfit Mother had spent all our coupons on was taken away.

I followed the woman back downstairs to the cloakroom where my gabardine coat had been hung on peg number 34. A black apron on peg 34, next to the dining room door, was measured against me, folded shorter, put over my head and tied in the back. The woman called it a "pinifor"[18] or "pinni." This was my first English word in this new home.

A tour of the house took me back upstairs to the bathroom where I left my sponge bag containing my toothbrush and hairbrush on peg 34. Downstairs again, through the kitchen to an adjoining room with a concrete floor and a drain in the middle. She called this room a "skuleri."[19] In the dining room, I was shown where to sit. In the shoe room I was given slot number 34. We then left the house through the back door to the outside toilets across the concrete playground. The toilets in the playground were lidless bowls in open cubicles, the same as I remembered from Hausberge.

We were to use it at all times except in the middle of the night, when we could use the toilet in the bathroom.

The woman did a lot of finger wagging, meaning "no." The same rules and regulations were applied here as at the hospital: no one allowed into the bedrooms except at bedtime, and no leaving anything personal anywhere except on your own peg and in a drawer in a long chest of drawers that ran under the windows in the bedroom, which the woman called the "domtri." I started memorizing words by their Estonian sounds.

When I had seen what I was supposed to see, I was told to sit on the church pew by the dining room door and was left there, to be looked at and examined by anyone who went by. No one spoke to me and I did not expect them to. This was definitely a prison. The two times I had ever been punished had had to do with chocolate. Not sharing my chocolate with Ursula had got me a beating from Mother. The consequences of accepting an extra cup of cocoa from Mrs. Boller had sentenced me to this place. Mother's contract was for five years. She had been in England for one year and still had four to go. Mother had made it clear I could not live with them again until their contracts expired.

It was not until I was in bed that night, wide-awake, that the full impact of my new situation struck me. When we had been separated before, as on the train platform on the way to the Münster transit camp. Some nice English soldiers had helped me find her again. Even now I knew I could climb out of the window and find my way back to the hospital, but Mother had forbidden me to even attempt to return to them. She said they would be forced to send me back. I must have done something so terribly, terribly wrong that there could be no forgiveness. My throat became tight, and before long tears began to flow. I pressed my face into the pillow to keep from making a sound. There were nineteen girls in this "domtri." Their presence kept my sobs down. Shaking, hiccuping, and choking, I soon realized I was not fooling anybody. The room was too quiet for so many people. They were all awake, listening to the new "foringel" blubbering in the dark.

Mother had told me that in England crying was like wanting to be warm, a character weakness. She had advised me not to show my feelings. I remembered one of her letters: "I don't see if I don't want to, I don't hear if I don't want to, and I don't feel if it interferes with the goals I have set for

---

[18] Pinafore, an apron.
[19] Scullery.

166

myself." In the letter she had said she was clenching her teeth. I had seen her clench her teeth many times after one of Matron's summons on her day off. I could clench my teeth all I wanted to, but no one was going to rescue me if Mother and Grandmother could not take me back.

In addition to turning out employable individuals, the orphanage system also adhered to certain principles established in the 19th century for the building of strong moral character. A similar curriculum prevailed in English boarding schools, geared to turning out future world leaders. Headingley Orphan Homes was not interested in raising Prime Ministers, just employable maids and domestics. Training included strict discipline developed on an institutional level where many physical and neurological anomalies such as left-handedness and bed-wetting were counted as character flaws, to be corrected by ridicule and punishment. My squint was also a flaw, but my greatest demerit was being a foreigner from a country no one had heard of. Due to an initial misunderstanding, they thought I was German, which was not so good in 1948 England. The war was barely over, feelings ran high, and although they had agreed to accept me, I was not welcome. In Germany they had thought we were Russians. In England they thought we were Germans.

In 1998 I obtained a paper from the Leeds archives that gives my nationality as "Austrian," even worse than German. Hitler had been Austrian, but what really shocked me was the next line: Parent or Guardian. "No parent or guardian named." Yet Mother and Grandmother were only a bus ride away.

The misunderstanding could have come about when Mother told them I was Estonian, but they heard "Austrian." Then Mother further compounded the misunderstanding by thinking it helpful to ask if someone in the orphanage spoke German, so they could communicate with me. Again they only heard the word "German." The rest fell on deaf ears.

My first days and weeks passed in a blur. Orders, orders, instructions, instructions. Earnest faces and patiently wagging fingers soon became fed up and turned to: "Putis on! Tek datof! No! No! No! Cum. Go. Sit. Veit. Cumhir! Sitther! Standup! Eiprenon. Eiprenof." When I did not understand they spoke louder. The problem was not lack of hearing; it was that what little English I had learned in the DP camp had totally disappeared. Still there was enough emphasis put into the commands to give me clues.

Clean clothes were left at the foot of the bed once a week. Dirty clothes were put into a large hamper in the bathroom. At night shoes were to be placed neatly under the bed, otherwise kept in the shoe room. (I remembered Grandmother being taught the same rules and laughing. She had thought it a joke.) The washcloth was a "flannel," hung over the sponge bag. The bed was to be made in the morning by turning the mattress and tucking in the blanket corners so tightly that Matron could bounce a penny on it. She checked the bed for warmth to make sure the mattress had been turned. The bedroom windows were kept open. Because my bed was directly under the window, my pillow was often wet when it rained.

167

I did not know what had happened to my camel coat, felt hat, green velvet dress, or patent leather shoes. A pair of scuffed shoes became my own. My watch, too, was taken away. Mother had overlooked it.

Eating became my first conflict with the staff. A full plate was set before me during the midday meal with food that I did not recognize. I was watched through each forkful. When I did not clean my plate the leftovers were put into the larder[20] and served again at the next meal or meals until the plate was empty. Sometimes, after days of whittling and picking at the mess, all that was left was a dry brown stain. Wallowing in self-pity and with my throat constantly constricted, I was made to move and "gerron witit."

English names were another problem. Because I did not see them in writing, I had to go by sound. The *English Reader* at the DP camp had centered on Jack and Jill, Mary and Jane. There was only one Mary.

At the Home the matron had a name, but we had to call her "Matron." I had no reason to address her, but she called me something that sounded like "eeling." When she was talking about me to someone on the staff, she used the word "foringel," and when she saw me eating with my fingers she called me "filfi forin bagij."

School was still in session, but as it was close to the summer holidays, I was spared the dreaded encounter with another Herr Koch. After breakfast, after the washing up, after the spastics[21] had been picked up by a special van and everyone had gone to school, the house became so quiet I could hear the clock ticking in the dining room. That was when my training began, not just to become English, but also to become an orderly, as I had witnessed at the hospital. That was the way I understood it.

The woman who had helped me change into orphanage clothes and whose name as far as I could determine was "Misses Waaker" was going to be my teacher. She was a middle-aged angular woman who was not only steeped in wet aprons, but also in deep misery and had no time for nonsense.

Misses Waaker tied the black work apron around my middle and led me into the "skulleri," the concrete room off the kitchen with the drain in the middle. It contained two large sinks, a tub washing machine, a large wringer, ironing tables, and a drying rack, as well as a gas stove—items I had seen at the hospital. The drain in the center of the sloping floor was to catch all the water activity that took place in the room, including the emptying of the mop bucket, the water from the washing machine, and the run-off produced by the mangle. [22] The sinks were for washing and rinsing dishes. A sloping wooden draining board with grooves was attached to one of the sinks, so that the water from there could also run off into the drain in the floor. Everything wooden was waterlogged and smelled of wet washcloths. The entire scullery was a dark, dank concrete cell dominated by drain odors. It reminded me of Berlin's abandoned cellars and *U-Bahn* stations as well as my grey-mud nightmares in Hausberge.

---

[20] A cool place for storing food.
[21] Children with neurological disorders.
[22] Mangle is the same as wringer for the washing machine.

My first lesson was on how to use a brush pan, the broom, and the mop bucket. From there we moved on to the cellar. The cellar had a trap door in the ceiling known as the coalhole. I recognized the coalhole from the Bollers. It was where they had told me to shelter from the rain until they came home in the evening.

Misses Waaker watched me fill a bucket to the brim with shiny black pieces of coal, like jet beads, but terribly dirty. With an empty bucket in one hand and a full one in the other, I went back up into the kitchen where I emptied the grate ash into the spare bucket and under the watchful eye of the Waaker woman, I "leid" a fire and lit it. It took several tries before I got it right. We then moved on to the other fireplaces on the ground floor, including the one in the Matron's sitting room. The third fireplace was in the dining room. That was usually lit first, but I was in training so we had started with the closest one to the cellar stairs. The coal bucket was heavy. No other bedroom fireplaces were lit except the one in Matron's bedroom, where I got a good look around. Wall to wall cozy. No bracing cold air or open window for the Matron.

There were three bedrooms in all. One was for the "little ones," which included boys from age's three to five. The girls in my room were ages ten to thirteen. The third bedroom was for the oldest girls, supervised by the girl with the red hair and freckles who had been introduced to me as Heti. Between Matron's bedroom and the oldest girls' room was a spy window with a curtain on Matron's side of the glass. This ensured that the big girls were under constant surveillance. In addition to being watched and listened to, they had no heat, but lots of cold. Mother had been right about many things.

Being spied on was a surprise. I remembered the torn posters in the U-Bahn stations: THE ENEMY IS LISTENING. I had seen the same in London, only this time in English, but this was supposed to be peacetime, and this was supposed to be a home.

The placing of my bed directly under the window gave me an advantage the other girls did not have. I could see down the corridor. After lights-out and the seeming departure of the staff, one of the staff always returned on tiptoe to listen outside our door. She stood there for about ten minutes, listening to the chatter and laughter that erupted after everyone thought we were alone. Sometimes, suddenly, the light was snapped back on and the Matron or whoever was out there, rushed in with a slipper that was applied to every backside out of bed.

During instruction Misses Waaker kept up constant chatter that was gibberish to me until I noticed something interesting. English had many German-sounding words in it. Words like house and *haus*, bed and *bet*, read and *brot* were so similar that all I had to do was change a sound or two and, I got a good idea of what she was on about if I listened carefully. Mother had told me that the current English royals were of German descent, but had changed their names.

As most jobs began and ended in the scullery, it meant going back and forth through the kitchen. Redheaded Heti was usually chopping or slicing

169

something by the kitchen table. She still favored me with that mocking expression she had directed at me in the hall. It was as if she were waiting for a pot to boil that had only just started simmering.

The orphanage dog, Kim, was a lazy animal glued to the dining room hearthrug. He had already noticed the barked orders directed at me, and it had confused him at first. He had lifted his ears, but now that he knew the orders to "Kumhir! Sit! Veit!" were not for him, he lay back down again, muzzle over paws, but with raised eyebrows, as if to say, "Look, just do as they tell you. I learned that way, too and here I am, nice and comfy. Give in, and you may get a butcher's bone for Christmas." Twice a day Kim lumbered into the scullery to his food dish and only balked when he was forced outside to pee. It was easy to see why Kim did not run away. The dog had chosen comfort over freedom. Unki had told me many men did the same sooner or later and got married.

None of the children had bothered me so far, not even the girls who had smirked at me from the stairs, but then I was seldom alone, always a few steps behind Waaker with my mop and bucket.

Mother had said it was not a prison, but it felt like a prison. We had played prisoners of war and politicals in Meerbeck. A prisoner's first duty was to escape. I had nowhere to escape to, but I could resist. I did not have to obey them. The people around me were meaningless, total strangers. I felt no obligation. I did not love them or even like them. I had only been obedient to Mämmä because I loved her and wanted to please her. These people could not even pronounce my name. Unki would have felt the same way.

Rather than sit in front of the same piece of meat for days, I slipped the roast beef into my apron pocket and from there into Kim's mouth. Everybody thought Kim had taken a special liking to me because he followed me around the house.

Because the bedroom was cold and the blanket left my feet bare, I waited until everyone was asleep, then got the bathroom rug and spread it on my bed. I trained myself to wake up early enough to put it back before Heti came to wake us. When I was left alone to polish the bedroom floor, I tied the dusters to my feet and skated around the room like I had always wanted to on the lagoon. I had fun and wished I had music. The Matron had a radio in her sitting room; I could hear it when I cleaned her toilet. Sometimes I used her toilet, although it was forbidden. I was not breaking anything, but I knew I was doing wrong. Turning the mattress was another waste of time; I stopped doing it. I continued to drink my tea with my mouth full because Waaker did it, too, and I needed something to wash down the potted meat sandwiches and Brussels sprouts. I reasoned that, if they no longer wanted me here, they would send me back to Mother and Grandmother.

I was scrubbing the draining board one morning when I was called into Matron's sitting room to take a phone call. There had been a phone on Mother's Madame's desk, but I had never touched it or used one. When I was handed the receiver, a black heavy object with two ends, I didn't know which end to put to my ear until Matron showed me. The call was from Mother. She came straight to the point.

170

"They want me to ask you why you are not obeying them. They think you are playing some kind of game. This is not a game. You will not be able to visit us until these people see progress. Am I making myself clear because....?" At that point the telephone was taken from me. Mother's unfinished sentence was left in the air.

The call came as a shock. In the background was Grandmother's voice, urgently asking to be given the receiver. Mother must have taken the call at the hospital reception desk. The thrill of talking on the telephone had not obscured the object of the call or the desperation in Mother's voice. She had guessed that I was playing politics, and I had been wrong in thinking I would be sent back to them. Instead I was being blackmailed. My behavior was ← going to punish Mother and Grandmother instead of me. "The filthy Fritzes," as Inge would have said. Seeing the dismay on my face, Matron considered the call a success. She ushered me out of her sitting room with the satisfied knowledge that the reprimand had been accepted on both ends of the telephone wire. My training was stepped up another notch. Instead of just being told "no," I was led to the punishment bench, the real object of the church pew, and left there to ponder over what I had done wrong. Unfortunately I had forgotten about the religious instruction Mother had mentioned as being part of my sentence. Maybe I was being trained to become a nun.

The religious instruction began a few Sundays later.

"No runin! Slo daun!" No running! I slowed down.

"Stop lafin! No lafin." No laughing. I took note.

There was no cooking on Sundays. We ate cold beef and potatoes for dinner and no chores. That part was fine.

We did not wear uniforms during the week, but on special days and on Sundays we wore American dresses and American shoes donated by the Red Cross. They were all alike except for small details like a different shade of check, a different collar, or different buttons, but basically they were cut from the same pattern and cloth.

Matron had plunked me on the bench and mimed for me to observe. I observed, but soon got bored. There was a shelf of cloth books and snap cards nearby, kept for the little ones and the spastics, the only ones who had time to play. In the general milling around the hall and shoe room, I picked up a book and a pack of cards, just to look at them. The book was especially interesting because the words and sentences were short. I was thinking how easy it would be to learn English that way, when suddenly Matron appeared beside me and ordered, "Put dat buk daun rait nau!" I put the book back on the shelf, but dropped the cards. I bent to pick them up, but she had already acted as if I had picked up a hand grenade. "Livdem!" she shouted.

No handling of books or cards on Sundays.

When she determined that I had observed enough and was ready to go to church, I was dressed in the American dress uniform and black patent leather shoes, not as new and shiny as the ones I had brought with me, but still nice.

Secretly I was thrilled. I had not yet made the connection between Grandmother's God, my Jesus, Mother's religious crackpots, and the church.

I had never been to church. Grandmother had told me it was God's house, and I was looking forward to speaking to God about some things going on in his country, in his name. Our religious instruction was definitely going to shock him.

The church was not far from the orphanage. Matron led the way. The matron of the babies and toddlers' house brought up the rear, prompting stragglers to walk briskly and stay in line. Her name was Miss Robinson, another elderly spinster in tweeds. She had the same chin hairs as our Matron, but was the exact opposite when it came to manner and attitude. She was strict, but had a sense of humor. She barked her orders military fashion, a drill sergeant having fun with the recruits. She used her cane the way I had seen British officers use theirs, not for walking, but for keeping pace. A tap on the shoulder got our attention. A tap on the side straightened the line. A tap on the rear made us step lively. "Geralongder!" she bellowed, prodding the cane against the nearest set of calves, the closest bottom, but never maliciously or painfully. The smile at the corner of her mouth, even when we were merely standing at a traffic light reflected good thoughts. It was obvious she enjoyed life and liked children, even those with flaws. Our Matron only liked the perfect ones and barely tolerated those with flaws.

The master and matron of the big boys' house managed a separate marching column. It was one of the few times we saw the boys. The boys' house was the other wing, separated by locked doors and keyholes plugged with wax. The master and matron was a married couple, capable of handling boys from ages five to fifteen. At meal times we could see the boys across the way, seated at identically placed tables in an identical dining room. Occasionally we could hear screams through the walls, and when the master raised his voice it was followed by the sound of the cane coming down. "Whack! Whack!" Like someone beating carpets.

The war was over, but the fear of being different from other children and singled out for stoning and punishment had remained with me since Germany. I had feared the same treatment because I was the "foringel" and Matron did not like me, but for the first time in years I felt safe on the street. It was especially wonderful when we were going somewhere in a group, walking in crocodile, in twos, all dressed alike. It was as if I had put on an invisible garment and was neither *Ausländer* nor "foriner" to passers-by. When we appeared people stepped aside for us. They stared at us with curiosity, some solemnly, like watching a funeral procession. Their eyes slid right over me as over the others, all "homegels" from Headingley Orphanage, Cliff Road. Our American dresses assured them we were all English and could be trusted. Me too. It was wonderful.

Though my euphoria soon turned to guilt. Grandmother would have been hurt to know I no longer wanted to be an Estonian refugee like her. I had a traitor's heart and on Sundays, on the way to God's house, of all places.

The moment I stepped into the English church, I felt right. Smells were familiar: musty graves, cold cellars, funerals. Just as I had expected. Of course the way to heaven was through graves and funerals. Dust, too, as befit tombs and mausoleums. Marble-garbed figures of dead knights and their ladies reposed on elaborately raised stone caskets. Brass plaques paved

172

the floor where more bodies were buried underfoot. I stepped around the brass plates respectfully to avoid stepping on anyone's face. It was all very impressive. The stained glass windows, I noticed with relief, were also peaceful. Jesus' expression was not the desperate "Dear God! Please help me get out of here!" Instead he looked resigned to his job as shepherd, surrounded by sheep. I recognized Moses under the heavy weight of the Ten Commandments looking around for a place to put them down. Baby Jesus was on his mother's knee, looking at least five years old, but still in diapers.

In another window Jesus was older, getting baptized by John the Baptist, who was dressed like a caveman. In side panels Jesus was surrounded by sheep, children, and angels; no adults. Most adults, I had discovered, did not like him.

Mindful that we had come to God's country through the service entrance, I still looked forward to meeting Him in spirit. I had a long list of things to tell Him about our new situation. I did not know how it would happen, what the protocols were, and whether He would speak to us directly or into our minds, as He had in the past or in some other way, like through His mysteries.

The sound of a penny rolling along the tiled floor brought me back to the present. We had each been given a penny for the collection plate, and the big girls were acting up. I was still amazed that they had not beaten me up yet.

Matrons and staff were sitting at both the ends of the first three pews. Heti and Waaker had the big girls' pew. The master and matron provided bookends for the boys. All exits were covered, but first in order to hear God's message, the scene needed to be set. I knew enough about theater productions to recognize the need for proper staging.

Paraphernalia was already on stage: costumes, different roles, lead actors, candles, smells. At the opening bars of the organ music the dignitaries, with stern faces and measured steps, proceeded down the center aisle, no running here either. First came the altar boys in white smocks over their street clothes, carrying candles. They walked ceremoniously, their ears red and their hair slicked down with water. Then the singers, wearing identical robes. A few more men wore dresses over their trousers, and finally the principal actor, called a "viiker." He was the man who had greeted us at the door. Robinson had introduced me by touching her cane to my bottom and saying simply, "the germingel." It was not until I was sitting down that I worked out the sounds and realized she had introduced me not as "foringel", but "germingel," the "German girl."

The "viiker" was a small man. His stiff garments made him look lost in cloth, but suitably dignified in his role as God's agent. I was getting a quick lesson in what was going on and what would happen next. God would not be delivering the message Himself. He would be speaking through His stand-in, the "viiker." That, then, was the function of pastors. What a wonderful job it must be, I thought, to open your mouth and hear God speaking through you.

The service began with a prayer. Heads bowed. We opened our hymnbooks to the numbers posted on the pillars. I did the same. The musical notes were familiar, but I could not read the words. I moved my mouth "esses," closed my eyes, and marveled that I had arrived in His _____ at last. It made sense that God would be in England and not in countries ravaged by war, just as there would be no foreigners in heaven—only angels. Lulled by Grandmother's assurances of God's love, I stilled my mind and waited for Him to speak first. No yammering off a list of panicked petitions.

There was a long hush while the "viiker" put on his spectacles and stared down at us from his tower. He did so with a secret smile, the way God might have looked down at the Israelites to let them know He knew which one had hidden the Golden Calf in his bathrobe pocket. His gaze was fixed on the first row where one of the big girls had deliberately dropped the penny. Further sounds of pennies rolling down the aisle did not faze him. He identified the culprits with a signal and a nod to the matrons, to deal with later. He then proceeded to speak or rather to scold us in a high-pitched voice that continued to rise until he was shouting, pounding the pulpit, and turning red in the face. At first I thought he was still upset with the girls who had rolled the pennies, but it soon became clear he was upset with us all, even the old ladies sitting quietly behind us in their hats and white gloves, and the English gentlemen who had already looked uncomfortable before the shouting had begun.

Using my method of picking out German-sounding words, I recognized the word *Sünde* as sin, *Hölle* for hell, *Feuer* for fire, and *Gott,* which all added up to the Lake of Fire that Mother had been upset about. Nothing about *Himmel,* but surely heaven was what it was all about. The word "damned" was easily recognizable as verdammen, as in *verdammte Ausländer,* and "damnt foriners." The viiker continued. It was easy to see why few people attended church, why Mother did not want to go, and why Grandmother had never been, although she had been born to a church organist.

The sermon ended with a rousing hymn about Christian soldiers (*Christen Soldaten.*) The war between Hitler and Stalin was over, but definitely not over yet between God and Christians. God's agent had spoken. I was stunned, shocked, and dismayed.

With my head still full of questions, I was ushered back out into the cold mid-morning. The grey sky, which I had thought to be the way to heaven, had shut its door on us. I was going to have to tell Grandmother that we had not only lost our country, we had also lost our God. I had lost her, too, and there was no one left for me to tell my troubles.

All the way back I was confused and disoriented. I had to be prodded several times, once severely enough for Matron to yank me back into line.

Lying in bed that night I thought about God for the first time. Did He come to all churches to hear what people were saying on His behalf, or was the "viiker" sometimes forced to ad-lib to cover up for His absence? Ad-lib, as when actors forgot their lines. Our God had been faith and hope, not religion and fear. We already had fear. My Jesus had become the angry God of religion; I suspected it had to do with the war. He was fed up with us all for complaining about a world He had already told us was bad and was tired of telling us how we could be saved. There had been no evidence of His presence in that church, not His ghost or His spirit, just the "viiker" and his

174

production. If anyone could save me now, it would have to be Unki, but he was in Brazil and probably did not even know where I was.

→ Feeling abandoned and not understanding what people around me were saying, I got into a fight with one of the big girls during the washing up. She hit me in the face with a serving platter and broke my front tooth. I kicked her in the shins, causing the platter to fall and break. Before anyone could call Matron, Heti appeared, put a finger to her lips, and quickly picked up the pieces. It happened so fast, it might never have happened at all except for the broken tooth.

→ Not God, but Heti had rescued me and saved me from the punishment bench. Now it was up to me to figure out the reason why she had rescued me. I had noticed that I was the only one who was put on the punishment bench day after day, while the big girls around Heti didn't even bother with the rules. They even bullied the little ones on Matron's day off, but no one told on them. Matron did not appear to have any idea what was going on in her own house.

→ Heti had shown me that punishment could be avoided. Heti was the key to a better existence. Now this was the kind of instruction I welcomed. Unable to speak to her, I was going to have to start listening with my eyes and common sense.

The scullery really did resemble a prison cell. There were even bars across the back windows to keep out burglars, but the atmosphere was of dungeons and sewers. In contrast, the warm and cozy kitchen with the fireplace and food smells from the pantry made it the place to want to be.

After the dinner dishes had been washed, the big girls gathered around the kitchen table to do their homework. Matron took a look around the kitchen to make sure everyone was busy, and then collected the spastics and her favorites into her sitting room. There they sat around her chair, mending clothes, knitting pot covers and crocheting doilies for the Christmas bazaar. I remained in the scullery where there was more work to do—the stove to be cleaned and the laundry folded while Waaker peeled potatoes. She did all the heavy work and dirty work and was constantly up to her elbows in soapy water, her apron wet from bending over waterlogged sink boards, clogged drains, and lint traps. I had not seen her smile since my arrival. From the bedroom chatter I had learned that she was a widow. She had a small son in the toddlers' house, but was only allowed to see him on her time off. A familiar situation existed for her as for the orderlies at the hospitals. Sometimes I caught her glancing wistfully out of the barred window to where her little boy Bili was playing in the sandbox. She showed the same desperation that mirrored most of the faces I had ever seen. I wondered whether there was a person in this entire world whose leg was not tethered to a string just long enough so they could reach their food dish, while even the people who pulled the strings lived in fear. The plight of the woman in the private wing had started to haunt me.

To make Waaker feel better I tried not to upset her any more. As she had only two expressions, grim or sour, depending on the chore, I tried to anticipate her needs before she could yank my arm. There was always perspiration running into her eyes and dripping off her chin, so I sometimes

175

handed her a towel to wipe her face. At first she could not understand what I was doing, but then caught on. She continued to box my ears, but no longer unkindly. Ours was a slow journey with the bucket from the scullery to the kitchen, down the tiled hall to the front door, then upstairs, leaving behind the smells of lye and carbolic.

Bit by bit I got to know names of things that English people needed just to have a simple meal. I washed platters, sieves, colanders, graters, cake pans, jelly molds, servers, pickle forks, ladles, and gravy boats. The work gave me a new understanding of what it was like to be civilized. The endless rooms, too, had certain functions. Apart from the obvious, like the kitchen, the pantry, the scullery, the bedrooms, the dining room, and bathroom, there was also a shoe room, a lumber room, a cloakroom, an ante-room, a mud room, a luggage room, a box room, a linen room, Matron's sitting room, Waaker's room, and the most mysterious room of all, the playroom. The playroom door was kept locked and only opened for special occasions and important visitors. Before visitors arrived the room was aired, the fire was lit, and we were all ordered to go in and "plei."

Hetty (I finally saw the name written down) came down with us in the morning, yawning and stretching. The buttons on the front of her dress ex-posed her brassiere, but her apron, once tied, covered the gap. Her beautiful red hair was like a halo around her head; she was unlike anyone else in the house. She was a domestic and the cook, but also on the staff. When given an order, she deferred to Matron, but did not seem to be afraid of her.

After I mastered the mop bucket, the fireplace grates, and the general cleaning, I was moved on to help with laundry and taught how to operate the washing machine and wringer. The washing machine swirled clothes around a large tub. It did not call for special skills, but the wringer did. The wringer was a larger version of the gadget Mother used to roll cigarettes. You cranked a handle and pulled the sheets through the rollers. If you cranked too quickly the sheets got caught and ripped. I earned a box around my ears before we moved on to the clothesline. The sheets were long and flapped around until the clothesline was propped up with a wooden pole. I could see why Waaker's apron was always wet.

Cleaning the bathtub was done by using a brush and something called Vim, but I confused the powder with something else called Talc. Vim was for the sink. Talc was for the body. Waaker snatched the Talc from me, but we were starting to get used to each other. When I was wrong she put the cor-rect item into my hand and made renewed motions to "gerronwit it!" Clean-ing too, was not simply wiping, dusting, or sweeping, but included mops, buckets, brushes, polishes, powders, oils, and Brasso (one for brass, one for copper, and another for silver.) There were floor brushes, vegetable brushes, clothes brushes, nail brushes, shoe brushes, furniture brushes, even a dog brush. It was easy to see why civilized people needed big houses and all those rooms. Where else could they put things except into dining room cabinets, cupboards, wardrobes, dressers, chests of drawers, bureaus, and closets?

176

Every doorknob had to be polished, every hinge oiled, every floor swept, every shelf tidied, every window washed, every windowsill dusted, and so on, until Saturday afternoon.

Then came Sunday with church, followed by walks when it was nice, and a cold midday meal. Then back we went to church for Bible study; I still did not understand a word of it, but was reminded we were going to be worse off after we died than we were already. On Monday morning the chores began again, and there was no more time to worry about the afterlife.

Matron at the Headingley Orphan Homes with her "little ones," 1950s.

Then one day Matron took me back to the scullery, away from scrubbing, polishing, and dusting. She led me to the long table where we ironed and folded sheets. On it she had placed two large cooking pots, an enamel bowl, and a strange gadget. On the floor nearby were a bucket and a sack of potatoes. She mimed her requirements. My new job was to fill the two large pots with peeled potatoes. The gadget was a potato peeler. I was going to take over Waaker's job.

"Filup!" She pointed a bony finger to the top of the pot and put the gadget into my right hand. I transferred it to my left.

"No, no!" Her chin flapped and her hands clawed the air as she yanked the gadget from me and put it back into my right hand. "Riteand!"

However, I was left-handed with knives, scissors, needles, and with throwing a ball. I was right-handed with spoons, pens, and pencils. In fact I never knew which hand I was going to use until the moment arrived. In this case my brain decided that the gadget belonged in my left hand, only to discover that the blade faced the wrong way. The pointed end of the peeler was no good either. It was a right-handed peeler. How could I tell her that what I needed was a paring knife? I changed the peeler to my left hand and showed her I could not use it.

177

"No, no! Riteand." Matron grabbed the peeler again and slapped my hand down on the table. "Riteand!"

"No." I held up my left hand. "And."

"Hand," she corrected me and got scrappy. We began to slap the peeler back and forth. She was forcing me to become right-handed, but I could not even hold a knife in my right hand, never mind the peeler. I could not understand what the fuss was.

"Neif," I ventured. "Neif." I made cutting motions to show her what I needed.

"No, uus riteand," she insisted. To give me better access to the bowl, she brought a wooden box for me to stand on.

"Gerronvitit!" She stalked off, leaving me alone to contemplate this new challenge. Of course I knew what she wanted. I needed to fill two pots with peeled potatoes before bedtime, using the right-handed potato peeler. With my right hand folded around the handle, my hand remained limp. In my left hand, the blade faced the wrong way. Gripping it as hard as I could and using it like a dagger, I managed to rip out a few chunks and chips.

When Matron returned I quickly switched the peeler back to my right hand. Matron sorted through the chunks until she found two short peelings she liked and dangled them before my eyes. "Luk! Luk!"

I looked.

She held the thinner of the two to the light, throwing the other back into the bucket. "Undestand?" She continued to hold the thin sliver of peel so the light shone through it. "Tin! Tin!" I understood. She wanted them thin.

Everyone had gone to bed when she returned to find one pot half-full of gouged-out potato pieces. She snorted disapproval and sent me to bed. Waaker was going to have to finish the job in the morning.

The secret of Hetty and the kitchen soon became clear. There were two camps in operation at the Home. One was Matron and her favorites, including the little ones. The other was an unruly and unwanted group of girls whom Matron had no more interest in and could not wait to get rid of them. These were the girls who congregated around Hetty. They included the girl who had broken my tooth and the crows who had stared me down on that first day, but had not yet beaten me up; I suspected it was because Hetty was holding them back. The two girls I feared most were Helen and Enid. Hetty had lied to Matron, telling her my tooth had been broken in an accident.

Peeling potatoes became my regular chore, and it had to be done with the potato peeler in my right hand. When Matron was back in her sitting room with her favorites, I used my left hand, but only managed to fill half a pot. Waaker had to do the rest in the morning while I lit the fires and set the tables. When Hetty came into the kitchen to start the "porig," I helped her to butter the bread. We made eye contact without speaking. Her green eyes were like green traffic lights, telling me to go ahead, but I had no idea to where.

Some of the big girls followed Hetty around and hung on her every word, especially in the evening after Waaker had gone to her room, the little ones were in bed, and Matron's sitting room door was closed. When there was no

178

more chance of hearing Matron's footsteps in the hall, the kitchen came alive. From my box in the scullery I could hear the scraping of chairs, the giggling, the laughing, the opening and closing of drawers and cupboards, followed by the smell of cinnamon toast and cocoa. Toast and cocoa were allowed, but definitely not the other activities, which interested me even more than the snacking. What had caught my eye were books, though they were not really books. The girls called them "komiks." I had seen them hidden behind the pipes in the outside toilets and had found them to be a marvelous invention for learning English, even better than cloth books. The dialogue was inside small bubbles coming from the speakers' mouths, showing the sentences in the pictures, but "komiks" were forbidden.

In addition to "komiks," the big girls were poring over dog-eared soft books with their covers off, like the ones Unki used to read in his chamber. These books were stashed under Hetty's basket of women's magazines, another thing I had never seen before.

Only one girl actually did her homework every evening. Her name was Poliin. She was studying to become a nurse and was sponsored by one of the committee ladies. Hetty made sure the other girls did not bother Poliin. There were many sides to Hetty.

One evening while the big girls were reading "komiks," I sat down next to Poliin to see what she was doing. As she did not chase me away I became bolder and picked up one of her textbooks. It was a medical book. As she still did not forbid me, I leafed through it. The pictures were interesting, showing the human body, the human skeleton, the bones and internal organs with muscles and veins wrapped around them. I had never seen anything like it and became completely engrossed. There was a picture of the heart, of the brain. One chapter was about babies. I had always wanted to know how babies were born, but what I really wanted to know was how they got started. How did the father put the baby into the mother in the first place? I turned back until I came to the section about men and women and sexual organs. I knew what men looked like, but had only a vague idea of how the male part worked to make babies. I studied the pictures and saw that the male put the baby into the woman from the end of his penis, so that was what that soldier had tried to do to me. He had wanted to put a baby inside me. No wonder Mother had panicked at the thought of having another mouth to feed.

It was about that time when I began to suspect that Hetty's reason for shielding me was not really what I had hoped for, it had to do with choices. There were only two choices. You were either one of Matron's favorites or one of Hetty's girls, but the choice was not yours.

Mother had told me that the orphanage only kept children until they were fifteen, then either sent them into service or put them out to fend for themselves. I had witnessed one of the sendoffs. "Dontcumbak," Matron had told the girl.

I had been watching from the bench and caught the name Megin.

"Noton yer nelli!" Megin had replied and made a rude hand gesture, upon which Matron shut the door on her. I wondered where Megin would go if she had no other home. Where did one go? Maybe the park?

179

I had no intention of being one of Matron's favorites and knew it could never happen anyway, but becoming one of Hetty's delinquents could mean I might never see Mother and Grandmother again. They wanted me to be good and there was no choice. Matron hated me and Hetty had already recognized me as one of hers from that first glimpse of me in the hall. Her message to me had been, "Don't waste your time with Matron, you're already flawed."

It was true. Matron's dislike of me and my dislike of her had been mutual. It had nothing to do with my squint or my running my tongue across my dry lips. She thought we were Germans. My other moral weaknesses and character flaws were already built in. I was not a nail- biter like Helen, whose fingers were routinely dipped into the mustard jar, which is why she had yellow fingers. I did not have spots and pimples like "Dirty Enid," who appeared regularly with purple lotion on her face yet still picked the spots until they were bloody. Nor was I overweight like "Fat Lori," who had to run around the yard after school and was never given baked treats; yet no matter how long she stumbled around like a sack of potatoes, she remained fat. Public humiliation was supposed to cure weakness. I did not see a single cure.

The happiest children in the Home were the spastics, who were treated better than anyone was. A van took them away in the morning and returned them at suppertime; they were allowed to play in the yard and dining room, where they drooled, mumbled, and talked gibberish. Sometimes they just sat on the floor and banged things about, until one of them got so agitated she was taken upstairs to the bathroom and held under the cold-water tap until she stopped screaming. After that she was put to bed and was fine again next morning.

I knew Matron hated my squint. "Luk at mi!" she would order and shake me, as though she could jiggle my eyeballs into place by force. As my squint was not fixed, it shifted from eye to eye; so she thought I could control it, but I couldn't.

When I was fourteen I had the necessary eye surgery, performed at Leeds Infirmary by a leading eye surgeon in England, a Mr. Foster. I saw him again one day in 1960, in the Tate Gallery, and wanted to go up to him and thank him, but I was too shy. The moment passed.

The cruelest punishment was meted out to the bed wetters. I remembered my wet pants during our flight from Estonia. All my worst memories had to do with needing a place to pee, being peed on, and finally having to pee in my pants. I felt her pain.

Poor Valri's ordeal started after supper, no more drinks, forced visits to the toilet before bedtime and again when the staff went to bed around midnight. I suspected she stayed awake for as long as she could, terrified of falling asleep; yet the inevitable happened and she was wet in the morning. Sobbing and sniffling, she dressed quickly, stripped her sheets, and took them into the scullery where she had to wash them and hang them on the line before breakfast. By that time she was late for school and was further humiliated by having to take a note to the teacher to explain her lateness. If she was dry, Matron came in and praised her and we applauded, but that had happened only once since my arrival at the Home.

Learning to speak English was paramount, but I vowed not to speak aloud until I was perfect. The few times I had tried had already earned me my nickname "Voolly," as in "Eelin vants her vuuly west!"

One morning, while waiting for Waaker to get back to my training, I noticed Valri's arithmetic homework on the hall table and took a quick peek. I wanted to see what English girls did in school. Every sum on the page had been marked correct. I turned more pages. Everyone had a five on it. At the same time I could hear Valri weeping in the scullery and Waaker shouting: "Yul hev to rins thet agen, gel. Hurri up! It's still got a pong to't thet goes riit up yer nose!" Valri's nickname was "Odecowshed."

Age-wise I belonged to the middle group, the ten to fourteen-year-olds and with my flaws and weaknesses I was definitely one of Hetty's, the "filfy forin guds" who puts food in her pockets, snacks on raw potatoes, and has never used a toothbrush properly. (Everything had to be done "proprli"). Waaker taught me how to clean my teeth. "Upnd doun. Upnd doun." She guided my hand so hard my gums hurt. We were in the middle of this exercise one morning, when Matron came in and watched for a while, then said something that sounded like "un-tsivilised retch." I knew the word "tsiviil." She was saying I was uncivilized. The word "retch," sounded like it belonged with "forin baggidge and nasti pis of forin guds." Waaker often called me "titch." I did not know what it meant, but her tone of voice was kindly. Perhaps some Yorkshire expression. In Matron's eyes I did not appear to have made any progress, but I could feel a change in myself that scared me. Like those traveling stones in the hospital woods, I could feel the metamorphosis. I was changing into a domestic like Waaker, or worse, into a maid and servant. I had seen what it had done to Mother and was determined not to let it happen to me.

The answer to everything important lay in learning English as quickly as possible without anyone being aware of it. I wanted to know what was being said about me. The quickest route was by way of one of the spastics named Betti. She sat at an old school desk for hours, banging beanbags, blocks, small toys and other objects against the desktop. The items were kept in a basket next to her. She pronounced apple "appe," but she announced each object loudly as she whacked it down. I tried to find myself near her and paid attention. When she picked something out of the basket, she named it, and down it came with a satisfied whack that gave me the word. I started to add things to her basket. Nothing obvious. Somewhere in Betti's mind she was having fun, and when I began to help her we had fun together. If she did not name something or if I could not understand the word, I picked the object up again and held it out to her. She misunderstood and started screaming for Matron. "The forngel tuuk mai blok!" I threw the block back quickly, but my bright idea was working. "Blok." Sometimes someone else came along and said, "Give Betti bek her heir slaid. Now!" Hair slide. Hair ribbon. Shoelace. Pencil. Crayon.

On Saturday mornings the doorbell did not stop ringing and the front door did not remain closed for long. Matron stood in the hall and greeted the visitors. The playroom was open. The little ones were in there, dressed in their nicest. They were told to "plei." No one else was allowed in. Waaker was upstairs supervising the clothes closet, helping with buttons, hair ribbons, and clean socks. When a girl was dressed she came downstairs to get her best shoes, and when she was ready she was delivered to the visitor. I had kept an eye on the front door for weeks, thinking Mother would suddenly turn up, but she did not.

Some visitors were called "goinout anties." They were also the "komiti leedis." The children who were taken out by them would become the ladies' future, handpicked maids. They were already forging a relationship with their future employers. These girls were considered the lucky ones.

The rest of us drifted in and out of the hall, anticipating the arrival of a parent so that we could watch hugging and kissing. Everybody wanted to see hugging and kissing. It was in that anticipation that the girls had gathered in the hall the day Mother and I had arrived. New girls were most likely to be hugged and kissed when they were dropped off, but some girls still had a parent who hugged and kissed them, much to a girl's embarrassment. The girl was ragged mercilessly for days afterwards. Only the spastics could be made a fuss over. Secretly I suspected most of us would have liked a day or two of being spastics, especially after seeing Betti clinging to her mother, making strange, happy noises. Jealousy touched us all—me, too, although I would never have admitted it.

A different type of visitor caused the opposite reaction. It started with Matron nervously hovering around the playroom, making sure the fire stayed lit and the little ones were playing "neisli". At the same time, Hetty stood positioned at the kitchen door, fidgeting with her apron and waiting for Matron's signal to put the kettle on.

These visitors were usually couples, hesitant, but determined. When they arrived Matron directed them into the playroom, where they were asked to sit on chairs placed against the wall so they could watch the little ones at "plei." Periodically Matron called to one or another child to "kum shou anti yer toi," which she did, shyly. The wives spoke kindly, the husbands looked uncomfortable. I hovered near the shoe room and wondered what was going on.

Then there was another type of caller. The playroom was closed. It was an interview situation conducted in Matron's sitting room. The visitor was usually a solid-looking type who marched in and knew the routine—usually a strapping woman with large arms, swollen legs, and a barrel body. When one of those visitors showed up, I saw the big girls make haste towards the outside lavatories. Hetty went to the back door and summoned one of the big girls back into the kitchen, to prepare a tea tray. The girl came reluctantly, but Hetty was adamant. In some things she had no choice. When the tray was ready the girl straightened her pinni, braced herself, and carried the tea tray into Matron's sitting room, as though the teapot were her own head on a platter.

182

When I finally spoke enough English I understood that the first couples came to adopt and the barrel types were housekeepers looking for domestics, like Mrs. Walker. I don't know if it was true, but as soon as I heard it I joined the exodus to the toilets, terrified that Matron might have the authority to give me away.

Only one girl in the orphanage was perfect, the same girl who had opened the door to us when we first arrived. Her name was familiar from the English storybook read to us in Meerbeck about an English Queen forced to paint her own roses to give them color. I could see why. England desperately needed color. The girl's name was Alice. She was Matron's absolute favorite and was held out to us as the perfect example of how to behave; we should all be like Alice.

One Saturday afternoon the playroom was open again. Important visitors were expected. The fire was lit and the piano was open. Alice was the only girl who could play the piano. She sat on the stool and nervously fiddled with the hem of her American dress. We all wore the dresses although it was not Sunday, and we had all been ordered to "plei."

Although the room was full of toys, only the little ones had picked them up. We knew better. It was a terrible temptation for me, too, to touch those English toys, but no one was allowed to hog a toy, to really get to like it. It was better not to become too interested or attached to anything that was not ours.

At the sound of the doorbell, Alice started to play a pretty tune. I recognized it as one of Aunt Alma's exercises for her more advanced pupils. A burst of women's voices filled the hall, and the visitors stepped into the playroom as a group. The prominent features that distinguished them were their big hats and large handbags. The size and uselessness of an English woman's handbag was an indication of her status. I recognized instantly that I was finally in the presence of the authorities, in this case the "komiti leedis" (committee ladies) in their official capacity. Even Matron was nervous. They were her employers.

The leading lady I recognized as our patroness and benefactor. Her portrait hung over the playroom fireplace. She was wearing a similar blue dress and matching hat in case anybody still did not know who she was. Her handbag was the size of my small suitcase.

The women wore make-up, not just a bit of eyebrow pencil and eyeliner like Mother and Grandmother, but thick and heavy paste, like actors. Their cheeks looked like floured buns. Where the blood red lipstick smeared their prominent teeth, it looked like blood.

The patroness entered first. She held her arms out to the little ones, who ran to her for a quick half-hug, a pat on the head, and a kindly hand on the cheek. These women owned us, I reminded myself.

"Helo childrin," she said to no one in particular.

"Good morning mis..." I did not catch the name, but made a note to read the plaque under the portrait as soon as it was polite to do so.

Waaker brought in the tea tray, helped by Helen of the yellow fingers. Matron and the lady exchanged chitchat while Alice continued to play softly in the background. Teacups rattled against saucers, the little ones giggled, and the ladies laughed out loud. I could see why Matron loved her little ones; they really were like little angels. Anybody who did not want to adopt them had to be crazy.

The ladies walked around the room, speaking to the big girls individually and, I noticed, avoiding certain ones. The patroness had a kind word for Alice as she looked over Alice's shoulder at the music sheet. Alice's cheeks turned pink with pleasure.

Suddenly the patroness who was also our benefactress and owner was standing over me instead of Alice. The piano fell silent and every eye was upon us. Matron came over and spoke quickly. I caught the words "jermin gel" clearly. The woman smiled and touched my face. I thought she was going to inspect my broken tooth, but no, her hand moved on to my head. She pushed her handbag up the crook of her elbow and parted my hair. I knew the gesture from the transit camps. She was checking me for lice.

Satisfied that I was clean, she said something to her friends. They gathered around me in a circle. Mother had mentioned an exception and guessed my sponsor might have been the patroness herself. I tried not to look directly at her, because of my squint. She did not say anything, but bent down on one knee and then, surprisingly, began speaking gibberish that I recognized as an attempt to speak German. Her voice was earnest, but I had no idea what she was saying. The problem was that she spoke it so badly I could not understand a word. The other women stood around adoringly. She must have boasted that she spoke German. It was very embarrassing when she realized I could not understand her. The benevolent expression underwent several changes before she saved herself cleverly and inadvertently to my advantage. Seeing that I did not respond appropriately she flushed and reared up in displeasure. "Tis cheild isnt germin! God nous vere she's from!"

This pronouncement was accompanied by a general swing of the handbag away from the awkward moment and towards the door. The group followed hastily. I saw Matron and Waaker exchange glances and the big girls begin to whisper among themselves. Not German! The "forin gel" is not German!

The visitors went on to inspect the rooms, unaware of the gift they had given me. Not German! Not German! Everyone, including Alice, was looking at me. So who is she, what is she? It did not matter to me who they thought I was or where I came from. The important thing was that I was no longer the dreaded enemy, the Nazi kraut they had taken me for. It was a sweet moment and the turning point in my more than four years at the orphanage.

Not everything changed. The potato peeler still remained useless and Matron continued to snort and berate me, but at least the biggest black mark against me had been erased. Mrs. Walker (I finally saw her name written down on a laundry list) was not happy to have to finish peeling the potatoes as well as supervise Valri's wet sheets. I felt badly about adding to Walker's misery, but understood the way the training worked. Just as my bad behavior affected

184

Mother and Grandmother, my failure with the peeler gave Walker extra work—all was designed to make me feel guilty, which it did.

Standing on the box in the scullery, night after night, I really wanted to fill those two potato pans and pass the test, but my right wrist was not strong enough to wield the peeler. Filling even one pan was a struggle, and the bits and pieces of potato ended up having to be mashed. My failure with the potatoes had caused Hetty to step up her recruitment of me. She had started rattling the kitchen drawers and deliberately opening and closing the central knife drawer, where the paring knife was kept. She was telling me it was time to stop trying to please Matron because that would never happen and did I really want to? She was right; I did not, but taking Hetty's paring knife could have serious consequences if Matron found out. I could even be sent to something called "borstal."[23] Mother had warned me about it in the taxi. It was a kind of juvenile prison for children who disobeyed repeatedly or ran away. The warning kept me from returning to the hospital, but the main reason I was not taking the paring knife was because Grandmother would be devastated if she heard I was cheating.

Hetty's offer was tempting, and for her it was a game. I suspected Matron herself was in on it because it served them both. The punishment bench's purpose was to observe your options. It was Matron's job to train the girls who were trainable, and it was Hetty's job to keep the failures from causing trouble until they could be put out legally. Hetty had already shown me what to expect under her authority: dried apricots, handfuls of raisins, forbidden reading matter, and a general good time, but in the end I would be put out like Megan and "dontkumback!"

As soon as Matron was safely out of the way, Hetty came and leaned on the scullery doorjamb, one eyebrow raised. What was my problem? Was I daft or just stupid?

I wondered how long I could hold out.

Another Saturday morning I was coming out of the shoe room when in the hall I saw Alice wearing my camel coat and the green velvet dress outfit Mother had spent all our clothes coupons on. I was shocked to see my clothes on someone else. Not having the necessary English, I ran up to Alice and grabbed at the cloth. "Mein!" I shouted. Alice looked confused, but Matron had already seen us. She pushed me aside, handed Alice some money, and shoved her out the front door.

Alice hurried away and Matron returned to her sitting room, leaving me in the empty hall, confused and wondering what had happened. Another puzzle. I had not meant to accuse Alice of stealing my clothes. I had only wanted her to know they were mine.

Alice was so far above me in goodness that I had never been near her. I had, however, heard things about her in the dormitory gossip. Her mother was dead and her father was dying in a hospital somewhere in Leeds. She visited him every Saturday. Matron must have dressed her in my best clothes because she felt sorry for her. That part was all right, but what if her father

---

[23] Prison for youthful offenders.

185

was ill at the same hospital where Mother and Grandmother worked? What if Mother suddenly spotted my coat in the hospital corridor and ran after the wearer - to discover it was not me?

My lack of progress with the peeler spurred Matron to extra effort; instead of wasting any more time with me, she recruited Alice to be my teacher. If I failed we would both be punished together. The standard blackmail routine had now extended to Alice. Here was a girl who had never been in trouble, who was perfect, but was now being punished because of me.

When we were sent to the bench, Alice kept as far away from me as space allowed. Her pale face was paler than porcelain, her neat pigtails were braided to the last hair, but her lower lip was trembling and her handkerchief was bloody from blowing her nose. I feared that if her father died while Matron was still training me, it would be my fault if she were not allowed to go to his funeral.

Another dismal Saturday afternoon. Alice was back from seeing her father. Matron had caught me reading one of the cloth books in the shoe room while I was supposedly polishing shoes. Alice was sitting on one end of the bench, I on the other, when the front doorbell rang. It was not a time for the usual visitors.

Alice became alert, jumped off the bench, and hurried to respond to Matron's, "Go see who that is, dear!" The "dear" made Alice flush with pleasure. I was glad. There was still hope that Matron would love her, despite me. Alice opened the door.

I could not believe my eyes. Mother was standing there, hesitating, as if I had actually brought her to me with my thoughts. She had on a new suit and looked thinner, but there was still a bit of the Snow Queen in the way she strode in and squared her padded shoulders. When she saw me on the bench, she might have come forward, but I put my finger to my lips. Matron also spared me the hug and kiss by blocking her path and my view by arriving quickly enough to let us both know I was now under her authority, not Mothers.

"Shall we go into my sitting room?" I heard Matron say smoothly.

Seeing Mother again was wonderful. We had not seen each other for months. I should have been happy, but instead I was traitorously relieved to have escaped hugs and kisses. Had I really sunk that low?

"Matron will see you now," said Alice, having approached me silently. She spoke formally and stiffly, as though she did not even know me.

As soon as I entered the sitting room, Mother stepped forward. Despite the atmosphere, she hugged me anyway. I saw Matron's pursed lips of disapproval. "Ten minutes," she announced and left us alone.

Mother's reserve unbent after Matron left. She was holding a wrapped parcel in one hand and a sheet of paper in the other. She offered me the parcel. "Mämmä sends her love and these, for your birthday, which we missed, of course."

186

As I did not take the parcel, she put it on a chair. From the shape I could see Grandmother had sent me colored pencils and a sketchpad. Because we were not allowed personal possessions, I resolved not to even look at them.

Perching on the edge of a chair, Mother took my hand. "How are you?" she asked in Estonian. Was I learning English? Was I being good?

I told her "no," also in Estonian, and was shocked to hear my own language sound strange to my ears.

"I see." Mother shook herself, then tapped the paper she held in her hand. "I've been called again to explain a few things to you. You'd better listen. Here's a list." She adjusted her glasses. "Let's begin with the food. What's wrong with the food?"

"I hate it," I told her truthfully.

"The food here is better than anything you've ever eaten. Do you realize that?"

"I don't like it," I said stubbornly.

"You are still eating raw potatoes."

"I like them and I'm hungry."

Mother cleared her head and referred to the list again.

"It says you are left-handed. I didn't know that. She's training you to use your right hand, but says you're resisting."

I remained silent.

"And here, she says you refuse to look her in the eye. Probably because of the squint," she spoke more to herself and sounded very, very tired.

She tapped the list again. "You refuse to speak English? By now you should have learned enough to speak to them."

"Everybody laughs at me. I'm not going to speak until I can speak properly."

Mother cleared her brain once more by shaking her head and read the next item on the list. "Spreads bath mats on her bed?"

"I'm cold."

Then she nearly jumped in the air. "What's this? Bit one of the staff?"

"I had to. They held me down on the bench. Hetty held my legs, Matron squeezed my nose until I opened my mouth to breathe, and Walker shoved a boiled egg into my mouth. It wasn't cooked. It was slimy, like snot. I had to bite her finger to make her stop. I'm sorry I had to bite Mrs. Walker. It wasn't her fault."

There was a moment of silence. Mother folded the list and put it in her handbag. She had had enough and jammed her glasses higher on her nose, at which point Matron returned, obviously having listened behind the door. Matron was frustrated that she had not understood the language. She took charge again.

"Are we clear yet?" she asked Mother.

Not yet! Mother's face was red. She turned back to me. "She says you refuse to sing. She says all the girls have to sing."

"You know I can't sing," I whispered in Estonian.

Mother could see the subject upset me greatly. Only she knew how much.

"She's tone deaf," said Mother in English.

Matron would not accept the excuse. She began to explain to Mother about "bilding bloks" to a stronger moral character. Ridicule was an important training technique. It had proven itself time and time again. "Mister Churchill was ...!"

Mother had worked herself into a state and did not want to hear about Mr. Churchill's strict upbringing or the wonderful benefits of child abuse. She did not want me to become a prime minister; she just wanted me to stay out of "borstal." She grabbed my shoulder and spun me into a corner of the room. "Have done with this nonsense," she hissed at me in Estonian. "If you keep this up, they'll put you into a state home and there's nothing I can do about it. Do you understand what I'm saying?" Mother took my hand. "Excuse us again," she said to Matron and motioned towards the door for her to leave us alone.

Mother kept my hand in hers. I braced myself. Hausberge came to mind. Instead she measured her words, speaking slowly and firmly.

"I know you and I do not have the best relationship, but this is not the time for childish indulgences. You are eleven years old, but in an adult world where nobody is going to make allowances for you. I have tried to tell you about the advantages of living in England. These advantages are real. This is not a test of wills, but it really is a test of character. You are nothing to them except a case number. Matron is merely doing her job." Seeing my lips forming the words "I don't want to be a maid," she held up her hand.

"You will never be a maid, thank God! Not with your attitude, but you could end up in serious trouble by the time you are fifteen. I still have over three years to serve on my contract before I can find a place for us to live together. Estonia is lost to us. What the woman says about a British upbringing is true. People all over the world pay money to be ridiculed, slapped, and caned in English boarding schools. You are getting the training free. If that woman listening out there treats you like dirt, it's because to her, you are dirt—a bloody foreigner. It's human nature. Nobody wants to be a foreigner in any country. You remember Bernau? You remember Hausberge? After I leave the hospital, even with Hilda's help, I'll be lucky to get an office job because of my accent. Yet the English themselves travel all over the world where no one expects them to speak other languages. Instead they learn English and are proud of it. I can't take back some of the things that have gone wrong between us, but I do have a practical brain and a cool stomach. I can see advantages here that will serve you for the rest of your life. Accept the training. Dismiss the nonsense."

She waved her left hand twice in exasperation to indicate it did not matter which hand I used, as long as the potato pans were filled.

"But the language, the English way of doing things—treat that knowledge like gold. If you leave here sounding and acting English, no one will ever again ask you where you came from." She cocked her head towards the door. "And that woman out there is your free ticket to that world. No more *Ausländer*, no more 'bloody foreigner' anywhere, no more licking their boots. Yes, Mum! No, Mum! Do I make myself clear?" Mother's lip was trembling; she was controlling herself with great effort.

188

When Mother had lectured in the past, I had usually put a barrier between us, tightened my muscles, and tuned her out, but this time I was listening for all I was worth. Mother was telling me there was a way out of this nightmare. In Hausberge, when the Allies had arrived, Grandmother had told me that half the world speaks English, and now Mother was telling me the same. If I behaved like Alice I could become Mr. Livingstone, explore jungles and discover natives who would call me "masa." (Mother had used that word and laughed her nastiest, setting the cork to barking.) I knew what she meant. I knew what she was telling me.

Mother saw the comprehension on my face instead of my usual sullen expression that she hated. She was pleased, nodded, and kept on nodding. Her hand on my shoulder relaxed.

Matron had picked up the silence and with a discreet cough stepped back into the room. "Well?"

Mother turned me around, smiling her actress smile. "I have explained everything to her. She understands fully, don't you?" she said in English. "She will try harder. We are very sorry." She nudged me and raised her eyebrows so they almost met the rim of her hat, encouraging me to speak, reminding me that it would take courage to get through yet another round of trying times. Had she not been brave herself once? Even now she was being brave, although she had told Grandmother that peacetime did not require heroes, only workers.

Matron was waiting.

I lowered my head and mumbled, "Sorry."

The Englishwoman nodded graciously and accepted my apology.

Mother took a deep breath and spoke Estonian again. "The woman told me that, if you make progress, you can start visiting us one day a week beginning New Year."

After Mother left, I heard Matron rustling through the wrappings of Grandmother's gift and tried to push the sound out of my mind. Instead I imagined a tree. Grandmother had told me that trees and hands were the most difficult things to draw because they demanded full concentration. Hands were the practical portrait of a lifetime of toil or lack of it. I was glad I still had memories of trees.

The next days felt strange. I did not want Alice to notice that I was copying her, but it boiled down to that. I had to become English by Christmas. The only physical obstacle to becoming a future statesman was still the potato peeler. Mother's visit had shocked me in more ways than I dared admit. A few more months and I would not be able to speak Estonian any more. I was already dreaming in English. If I was still hacking potatoes by Easter, Grandmother and I would become strangers who no longer had a common language.

There was another thing that bothered me. I did not want to be called a foreigner, but I did not want to stop being foreign. During the screening at the DP camp, one of Mother's friends who had jumped off her ship and lost all her documents, laughed about taking ten years off her age. "Can you imagine, being born again?"

"Yes, and when you're sixty-five you'll have ten more years before you get your pension," Mother had replied. "Making yourself ten years older would have been the smart thing so you could retire while you can still enjoy life."

I did not want to be reborn English or anything else while Mother and Grandmother remained Estonian. My metamorphosis was happening too fast. It was time to act. I marched over to the draining board and took the paring knife from under the ledge where Hetty had left it for me. With the knife in my left hand I lifted my face towards the night sky and whispered, "Sorry, God! Please forgive me. I just want to go home."

With the paring knife in my left hand and the peeler ready by my right hand, I finished two pots of potatoes in less than an hour with time to spare.

"You are learning," said Matron with approval.

Was I ever!

Becoming part of Hetty's group was wrong. I hoped God would forgive me and not punish me too much. The turnabout in fortune was not a gift. I had known it would not be. In the DP camp I had gone through a similar test, nothing drastic, just wanting to make friends, but this was different. This was not about making friends, but knowing my enemies and getting through Mother and Grandmother's contract years.

Unki had explained that once you joined a gang you had to have a blood-letting, and once you sided with the devil you paid a price. He had learned that in Africa. "Honor among thieves," he had called it. The bloodletting would be real and the blood was going to be mine.

So who would be sent to test me, I wondered? "Bony Helen" or "Dirty Enid?" Hetty's prediction about me had been right on. She had known me better than I knew myself. The crows, too, had recognized me immediately as one of theirs, and much as I hated to admit it, it was true. I was flawed from top to bottom and lacked all the attributes for becoming a great states-man.

The initiation took place in the outside lavatories. It amazed me how many of my trials had taken place in similar locations, at the hands of similar people. Only the languages had changed.

It was a Saturday morning again. Matron was busy at the front door, and I was coming out of the toilets when I was surrounded by the biggest and toughest of Hetty's girls. They formed a circle so I could not leave and herded me back inside. Helen and Enid blocked the door while Hetty kept an eye open for Matron.

Helen hit me first. She came at me like a workhorse, snorting and pawing the air with her big yellow fists. Enid landed an experimental blow to my chin to see how I would react. She expected me to burst into tears. The other girls backed into the stalls and stood on the toilet rims, feet apart.

I hoped to come out of it alive, but I did better than that. Inge had taught me some good moves. It was not always better to be bigger. Bigger people expected to win and started showing off. Their concentration became divided. The secret was to throw your fist directly at your opponent's nose

190

or eyes, using all your strength, surprise them, and while they are unbalanced, kick them in the shins. If that didn't stop them, you closed your eyes and let loose with your fists, firing blows like bullets from a machine gun.

"Never give the enemy a chance to recover. It's not important that you land your blows only that you keep swinging." Thanks, Inge!

I was swinging and kicking so furiously that I never even felt the blows that landed on me. All physical sensation disappeared. I was even enjoying myself when Hetty reached in and pulled us apart.

"All right, all right, that's enough!"

Still I did not stop until she boxed my ears so hard I fell to my knees. Hetty then steadied me and looked pleased. She handed me a hanky and told me to wipe my face. There was blood on the hanky. Helen and Enid were also wiping their faces, and there was more blood on their hankies than on mine. They grinned at me while they wiped.

Hetty, too, was smiling. Her green eyes twinkled when she reached forward and dusted me off, straightened my clothes, and told me to keep my head back. The nosebleed would stop by itself.

The onlookers jumped off their perches and also attended to my clothes and hair. While they fussed over me, I felt the first surge of pleasure since coming to England. When we were all clean and tidy again, Hetty handed each of us a dried apricot, and we returned to our chores.

My English lessons with Betty (y not i) began in earnest. Saturday mornings were still the best times to escape Matron's attention, when she was too distracted to hear extra screams. Luckily Betty remembered me and soon caught on to the newer version of the game I had taught her. I took her into the kitchen and the scullery, the hall, the shoe room, the cloakroom, and outside. In the yard we slapped the drains and dustbins, the toilet fixtures, the things in the sandbox. In the kitchen we went through the cupboards, the drawers, the sink parts. I never handed her anything breakable. Our play was accompanied by wild laughter until Alice noticed us and realized what was going on.

"Yur in fert nau," she hissed, grabbing Betty's hand and leading her back to the dining room, but she didn't tell on Betty, and me and I continued the game from a distance. I would hold something up for her to see it, and she would bang her fist down, use the word, and laugh insanely. They couldn't blame me for that, could they? They thought Betty was daft in the head! Betty was cleverer than all the rest of us.

"Oh to be beside the seaside; Oh to be beside the sea!"

We were going to place called "Skaboro." I had not seen it written, but that was how it was pronounced. The word "siiseid" meant nothing to me.

Mrs. Walker had been packing for weeks, filling wicker baskets with linens and blankets, kitchen utensils, and clothes. I was anxious to see if my paring knife was included among the cutlery and got a wink from Hetty to confirm that it was.

191

The hampers were sent ahead. We boarded two buses. Kim, the dog, was the last to be shoved aboard the second one, reluctantly. He had probably been to this "Skaboro" before and wanted to stay home.

The drive was long and pretty, most of it through wild country and much of it the same kind of moorland that surrounded Cookridge.

We arrived in Scarborough (I saw it written on a sign) in the late afternoon. We were going to live in a church hall. Matron made a room for herself on the stage, with curtains drawn. Walker and Hetty got the anteroom and the rest of us were spread about in the large hall. We slept on cots.

There was a complete lack of organization as I had come to know it. The only rule was that we were forbidden to enter the church itself, but could use the toilet off the sanctuary. There was a small kitchen from which we drew water, and instead of a bathroom a folding screen was placed in a corner of the room with a washstand, buckets, and washbowls.

In the morning after the cots were folded away, they were replaced by long refectory tables. After breakfast the tables were folded away, and small groups were readied to go to the "frunt." The hall was going to be locked; we were forbidden to return until noon.

Matron's pets and the little ones would go with her and were clamoring excitedly for her attention. Walker took the spastics. Hetty had her usual hangers-on already whispering and bustling about furtively. "We're going to the 'frunt,'" Hetty repeated, gesturing over their heads, but not asking me to join them. The front of what?

"Nuun," said Mrs. Walker, handing me a silver coin and pointing to her watch, to the number twelve. She pocketed the hall key and walked her girls across the street. Each had a nametag pinned to her collar.

No one had included me. I followed them until they dispersed in different directions and I found myself alone, completely unsupervised, in a strange town, with limited English, no idea where to go or what to do—a thrilling moment! I had not been alone for months. I clutched the coin tightly in my fist. English money! First I had to find this "frunt," which I guessed might mean the front of the sea.

The traffic was driving on the wrong side of the road. I dared not cross, so I remained on the same side until I came to a bridge and an underpass. Hetty, Helen, and Enid were ahead of me. I called out and caught up with them. I could see they had hoped to lose me. Hetty slowed down, but shook her head. "No, not now. Not tudei." She told me firmly. They did not want me with them.

"Where you going?" I asked.

"Geilaland," said Enid.

I had no idea what "geilaland" was.

"Oh, come on," said Hetty annoyed, but aware of my plight. "We'll take you as far as the 'frunt.' Then you're on your own, understand?"

The "frunt" yes. Whatever.

"Come on!" Hetty gave me a push forward.

The underpass went through a garden-like park and came out again at street level. We climbed up the steps, and there was Matron with her little ones at the other side of the road.

192

"Oh-oh!" said Hetty, but she could not turn back quickly enough.

"What are you standing about for?" Matron called over to us.

"Enid's sandal strap broke," Hetty, shouted back at which Enid smartly bent down to her foot.

"Take care of it then," shouted Matron and continued shepherding her flock to a crossing, satisfied that all was well, but how well was it, I wondered. What was going on? If I had been Matron, I would have asked to see the broken strap or would have noticed that Enid was not even wearing sandals. She was wearing plimsolls[24] like me.

We reached a road junction; after a hasty look around, Hetty gave me another push. "See you later," she said, turning me to face the rest of the way alone. "The prom," she pointed to where the road ended with a broad promenade and metal railings. The "frunt!"

The sea was a dark grey strip under a line of black clouds that promised rain. The wind was cold and tangy; a mixture of salt and rotting seaweed, familiar smells from long ago.

I hurried to the railing. The pewter-colored water was ridged with white-caps. Undersides of waves were luminous green before they spread out across the dirty sand. Visibility was limited because of low clouds, but I could see a bristling of masts and a large ship at the end of the pier. About a half dozen donkeys, tied together, stood huddled under a canvas awning. Their owner sat on a deckchair reading a newspaper. I could not tell how much it cost for a donkey ride, and did not have the English to ask.

The few people who were about were heavily bundled into overcoats and holding their coats closed while making short forays to the railing. A few people walked backwards to avoid the stinging spray.

Normally I would have gone down to the beach, but the shops were pulling me towards warmth and an interesting sound like coins falling into metal containers. Was someone throwing money away? The sound was coming from one of the cavernous arcades. I was not familiar with English money, but knew the coin I had was a shilling. I remembered Unki burning a wheelbarrow full of German Marks for the fun of it, but this was real money. Mother and Grandmother counted it carefully to make their hire purchase down payments at Leeds market.

Alice could help me with the money, but she had gone off with her friends. She was avoiding me. I could not blame her. She wanted to enjoy this unexpected freedom without me.

Nobody was swimming. A few children were building sandcastles with small buckets and spades while their parents built themselves shelters out of deck chairs and huddled under them, wrapped in beach towels and sipping hot tea from a thermos bottle. I wondered whether I should spend my shilling on a bucket and spade, but remembered I would not be allowed to keep them.

At an ice cream shop a man was dispensing ice cream "kornets" and some pink fluff on a stick asked each person a question when they came to the counter. I did not want to make a fool of myself by not understanding what

---

[24] Light canvas shoes with rubber soles.

I was being asked, so I parked myself next to the door to listen to the questions and answers. I wanted the ice cream, not the pink fluff.

The first question for ice cream sounded like "Vat flever?"

What was this "flever?" I watched and listened as each person was served, until I had matched the next words to the colors of the ice cream he piled on the cone.

When it was my turn I said, "Isekrim, plis?"

The man looked at me. "Vat flever?" he asked.

Darn it! I could not remember!

"Strobry, venila, or chokolat," the man prompted impatiently.

"Chokolat plis?" Of course! How could I have forgotten chocolate? An unfortunate, but appropriate choice. Eve might have vowed never to eat another apple, but I bet she did.

The man handed me a cone piled so high with chocolate ice cream I dared not take it outside to eat. I had seen the seagulls snatching ice cream cones from people's hands. Instead I sat at one of the small metal tables to marvel at my accomplishment. I had not only bought myself an ice cream, but the man had given me back a handful of pennies. Pennies were the source of the noise around the arcade machines.

While eating the ice cream, I noticed a rack of postcards in the doorway. I thought about Mother and Grandmother. With no writing paper, envelopes, or stamps I had not been able to write to them, but I could send them a postcard. Stamps cost money. I had money, but how to put it all together. I would also need their address. The more I thought about it, the better I liked the idea and hoped Hetty would help me. I looked through the postcards, views of Scarborough, but there was another rack of cards with funny pictures. I picked a card where a girl was sitting sideways, looking at the painter. She looked like me! I bought the card by holding out my palm and letting the woman behind the counter take the right amount of money. It was my second purchase. I tucked the remaining four pennies into my hanky, hoping it would be enough for the stamp and maybe one of the games in the arcade.

There were many amazing things to see so I watched and copied what other people were doing and inserted a penny into the slot under a wax fortuneteller's torso. The penny dropped, lights flashed, music began to play, the gypsy's eyebrows shot up, her eyes rolled, her hands moved around the crystal ball until a small card fell out of the machine onto a tray. I could not read the card, but was going to treasure it until I got back to the hospital. Mother would be surprised to know I had my fortune told by a machine.

I had only three pennies left and was wishing I had more when I again heard the sound of money falling, this time in a steady flow. I followed the sound and saw two of Hetty's girls behind one of the machines. Instead of putting pennies into the front, they were kneeling at the back by a loosened board and were catching money as it fell out. Hetty, Helen, and Enid were not with them. I guessed they were up to no good somewhere else. The sight of free money was troubling and tempting, but I hurried away mindful of my conscience and what was left of it. Since taking the paring knife, I knew how easy it was to be bad.

194

A few minutes later I saw Matron and her favorites coming out of the lifeboat station. They were eating snails, pulling them out of the shell with a pin. I bought a pennyworth. The pin came with them. I poked the pin into my dress for Grandmother who always needed pins. The snails tasted good. They were called winkles.

The tide had gone out when I returned to the prom, or the "frunt." I walked down to the water's edge and put my foot into the foam. The water was freezing cold. Farther along the beach, on rocks exposed by the outgoing tide, several children were poking around with sticks. When they had moved on, I went to see what they had been playing with and discovered pools of small fish and crabs, trapped by the outgoing tide. Feeling sorry for them, I collected as many of the fish and crabs as I could into the hem of my dress and threw them back into the sea. The crabs I handled carefully, holding only the shells between my two first fingers. Because they did not know I was rescuing them, they waved their claws, frantically anxious to hurt me. Nature expected nothing good from human beings. I rescued about fifty small fish and a dozen crabs until my shoes fell apart. Wet and chilled I hurried back to the arcades with a hard knot of seashells tied into the hem of my dress. They clonked against my knees as I ran across the street. A tall clock tower at the end of the promenade warned me that it was nearly noon. I started back to the Church Hall.

In the Valley Gardens underpass I spotted Hetty, Helen, and Enid on a bench, laughing and poring over the contents of a paper bag. I joined them and barely recognized Helen behind the heavy black eyebrows and blood red lipstick she was removing. Enid was even more bizarre with glittery blue eyelids that Hetty was cleaning up with a wet hanky. Seeing me stare, Hetty gave me one of her love pats, a sharp slap on the back of the head. "When you're older," she promised. She did not remark on my being barefoot. That was the whole idea. We were supposed to use up the old shoes. I took the card out of my knickers and showed it to her. "Cad fer Grandmother, wid stamp you by?" I gave her the two pennies.

Hetty took the card and the pennies. When she read the card she put a hand over her mouth as if she was stifling a laugh, but let it go. She understood what I wanted. "Hey up," she said, "not ere. Tonite." She put the card into her handbag. I feared she might forget.

One evening when I was peeling potatoes Hetty came in and handed me a stub of pencil. "Wreit it nau," she said, putting the card on the sink board. She read the address from a slip of paper I was to address it to Mother, Hospital for Women, Koventry Place, Leeds 2. "It's Coventry Place, with a cee," Hetty corrected me, but I had no eraser so we left it. I wrote:

Dear Mimma and Mämmä, please come to see me if you can.
Elin

I was not used to writing in Estonian and had to cross out several more mistakes before I was finished. Hetty slipped the card into her apron pocket and promised to buy a stamp and post it as soon as she went near a post office. The stamp would cost two and a half pennies, she told me. She would make up the difference. I was so thrilled by my new independence that I was ready to write to Inge next, but Mother had said the DP camps had closed. I did not know where Inge was.

That night, lying on my cot next to Alice and almost asleep, I sat up with a jolt. The address Hetty had dictated had not sounded right. What had happened to Ida Hospital and Cookridge? This Women's Hospital was not where I had left them.

The card was posted on the 4 August 1948. Mother and Grandmother got the card and mused over the naughty message under the innocent picture. Sexy seaside postcards with a double entendre were a popular English seaside novelty.

When it rained too hard to go out we stayed in the hall. With a ready stage and auditorium, the hall was an ideal theater. On one such afternoon Matron decided we should all get up on stage and sing. As a reward each girl was given a sweet.

The concert began with the little ones. Matron and Walker sat on stage. Walker had a faraway look, as if she was not really there. The toddlers, including little Bili, had gone somewhere else for the summer. Without the wet clothes, the wet apron, and with her hair in a tight perm, Walker looked like someone's lost poodle, hoping to be claimed by a loved one. It was not going to happen, not to her, not to me.

When a girl called Dorin was pushed on stage, everyone began to hoot and whistle even before she opened her mouth. I guessed she was also tone deaf. She tried to turn back, but Matron reached out and shook her. "Geton witit!" she ordered.

Dorin sounded like the pig I had seen killed in Hausberge. When the squealing stopped, she was mercifully drowned out by raspberries and jeers, given a sweet, and allowed to leave the stage in tears. The same gleeful anticipation was on every face when I was pushed up by Hetty. The "foringel" would give them a real treat, but I stood defiant. I did not know any English songs anyway.

The silence in the hall lengthened. Seconds ticked by. I was frozen into what Mother called my attitude, which had prompted her to slap my face in the past. A few seconds later I heard Matron sigh. She signaled for Hetty to remove me.

As Hetty helped me down she whispered into my ear. "Yu did't hav to sink, ya silly birk, yu kud hev reseited a poem."

My eyes opened wide. She was right! I had missed a unique opportunity to baffle the lot of them by reciting one of Grandfather's poems, in Estonian, or I could have recited the French-German rhyme about the ox and the cow, that Unki had taught me. Until that moment it had not occurred to me that character training had a real purpose.

196

Learning to swim was another of Matron's goals designed to conquer personal failure. She supervised the lessons herself from inside a shelter of four deck chairs and an umbrella.

"Its varmer if you hould yur breth," the girl next to me whispered.

I tried holding my breath, but it did not help.

"Stat svimming!" shouted Matron from the beach. "Doun't chust stend der!"

I braced my whole body and plunged in, surprised that it was warmer under water and definitely better when I relaxed. I crouched down, but not for long.

"Furder out!" ordered Matron from shore.

We waded as far out as we dared, jumping up to avoid each wave before it could break over our heads.

"Nou svim bek!" she instructed.

I had never tried to swim and only had a vague idea of what to do, but hopped along quite nicely, keeping one foot on the bottom.

"No! No! Sho her!" Matron ordered Pauline, the future nurse, to take hold of the back of my bathing suit. She was supposed to float me through the water, but was actually dragging me along the bottom or holding me in the air. I could not tell if she wanted me to swim or fly. Back on shore, with our lips blue and our teeth chattering, we huddled together in a ragged line begging to be allowed out.

Matron looked at her watch. "Not jet."

I never did learn to swim.

Although I was registered at Quarry Mount School on 24 May 1948, I did not actually begin classes until the autumn. Quarry Mount was a small elementary and infants school, not far from the orphanage.

My first day in school was not the nightmare I had expected. Alice took me and introduced me to the headmistress, Miss Moffat. The headmistress in turn took me into a classroom, where everyone was already seated, and introduced me to Mrs. Brown, the teacher. The girls in the class were all about my age and stared at me with curiosity; a few of them giggled when they found out I was foreign, but Mrs. Brown stopped them at once. She made the girl who had led the giggling give up her desk for me and sit with someone else.

After I was seated the class returned to normal. Everyone had a book in front of her, and each girl stood up and read a paragraph. I saw the peril approaching. When it was my turn everyone swiveled around to see what I would do.

"Plis rid vat you kan," said Mrs. Brown kindly. She came over to me, handed me her own book and showed me the paragraph she wanted me to read. "I no you kan rid," she said, nodding encouragement.

She was right. Any idiot could read, but I had already discovered that in English the words were not pronounced the way they were written. I stood up, ready to clench my teeth in the usual attitude, but Mrs. Brown was not like Matron. She had not already judged me and was even leaning forward,

197

willing for me to succeed, ready to help me. The class was so silent I could hear the teacher's breathing and the sound of cars outside on the road.

"This royal throne of kings, this skeptered...."I heard a snort nearby.

"Sceptered," Mrs. Brown, corrected me. She cast an angry glance at the interrupter, and then turned back to me. "Yu dont sound the sii. Yu ar duing veri wel."

Thus encouraged I stumbled along until I came to the word "island." I pronounced "is-land." Now someone did laugh.

Mrs. Brown rapped the desk; putting her hand on my shoulder, she spoke to the class in angry, rapid English. When everyone hushed, she glared down the rows of desks and patted my arm to let me know she was on my side. "Ai-land. Not is-land," she said, but veri gud! Thenk yu. Yu mei sit doun." She took the book back and returned to her desk. I saw the cover briefly and the word "Shakespeare." I did not know if it was the title or the author. I had no idea what I had just read.

After the bell rang everyone rushed for the door, I was forgotten. Mrs. Brown asked me to follow her to another classroom where she handed me to another teacher. From the sums on the blackboard I guessed it was arithmetic class. Easy as mud pie, I thought. I quickly added the numbers up and got a shock. My answers were all wrong. I was supposed to add £3. 7. 8d. to £6. 4. 8d. The answer I got was £9. 12. 6d, but the correct answer, written into the margin was £9. 12. 4d. I added up again, this time carefully. Eight and eight were sixteen, six down, one to carry and so forth, but it was still wrong.

The teacher was young and impatient; she tried to explain in words, and then did the sum over and over, coming up with four pence instead of sixpence. She was saying that eight and eight were fourteen instead of sixteen. Eight and eight had always been sixteen as long as I had lived! "Eit and eit, sixtin," I persisted.

"No, no! Forpense anashilling." She looked exasperated, like Matron with the potato peeler. We were both glad when the lesson ended.

After the tussle with the eight pennies, I was handed to yet another teacher whose name sounded like "Banana." It was an art class. Miss Banana looked a little strange; then I realized she was wearing a wig. Her real hair and wig hair did not quite match. Seeing I was good for only a few English words, she put a pencil and blank sheet of paper in front of me and said "plis dro somsin for us so vi willget tu no yu."

I understood what she wanted and drew a picture of me and Grandmother walking together. It had been a long time since I had drawn on a clean piece of white paper. Miss Banana was surprised by my picture and held it up to the class.

At last I could do something right!

Art became my favorite subject and Banana my favorite teacher, a close second behind Mrs. Brown, who started teaching me to read English during playtime. After the bell rang and everyone went into the playground, she took me to an empty classroom and we read together. She praised me at the end of each session, even when I did badly. I was baffled by the disparity between the written word and its pronunciation that did not happen in Estonian or German. In Estonian especially, what was written down was what you pronounced. It was frustrating not to know ahead how to pronounce anything until I heard it; or if I only heard it, I had to wait to see it written down. For spelling tests I learned each word twice. First the English pronunciation, then the Estonian spelling. The word beautiful or "buutiful" became "be-au-ti-ful" for the written test. The method worked wonderfully, but there were still words I had not heard pronounced. One such word was on a shop sign I passed on my way to school. The word was "Antiques." In my mind it was "an-ti-ku-es." To pronounce it I had to hear it. There was one girl who lived near me, at the bottom of Cliff Road, and I started walking with her. Every time we passed the sign I pointed and said, "Oh, look."

"So what?"

I said, "Look at that sign."

"What about it?" she asked.

Another time she got annoyed. "Do we have to look at that bloody sign every day? What's wrong with it?" Then one day she really got angry. "Not again! I'm not coming by this antik shop anymore!"

I had it! "Antik, antiks!" I repeated and skipped all the way up the road. The girl called me a daft "pilok!"

Mrs. Brown was amazed when I started getting high marks on spelling tests, spelling words correctly that did not even know the meaning of and had only seen written down once.

One evening when I was struggling over my arithmetic homework, still getting it all wrong, Hetty came and stood behind me. She shook her head and sat down next to me

"Pei atenshun," she said, pulling her chair closer. I was not sure what was going to happen, because Hetty could also be very nasty if she wanted to.

"Thiis ar penies," she spread a pile of church collection pennies onto the kitchen table. She counted out eight pennies and placed them in a pile. "Sii eit penies?"

I could see. Eight pennies.

She counted out another eight pennies and built a second pile. Sixteen pennies in all. Eight and eight are sixteen. I knew that, but Hetty shook her head and took away twelve pennies from the sixteen, leaving four on the table. She then rummaged in her purse and produced a silver shilling piece. She put the shilling coin on the table with the twelve pennies. "Tvelv penies, vun shilling." She swept the four pennies to one side and wrote on my homework page, "8 + 8 = 16 = 1 shilling and 4 pence."

"Vat du yu sii?" she asked smiling.

What I saw was another mystery solved. I had a shilling in Scarborough, but had been too excited to count the change. Twelve pennies, one shilling. Twenty shillings in one pound.

Having conquered most English names from writing to sound and vice versa, there was still one name that left me shaking my head. There was a girl in my class everyone called "Fibi." I thought it began with an F. When I finally saw the name written on her composition book, I saw that it began with a P. "Fibi" was "Phoebe" or "Fo-eh-bi!"

Christmas was approaching. One Friday afternoon, having dawdled as long as I dared on my way home from school, I barely got inside the door when Hetty grabbed my arm and pulled me upstairs to change my clothes. The other girls were already in their Sunday best, "ironing" their hair ribbons on the hot water pipes and talking excitedly about a "parti."

We were divided into three groups and taken by bus into the city center. The word "parti" was never explained, but everyone was excited; so I believed it would be something good.

We were taken to a big building, which turned out to be the offices of the *Yorkshire Evening Post* newspaper. Mr. Boller used to read the *Yorkshire Evening Post* every night before going to bed.

Men and women in colorful paper hats lined the entrance hall to greet us and take us into a hall decorated with paper chains and balloons. At the far end long tables had been set up, laden with food. In one corner stood a tall-decorated Christmas tree. A gramophone was playing Grandmother's favorite Christmas carol, "Lo, How a Rose E'er Blooming." I wished Grandmother could be with me. So much was happening to me that I could no longer share with her.

Elin at Headingley Orphanage, Leeds, 1948.

Just as I was taking note of everything from the doorway a photographer let off a flashbulb in my face. It stunned me. I thought he had shot me. There was no pain, but I was blinded. Unable to move forward or turn back I felt someone put a paper hat on my head and tie a balloon to my left wrist. The hat was too big and fell over my eyes, bringing some relief from the dazzling blindness. Before I could adjust to it, someone else placed a bowl of something into my right hand. With my left hand hampered by the balloon string and my right one holding the bowl, I could not move either hand, but could see a part of the bowl from under the rim of the hat. Red jelly was sliding towards the floor. Just then another flashbulb went off in my face. Blinded once more, I heard my name called over the loudspeaker. I knew from the DP camps that the only reason for being called on a public address system was because there was an emergency. The only emergency I could think of would have to do with Grandmother. Letting the jelly slide away with a *plop*, I got ready to panic when Hetty's face appeared under the hat rim, along with the face of a jolly man in shirtsleeves. Both were grinning like idiots, thinking I looked funny. Hetty pushed my hat back and told me I had failed to find my "friend" for the evening. I had not known to look for one.

200

The man with Hetty was fat and friendly, with grey bushy eyebrows and tufts of hair growing out of his ears. He smelled of cigarettes. "Call me Fred," he said, pointing to a label on his shirt with FRED written on it.

Fred soon found out that he was dealing with a foreigner and told me he had been to Moscow. When he saw that my dish was empty, he took me to the food table. He ladled in more jelly, but it slipped off immediately, down my dress and onto the floor. I looked around in horror, but everybody else's clothes were even more stained than mine were. "Never mind," said Fred, cleaning off the thicker gunk with a corner of the tablecloth and filling my dish once more with jelly. This was fun! There was also a big bowl of custard, another of ice cream, and plates piled with buns. Small squares were fish-paste sandwiches and the drink was lemonade.

The jelly, when I finally tamed it, turned out to be the best. It tasted of strawberries. I ladled myself a combination of jelly, custard, and ice cream, but Fred showed me that had already been done for us in another bowl called a "treifel." Except for constantly using the Russian words *da* and *nyet*, Fred did his duty and even took me across the hall to the newsroom. I had heard typing and had noticed an open door and wanted to see the typewriters. Fascinated by clattering machines, ringing telephone bells, busy voices, and thick cigarette smoke hanging over every desk, I wanted to stay longer. By now I had ascertained that the word "parti" meant enjoying yourself mind-lessly and without restriction.

Fred sweated and performed his tasks with gusto. He attended to my every whim and took better care of me than any cavalier; an international word I had no problem understanding. When I did not know which way to turn in the ring-games, he was right there to turn me, guide me, and lift me over the benches when the paper hat was again over my eyes. Stupid hat! I was truly grateful to my friend and tried to imagine him as a house owner with a wife and family, washing dishes and changing diapers, as Mother's friends had boasted about Englishmen. I wondered if he also owned a refrig-erator.

I had never in my life eaten so much; after the fish paste, I began to feel sick so as not to throw up in the middle of musical chairs, I crawled under one of the tables. Shielded by the long white tablecloth, I upchucked. It was a relief to discover that I was not the first. Someone else had vomited there before me.

One good thing about vomiting: once you were empty you could start over. Fred had lost me for a while, but now I knew to look for him. We celebrated our reunion with a bowl of "treifel." His entire front was covered with jelly and custard, as was mine. We sat together on the floor. Finally he noticed that my hat was too big for me. We exchanged hats. I hoped I had not looked as stupid in his hat as he looked in mine.

There were also female friends for the smaller children. Matron walked around with the photographers, snapping pictures of her favor-ites before Santa Claus arrived.

Santa Claus was a new experience for me. He was dressed in red pajamas and carried a big post office mailbag. "Ho-ho-ho!" he boomed and explained that he had come to Leeds early because he had such a big world to get through before Christmas Day. "Ho-ho-ho!" He used short sentences and short words.

For the sake of the little ones, we pretended that we believed he was not just another man in badly fitting red pajamas. This man represented Saint Nicholas, whom I had heard about. Like the "viiker" he was another of God's representatives. I had come to accept that the robes, false beards, pajamas, rubber boots were all man could provide in the way of divinity in the absence of St. Nicholas, Christ, or Kristus. I did not expect miracles, but then a miracle did happen. I was called to the tree to receive a Christmas present. It was from Fred. The miracle was that he would give me anything at all. We were strangers. This time I was more than ready to recite my French/German verse, but the English Santa did not require a rhyme. I took my present to a corner of the room and unwrapped it in private. It was a mouth organ!

The evening ended with everyone escorting us out to the bus, singing "Nau is the our, ven ve must sey good bei."

"Sun eil bi seiling
Fer ekross de sii ...
Then something, something "rimember me."

I would never forget!

The next day our photos were in the newspaper. "Headingley Orphans at Yorkshire Evening Post Party." I did not expect to see Fred ever again, but would always remember him as my first adult "kavaler," the Estonian word for boyfriend.

I hid the harmonica in my knicker leg, and the next time I went to school I buried it under the roots of an oak tree in a small park at the end of Cliff Road. I marked the tree in case it moved, but of course trees never move. Little did I know.

One morning, when I was not yet fully awake, I felt something cold tickling my nose. I put my tongue out and jumped up in bed. "Snow!" Glorious snow! It was snowing heavily. The garden, the road, the bushes were all covered with a white bed sheet. I dressed hurriedly. Hetty came and closed the window. There was no water in the bathroom because the pipes had frozen. From the kitchen arose a smell of scorched milk and burnt "porridj." Kim lay growling, steaming and stinking resentfully on the dining-room fireside rug. Someone had forced him outside to do his business. When Matron came into the room I discovered that wet dogs and English tweeds smelled the same.

"No school today." Matron hoisted her skirt towards the fireplace and heated her rump. The backs of her legs were already mottled. When she saw me pressing my nose against the window, she gave a tight smile. Alice followed it with a withering glance reserved for little ones when they got overly excited. I wanted to go out, but had to remain satisfied with seeing the snow through the frosted dining room window, and also through the memory of a cat's measured paw prints walking out of my life. The snowbank I was looking

202

at was marked by a set of dog prints and a yellow stain where Kim had lifted his leg.

The snow melted as suddenly as it had appeared.

English life continued; I never knew what to expect. One afternoon we went by private bus to a "pantomime." It was already dark, and streets were lit by gas lamps. On the main road workmen had begun erecting long poles and electric streetlights that hummed, buzzed, and turned your face green or orange. It being near Christmas, colored lights had been strung between the poles. The wind and rain made the lights swing violently from side to side; making it look like an ocean liner was sailing up the road with its cabin lights on.

Other changes were also taking place around Leeds. Apparently peacetime was going to last a while. Shops that had been boarded up were repainted. Some had already opened for business. Windows that had only displayed National Dried Milk Powder and Ministry of Food tins, had built pyramids of colorful boxes and packets that appeared to contain edibles. I had no idea what tins and boxes contained. I knew very little about shops. One display I did recognize from my time with the Bollers was a stack of Cadbury's cocoa tins. I was beginning to see chocolate everywhere. There were long queues outside the shops and the pavements were crowded.

When the bus stopped, I followed Alice as usual, with no idea where we were going until we arrived at a theater. This auditorium was bigger and starker than any theater I had ever seen. The steps and seats were made of concrete. The rows were so narrow that you had to place your feet sideways to reach your seat. We were led to the top rows, under a steel-girdered ceiling. I guessed that instead of a theater we were in some kind of sports facility.

This "pantomime," Alice explained, was a famous English Christmas tradition. She told me the leading lady was a man, the leading man was a woman, and the main character was a dog. I did not know whether to expect a comedy or a tragedy.

The auditorium was cavernous and the noise deafening. It reminded me of railway stations where thousands of starlings nested under the domed glass roof girders in Berlin, in London, and in Leeds.

The seats filled up around us with children in the different uniforms of the many other orphanages around Leeds. Some were familiar from the Christmas party. Matron sat on the end of the row. When we were all seated and before we could become overly restless, the lights dimmed and the curtain rose. A woman, dressed as a man, pranced onto the stage in a tight embroidered vest and short pants. A man, dressed as a woman, came out of the house with a laundry basket. He/she bent over the basket and began to hang sheets on a clothesline. Then a small dog dressed in a red velvet jacket with a white ruffled collar, jumped out of the basket and sank its teeth into her/his behind. The dog dragged her/him offstage by the knickers. Everybody laughed and clapped. Alice bent forward to show me that I should applaud, which I did.

I wanted to please Alice for different reasons, and one of them was that I recognized her decency. It surrounded her like a closed fence. Even Hetty respected the boundary of her solid, but solitary competence within which she moved. It kept people from teasing her and resenting her for being Matron's pet, but nobody wanted to change places with her. I wondered whether that was because her father was dying or because they recognized that wanting Matron to love her was going to cause her another death in the family when she turned fifteen. I hoped we could be friends but feared it could not happen while I was her first failing. What really drew me to her was that I saw a terrible deep emptiness under her perfect poise, as if her entire insides had been scooped out to remove all impurities and her insides rattled like the filament in a spent light bulb.

Because Alice was on duty that evening she continued to explain what was happening on the stage. The washerwoman (man) had a beautiful daughter who was not allowed farther from the house than the washing line and back. The washerwoman forced her to work from sunup to sundown (as in hospitals) with no holidays and no tea breaks. One day a handsome young man (actually the woman with the big hips and fat thighs) was passing the garden fence. When he/she saw the girl at the washing line, she/he fell in love with her/him and he/she fell in love with him/her as well. It was then revealed that the young man was a handsome prince and the girl a beautiful princess who had been kidnapped by the washerwoman/washerman. All this was set to lively music, singing, and dancing. It was too bad that the prince could not close the front of his/her vest over his/her large bosoms and that the princess cavorted around the stage like a rugby player in high heels and worse, the prince was prettier than the princess. In the end nobody knew who was who, not even the dog. The pantomime ended with a gunshot, which woke everybody up.

The audience clapped wildly, cheered, and whistled appreciation. I joined in without a clue as to what had happened, but it did go through my mind that if women could become husbands it would certainly solve the shortage of men. Single women could then marry each other and immigrate to Canada.

After the curtain came down and the houselights came on, we could still smell smoke from the gunshot. In a moment of dizziness we teetered on the edge of the steep upper balcony. Our orphanage had been sitting in front of a government orphanage. They had been poking, shoving, and swatting at us with their programs throughout the show. Now that the lights were on, we could see each other clearly, and the fighting began in earnest. I felt someone behind me yank my braids and then tie them into a knot. Alice's hat was sent flying down into the stalls. Scuffles broke out on every row between the orphanages, first with programs, then with fists, hats, or whatever came to hand.

Teachers and matrons with each group blew whistles calling for order, but they were powerless against the surge of whoops and screams of delight. The gunshot had roused everybody, and the response was to break free of the constant discipline, the endless restraint and regimentation.

The teachers were outnumbered. Shoved from all sides, I, too, became part of the tidal wave of screaming, a heated lava that surged down from the balcony into the stalls and out into the street. It was a river of all-consuming anarchy, a jumble of hats and gymslips, children screaming mindlessly, oblivious of whistles and orders. I recognized the children from Dr. Barnardos by their uniforms. I recognized the kids from Street Lane. Our boys were fighting their boys, shirts rumpled, blazers askew, and socks down by the ankles. It was wonderful!

However, the excitement was short-lived. As we surged through the outside doors into the street, we were immediately met by a barrier of ushers and staff who separated us by uniforms, corralled us into groups, and led us back to our respective buses. Our uniform was the navy blue gabardine coat. I was distracted, but not enough to miss seeing that it had started to snow again.

Matron stood at the front of the bus and called the evening a disgrace. "Straight to bed! No cocoa!" she shouted, revealing that there might have been a cup of cocoa planned for the end of the evening.

On the way home the bus passed the Civic Hall where we had lined up to admire Princess Elizabeth's wedding dress. The English princess had married Prince Philip the previous year, and now her wedding gown was touring the country. Still trying to make sense of the pantomime, I was glad the real English princess, Elizabeth, had married a real prince and not a woman in disguise. I hoped Prince Philip was a real man. According to Mother's friends it was as difficult to find a real prince as it was to find a hard-working husband.

It was snowing heavily when the bus drew up at the orphanage gate. We were pushing and shoving to get off, when suddenly Hetty screamed and ran ahead to the covered vestibule. She picked up a basket and held it up, revealing the edges of a blue blanket. The words "baby" swept down the aisle of the bus, even to me, who had not yet left my seat. A baby? I was shocked. Blue meant it was a boy.

"Its baby Jesus," one of the little ones shouted, jumping up and down and clapping her hands in delight.

We all got off the bus quickly and stood around the front door while Matron, Hetty, and Walker fussed over the basket. Hetty opened the front door, and Walker was sent to telephone the police.

It was almost Christmas. Could the baby be the Savior? I still believed in miracles, in Jesus Himself, despite Him becoming the angry God who berated us every Sunday—if it were truly He! Hetty came back outside a few minutes later, joined by Enid and some of the big girls from her kitchen group. I watched them draw towards the side of the house and begin to whisper with agitated hushes and glances across their shoulders at Matron's sitting room window. Every time they whispered like that, I knew something else was happening, other than the obvious. Hetty's group must somehow be involved in this miracle or trouble. I wanted to join the girls in the shadows, but I was only days away from being allowed to see Mother and Grandmother, so I went into the house.

In her sitting room Matron was telling the little ones her version of what had happened. I joined the back of the crowd and heard her say it really was Jesus; "come for a brief visit."

"He will have to go home again shortly," she warned us. It meant He could not stay. Home was where? With my other ear I heard Hetty tiptoe across the tiled hall towards the kitchen; I decided to follow. Thus I heard the words "Megan" and "shame." Hetty slipped out of the back door. I remembered the girl who had left abruptly without ceremony and with a rude gesture.

That "dontkumbak" still rang in my ears; I wondered if the baby had anything to do with Megan. Maybe she had gone to have a baby and was hiding in the outside toilets, worried that her newborn would not be found and fed quickly enough. It made sense. If you had nowhere to go, nowhere to put your things, especially a baby, the sensible thing was to leave it on a familiar doorstep with people you knew.

Two police cars arrived, sirens blaring. An ambulance followed, lights blazing, bells clanging. Police and men in white rushed into the house and into the sitting room. Matron was holding the baby in her arms, cuddling him and making mothering noises. I was surprised at how tenderly she treated children who did not have flaws. I guessed she had always yearned to hold an angel. Her wish had come true.

The baby was taken away.

Newspaper headlines the next day informed Leeds that a Christmas miracle had been left on the steps of Headingley Orphanage. A picture showed Matron cooing over the baby, which they called a foundling.

It was hard to fall asleep that night. The foundling was now lying in a government cot. If it had been Jesus, someone would be changing God's diapers and wouldn't even know it. Grandmother told me it was just as well He had not come back, because the world would crucify Him all over again. Thus it was better to believe in Megan's shame than to have to rewrite the Bible. There would be total chaos if Jesus were suddenly to turn up at the Civic Hall and say, "Here I am!" No more Christmas, no more Easter. Churches would shut down. Vicars and pastors would be out of work, and thousands would be stewing in their own juices, as Grandmother had put it.

On the other hand, Hetty had been conveniently placed and awfully active behind the scenes. I wondered whether Hetty had not somehow engineered the entire miracle as a favor to one of her own, the way she had covered for my broken tooth. I was still confused about religion; it certainly seemed to be the cause for people to be constantly fleeing from one war to another. With all that new information pouring over me in Bible study I had come to think that no one really knew the truth about anything on this planet, until they were dead.

"Get up," said Alice, shaking me. I opened my eyes; it was still dark.

"Don't you want to know what Santa has brought you?"

"Senta Klaus?" I thought that was last night.

"It's Christmas Day. Don't they have Christmas where you came from?"

"Kristmas, yes."

206

"So get up!"

Pushed from behind I joined the surge down the stairs into the playroom. A large Christmas tree stood in the middle of the room, surrounded by presents. The tree decorations were the kind I remembered from Estonia: silk angels, colored glass balls, silver tinsel, but no candles. It was Christmas Day. I had missed Christmas Eve without anyone even mentioning it.

Matron, Hetty, and Walker, in their dressing gowns, sat on chairs along the wall, yawning and watching us. Matron had her hair in a long braid that reached her waist. Presents passed from hand to hand. "This is for you," and "Here's yours." Alice handed me a small box wrapped in colored paper with colored string around it. I untied the string and removed the paper carefully. I had never had such a neatly wrapped present before or such nice paper or string. The little box contained two hair slides. Who to thank? Alice pointed to Matron. I went to Matron and said, "Thenk yu!" I remembered not to curtsy.

"Don't thenk me. Thenk Senta Klaus," she replied and pursed her lips in a half smile. I remembered lining up with everyone else to shout up the chimney and tell Senta what I wanted for Christmas. I had felt pretty stupid doing it, but had called up "bali slippers" just in case someone was listening. Matron had smiled and said: "yul get a bali supraise!" And this was it.

Chapter 12

THREE WHITE DOVES (OR THREE PIGEONS)
1949 - 1950

The New Year, 1949, started cold and grim. Rain pelted the window above my bed with droplets straying to my pillow, but I did not notice the cold or the rain. I was awake already. I had been awake for ages, even before Hetty came in with my clothes.

"Happy New Year!" she said, then bent down and whispered, "Starting all right then?" She winked to let me know she was happy for me. I was going to the hospital to visit Mother and Grandmother—at last!

Mother arrived to collect me after breakfast. I was excused from washing up. Walker fussed with my hair and got my Wellingtons[25] while Mother stood in the hall and watched. There had been no time for her to hug or kiss me, because Matron was to see us off. When I was ready Matron held the door open, and before she closed it again she put a bony hand on my arm.

"Now remember, no foreign foods." I remembered.

Mother held her umbrella over us. I could see something was bothering her. When we were seated in the taxi and on our way she asked, "What was that about foreign foods? What did she mean?"

"Oh, Polish sausages, things we usually eat." Seeing trouble ahead, I tried to make light of it. Mother's jaw had acquired that rigid look. She stared out the window, trying to find the right words that would not spoil our reunion, but at the same time get what she needed to say off her chest. The taxi had not turned right at the end of Cliff Road, I noticed. I wondered where we were going. Obviously not to Ida Hospital.

Mother took a deep breath.

"I'm very proud of you," she began. "It has not been easy, but you've come through. I knew you would. You're a strong girl. I commend you for that, but I want you to remain strong because I'm going to tell you something important that you're not going to like. It's about foreign foods, as the woman put it. Your grandmother has been waiting for almost a year to have you home and has prepared for your homecoming in the way she always does, with food. That means Polish sausage, rye bread, salt herring, and many of our favorite foods, which we can now buy from the Polish delicatessen. She has collected them especially for you, and I won't have you break her heart by not eating. Do you understand what I'm saying?"

I always understood what she was saying and would never break Grandmother's heart. She did not have to tell me that. I would eat everything.

---

[25] Rubber boots.

"And I don't want you to tell her what you've been through these last months. It would upset her."

I stared at Mother in horror. I had waited eight months to tell Mämmä what a terrible time I had had since I last saw her. I had stored it all up and could not wait to sit down with her and complain about the punishments, the unfairness, and the terrible church services. I had always confided in Grandmother and was even going to confess to using the paring knife, although I had a feeling that Matron already knew about it and didn't care.

"It isn't fair," was all I could think of to say.

"Life's not fair, my little love," said mother sadly.

"I thought you said I was to become English?"

"Not that English," she retorted and began lighting a cigarette, drawing on the smoke as she always did to help her think. She sounded strong, but did not look well. Her hands were bone thin and her knuckles red-raw around the old amber cigarette holder.

"I can see you're upset, but there's something you need to know," she continued. "Your grandmother's asthma is worse. These last months of worrying about you, not knowing what is happening to you, have worn her out. Your postcard was well meant, but what you wrote did not help. You knew we could not come to see you."

"I didn't think. I'm sorry. So what am I going to be able to talk about if I can't talk about myself?" I asked, lowering my voice because the taxi driver was watching us through the rearview mirror.

Mother gave a quirky smile. "You'll find something." She stubbed the cigarette in the ashtray. "Now we understand each other, don't we?" She patted my hand.

"Can't I tell her that one of the girls broke my front tooth? She hit me with the platter."

"I noticed the tooth. And no."

"She'll ask about it," I persisted stubbornly. Our first day together was already withering on the vine.

Mother adjusted her glasses and turned to me directly. "If Mämmä asks you what happened to your tooth, tell her you fell."

"But it would be a lie."

"Better than letting her know you are fighting. I don't even want to think about it. No." She shook her head. "Even I don't want to hear about it." Mother put her head into her hands.

"It's all right," I touched her arm. "I won't tell her anything. All right?"

"It's not all right, but for now it will have to do. There are more important things at stake, like your Estonian. You've developed an accent. Oh, God!" Mother gave a loud groan. This time the taxi driver did look at us and started to slow down.

Mother waved him on and sat up straight. "I have a headache." She adjusted her posture. "We're almost there."

It was not until then that I noticed where we were. We had only skirted Hyde Park. The taxi stopped outside a small square building with a weathered wooden sign by the gate: LEEDS HOSPITAL FOR WOMEN. This was the

216

same address I had written on my postcard from Scarborough. I had not known they had moved.

Their room was on the top floor again, about the same size as the one at Ida. Grandmother was standing in the open doorway. Never mind being English! I rushed forward and she caught me to her chest. We fell back upon the bed. My first impression was that I had become taller and she smaller. My Englishness melted away as fast as English snow. The months of trying to make sense of senseless situations were no longer important. I was home again and so overwhelmed by relief that I burst into tears despite Mother's look of alarm.

Grandmother's eyes were bright and watery, as she looked me over, inspecting me for changes. "Your hair is cold. Don't you have a hat or scarf?" she asked.

"We came by taxi," I explained.

Seating me on the bed, she began to pull off my boots and immediately noticed the thin ankle socks. "Don't they know there's still slush on the roads? Why are you not wearing the warm stockings I sent you?"

The stockings! Matron had forced me to wear them as punishment, part of the ridicule therapy, to make me ashamed of being foreign. English children did not wear long stockings. I made sure to have big holes in them before very long, holes too big to mend so that I could discard them.

I did not reply, and Grandmother had already moved on. Truly dismayed now, she fingered the wet hem of my coat before hanging it over the back of the chair.

"What happened to the camel coat we bought you?"

"It became too short for me," I replied quickly.

"If you had brought it with you, I would have let out the hem."

I made a regrettable noise and could see why Mother had warned me. We were getting into dangerous waters. Grandmother was my rock, but I was slipping into the undertow of her obvious concerns.

"And you've lost a lot of weight. Are they feeding you properly? You need to eat more oatmeal. Thank God we can feed you again." With those words she went over to the wardrobe and began to rummage among the tins and packages piled into the back.

"We now have rye bread, and *rollmops* (pickled herring in a roll). I made some *rosolje* (Estonian beet salad). Our Estonian friends gave us a small blood sausage for Christmas. You must be hungry." She looked up suddenly and just missed the despairing glance I had thrown at Mother.

"Elin speaks very good English now," said Mother quickly. "She's at the top of her class in art, spelling, and composition. Aren't you?" she prompted me.

Art yes, composition not really, but I was getting ten for spelling by using my Estonian pronunciation method.

"Art is my favorite. We have real art paper and paints. I drew a vase of daffodils for the headmistress, for her birthday, and composed a poem to go with it. It was Banana's idea."

"You did?" Grandmother straightened up, holding several packages in her hand. She did not ask who Banana was. "What was the poem about?"

"Daffodils." I said the word in English. I did not know the Estonian.

She frowned. "Daffodils?" she repeated.

Mother rolled her eyes to the ceiling and started lighting another ciga-rette. We were so anxious for everything to go right that we were like actors in a play. My part was to keep the mood light, like a balloon that could burst if it hit something sharp.

"Let me recite the poem for you," I offered. "I am a little daffodil," I began. "You know those yellow flowers?" Grandmother did not know.

"*Kullerkupud*?" she asked (Globeflowers.)

"No, not *kullerkupud*."

"Dandelions?" Grandmother guessed again.

"No, not dandelions." I looked to Mother, but she could not help either. She knew daffodils, but not in Estonian.[26]

"So go on," Mother urged me.

"I live upon the windowsill ..." I continued, but Grandmother looked puz-zled again. She probably knew window, but not sill.

"Here, let me write it all down so you can use your English dictionary," I suggested. I wrote the poem into her lined notebook, which she used to practice English words:

I am a little daffodil,
I live upon the windowsill.
I cannot walk, I cannot run,
The only friend I have's the sun.
I watch the children as they play,
And think so many times a day,
If I could speak, then I would say,
I wish you'd let me come and play.

After I had finished I realized it was the stupidest poem anybody could ever have written. Repeating the words over and over, made it even stupider. There was such a large lump in my throat I thought I would choke. The im-pulse to tear up the poem and run out of the room was overwhelming, but where would I run? If Mämmä did not know what I was talking about, then nobody did, and nobody knew me anymore. Except Mother, who was shaking her head behind Grandmother's back.

Grandmother had begun buttering a slice of rye bread by the sink. Una-ble to stand the tension another minute, I grabbed her around the middle in a bear hug, giving her time to put the knife down, and twirled her around and around the room, the way she used to hug me when she could still lift me. The room was too small for my outburst of emotion; I began to sob uncontrollably. I had not dared to weep for so long that it was like a river bursting the banks. Mother moved forward, truly alarmed now, but Grand-mother continued to hold me. "There. There." She let me cry, then took my hands and kissed them. I could not explain why I was crying and I kept saying, "I'm sorry, I'm sorry!" I knew only that my world had ended because I had

---

[26] *Kollane nartsiss.*

218

done everything wrong from the day we arrived in England, and there was no going back.

Mother got off her bed and reached under it for the gramophone. I could see it out of the corner of my eye. She cranked it up and quickly grabbed a record to change the mood. I remembered how in Haapsalu she would get up and go to the piano to play some Chopin after a heated discussion about Father. Instead of soothing music, however, a terrible screeching filled the room. I recognized that, too.

"That damned *Largo* again," said Mother, snatching back the needle and the record. She chose another one. Beethoven's *Moonlight Sonata*. Grandmother wiped my face with a corner of her cardigan. The noise had done its job and dried my tears.

The Beethoven skipped. "Scratched," said mother in disgust. "One of these days we'll have something that isn't damaged." She returned to sit on her bed and let the music hobble along as best it could. I slid to the floor at Grandmother's feet. The lump in my throat had turned into hiccups.

"Why does everything we own have to be broken?" I asked.

"Because we can't afford anything that is whole," sighed Mother.

Grandmother returned to her buttering. "We have each other," she pointed out. "We have not broken." She turned her head and looked down at me with a smile that was for me only.

I was broken I wanted to shout! I was so broken that I did not know what piece belonged where.

Suddenly, there was loud banging on the wall. Mother leaped up and lifted the needle. "Oops! I forgot. Velda's on nightshift." She made a comical face and put her finger to her lips. "If Velda thinks this is bad, wait until I get my Verdi and Puccini." She pushed the gramophone back under the bed.

With a towel spread over the blanket, we began to eat. There were *rollmops*, different kinds of European sausages, and *rosolje* made with salt herring, beets, gherkins, cooked potatoes and sour cream. There were German *Pfefferkuchen* (ginger biscuits) and a piece of cold blood sausage with cold sauerkraut, left over from Christmas. I ate everything under Mother's watchful and approving eye.

Finally Grandmother mentioned my broken tooth. "What happened?"

"I fell," I lied and felt terrible for lying.

She accepted the lie. I hoped it would be the last lie, but feared it would not be so. She had not yet noticed that I was missing my watch. What if she asked me if I were enjoying the coloring pencils and presents she must have sent me for Christmas, the ones I never got.

"So, tell me what have you been doing since we last saw you?" Grandmother asked. "I thought about you all the time, wondering what is my Mussa doing. I knew the day would come when she would be back with us, sharing her adventures." Grandmother looked at me expectantly, her mouth full.

In the DP camp, under the Christmas tree, Grandmother had told me stories that I suspected had not been true. She said Father had missed the last train from Tallinn to Haapsalu or he would have come with us. Uncle Richard had not known we were leaving. I had not known Father had a brother. With Mother's eyes upon me, I began a story of my own that I hoped would please Grandmother.

"I've been learning about English life," I told her. "It's not what we thought it would be, and it's not what we see here. Real English life is like having two picture books, one in black and white, and the other in color. We are in the black and white one."

"More like a dirty grey," added Mother with disdain, lighting a new cigarette with three flicks of her match. I knew I was doing well.

"What's in the colored book?" asked Grandmother, catching the mood.

"We're not supposed to know that. It's a secret, but I'm finding out slowly, bit by bit. We'll be in the colored book one day," I finished.

"When pigs fly," said Mother, but she laughed. She was kidding. "You should hear Mussa speaking English already, better than me." She beamed with approval. "Our next job is to restore her Estonian." Then to me she said, "When you come next Sunday we'll start reading, writing, and grammar."

"Uhuh," I replied, trying not to make it sound like a groan. I had been looking forward to playing Black Peter with Grandmother, sketching, and taking long walks again. The hospital was close to the city center and the Town Hall. The Civic Hall was just down the road.

"And Mussa can teach me English," Grandmother added, giving me a wink. She was still the only person in the world who could read my mind.

Suddenly Mother slapped her forehead and jumped up again. "I almost forgot! We heard from Alma."

At the mention of her sister Grandmother also jumped off the bed and opened her bedside drawer.

"I have the postcard right here. It arrived in August, but was written in June. It was sent to Ida. We are lucky to get it at all." Grandmother put her glasses on and sat back on the bed. The postcard was brown, torn and stained with several addresses on it, most of them crossed out. At the very top it said "England," then "Try the Women's Hospital" with "Ida Hospital, Cookridge," scribbled over.

Grandmother touched the card to her lips. "You do remember your Aunt Alma, don't you?"

"Tätä, of course!"

"Here, let me read it to you." Grandmother pushed her glasses higher on her nose and began to read.

Dear sister!
I was overwhelmed by happiness when I received your letter. I have been very worried about you. It is good to know you are all safe and well. Despite some changes I am living as before. I was ill last winter, but am better now. The house is holding up, but I can no longer tend the garden. I have rented out two rooms and my income is still from piano lessons. They let me keep the piano. I pray we will see each other again someday. Please write again.
From the heart, your sister,

220

Alma Saul's postcard, 1948.

Grandmother wiped a tear.

Mother said she had also written to Father, but had not yet received a reply. Her glasses glinted while she blew her nose. "Estonia will always be our home. When we go back, all this will have been a terrible nightmare."

I did not know what to say. The reunion with Mother and Grandmother had pointed out several upsetting things. First, my relationship with Grandmother was no longer the way it had been. Mother would not allow it. I could see she was right. I had become separated from them, like a piece of ice broken off the main berg, the current moving me away from them. I had felt the separation keenly while trying to translate my English poem into Estonian. Aunt Alma's card also illustrated clearly that they were on a different course, still looking to Estonia while I was moving on. A crack was opening between us, ready to become a gap. I decided then and there that it would not happen. It must not happen! There would be no broken hearts, only disappointment for those people who had no heart to break.

"You don't look happy," said Mother.

"I am, I am!" I took a large bite of kielbasa so my mouth would be full and not twist in the involuntary grimace that precedes tears. Munching on pungent sausage and licking my fingers, I was aware of the strong odor of garlic. Matron would notice it as soon as I walked in the door. English people did not smell of garlic. Only foreigners smelled of garlic.

When it was time to return to the Home, Mother and Grandmother walked me to the bus stop, just a few yards from the hospital gate. The street lamps outside the hospital were still the gas type, half of them broken. Springfield Place was the main road, a steep hill to the top of Mount Pleasant and Hyde Park. We now lived so close to each other that I could have walked the distance. So why could they not visit me? Mother stood behind us, sheltering us against the wind, assuming the bomb shelter formation of the past. It had been a wonderful reunion in some ways, but terrible in others. Grandmother was too quiet. She sensed that I had lied to her for the first time in my life, and she was troubled by it. As was I. I wanted to tell her not to worry, I was still me, but that was not true either. Changes in the past eight months had gone beyond my growing taller. Actually, I felt I had grown smaller.

We were glad when the bus appeared. It was a request stop. While the bus slowed down, Grandmother pressed a two-shilling piece into my palm. "Buy yourself something you want," she whispered, blinking back tears. "*Bientôt!*"

"Keep your chin up," said Mother, giving me a quick hug and peck. "See you next Sunday."

And so it began. Games, secrets, lies. Sometimes complete dishonesty, as I tried to juggle the two worlds I inhabited, to keep one from crushing the other. The real dishonesty began with the money Grandmother had given me. The value of money in peacetime was not for the fun of seeing it burn, but for buying what one could not get otherwise. After I got off the bus I went into the newsagent and changed the silver florin for sixpences, then dealt with them the way a banker would.

I squatted by the same tree roots under which I had hidden my harmonica. I put two sixpences into an old tin that already contained other treasures. There were the harmonica, my champion conker—a tough chestnut on a string with which I won sweets in schoolyard tournaments, and a bit of candle and matches, because Grandmother had taught me the importance of having a candle and matches handy for dark days. There were also a skein of string and a champion marble. I closed the tin and buried it again. Any passersby who saw me digging around the tree would simply dismiss me as another of the Headingley orphans goofing off.

It was my intention to save enough money to buy presents next Christmas. For Mother, a small calendar on which she could mark every day off with a cross. For Grandmother an embroidered handkerchief to wipe tears at Estonian gatherings, during the singing of the national anthem. (A small group of Estonians had started meeting once a month in a church hall.) One sixpence I slipped into my shoe and the other I tied into the hem of my dress. That sixpence would go into Matron's Black Book, a bank account which she kept for us and from which she deducted breakages and fines.

When I arrived back at the orphanage Matron's first question was, "You didn't eat any foreign food, did you?"

I said, "No. Nothing like that." The food was not foreign to me.

"Did your grandmother give you any money?"

"Yes." I handed her the sixpence.

"I'll put this in the book," she nodded.

When Matron had gone back into her room, I entered the kitchen where Hetty was reading a magazine. I handed Hetty the other sixpence. Grandmother had told me to buy myself something I wanted. I wanted independence and I wanted protection. I had learned the value of money in Scarborough, and Hetty was the only one who could protect me. Hetty's services were priceless—the paring knife, the warnings that Matron was approaching the scullery, and especially the occasional quick read of a comic book that helped me learn new words without being punished. It all added up. Unki had told me never to expect something for nothing. Hetty looked surprised, then nodded and slipped the sixpence into her bra.

When I found out bony Helen was leaving, it came as no surprise. She had started leaving for weeks. First her coat disappeared from her peg. Then her apron. She was no longer given chores. Her towel did not come back from the wash. Slowly, she began to be erased like a pencil drawing until the page became blank and Helen was standing in the hall with her suitcase. Only Hetty was there to see her off. Her former friends, even spotty Enid, ignored her in the end. I would have missed seeing her off myself had I not been on my way to the shoe room. When she saw me in the doorway she raised her hand, and then turned her thumb down in the direction of Matron's sitting room. I recognized it as a friendly good-bye and a warning. "Look out for yourself." She then gave Hetty a playful slap on the shoulder, which Hetty reciprocated by gently boxing her ears.

After she had been gone an hour, it was as if she had never been.

In Estonia, the Soviet Government decided to accelerate the process of genocide. In the early morning of 25 March 1949, another wave of deportations began. Just as in earlier years, families were separated, taken to the train stations, put into cattle cars and sent on their final journey east. The focus was on farmers and their families who were resisting the collectivization of their farms and on the organized resistance of the Forest Brothers who were still active in the woods and marshes.

A. Rahi-Tamm

One afternoon I was peeling potatoes in the scullery when Hetty told me Matron wanted me in the sitting room. I panicked, thinking I was going to be punished for using the paring knife, but instead Matron asked me to run down to the grocery store to get some Paxo. Hetty needed it for what she was cooking.

Paxo? I had no idea what that was. There was no need for money; the store kept an account. I was told to hurry.

I set off down Cliff road with absolutely no idea what I had been sent to buy. I wondered if Paxo was a spice or maybe a vegetable. It was the first time in my life that I had been sent to a store to buy anything specific, and so as not to forget the name of the purchase, I found a chalky stone and scratched the word into the pavement slabs at about every twenty paces until I arrived at the store.

"Taxo" I said to the shopkeeper, when it was my turn.

"Taxi?" the man looked at me in astonishment and pointed to the taxi stand in the street.

"No. Taxo. Box." I remembered the word box.

The shopkeeper scratched his head. Other shoppers gathered around all repeating the word "Taxo," like idiots. No one knew what I wanted, but they knew where I was from. Someone said, "The Home. You had better call and find out what she wants."

"No! No!" My first real errand, my first chance to be trusted and I had failed! I ran out of the store and began to walk back; passing all the TAXOs until, hey, the next T was a P! PAXO! I rushed back. "Paxo! Paxo!" I shouted joyfully, hoping they had not yet called the Home.

"Paxo, of course," the shopkeeper handed me a little box.

Matron was waiting by the gate. She took the box from me and scolded me for dawdling. Instead of arguing I dropped my eyes meekly and followed her to the kitchen. I was dying to find out what this Paxo might be. The cover of the box showed a chicken.

I hovered around until Hetty opened the box and shook out some reddish artificial-looking breadcrumbs and started rolling chicken pieces in it. Breadcrumbs? But why call breadcrumbs, Paxo? I knew that tea was Typhoo, and Lyons, coffee was Nescafé, oranges were Jaffas and bananas were Fyffes. It made no sense, but there was so much about England that was different by design so that foreigners couldn't pass as English.

One Sunday when my weekly visits to the hospital had become routine I arrived upstairs to good news. We had received a letter from Unki with a special enclosure marked "For Rin-Tin-Tin." I tore the envelope open. Out fell a photograph, a newspaper clipping, and a piece of carbon paper folded around an American dollar bill. I wanted to examine the money right away, but knew it would be rude to gloat over it without reading the letter first. Mother and Grandmother were waiting to hear what Unki had to say. The handwriting was small and spidery. I began to read carefully, emphasizing the "L" sounds, the cause of my foreign accent in Estonian.

Dear Rin-Tin-Tin!
I hope you are growing up to become a beautiful young lady. I miss you. I'm enclosing a newspaper clipping from today's newspaper so you can see what is happening over here in Brazil. The snake was in the basement just a few houses down from us. After it was shot and dragged away, it was almost as long as the street. It's an Anaconda....

224

"Let me see that," said Mother, and grabbed the clipping so quickly that all I saw was a huge snake rearing out of a basement window with soldiers kneeling around it, rifles aimed. Blood was pouring out of dozens of holes in the snake's neck.

"But I haven't finished," I protested.

"You don't need this," said Mother. "We don't need any new nightmares." She handed the clipping to Grandmother who looked and gasped.

"I'll read the letter for you," said Mother, now suspicious. She began to read, but I suspected she was skipping lines if not entire paragraphs.

"Hmm... 'er, 'I have not forgotten my promise to leave you my gold watch and my gold teeth in my will.' "

"That's Paul all right!" said Mother. "And hear this," she was speaking to Grandmother, although the letter was for me." 'When you turn eighteen, you must always carry a pistol in your purse.' "

Mother made a face, but she was not angry.

Paul Enno and wife Steffi in Brazil, 1949.

"Your Uncle Paul is living in San Paulo," she continued, no longer reading. "He married a German woman named Steffi, so," she glanced at the letter again, "he can have gravy on his potatoes. I love it!" Mother tapped the page, reading here and there, but mostly telling Grandmother things she did not think I would understand. "Steffi is looking after him, protecting him from getting rolled. If he doesn't come home by a certain time, she goes out to look for him, armed with a frying pan." Mother laughed and wiped her eyes. "He says the town drunks are afraid of his wife, because she beats them with her skillet if they don't return the money they took from him.

"Looks like Steffi and Emilia will refine Paul between them like a grain of rye between two millstones," pronounced Mother. Emilia was Paul's sister still in Estonia, living in a Baptist Convent. She was urging her brother to convert and avoid the same fate laid down for us, namely the Lake of Fire.

"Paul is being finely sifted," agreed Grandmother. "He has a good heart." Mother's reply to that was a grunt.

The photograph was still on the floor. I picked it up and saw Unki, straight and proud in a real suit, next to his wife who had the piercing eyes and jutting chin of a household warrior. It was easy to see why San Paulo's drunks were afraid of her.

My Estonian was coming back gradually and Grandmother's English was improving under my tutelage. We liked to walk for at least an hour on Sunday afternoons before I had to leave them again. The area around the hospital was falling into ruin. It was becoming a ghost town. Mother had told me that

225

Leeds was undergoing slum clearance and was going to be completely re-built. The area around the hospital would be cleared to make way for an extension to Leeds Infirmary. Mother held her fingers crossed that she would not have to go back to Ida. Life at the Women's Hospital suited her fine. The rules were relaxed and the sisters were more interested in their own futures than whether foreigners were keeping food in their rooms.

Sometimes we walked in a different direction, downhill towards the river Aire and the Leeds-Liverpool Canal. It was there we had seen the worst factories and row houses upon our arrival. The factories were closed on Sun-days. Without the smoke we had a clear view of the river, the canal, and the narrow blocks of row houses. Each with their one-up and one-down windows, identical front doors, and washing lines strung across the street.

Grandmother said she had come to know the area well. She had been shocked by the soot and smoke, but had found the English people who lived in the row houses both cheerful and friendly. When we passed, some of the women sitting on their doorsteps recognized her and nodded. She said she wished they would speak to her so she could use her few words of Yorkshire, but so far no one had. The prams were still outside. We peeked under the canopies and saw well-fed babies sleeping peacefully despite the cold, the soot and coal dust. Every front step was still painted the light beige we had seen before. There was always someone on their knees, chalk in hand, re-freshing the one area in their lives where they could still express pride. Grandmother said it was the human spirit yearning for beauty, no matter what the circumstances. "England is not only rebuilding its cities, but also its citizens and teaching us valuable lessons," she said firmly.

It being a sunny day, children played in the street, skipping under the clotheslines. Men clustered around a pub where several streets came to-gether, laughing, talking, and clutching large glass tankards of beer. I half ex-pected to see Mr. Boller. Men had defi-nitely enjoyed the war more than women had. They had now settled back to becoming husbands and breadwin-ners again—until next time. I was think-ing of Unki, trapped into a shirt and tie, tight collar, and leash.

We walked a little farther until we reached a church. Grandmother sat on the low wall to rest. We could hear or-gan music through the open door, but she did not suggest we go inside. A few elderly ladies straggled up the path to-wards the door. They were the same kind of stiff-backed ladies who at-tended our church. The stiff backs were

Mother and Elin in Leeds, 1948. Elin is wearing the American Red Cross uniform dress.

created by corsets, which Grandmother refused to wear. Mother sometimes molded herself into a girdle so she could close the zipper of her skirt. More people went into the newsagent's and came out with a Sunday paper than went into church—more interested in *The News of the World* than news ₁. God.

I had thought to tell Grandmother about the orphanage church services, but decided not to.

One Sunday Mother said she was going to take me to a Cartoon Cinema in Leeds Station. We went together, but when we got there Mother bought me a ticket and told me to go inside alone. She would pick me up in an hour. I was a bit surprised, but I went in anyway. I had never been inside a cinema. The newsreels came first, called *Pathè News*. The cartoon characters were called "The Three Stooges." I thought they were silly and was glad when mother met me outside again after an hour. Mother, too, seemed happy. We went back to the hospital, but before we went into the room, she asked me not to mention to Grandmother that I had been in the cinema without her.

The trips to the Cartoon Cinema became a regular outing. It was not long before I became bored with "The Three Stooges." One Sunday I decided to leave early and walk around City Square. That had been our first glimpse of Leeds. I was sitting on the base of the statue of the Black Prince, still green, when I saw Mother frantically talking to the cashier at the cinema ticket office. I had meant to catch her before she got there. I ran quickly to her, but she was so upset that she could barely speak.

"I was just over there," I told her, pointing to the statue.

Mother's face was still red. I remembered all the scenes we had previously. She took my arm, but instead of shaking me she led me to a bench.

"You're a big girl now, and I'm going to ask you a big-girl question. It's very important to me." She began to dig in her handbag for a cigarette. She lit the cigarette, took a drag, and looked me in the eye. "How would you feel if I got married again?"

"I thought you *were* married?" It was my first thought, but in truth there was no husband. I could barely remember Father.

"I am, but your father already has someone else."

"What does Mämmä say?"

"She doesn't know. I haven't asked her. I'm asking you. If you say no, then things will remain the way they are." She blew out a cloud of smoke and continued to look at me. Behind us I could hear trams clanging and cars passing.

"Would Mämmä and I live with you?"

"I can't answer that right now. First I need your answer."

"Then no."

Mother looked shocked.

"Can you tell me why?"

My answer had also shocked me. How to explain it? It just came out. Mother continued to look at me. She was upset.

"Would I have to stay at the orphanage?" I asked finally. I could not grasp her question in any other context than what I had heard from conversations around the hospital about getting married to go to Canada. I did not want her to leave me in the orphanage and Grandmother at the hospital, just so she could go to Canada. She had always gone ahead and left us, but now Grandmother was also trapped in an institution. I was panicked.

"Are you going to Canada?"

"Good grief! Of course not. I would stay right here."

"But I would still be at Cliff Road?" I persisted.

"The orphanage? I can't do anything about that."

"Then the answer is still no." I started to cry.

Mother sat motionless for a long minute, not even smoking; she threw away the unfinished cigarette.

"All right, I asked for it." She patted my arm. "We won't mention this to Mämmä and we won't talk about it again."

Mother could have remarried, but after my vehement reaction she never did speak of it again until I was an adult. I deeply regret my part in denying her a few years of happiness after all she had been through; I was too young to understand and did not know that Father had already divorced her under Soviet law. Had I agreed, it is doubtful she would have got the divorce papers out of the Soviet Union, but she might have got some different kind of legal divorce. Unfortunately her friend died a few years later of a sudden heart attack. One of the greatest cruelties caused by the Cold War was that bureaucrats not personally touched by war were holding the survivors to a criteria only possible in peacetime.

Another Sunday morning. Mother and Grandmother already had their overcoats on when I arrived. We were going to visit the Elmers. Unki's friend Juhan and his family were also living in Leeds.

"We're going to their house," said Mother.

"A whole house?"

Mother laughed and told me not to take things too literally.

Grandmother was happy to be seeing her friend, Mrs. Grigorjev, again. Leena had not been as good a friend as Inge, or maybe I had been too jealous of Leena. They lived only a few streets away, at the top of Mount Pleasant. We went by bus. Grandmother was wearing her elastics and did not think she could walk up the hill.

Their street was in an area marked for demolition. Only a few houses looked lived-in. Grass grew on the pavements. Gates had broken off their hinges and front doors were boarded, but the Elmers' door was newly painted a bright blue. When we were ready to knock we could hear loud voices in the basement, speaking Russian.

Mother rapped loudly. There was no knocker, just holes where one had been.

"*Vhodeetje!*" A Russian voice yelled from deep inside the house, to come in. Still we waited. After a short minute the door was yanked open by a woman smelling of garlic and incense. The hall itself smelled of cooked cabbage. Tattered rugs and bits of linoleum covered the hall floor. I guessed everything had been put together from the same stalls at the back of the market where Mother and Grandmother shopped, but what really caught my eye was a cardboard box under the stairwell, covered with a rug. There was no mistaking the black sides of an iron stove. My heart leaped. Our Meerbeck stove!

228

The woman who had opened the door was Ukrainian, which I was told meant that she was not a Communist Russian since Ukraine was a separate country.

While Mother groped through her meager Russian vocabulary, Grandmother interrupted and asked for *gospodin* Grigorjev.

"Ah, *da, da!*" The woman threw her head back and bellowed behind her. "For you!"

There they were! Leena's mother, wearing a flowered housedress, work apron, and long cardigan down to her knees, and much fatter than I remembered her. She was coughing into a hanky. Leena was behind her, older and taller. Babushka was in the background, adjusting her headscarf and wearing her usual shapeless skirt and loose top. Her appearance shouted *Ausländer* to any ethnically prejudiced eyes.

Mother and Mrs. Elmer clasped outstretched hands, and Mrs. Elmer broke into tears.

"Mein Gott! Lenuchka, com', look who ist here!" she called behind her.

I had forgotten that Leena's mother spoke six languages—all at the same time.

Babushka and Grandmother fell into each other's arms. Thus, I had seen them say good-bye. Here they were again, saying hello in excited Russian.

I watched Leena pull back and saw in that instant that Leena had also started sorting the foreigners from the English.

We were led into the interior of the house, the back part, into a big room with two side doors. One door was ajar, the second closed.

"Juhan *on* asleep," said Mrs. Elmer, indicating the closed door. "I *arbeit* day shift in *asbest* factory, he *nachts* in steel mill, we only one *bett.*" She laughed and broke into a fit of coughing.

Mrs. Elmer explained that the house was scheduled for demolition, but there was still time to rent the houses to foreigners who did not mind the conditions. She said it was a godsend because it enabled them to send Leena to private school. We were shown around.

Leena and Babushka had one room. There was a scullery that opened onto a backyard. They had plans to keep chickens and maybe a pig. Mother thought they should first check for permission, with the Council. "They have a lot of rules in this country," she cautioned.

"Permission *ver* for? Is *mein* own yard in back?"

I could see the Elmers had not yet grasped the rules of living in a civilized society.

The kitchen was off a main corridor shared by three families. There was a gas ring propped onto orange crates on the second floor landing for people who lived on the top floors.

Mrs. Elmer opened cupboards to show us all kinds of dishes—plates, bowls, cups, saucers. Mother and Grandmother "ooh'd and aah'd." We also admired their furniture and the view of the backyard brick wall.

Leena and I did not speak while we trailed the adults from one piece of furniture to another, but once in a while she rolled her eyes to the ceiling and smiled to let me know that all this foreignness had nothing to do with her. I smiled back and felt guilty because I agreed.

229

Finally we all sat around the kitchen table. Mother and Mrs. Elmer remembered mutual friends. Babushka and Grandmother recalled old times. Babushka could not believe that Grandmother was *"Rhabochina rot!"* Also a worker! She marveled, shaking her head. Mrs. Elmer was sorry to hear Mother had signed an indenture. "Vurst ting you do, sign kintrakt, become *comme une nègre*," a nergo slave. She patted Mother's arm sympathetically across the table. "You *muss* married. Cannot *lebe gut* in world *ohne mann*." (*Cannot live well without a man*).

Mother reminded her that she was still married to Father.

"So *wehr* vill know?" She broke into another fit of coughing. When she was able to draw breath again, she continued. "We *alle* taken from de water *mit* nossing. No *papiere*. Nossing! *Femme* all single. You come verk in asbeste, *gut* money." She pressed a handkerchief across her mouth.

"I heard many asbestos workers are becoming ill," said Mother carefully.

Mrs. Elmer would not hear of it. "Verk *schnell*. Work quickly, later live *gut*." She told Mother she had applied to work in a coalmine, but had been turned down.

Babushka had meanwhile gone and come back with a platter of *pirukad* (meat pasties) and a bowl of *smetana* (sour cream) to dip them into. She was heating some *shchi*, cabbage soup, and the water was almost ready for *chai*.

I took a pasty. *"Spasiba Babushka!"* I thanked her shyly, to let her know I remembered.

"Krasaavitza maya!" My pretty! She reached over and kissed the top of my head. They continued their conversation in Russian and French while Mother and Mrs. Elmer spoke a mixture of Estonian, English, and German.

Leena raised her eyebrows for me to follow her to another room. I had hoped we could be alone and followed her eagerly though not entirely happily. They had obviously known we were coming. Leena was wearing a beautiful lace-trimmed blouse and pleated skirt. I hoped she would not know my American dress was a uniform.

We had not yet decided what language to speak and I was glad when Leena chose English. Leena's English was as good as mine was. I had hoped it would be worse. The Elmers had more things than we could ever dream of, I really became jealous when I saw Leena's and Babushka's bedroom. How to describe such a sleeping chamber except as a room-sized bed or a bed-sized room? Their clothing hung on nails on walls covered by sheets. Bundles were wedged between the walls and mattresses, forming a bulwark against the wallpaper. The room smelled of incense from Babushka's icon. The Black Madonna and baby Jesus that I remembered from Meerbeck were inset into a silver frame and placed on a shelf above the bed. It was a wonderful room. One could laze around such a room from morning until night, sleep or read, lie down or jump on the mattresses without anything breaking.

Leena's mother was still coughing when we went back into the main room. Uncle Juhan had joined them; he sounded sleepy, but looked tamed without his wild hair and greatcoat. Marriage did that to men. Juhan went to a cupboard and got out a bottle of "white." What else? The merry clinking of glasses followed in due course.

"Zavasheh sdarohvyeh!" said Uncle Juhan, saluting the occasion in Russian.

Mother said *"Prosit"* and *"Tervist"* in German and Estonian.

Grandmother added a quiet *"Salut!"* in French, as she and Babushka touched glasses.

With one ear cocked to what the adults were saying, I pretended to listen to Leena boasting that she was head of her form in school. I watched Uncle Juhan showing Mother and Grandmother his scars, "caused by flying sparks of molten metal," and when I got back to Leena, she was waffling on about some 11+ examination she had missed, but had still been able to take because her parents had put her into a private school. She called it a public school. I had no idea what she was talking about.

The information I had missed was going to affect the rest of my life!

The foreign workers from the DP camps only solved some of the labor problems. They were offered jobs English people did not want and it was only a stopgap. It did not incorporate England's own lower classes or give the poorer children a chance to rise out of their ghettoes, even if they had the mental agility to do so.

The solution came in 1944 with the passing of the Education Act. Although not implemented until 1946, it raised the school leaving age to fifteen, with the Minister of Education having the discretion to raise it another year. Henceforward the state was bound to provide free education for everyone, education of a kind, which was divided into three categories: primary, secondary and further. Everyone had the first and then, just after the age of eleven, there was a competitive examination. Those who passed it went on to grammar school for an academic training. Those who did not went to secondary modern schools, where the stress was on manual skills. The old fee-paying public schools and those which were called 'direct-grant' from government were left untouched. This Act was of fundamental importance for the future structure of British society, which was to be transformed within a generation into a meritocracy dependent on talent.

Sir Roy Strong

Leena was not the only child in the Estonian community whose parents overcame the 11+ exam disaster by putting their children into public school. There were other examples. One Estonian maid's titled employer paid for the maid's two daughters to be privately educated. Both became nurses. A Lt. Colonel and his wife went to work in a boarding school as cook and gardener so that their daughter could attend classes. She was already twelve years old, but the boarding school gave her the 11+ examination anyway and she went on to grammar school, then medical school, and became a pediatrician. The dean of the Estonian Lutheran Church sent his twelve- year-old son to be educated in Ireland. Although Mother could never have found the money to send me to a public school (private school) she should have at least been aware that under the new English law I would be barred from higher education for the rest of my life.

231

Leena was launching into a list of her further accomplishments when Babushka said she had something to show me. She smiled mysteriously and reached into a wooden crate. After a suspenseful hesitation she removed the cloth wrappings and brought forth our old cooking pot, the same one Grandmother had pressed upon her before we had climbed into the truck. She patted the pot's full belly with satisfaction and thought I would be pleased to see it. I said "*da*", but was close to tears. What good did it do for me to know that Leena also had our old cooking pot? Leena already had more than enough things and was also eating out of our soup kettle. Mother and Grandmother could not even heat water. The stove I had glimpsed under the stairs was definitely ours.

Babushka called us to the table for bowls of cabbage soup and home-baked rye bread. The soup was ladled out with a hand-carved wooden ladle that also looked familiar. This life was definitely close to heaven and much as I hated to admit it, this heaven belonged to Leena.

After we had eaten, Leena took me to her room to show me her toys.

What a day! We left with promises to come again. "*Preekhodeetyeh snova!*" Come again. To which Leena piped up with an invitation of her own. "Do come back!" She had not had time to show me her clothes yet.

Back at the hospital and facing imminent departure to the orphanage, I could only stare out of the window at the gathering dusk. The orphanage was no longer the confusing place it had been at the beginning, but it was not where I wanted to be.

Grandmother walked me to the edge of Hyde Park. It was slow going as she struggled up the hill. When we entered the park she plopped down on the nearest bench. It was early evening and the gaslights had come on while we sat there. The lamplighter nodded to us as he passed with his little ladder. Old rain puddles were shiny like glass. A damp cold wind was gusting up my skirt. I waited for Grandmother to catch her breath. It was no longer a mystery why Mother and Grandmother did not visit me at the orphanage. Matron had said that Grandmother was a bad influence on me, and Mother did not want them to meet.

"Do you think we will ever live like the Elmers?" I asked, watching a well-dressed couple stroll by arm in arm.

"No reason why not." Grandmother sounded doubtful.

"Leena has all the luck," I grumbled.

Grandmother did not reprimand me, but followed the couple with her eyes. "Luck is an illusion," she sighed. "You don't really know what goes on in people's lives."

"But some people have more illusion than others," I muttered darkly.

"You thought that woman in the private wing had all the luck, remember? Until you found out she was dying."

"Even so. And Leena isn't dying."

"Heavens forbid! You must never wish you were somebody else. You don't know what is in that person's future."

232

"I don't know what is in our future either." My bottom lip began to wobble and I hid my face in Grandmother's shoulder.

"Nobody knows, but we have each other." She squeezed my arm. "If you were someone else, I would not have you to play Black Peter with." She got up. "We'd better keep going. I don't want you to be late."

She was right. Mother had not told me to be somebody else, only to speak English and act English. She did not know that sometimes I did wish I were someone else. Mother's friends had started to call themselves "Estonians in exile." It was supposed to sound good, but to me it sounded like having been kicked out and told not to come back. I took Grandmother's hand and gave it a hard squeeze. No matter who we were and what we lacked, one thing was still certain—I would never swap my Mämmä for anyone, not even the King of England. As for giving her to Leena in a trade of homes and grandmothers—that, too, was absolutely and totally out of the question.

In the hospitals the labor contracts were expiring. The foreign workers were leaving England in droves, desperate to get away from the class discrimination that was ruining lives.

Mother tried to put our name on the newly developed housing lists for Council houses, but we were not eligible. "English only." She was particularly anxious because she needed to be able to show a proper residence for me before I could be released from the orphanage.

Banana was going to petition the Leeds Board of Education to allow me to take the 11+ examination out of turn. I had only missed it by three months. She collected all my report cards and some drawings that had been shown at the Children's Art Exhibition in Leeds Town Hall. With these she planned to explain to the Board of Education my special circumstances and plead with them to overturn the terrible consequences should I not be able to continue my education. She had explained it all to me beforehand. "That way you can go to Leeds College of Art. You have talent." It sounded good. Grandmother had studied at the Helsinki Ateneum, a famous Finnish Art School.

Banana meant well, but I had already noticed how so many well-meaning people became helpless when faced by the authorities. Banana was one of them. The orphanage training had given me insight into why certain people were dismissed and others accepted. The same failings that worked for Matrons operated everywhere else as well. Banana was too emotional. She took things to heart. She showed her feelings and worst of all, she wore a wig.

Banana's presence at the orphanage brought the gawkers, the eye-rollers, and the gigglers into the hall. Everyone knew her from school, where she was called "the wig." They wondered why she had come. Matron welcomed her politely, but with that "you're wasting your time" look on her face. At least she did not forbid her from taking me out of school for the appointment.

We traveled by tram and then walked to a solid office building with long corridors and doors with nameplates. We found the correct door and were asked to sit down. We waited until a woman came and led us into another office. More chairs to wait on. Finally we were taken to a smaller office with a long table under the window where two men and two women sat and shuffled papers. We were asked to approach while they continued shuffling and talking to each other with meaningful nods until one of the men gathered all the papers together into a sheaf in front of him. It was all so familiar. I did not expect us to be successful.

The man with the papers finally looked up.

"We've gone over this carefully and don't see a problem 'ere," he said, pleasantly, in broad Yorkshire. "Anyroad, don't see nowt wrong wi't lass bein' a weaver, seen as most of 'em are doin' a reet good job. Like they say, where thar's muck thar's muney! But ta, for coming. Sorry we can't oblige!" He got up; the chair scraped. He tapped the sheaf of papers on the table. Two taps—a definite finality. The others at the table rose as well and began to gather their briefcases and jackets. They made haste to file out.

Not even a proper hearing. No one asked to see the papers we had brought with us. They had not even let Banana speak. Banana blushed to the rim of her wig, but still made a final attempt. "What about the...." she held up the folder from which several sheets fell to the floor.

"Sorry," the last woman to get up felt compelled to murmur with her head bowed, before she got up and followed the others.

The papers on the floor were my spelling tests and a report card. I handed them back to Banana who was standing by helplessly, silently, her mouth working as though the words she had meant to say had become clogged in her throat. She could not force them out. Only I knew why the interview had ended so quickly. Their entire focus had been on Banana's sideburns, a different color from the rest of her hair. They had judged her to be the kind of person who might make a scene. English authorities hated scenes. Besides, someone with a legitimate mission would at least have made sure that her hairpiece was in place.

On the way back in the tram Banana sat glumly with the folder and roll of drawings in her lap. I wanted to comfort her and my fingers itched to tuck those stray hairs of hers back under the wig. "I don't mind the mill," I told Banana, to make her feel better. "Many of my mother's friends are weavers." I did not tell her Friida was going deaf.

"Yes, your mother's friends might be helpful," Banana nodded vaguely, and kept nodding, clearly not paying attention to what I was saying any more. I recognized her pain. It was Mother and Grandmother's pain, too. Unfairness caused the greatest pain in everybody, no matter what their fitness for leadership or normal life.

Matron opened the door to us, having spied our arrival from behind the sitting room curtains. Banana began to explain, but Matron cut her short. "You meant well," she said crisply and thanked her for her trouble. At least she did not say, "I could have told you so."

Grandmother's asthma was getting worse. Mother continued to inject her with Asthmolisin. The asthma had not yet interfered with her job, but this time when I came into their room, it was not just another attack. Grandmother must have missed a shift and had her absence noted on her time card. It meant a doctor's signature was needed so she could stay in bed. The doctor was there too, a houseman.[27]

Mother acknowledged my arrival with a nod. She was into a heated argument with the man, who was facing her angrily with his hands in his pockets and barely moving his lips when he spoke. He was questioning her.

Mother was confronting him the way she used to confront me when I was acting up, her face red, her nostrils dilated. It looked like she might grab his collar any minute and shake him. That she was even speaking to him was unheard of.

"What do you mean you can get your own Asthmolisin?" The doctor's eyebrows shot up into his sparse and receding hairline.

"I have a friend in Germany," said mother, backing down a bit. "There is instant relief."

"You're not injecting her yourself, are you?"

"I ... it works."

"I don't believe I'm hearing you correctly, err ... Mrs. Turner."

"Toona."

I tiptoed past and sat down on the floor beside Grandmother's bed. I wanted to let her know I was there. Mämmä was half lying, half sitting against two pillows and a mound of towels. She could breathe, but her whole body shook and writhed with each breath. I found her hand under the blanket and felt her fingers squeeze my fingers in return.

"I want to know now, have you been injecting her?" the doctor bellowed.

"Of course not," Mother lied. "How could I?" Her expression changed to instant innocence. The actress was still in charge.

"Then who has?" he asked. "What do you know about Asthmolisin?"

"Oh, nothing. That was back in Germany," said Mother vaguely.

"If I thought you were injecting her, I could have you arrested," he said quietly, a flush spreading up from his neck to his cheeks.

"Arrested, for saving my own mother's life?" Mother's voice had an equally dangerous edge to it. Her glasses glinted in the light coming through the closed window. It was her turn to face the tiger. I felt a moment of exhilaration. Sitting on the floor beside the bed I braced myself for Mother's next move. If they started fighting I would jump on the doctor's back and pull out what hair he had left. We would then all be arrested and sent somewhere together.

The doctor took a step forward, then a step back. He appeared helpless. I wondered if he was going to call for support, blow a whistle, like the police did, or shout "Sister!" But the seconds passed. Instead he turned and walked over to the bed. He looked down at Grandmother, took her wrist, nodded, and then dropped it. He addressed her directly.

"Now then err... Mrs. Eno, is it? Obviously you're having some discomfort, but it won't kill you. People don't die of asthma." Then he did a strange thing. He laughed. "You people are so difficult, so excitable." He shook his head

---

[27] A houseman is roughly equivalent of an intern in American hospitals.

and continued laughing, thinking it was all too funny for words. "Can you imagine what would happen if we injected every asthma patient with Asthmolisin every time they have an attack? The National Health Service would be bankrupt." He looked for Mother to support his statement.

She would have none of it.

"I told you I can get the medicine." Mother looked at the floor.

"Illegally. I'm warning you!" The doctor pulled himself up to his full importance again.

"Then help her, please. You can see this is not just 'some discomfort.' She can't breathe," begged Mother.

The doctor was not used to arguing with underlings and was embarrassed at having to do so. He changed his manner abruptly. "The other alternative is that I can refer you as a private patient."

"How much would that cost?"

He named a fee.

Mother said she didn't have that much money.

"Then give her the Ephedrine pills." He turned to depart.

"But they don't work." Mother blocked his way. I thought he was going to push past. Grandmother half rose from the bed, waving her hand helplessly to tell Mother to let him go.

The doctor's eyes narrowed. "Enough! You know I can have this room searched." He looked around and glanced at me briefly, probably thinking, "If I arrest the mother, the Home Office will have its hands full."

"Then search." Mother stepped back.

I could hear voices in the corridor. The doctor had heard them, too. The moment had arrived for the "boil them in oil" line I remembered from the Pantomime. "To Siberia" was the Estonian version.

"So what am I going to do?" asked Mother in a normal voice.

"For God's sake, give her the pills." He threw his hands up and left the room, almost running in his haste to get away.

Mother closed the door on him and leaned against it. In her eyes were tears of anger and exhaustion. A few minutes went by. No sound of police whistles, no Sisters running towards our room. Grandmother had fallen back on the bed and was heaving as quietly as she could. Her breath had a whistly sound until she began to cough violently and turned a bluish white.

"Kurat!" Mother went into action. She marched to the wardrobe where she kept her medical kit taped to the back panel. There was the box of glass ampoules, the syringe, a packet of needles, and a tiny saw with which she sawed through the glass. She worked quickly to put the needle together, sawed through the tube, filled the syringe, sterilized the point of entry, pushed out the air, and gave Grandmother the needed injection. She then quickly re-assembled the kit and taped it back into the wardrobe. After the wardrobe door was closed and the clothes inside rearranged to hide the kit, she lay back on her own bed with her arms thrown over her face.

We waited.

It usually took about three to five minutes before Grandmother began to breathe normally again. While we waited I thought about the doctor. He had been angry, but he had not searched the room. Maybe he had not wanted

236

us to be arrested. I pondered the question for a while. It was an unexpected kindness on the part of the authorities. If only authorities realized that by being kind they could change the world.

There was movement from the bed. Grandmother was recovering and was trying to sit up. She was still pale, but no longer blue. Her words to Mother were said with wry appreciation. "I don't know which was more useful, your medical school training or the drama school. You should have stayed in medical school and married a doctor instead of an actor."

"And if Alma had wheels, she would have been a car," answered Mother, also sitting up and starting to act normal again. She laughed with a twist of her lips, a newly acquired habit.

The crisis passed. Mother was going to have to be doubly careful now that the authorities had been alerted to Grandmother's asthma attacks.

Alongside his heavy responsibilities for housing Bevan also crafted the centerpiece of the Labor government's social policy: the National Health Service (NHS). As with most initiatives between 1945 and 1951, the war had paved the way for rapid improvement in the system of public health benefits. The Churchill coalition, in 1944, proposed a National Health Service based on the twin principles that every citizen in the country had a right to the best medical facilities available and that these services should be free. (...) The real problem was with the doctors and their lobbying arm, the British Medical Association. They feared a loss of autonomy, a weakened relationship with patients, and of course, an inability to charge fees to paying customers who wished to have special treatment.

William I. Hitchcock

The next time I came to the hospital, Grandmother was sick again. Mother was traipsing back and forth to the kitchen with hot water jugs and camphor salves. She let it be known that Grandmother had a cold. It would keep the doctor at bay. Even authorities were afraid of colds.

Because the doctor had not yet betrayed us, Mother had started calling him "the good doctor." That did not mean he did not suspect Mother of continuing to inject.

When Mother saw me she said she had been waiting for me. I was to keep an eye out for the doctor or anyone coming down the hall. The syringe was already loaded, hidden behind her back. "Stay alert," she told me. "We don't need any surprises." Her face had the look I remembered from Haapsalu, when she had said the Gestapo was coming to arrest her.

The injection took a minute. As it began to work its magic, Grandmother's breathing improved. I had been watching her face fearfully, hoping she was not going to "cross over." In Germany I had picked up one of Grandpa's books and had read about death, dying, and "crossing over" into a new body. Grandmother had seen me reading it and felt prompted to tell me about death. "It's quite simple. After we die we get a new body to replace the old one, the one we are currently using."

"Will it look the same?" I had asked.

"No, it will be a heavenly body."

"But then how will I know you when I come to join you in heaven?"

"I will wear my old face, just for you," she had promised.

Grandmother looked better, but her recovery was not as complete as usual. She lay listless with her eyes closed, already looking dead. Mother had left the room to refill the jug. I panicked. Maybe I could get her to wake up and look more alive.

"Do you want to play cards?" I asked. "We can play Black Peter."

"Perhaps a bit later," said Grandmother. "I think I'll just rest a bit more."

"I could read to you," I offered.

She nodded.

I hurried to the storage cage. The bulb was still missing. It was pitch black in there. The other cages were empty. Mother told me that the Women's Hospital was next on the list for demolition and the maids were clearing their things out and going into rented rooms.

I dug among the books, taking them to the door to read the titles in the hall light. There was a book in German called *Das Mysterium von Golgatha* (The Mystery of Golgatha.) Grandmother had used it to teach me Gothic letters in Hausberge. It brought back bad memories, so I put it back. I rummaged some more, purposefully now because I was searching for the little book about Jesus. We had stopped reading it after my nightmares in Hausberge. I could not find it. The next book I saw was the Danish cookbook. It had always guaranteed a response. Grandmother was looking forward to cooking in her own kitchen again.

I carried the cookbook to the bed and opened it at red currant compote, a fortunate opening. I could visualize the shiny red berries. I held it up and Grandmother agreed, leaning on her elbow to look at the picture. She could not stay up for long, so I turned to a mousse that looked good enough to eat right off the page. Not much reaction there, so I turned a few more pages. I passed over paradise apple cobbler for obvious reasons. Grandmother needed to concentrate on something she could eat in this world, not in the next.

The recipes that I myself liked included good, strong words like "curdled" and "crisp." The French word "fricassee" had a robust sound to it. So did "waffle." The colors were also important. Vivid reds made you hungry. Those dishes were usually sweet because they contained sugar. (I had never tasted any of the foods myself except the pink *manna*, made with red currants).

From the meats, I chose baked calf's liver. It was Grandmother's favorite, done "*nach Berliner Art*" the Berlin way, which made the liver puff up instead of harden into a slab of shoe leather. I held the book under her chin so she could read it along with me. "Calf's liver, 3 onions, 1 egg, 2 spoons of bread crumbs ...."

Grandmother listened, opened her eyes for a second, and rose to her elbows. "Don't forget the sour cream," she gasped.

Pleased that I was getting a response and that she was no longer thinking of dying, I set the book aside and planted a kiss on her camphor-smelling cheek. The doctor had said she would not die, but I felt the doctor had said that in order to get away from us. He did not want to become involved with people who had their own syringes.

"The meat is chopped...," I read on. With an axe, I imagined, as in the DP camp, but Grandmother interrupted me weakly. She waved a hand in the air. "You turned two pages. Those are lamb ribs. Turn back."

She was right. In my excitement of seeing that she was feeling better, I had lost my place. "The liver is washed, skinned, deveined."

That did not sound good. One of the reasons I did not want to eat meat was because I had seen animals slaughtered and had heard their cries. Their cries were likely also heard by their loved ones waiting to be killed in another part of the slaughterhouse. I turned the page quickly back to desserts. Desserts did not have relatives in cowsheds or pigpens.

One dessert that sounded cheerful was Danish farm girl.

"Mix one half pint of fresh cream into a deep dish full of coarse rye bread crumbs, then chop eight apples, half a pound of sugar, half a glass of raspberries or cherries, a quarter of a pound of butter...." Reading about apples, raspberries, rye bread made me hungry.

Mother had returned and was listening by the door. She said the canteen was opening in a few minutes. With Grandmother officially "not well," she was allowed to bring her a tray.

"Maybe white bread and raspberry jam?" I suggested.

"I'll try to get some ice cream," she promised.

Mother went back down to the canteen. I stayed in the room, by the bed. I closed the book. Grandmother lay quietly on her back. She did look dead. There was a cold puddle of water sloshing in the pit of my stomach, reminiscent of Berlin mornings, flooded air raid shelters, broken drains, spring and autumn funerals under wet umbrellas, and people in black. It was definitely a dying kind of day. Were I still four years old I would have climbed under the covers with her so we could "go" together. Going together had been our goal. Now we could not even live together.

Grandmother did not die, but remained in bed.

The following Sunday, after the big blow-up and many more injections, the houseman came back into our room unexpectedly. Grandmother and I were playing Black Peter. Mother was reading. He paused at the door and smiled.

"I told you the pills would work!"

"Thank you, Doctor," said Mother meekly, casting her eyes down. Her tone was so phony that even the doctor raised an eyebrow, but he did not comment.

At the orphanage things continued to change. Hetty got married. We presented her with a rug made of dishcloths. Fat Enid took her place, but she had neither Hetty's charm nor deviousness. Matron caught Enid in the pantry making beef-dripping sandwiches; she was instantly dismissed.

When we sat around the kitchen table, notebooks open for our homework, we could not have looked gloomier. We mourned Hetty's sneaked raisins, fingers dipped in cocoa, tattered magazines, and stolen pleasures.

There was nothing left for us now, but to do our homework to the sound of logs shifting in the fireplace and Kim farting in his sleep.

The next news was that our school was going to be demolished. We had already seen the streets around it emptied house by house. The area had been turned into a ghost town.

The war destroyed 200,000 houses in Britain and left three and a half million damaged. Repairs and upkeep had been postponed due to lack of materials. On top of this, the population had increased by one million during the war, and birth rates were on the rise. Everyone agreed on the need for a massive house-building program, and Labour rashly promised swift action. "Five million homes in quick time," declared Ernest Bevin during the 1945 campaign, but the skilled labor force was scattered, with many still in the services; there was a terrible shortage of timber and the dollars needed to buy it; and the brick industry in 1946 was running at one-fifth its prewar level. (...) The government did manage to build over a million houses by 1951, which, given the terrible economic troubles of the country at this time, was quite an achievement, though well below its initial goals.

William I. Hitchcock

It was time to go to Scarborough again. Mother and Grandmother were going to visit me. They had never had a holiday since coming to England.

They turned up at the Church Hall early on a cold, but sunny morning and did not look too "foreign." Actually Grandmother looked very smart in her best coat and hat and was carrying a new slim line handbag. Alas, she had left the price tag on it; I berated myself for noticing.

Matron did not shake hands, but was gracious and asked them if they had had a pleasant journey. She hoped we would have a good day together. After the brief, polite exchange of pleasantries, everyone dispersed, and the door was locked.

As soon as we were alone Mother explained that they had to go back to the station to change into more comfortable clothes and shoes from their suitcase in left luggage. They had wanted to be presentable for my sake. Mother had also noticed the price tag. Ah, well.

Grandmother thought Matron had had an interesting English face and a man's chin. She had come to admire everything English, not just in the last century (like Mother), but what she saw daily.

After they had changed their clothes we went straight to the Front. I pointed out the landmarks, feeling important and knowledgeable about all things English. Grandmother tried to fish for a ring at the amusement arcade, but did not get one. Mother had her fortune told. She got the same card I had received the previous year. She read it:

Life has its heroes and its villain's, its soubrettes and its ingénues, and all roles may be acted well.

240

"I can't believe it!" Mother tapped the card in excitement. "You'd think she knows I was an actress." The wax gypsy had given her a boost. I suspected the cards were all the same or at least one in six, but who did not want to be a hero?

Elin in Scarborough, orphanage summer holiday, early 1950s.

Next, we walked around a big "tunny," a huge stuffed fish. Grandmother's feet began to hurt and she changed shoes again. While they fussed with their shopping bag I bought a bag of winkles. Mother did not want any, but Grandmother took the pin. I told her I had kept one from the previous year but had lost it since.

We sipped tea while Mother wrote postcards. "Wish you were here," she wrote on each one. "An English tradition," she explained. Later, with an ice cream cone dripping down my arm, we sat on a bench in the rose garden overlooking the bay. Mother had a strange look on her face as she gazed at the sparkling horizon. Grandmother closed her eyes and warmed her spirit.

Suddenly Mother looked at her watch and said, "We can't say we've been at the seaside without at least getting sand in our shoes." She had noticed black clouds rolling in. We hurried down to the beach, where we collected three deckchairs and placed them sideways to catch the sun. Mother opened the top buttons of her blouse and removed her glasses. Every time the sun came out from behind a cloud, she threw her head back and sunbathed, but Grandmother just sat there, rapt and absorbed by the moment. Once in a while she would reach over to pat my arm or smile at Mother as if to say, "What a happy day!"

Finally Grandmother heaved herself out of the chair, bared her feet, and challenged me to get our toes wet. We walked to the water's edge where the incoming tide made a wide sweep across the sand. Grandmother hoisted her coattails and we waded out a little way. The water was icy and she pulled back laughing. "At least I can say I've been in the water at an English seaside, more than some!" She waved to Mother, but Mother only waved back and lifted her face in anticipation of another break in the clouds.

When we returned to Leeds and the bus turned for the climb up Cliff Road, I got the shock of my life. Quarry Mount School had disappeared completely. There was only sand and fine rubble where there had been an entire neighborhood of streets of houses and shops. Bulldozers were parked at the bottom of Cliff Road alongside portable toilets, but the real shock was a huge mound of earth, almost the size of a small mountain, which had risen on the site of the little park I had walked through daily. The trees, too, had been removed, including the one under which I had my "bank account" and my most precious possessions. All gone! I stared in horror at the loss of my treasures, and then remembered Grandmother's warning about "treasures on earth." At the same time I was mindful that even while she had become reconciled to losing everything, she and Mother were busily acquiring new treasures through hire purchase. If the call came to return to Estonia, they would be encumbered with too many possessions to heed the call. I began to suspect that some of the orphanage training had a deeper purpose. It was ideal for people who had nothing, because only they could then count their blessings for anything that came their way.

I was in the kitchen doing my homework when one of our neighbors brought us a small orange kitten. The mother cat had been run over by a car. As the woman already had two cats, she thought to bring the little orphan to join us other orphans. Even Walker rolled her eyes at that.

I did not even look up. Cats had always been instant trouble for me, and caused me nothing, but heartache—Tondu in Estonia, Cat at the camp. Love affairs that ended in guilt were the worst. The orphanage had also taught me that love opened one up to emotional blackmail, so when everyone gathered around the kitten to pet it, I stayed away on purpose. Alice saw my reluctance and brought the kitten to me. She could not understand why I would not hold it.

"Don't you like cats?"

"Of course I like them." Alice could not understand and kept pushing. "Isn't he beautiful?" she asked again and again. I could see that she had already fallen victim to the cat's beauty and perfection.

"He is beautiful," I admitted reluctantly. My heart was crumbling.

We named the kitten "Boots" because of his beautiful white paws.

Matron made a fuss over him and then put him into the kitchen for the night, with a litter box, a bowl of water, and a food dish under the scullery sink. She closed the kitchen door and said, "Anyone opening the door and letting the cat out will be punished."

We promised not to let the cat out.

"That's no idle threat," said Matron, wagging a bony finger in our faces.

An hour later Boots was deeply snuggled into the bottom of my bed, by my feet. He was much warmer than any hot water bottle. I suspected he had got out through the serving hatch to the dining room and for some reason had come to my bed. Love stories and marriages began like that. Two people fall in love and in the next chapters there is nothing, but trouble until they get a divorce. That, too, was a pattern. When relationships became secure, they ended. The books and magazines in the outside toilets were highly educational, plus I had prior experience.

Nevertheless, Boots chose me to be his friend. Why cats always chose me was a mystery. It was no mystery that our marriage would end in divorce. Still it was good to feel his warm body at the end of bed.

When I was peeling potatoes in the scullery, Boots always found time to come by and wind his tail around my legs or just butt me, the way Hetty had sometimes butted my shoulder with her knuckles after she dropped a handful

242

of raisins into my apron pocket. Boots did not care that I still mixed my v's and w's. He would never tell on me or break my trust, unless I broke his first.

The sacred trust of an animal was far more exacting than having a human friend, because there could be no explaining circumstances or apologizing. I had learned that with Tondu and Cat and was on edge. Trouble was imminent. It was all right for him to hang around me by day, but by coming to my bed at night he put us both in jeopardy. If caught he would be returned to the neighbor and I would be punished, probably banned from visiting Mother and Grandmother.

Breaking Mother's rule not to tell Grandmother my worries, I confided in her.

"How can I keep Boots from coming to my bed?"

Grandmother suggested I should secure the serving hatch myself before going to bed. I was usually the last to bed anyway because of the potato job. I closed the hatch, but there was no fastener. The lights were barely out before Boots was bumping my nose to say he had arrived and to please raise the sheet so he could get under the covers. Thankfully he did not make any noise for the nightly spies in the corridor, but I could not stop him from suddenly deciding to leave while they were there.

Finally I went to Walker and told her that Boots was getting out. I did not tell her that he was coming to me, only that I had seen him about. Thereafter, Boots was confined to the scullery. The door was closed and there was no further escape for him, not even into the warmer kitchen. I had meant well, but I was wracked with guilt and my heart was broken.

One day, going through the kitchen to my potato peeling station, I saw Boots sitting on the kitchen table. He was washing himself and ignored me pointedly. Of course he knew I had betrayed him. All previous promises were off.

It was the end of the month. Walker had baked a birthday cake for the end-of-month birthday tea and had placed it on a cooling rack next to where Boots was now licking his tail. I was almost through the kitchen when there was a loud crash. Out of the corner of my eye I saw an orange streak leave the table and disappear. All that was left was an empty wire rack and broken pieces of cake on the floor. The crash was loud enough to bring people running from the dining room. Matron had been on her way upstairs with an armful of linens and arrived first.

The evidence was clear. There I was, looking shocked and confused, and there was the cake in pieces, on the floor. What more was there to say, except "The cat did it." The words came automatically. I never thought how they might sound.

"What cat?" There was no cat anywhere in the area.

Matron put the sheets down on the table and boxed my ears so hard that I saw golden flashes before my eyes. "So! You don't even have the decency to own up! You blame the cat! Shame on you!"

A new cake was baked. Later I listened to the birthday squeakers in the dining room. I had not been part of the birthday tea anyway and would not have enjoyed it had I been. Boots had punished me suitably for the crime that I had committed against him, a crime of betrayal. He had offered me love, but I had not been brave enough to honor it. It was only cat love, but I had failed that, too.

The next time I went through the kitchen, Boots was perched on the windowsill, again washing himself as if nothing had happened, but looking closely into his eyes I could see the narrow accusation in their depth. "Love is personal," he was saying to me in cat language. "And love itself punishes those who don't know how to love."

It was clear I did not know how to love anyone anymore except my Mämmä, which put me in the greatest risk of all and filled me with fear that she would be next, that I would lose her, too.

Another Sunday morning, Alice and I were walking down Cliff Road together. Her father, I had discovered, was not at Mother's hospital, but at Leeds Infirmary, not far from where I was going. I sensed Alice did not want to walk with me, but it would have been hard not to notice that we were going in the same direction.

Alice was white-faced and tight-lipped.

"So be like that!" I fell behind and we continued in silence, one in front of the other. I did not pass her and she did not pick up speed. It distressed me that I could not speak to Alice as a friend. Thanks to Alice, I sounded and acted, as English as she did, and that was why I stayed behind.

At the bus stop there was no way to avoid each other.

"What do you want?" Alice asked rudely.

I said the first thing that came to mind. "I hated you for wearing my new clothes, but it's all right now. My coat would be too tight for me. I used to have a coat that was too tight and too short and was glad when I no longer had to wear it."

"What do you mean your new clothes?" Alice turned to me in genuine surprise. "That's impossible. Matron bought those clothes especially for me."

I was stunned! To have a row with her when her father was dying was unthinkable. I changed the subject.

"I'll swap you six seashells for that petrified starfish you found in Scarborough. I'd like to show it to my grandmother."

"I don't want your shells. Besides, they've got holes in them," she replied, still being rude, and turned her back on me.

"And your starfish stinks," I told her angrily.

Instead of getting on the bus with her, I turned into the park and decided to walk. So much for wanting to comfort her. Something terrible was happening to her. I could see it in her face, yet she could not speak of it. It was impossible to force good feelings on people the way you could bad ones.

It was teatime when I returned from the hospital. I was late and expected to be scolded. I was hanging up my coat when Alice came out of Matron's sitting room, her eyes red and her face even whiter than it had been that morning. Matron barely acknowledged my return. She did not even ask if I had any money. She walked Alice to the tea table and held her chair for her.

The dining room was unusually noisy, but as soon as Alice appeared it became so quiet I could hear the clock ticking. The bread plate had already

244

been passed around and someone had put a crust on Alice's place. We all vied for crusts. Alice sat, but made no attempt to touch it. Nobody continued eating. No one had said anything, but we all knew Alice's father had died. That knowledge was confirmed when Matron took a bun from the Matron's table and placed it alongside the bread. When someone's parent died, that girl was always given a piece of cake from Matron's table.

After lights out, the dorm remained quiet. No giggling that night, not even talking in whispers. It reminded me of my first night and so I knew Alice was awake, lying on her back, fist stuffed into her mouth.

Only after the dining room clock had struck one did I hear Alice begin a strangled sobbing. I could almost feel the tears trickling down her hairline into her ears and the terrible pain in her chest that came from trying not to breathe out. I knew the drill. Alice herself had taught me.

Not being allowed to speak, I got up and went to stand beside her bed. Sure enough, her face was wet and she was stuffing the sheet into her mouth. I reached and touched her arm. That was within the guidelines. Alice had taught me that, too. "Don't run too fast, don't eat too fast, don't laugh too loud, and don't cry so others can hear you. And don't go around embracing, hugging, and kissing."

Grief, no matter how heartfelt, should not disturb anyone. Grief was shameful, ugly, and embarrassing like all those public shows of affection. Silently and privately was the only way to weep, but affection could be shown by a slight touch, a gentle slap, a playful boxing of ears to let the other person know that, by holding back, you are civilized and able to retain control of your most unseemly impulses.

I left my arm on hers, ready to pull back if rebuffed, but she let it be only turning her head away so I would not see her tears. I still wanted to extend my sympathy, but I also wanted to show her that I was no longer the kind of foreigner whose emotions ran amok. I wanted to show her that, thanks to her, I had learned not to grieve too deeply, but love was another matter. I feared that love was like being able to ride a bicycle. You could not unlearn it no matter how many times you crashed into a brick wall.

The following Christmas party was at a Teachers' Training College, near Kirkstall Abbey. It had been snowing for two days and the snow had not yet melted. We were in high spirits when we arrived. The party was already in progress. Children from other orphanages were already present with paper streamers and silly hats, screaming and shrieking with adults who were also prancing around them, singing off-key, sweating happily, and behaving as was usual at these wonderfully mindless events.

Off with our coats, on with the paper hats, on with the nametags. Ready for ice cream and trifle, for potted meat sandwiches, for Dandelion and Burdock, Tizer, and other fizzy drinks that get up your nose and spray out when you sneeze.

The party tables were laden. One quick look around the room marked where the tastiest foods were. I was getting into high gear around the ice cream when I heard my name called over the loudspeaker. There was no need to panic. It was the signal that I was going to be introduced to my new "friend" for the evening. I thought it might be fun to play a trick on him. I decided to let him find me instead, so I hid in the cloakroom among the wet coats and Wellingtons. A few minutes later I heard my name again, more urgently. I could see the hall from my hiding place. Matron appeared in my line of vision with a woman who looked like one of those teachers who grab you by the shoulder blades and make you leap like a flea.

When my name was called a third time, someone pointed towards the cloakroom. Walker had joined the search and came to check the coats. She stopped at the door. "I know you're in there, young Missy. Come quickly, we have to leave."

"Leave?" I stepped out meekly. "Why?"

Walker grabbed my coat with one hand and my arm with the other and dragged me with her, not into the hall, but outside into the snow.

"Where are we going?"

No reply from Walker, but she guided me over the icy ground to a waiting taxi. The motor was running. "Take her to The Women's Hospital, Coventry Place," she told the driver and gave him money. "Hurry!"

Mämmä had died! It was all I could think of.

Walker slammed the door on me, but not unkindly. Not unkindly was the English kiss on the cheek. She gave me a tight smile that I returned and congratulated myself on how far I had come from people who allowed themselves to panic.

The drive seemed endless through Christmas traffic. When we arrived at the hospital entrance, the driver let me out. I made towards the stairs, but heard Mother call me from the reception desk. "Thank God you are here!" She grabbed my hand and pulled me into an alcove. "You have to help me. I need to give an injection. Only you can help me now."

We half ran together to the first floor central ward. It was dimly lit. Some curtains were closed, some open. Drawn curtains meant someone was very ill or dying. Grandmother was behind one of the closed ones. She was lying on her back with tubes up her nose and great gasps of air gurgled through hoses like water through clogged pipes. She was conscious and tried to rise when she saw me, but fell back. A strange purring rattle came from her chest. Her lips were blue. I kissed her cheek. "Mämmä! Mämmä! It's me!" I cried, forgetting all the stiff upper lip stuff Alice had taught me.

"I have to inject, now," mother whispered. She patted her handbag. "The doctor had told the Sister to keep an eye on us. He suspects."

I was old enough now not to be confused. Mother was about to break the law and risk arrest, this time in public. The doctor had given Grandmother the usual useless pills. Same old story. The hurry was to get the injection in before mother would be arrested.

"Then do it quickly," I urged, feeling a similar panic. From orphanage to hospital to prison. So much for "famous institutions".

"I have to prepare the syringe. The Sister is on her supper break, but could return any minute. The doctor is in the area. I need you to keep watch." Mother was almost in tears, but I was beginning to discover that when things got worse, she was usually at her best. Instead of stiff upper lip, she jumped right in and let fly.

246

"I'm ready." I barely got out the words before the curtains parted and a Sister appeared. All she said was "Ah!" and noted my arrival. Walking around the bed she rearranged the tubes and left again.

"I'll prepare the syringe in the toilet," said Mother and hurried to the lavatory. I remained by Grandmother's side. Her eyes were closed and her graying hair was spread over the pillow. She already looked dead. The most dreaded moment of my life was happening. I tried to remember her assurance: Nothing to worry about, just stepping out of the old body into Paradise.

I was deep into my thoughts when Grandmother made a noise. She was awake.

"I was at a Christmas party," I apologized, bending over her. "I hid in the cloakroom. Otherwise I would have been here sooner. I'm sorry."

Grandmother opened her eyes and tried to speak, but the tubes and tapes around her nose and mouth just gurgled. I wished I had the Danish cookbook with me. I could have read the recipe for pink *manna* while Mother was getting the syringe ready. I wanted to keep Grandmother's attention so she would not slip away.

"Let's make pink *manna*," I had to shout because one of the machines was making a loud pumping noise. "Red currants are not in season, but we can use apples."

Grandmother moved her head slightly to show she had heard.

"First we'll make the juice. We have to cook the apples until the foam rises to the top. Then we add sugar... lots of sugar, then more water and a handful of *manna*." Manna was biblical. I had no idea how much was a handful, but I knew that "manna" in English was Cream of Wheat or Semolina.

"We are cooking now, I told her, bending over her face to see if she could still hear me. Her eyelids were moving. I had hold of her hand under the sheet when the curtains parted. It was not Mother, but the houseman doctor again. I recognized him immediately. He had laughed at us, but had turned kind in the end. He remembered me, too, and nodded. He asked how I was. What to say at a time like this, but Alice's training came in handy. "Very well, thank you."

At that moment Mother also returned. The shock of seeing the doctor was obvious and her intention equally obvious. She clutched her handbag to her chest in such a way that the doctor was forced to look at it.

"How is your mother?" asked the doctor.

"Your pills are no good," said mother, her voice shaking. "She needs the Asthmolisin. It's the only medicine that will save her. It always has. Can you not understand? This is my mother I am trying to save." Mother thrust her chin out and made a desperate gesture. "Please step outside for a couple of minutes," she told the doctor.

The doctor was too startled to be angry. He was still not used to being spoken to like that by an orderly wearing a scrubbing dress. His head rose an inch, but he lowered it again and appeared to be listening to Grandmother still gasping and gurgling in the background. He seemed at a loss.

"I warn you..."

"You already have," snapped Mother. Her glasses were askew. She looked like she was about to cry. I reflected again that I had seen Mother cry more often in English peacetime than any time during the war.

There was a hiatus of silence. The doctor looked deflated. Under his eyes were deep bags I had not noticed before. He rubbed his chin, probably thinking "these foreigners again," but he was not a bad person. He had already proved himself by not betraying us the last time. It was Mother, who was disturbing the peace with that look on her face—eye to eye with the tiger!

The doctor stooped over Grandmother to take her pulse and check the hoses. "We're doing all we can. Your mother is suffering a severe asthma attack. The machine is a help. As I have explained to you many times, I can only give her Ephedrine. In a day or two she should improve." He looked at me accidentally.

It was well known around the hospital that looking the doctor in the eye was like facing God, but I had already decided that God was not an Englishman and probably not even in England. It was a lovely country for some, but not for others. I kept the doctor's gaze and mouthed the word I had chosen clearly, in case he misread my lips.

"Murderer!"

The man reared, startled. He certainly had not expected to hear the word in English. A ripple in his cheek, a tight movement of his lips almost turned into a smile before he looked at the floor. Then he lifted his head again and seemed to have an idea.

"Sister!" he called outside the curtain.

I heard Mother gasp. He was going to tell on us.

The ward Sister arrived immediately. I suspected she had been hovering nearby. "This patient is ready to go back upstairs," said the doctor firmly. "Remove her from the respirator and have her taken to her room."

The Sister looked incredulously at the bed, at the doctor, then back to Grandmother. "Do you think? I don't see ... I don't think. She is my responsibility."

"Not any more. I take full responsibility," said the doctor in his most doctor-like voice.

A bright red spot appeared on both of the Sister's cheeks, but she dared not contradict him. Hospital rules were hospital rules.

"I'll get an orderly," she stated stiffly and hurried away, letting her squeaking shoes, elaborately goffered cap and starched under slip rustle a subtle protest for her.

We were not sure what was going on. Mother was wiping her glasses with a corner of her apron, her mouth slightly open, and she could not take her eyes off the doctor.

"She'll survive the journey upstairs. What happens after you get her into her own bed is none of my business. My responsibility ends here. You'd better know what you're doing," he said in a dark undertone, eyebrows raised.

Mother looked bewildered until his meaning dawned on her and she jumped into action. "Thank you! Thank you!" Mother started searching for

248

Grandmother's clothes. I thanked God she had not snatched the doctor's hand and kissed it.

The doctor touched Mother's shoulder. "Don't panic. She's not as bad as she looks, and don't bother to dress her. We'll take her as she is."

Mother calmed, but I did not. Why could he not inject her here where she could still be watched and monitored?

The doctor removed the tubes from Grandmother's nose. She drew a noisy, ragged breath of relief. No wonder she had found it hard to breathe.

Mother bustled to the locker and gathered up Grandmother's clothes and shoes. She rolled them up and tucked them under her arm, but was still unable to comprehend the situation, because the doctor remained standing by the bed, hands on his hips. Was he really going to let us go back to our room and let Mother carry on as usual with the injection? Apparently so. He still looked weary, but less official. He even looked relieved at not having to continue being a terribly important person with people who did not understand his importance. He could now go back to his Christmas party.

A Sister and porter arrived with the gurney.

When Grandmother was safely aboard, the doctor said to Mother, "I wish you all the best." Then before I could follow them, he leaned over the empty bed and whispered quietly to me, "I'm not a murderer, young lady, I'm just a civil servant."

I was shocked. A servant? He, too?

Mother sought Hilda's help again in the autumn of 1951. Her contract would end in January 1952 and she hoped she could get back to Philips Electrical. They had a branch in Leeds. Marga had also picked up her old job as a dental technician. Former refugees were regaining their lives and returning to jobs as close to their former professions as possible, everywhere, but in England.

The plea to Hilda engendered a swift reply.

Dear Madam:

I understand from my Head Office that you are desirous of obtaining employment in the Philips organization on the bookkeeping or clerical staff. I shall be very glad indeed if we can assist you in any way and would suggest that you contact me by telephone to make an appointment to discuss the matter.

Yours faithfully,
H. Morehouse,
Branch Manager, Leeds

The reference was helpful, but Mother was not the only DP whose labor contract was expiring, and the English workforce panicked. There was fierce resistance from the local trade unions and citizenry in general. An organized protest march with speeches paraded along The Headrow with banners bearing slogans such as "FOREIGNERS BACK TO WHERE THEY CAME FROM" and "FOREIGNERS WILL NOT TAKE THE FOOD FROM OUR MOUTHS." The result was that only two foreign workers in the Leeds area got white-collar jobs. One was a Ukrainian woman who spoke ten languages. She was hired by the Ministry of Labour to translate to other foreigners why there was no work for them. The other, a Latvian mathematics professor, became a bookkeeper at the same factory where he had woven carpets. Mother eventually got the office job, but only because of the direct orders from Holland. Despite Hilda's request that she be hired as an auditor, she became an ordinary clerk.

Chapter 13

AN UNEXAMINED LIFE
1951

The unexamined life is not worth living.

Socrates

It was a cold January morning when Mother came for me by taxi. I had become wary of taxis. This time she was her most bubbly, really happy, and not just keeping the lid on a pot of new disasters.

The taxi passed Hyde Park and turned right. We passed the Church Hall where Estonians now met once a month. Many of the maids had left the hospital and were renting rooms in private houses and working in factories so they could have their weekends free, cook their own food, and receive visitors.

The name of the street the driver was looking for was Caledonian Road. Mother was directing him. I remembered seeing it on our walks with Grandmother and had thought it was one of the streets being emptied for slum clearance. I was right! We entered it at the top end. At the bottom was Leeds Infirmary. The blocks of terraces in between were mostly abandoned. Plywood covered the doors, weeds grew between the paving stones, windows were broken, and gates were missing. "Keep Out" and "No Trespassing" signs were posted everywhere, but now and then you could see curtains in windows and the occasional spire of smoke from a chimney, so you knew people still lived there.

The taxi slowed in front of a house with curtains. The driver was not sure it was number 22, because numbers were missing, but Mother said it was the right house, and to "pull up by the curb."

The gate was down, but on the second floor a splash of white lace fluttered through an open casement. While Mother paid the taxi, I ran my eyes up and down the peeling paint and saw a hand appear to lift the fluttering curtain. It was followed by Grandmother's face. She saw me and tried to raise the transom higher, but it was stuck. She waved instead. That was all I wanted to see. I bounded up the front steps to the open door and up the stairs.

"Be careful," Mother called after me. "The stairs are broken!"

I barely heard her as I took two steps at a time. The treads creaked underfoot and the banister wobbled, but the hall had already released a familiar smell of cabbage soup. I knew this was not going to be another occasion where I was going to have to admire other peoples' good fortune. This was our own good fortune happening at last.

An open door on the second landing showed an old man sitting on a chair patching a pair of trousers. He looked up and smiled. From his wiry hair, broad nose, dark stubble-beard, and coarse features, I guessed him to be another foreigner. An Eastern European? Maybe another White Russian?

To the right was an open door. There was Grandmother with the light behind her, her arms wide, our old wooden spoon in one hand and a tea towel in the other. The wooden ladle at Leena's had not been ours after all.

"Oh, Mämmäl!" I ran into her arms, a scene reminiscent of so many times before. I hoped this was the great deliverance Grandmother had prayed for.

The flat at 22 Caledonian Road was our first official home since leaving Estonia. Because of her last severe asthma attack Grandmother had been released from her contract early and allowed to go on a pension. She showed me her Aliens Order stamped 20 January 1951, listing the Caledonian address as her residence with the comment: "Not now employed." Mother was still working at the hospital, but no longer as a "live-in." She was waiting for the Home Office to release her so she could start working at Philips.

Our room was actually on the third floor, the basement being the first floor. The room was crowded with two beds pushed against the walls and pillows along the back, so they looked like couches. A wardrobe, a thick plank table, and a horsehair sofa filled the middle of the room. The gas ring was on an orange crate. Another crate alongside that doubled as a pantry. Pots and pans were placed on a board divider. Food items filled the spaces with a tea towel across the front. A shiny red whistling teakettle held pride of place.

"When you come to live with us, I'll be sleeping on the sofa," said Grandmother. "My hip is bothering me and the dip in the springs is exactly where I need it." She showed me the hole in the sofa, filled with old rags and covered by "dear Erni's" prayer shawl. I knew she was telling me this so I would not feel guilty about sleeping in the other bed.

I had to sidle sideways and climb across the beds to give everything a little pat of welcome. Our own furniture at last, even though it was rented. I ran my hand over the table, feeling all the nicks and cuts. I opened the wardrobe door where their clothes hung on hangers, and checked out the bottom drawer filled with more tins and jars than ever before. It was our own food. Nobody could forbid it.

Grandmother became busy by the stove while I sat on one bed. Mother sat on the other bed and smoked, with a pleased and happy expression on her face. It had been her idea to come to England, and bit-by-bit England was starting to make us welcome—not just as workers, but as human beings.

A little while afterwards I began to hear the *plop, plop* of a pot lid being raised by steam. From the smell I knew the soup was hot and ready. I got off the bed to stand by Grandmother and got a pleasant surprise. There was no mistaking the rounded belly of our cooking pot. Babushka must have returned it to us. Grandmother lifted the lid so I could see the contents. Unbelievable! "Hope you're hungry?" she said with a pleased smile.

I was! Good-bye hospital canteens! Good-bye mothball gravy!

254

While Grandmother ladled the soup, I asked if I could set the table. I had yet to see our own knives and forks.

"Look under the bed, in the box," Grandmother directed me, her face red and damp with steam and happiness. I found the box and climbed across the beds to lay out the cutlery—knives, forks, and spoons, even though we only needed spoons for soup. The mismatched plates were only slightly chipped. Grandmother handed me a wooden board she was using as a chopping block and a loaf of fresh bread. I found the bread knife. No more axe. I was grateful to Walker for having taught me how to set a table, what knife to use to cut bread, and what knife to use for butter. We did not have a butter knife yet, but there was a small paring knife in the box, very like the one I was using at the orphanage. It was hard to believe these luxuries belonged to us.

When Grandmother had ladled the soup, we gathered around the table, sitting on the edges of the beds. We looked at each other. After a look like that someone usually gave a speech or lifted a glass for a toast. We each had a glass of water, and it looked as if Mother would do the honors, but before she could start I raised my fork above my head, grabbed the rest of the cutlery, and began to dance around the empty space between the door and the table. "Our own knives! Our own forks! Our own spoons!" I yelled. Grandmother waved her ladle to conduct the chorus.

"Shush! Not so loud," Mother warned, but she was also laughing, and saying, "Amazing! This is what I call *elurõõm*," the Estonian word for joyous living! "*Joie de vivre*," added Grandmother, not forgetting that being alive was still a worldwide celebration.

We were getting carried away by the moment, when a heavy pounding rattled the floorboards under the table. It sounded like a broom handle was being rapped against the ceiling from below. Two more raps and an angry voice bellowed, "Quiet up there!"

So much for joyous living!

"Oh dear!" said Mother, putting a finger to her lips. "That's our landlady!"

Grandmother was 72 years old when we got the room in Caledonian Road. For seven years she had slept on floors, straw mattresses, camp beds, hospital beds, and had only been able to eat what had been given to her. My own release was contingent on Mother getting the job with Philips and under the law, a girl my age had to have a separate bedroom and privacy.

My Sunday visits to Caledonian Road were the highlight of the week, but on my fourth visit Mother told me they would have to move again. The demolition program had reached our street. She found us two small rooms on Springfield Place, the same main thoroughfare where we always caught the bus to take me back to the orphanage.

A few weeks later the Home Office approved Mother's release, and she told me she would come for me after my separate room had been inspected by the authorities. That meant she would come on a Saturday morning, which was always the best day of the week for workers. They could sleep in, open their eyes to daylight, and start believing in miracles. It was on Saturdays

_____, too, began to re-believe in miracles. I believed God had started watching us again, at least from a distance, to see if we were ready to continue our journey.

My erasure from the orphanage began when Mrs. Walker tapped my plimsoles together and said, "I'm giving these to Alice to wear this summer." A few days later my aprons did not return from the wash. The next morning my bathroom peg was empty. When I returned upstairs after breakfast my bed had been stripped. In hospitals an empty mattress meant the patient had died. I knew then that the Saturday I had been waiting for had arrived and was not surprised to find Mrs. Walker right behind me.

"Your mother's coming for you around noon," she said. "I've already packed your suitcase." She handed it to me. It clonked when I picked it up. All it contained was my hairbrush, my toothbrush, and a new tin of tooth powder, a gift from Mrs. Walker who had first shown me how to use it. "Up and down, and mind yer gums!" I remembered.

When I came downstairs again Matron was in the hall. "You can wait in my sitting room or in the dining room," she said coldly.

"I'll wait in the dining room."

"Suit yourself." She took out her purse and counted out four shillings and eight pence, the balance on my account. Placing the money into my palm, she sighed heavily and added, "I want you to know you've been one of my greatest disappointments. I had hoped better for you, you ungrateful wretch." That said, she gave a sharp nod, straightened her spine and marched back into her sitting room. Strangers once and strangers again.

I went to sit on the dining table with my feet on the bench. No one stopped me. The rules and regulations no longer applied to me. The dining room was empty. Everybody was in the yard. I could hear the playground sounds. The boys were playing cricket. A group by the back door was counting, "One potato, two potato, three potato, four, five potato, six potato, seven potato more! You're out!"

"You're out!"

I was out!

I could have taken my suitcase and waited by the gate. That way I would not have had to hear the playground noises and feel my own absence so keenly every time the back door banged open and shut. The children who came and went ignored me on purpose. They were embarrassed to be seen with someone who no longer existed.

Like Mother, I hated long good-byes. We preferred sudden endings.

There was only one person I wanted to say good-bye to.

Finally the one I had hoped to see appeared. She was not alone. Her friend Julia was with her.

Alice stopped at the dining room door and smoothed her apron as though she'd forgotten something. I knew what it was. Our friendship. At least I had felt a friendship of sorts during the four plus years we had lived together in the same house. Julia continued on into the kitchen. Apparently Alice was not ashamed to show me that I had been replaced. Still, she stayed, then

256

stepped partly into the room and smiled as though we were going to see each other again tomorrow instead of never.

"What time is it?" she asked pleasantly.

"Ten minutes to twelve," I replied. I was facing the clock and could not get over my ability to see the time through my new glasses. During the eye surgery to correct my squint, they had discovered that I was nearsighted and needed glasses.

"Oh, so! Ten minutes to twelve." She smiled again and dug her hands deep into her apron pockets. "Did you get your clothes back? You know the coat, hat, and green dress?"

I shook my head.

"Then forget them. Don't mourn things that were never yours."

For a moment her glance became sharply personal, even intimate, recalling in my mind the words "cat love," before she turned on her heels and followed Julia into the kitchen.

With my head on my knees I tried not to think at all until I heard the familiar crunch of high heels on gravel. A few seconds later the doorbell clanged loudly and I ran for the door, determined to open it, but Alice reached it first. She hesitated, then comprehending my intent; she stepped back into the cloakroom.

I was grateful.

"Are you ready?" asked Mother brightly.

Matron came out of her room. She, too, had been watching for Mother. Alice smoothed her apron and assumed a maid's pose, hands folded, and eyes downcast.

"Get your suitcase," Matron told me curtly.

Walker had also been listening for the doorbell; she rushed in from the kitchen, drying her hands on her apron. She stopped when she saw Matron ahead of her. There was an awkward moment. I sensed she had hoped to get me alone and might have wanted to say something. With Matron present she merely stopped by the kitchen door. Even from where I stood I could smell carbolic and chlorine on her clothes.

Mother picked up the atmosphere instantly and said in Estonian, "Let's get out of here!"

I wanted to, but my feet would not move. I could not leave like this, after so many years of calling this place home. I looked at Walker beseechingly and heard her snort of disgust, same as when I had not done a proper job on the toilet bowl or mixed up Vim and Talc. She stepped forward, wiped her hands once more, and gripped my upper arm, giving me a slight push towards Mother. "Get on with ya, ya hefty lump!" she said, in her gruff smoker's voice, as cracked as the kitchen floor we had spent hours together scrubbing. I recognized the move for what it was a proper English good-bye. She stepped back and blew her nose noisily into the wet clout she called her "hanky," a torn bit of sheeting from the rag bin. That was it. It was what I had been waiting for, a final push and a final release and from Mrs. Walker of all people.

At the back of my mind, at the very back and farthest corner of it I had hoped for a decent good-bye from Matron and Alice. It was not to be. Mrs.

Walker filled that gap inadequately, but nicely enough. Now I knew I would not come back.

"What did the washerwoman say to you", asked Mother, when we were alone in the taxi. She could not understand the Yorkshire dialect.

I looked at Mother and groped for a translation.

"So?" Mother asked again.

"She said, 'Go on, fly away, you fat little pigeon!'"

Although I had left the orphanage, the school semester would not end until the 25th of July. Because Quarry Mount had been torn down, it did not surprise me when I was assigned to a new school. The new school was Blenheim Secondary Modern, a large school opposite Leeds University and not far from our new address in Springfield Place.

When I arrived at the school I was a bit surprised that there were only seven of us in the classroom, but I was not alarmed, because Mrs. Brown had come with us and was going to remain with us until the end of term, when she would retire. The only clue that something was not right was when I heard one of the prefects refer to us as the "seven dunces," but I quickly dismissed that as the usual hostility towards new girls. What did surprise me was that we were not taken into any of the other classrooms in the school, and we took no part in the new school's activities, although we were right next to the assembly hall and could see what was going on. Because there was nothing for us to do, Mrs. Brown began to read to us.

The weather was unusually hot. Despite the open windows and doors, the classroom continued to be stuffy and airless. Mrs. Brown kept nodding off, catching herself, then yawning profusely and saying she had never known such a hot summer. What she was saying was that she was as bored as we were.

The school was preparing for Children's Day, a major event every summer, in which I had participated in the past. I had run in the potato race in previous years, not placed, but had qualified to take part. One highlight of the festival was the choosing of the queen from among the schools in the area.

Because of the heat and the open doors, we could see into the assembly hall and follow the activities around the stage. The school had already nominated its candidate. She was being prepared for the final contest. From our vantage point we could see and hear enough to agree that they had made a good choice. The girl's name was Anita Lowther, the most popular girl in the school. She had long dark hair, a beautiful face, and wore clean clothes every day. Since coming to England I had only really seen English life in its famous institutions, and since getting my glasses I had noticed some nuances of normal peacetime living I had not known about before. I had learned to undress at night, sleep in proper nightclothes, clean my teeth every day, eat regular meals, and take a bath; there had been none of that during the war years. Even at the orphanage we had only changed clothes once a week. I was not picking bedbugs out of the hem of my dress anymore, and Grandmother was not combing lice out of my hair, but I still had a lot to learn. In Springfield Place we shared a bathroom with the other tenants, but basically still had to do with a basin and wash cloth. Our bath night was Thursday night. Grandmother did our laundry in the same water after we had all bathed.

The new school also gave me an opportunity to see that school could be a lot more interesting than what I had so far experienced. I learned this during trips to the toilet. When a classroom door was left open, I caught a quick glimpse of what was written on the blackboard and was puzzled. I had never been taught the things I saw.

During the last weeks hot spell when the doors and windows were open and when everyone was in the assembly hall. I had dawdled in the corridors on purpose, as long as I dared and had seen amazing things. On one blackboard the teacher had written numbers and symbols. Some kind of complicated arithmetic. In another classroom I saw words on the blackboard such as "noun," "verb," "genitive," and "gerund." I knew that was grammar, but only because I had picked up the words "verb" and "noun" from somewhere else. The other words were unknown to me. In another classroom I saw racks of colored glass bottles, vials, and tubes. The children had been wearing goggles. That classroom had emitted a chemical smell. I stood in the doorway until a teacher came down the corridor and waved me away.

Seeing those things had given me a feeling of unease. In fact ever since coming to this school my mind had been trying to tell me something I had desperately tried to ignore. It had to do with things I had overheard, been told, had perhaps misunderstood or had forgotten. Like, why were we called the "seven dunces" and why were we not allowed to see what was going on in the rest of the school? I thought we had been brought to Blenheim to finish the semester because our own school was being torn down. That had made sense. This did not. It did not explain why we were segregated, why we were not even included in Children's Day, and what about the autumn semester? No one had told us which school we should report to at the beginning of the next term. There was no one to ask except Mrs. Brown, but she was about to disappear into retirement. I thought of asking her outright: what was going on and what was the meaning of things I had seen in other classrooms? However, I had also developed a vague feeling that she was avoiding me. It inhibited me from speaking to her. I decided to wait until our last day, and then ask her whether I should come back here to Blenheim or go somewhere else. There were obviously still many things I had to learn.

Our last day arrived.

We were on our fourth book. We had lolled, dozed, and yawned through *Little Women, Lorna Doone,* and *Alice in Wonderland.* I had not been able to make any sense at all of the last one. The nonsense rhymes were still nonsense. The fourth book was *Ivanhoe* by Sir Walter Scott.

In the assembly hall Anita was on stage, learning how to stand and deliver her speech. Mrs. Brown stifled yawn after yawn, keeping a surreptitious eye on the wall clock, counting the minutes to her retirement. She was ploughing through our final book. The other girls around me were practically prone with boredom, legs stretched out, heads on their elbows, or thrown back, and eyes closed, but not me. I was listening to every word. The book

Ivanhoe had made me sit up and take notice of the story because I had become interested in the characters. These were people I could relate to. At Quarry Mount we had been given lists of English kings and queens to memorize, along with dates, but those lists might as well have been grocery lists. What I was hearing now was about real people who were battling the same kinds of situations we had come through.

Mrs. Brown read slowly and clearly. She, who had taught me to read English on my first day, was still reading to me on our last day together. I was used to her voice and inflections. As the story unfolded, and although I could not understand every word, I had become involved in the drama. Knights and ladies, Wilfred of Ivanhoe and Lady Rowena, made me think of the noble tombs and slabs in English churches. I had visited Scarborough Castle, and even the hymn "Christian Soldiers" brought to mind the eternal war between good and evil. There was an old Jewish man called Isaac who was said to be an outcast, like his people. He was called names like "Jewish dog," same as *Juden* in Germany. Another *Ausländer* being mistreated because he was different. Jesus had been a Jew, and look what happened to him!

Rebecca was going to be burned at the stake because she healed people with the same kinds of herbal teas and compresses with which Mämmä had helped people in the Meerbeck camp. Brown had said the book was about history. I disagreed. The book was about exiles and outcasts who would always be bloody foreigners, now and forever. I wondered how the book would end. Would there be deliverance or hellfire, the only solution to every situation on earth? There was also romance. Not quite the romance of Hetty's forbidden paperbacks, but Wilfred of Ivanhoe and Lady Rowena were definitely in love. I hurried to school every morning for those last few days to hear the latest news. Would Wilfred come back to marry Rowena? Would God deliver His chosen people not just once in a while, but in the reassuring pattern Grandmother and I had come to rely on?

When there were only twenty minutes of our class left, Rowena and Wilfred were still apart, Rebecca was staring at her unlit pyre, and Mrs. Brown was closing the book for good. I panicked. I forgot all about the next semester and the next school. All I wanted to know was how the book ended. Many students had already tuned out Mrs. Brown and were listening to the activities in the assembly hall. The constant blather of the loudspeaker was equally distracting. The headmistress came on stage to announce that Anita Lowther had indeed been chosen queen. There was loud cheering. Blenheim would be in the first float. Instructions followed on what time and where to board the floats.

Desperate now, I raised my hand. "Excuse me, Mrs. Brown."

"What is it?" She put her finger on the page to look down at me over her glasses.

"Where can I get that book," I asked, "so I can read it for myself?"

A look of confusion crossed her face. "What do you mean?"

The girls in front of me turned and giggled. I felt myself turn hot with embarrassment. I felt like a foreigner again.

"Where can I get that book?" I asked. "Is it very expensive?"

260

"Not if you go to the public library." Mrs. Brown looked at me longer than necessary, and then snapped the book shut. "Come girls, we don't want to miss the last assembly." She stepped down and faced us, her expression kindly but distant, in prelude to a short speech. That was when I remembered the other question, but it was too late.

"Girls, the time has come to tell you how much I have enjoyed teaching you. As this is your last day in school and tomorrow will be your first day as independent adults, it is a day you will always remember. Hopefully some of what you have learned in our school system will stand you in good stead in your future lives. I wish you every happiness. And now we need to go congratulate the queen."

My last day in school? Forever? It was as I had suspected. Still the news hit me like a whack across the head by a thousand matrons. I had already worked out that I had missed something important. On that day at the Elmers, Leena's mother had talked about an important test—so important that they were killing themselves with work in order to keep Leena in public school. I had heard, but had not listened. Mother had not been listening either. The visit to the education authorities with Banana also fell into place. It had not been about art school, but about continuing school—any school. I had not even understood the man's comment, "Where thar's muck thar's muney!" No wonder Banana had been upset. Mother was also going to go berserk when she found out that I was going to be the only uneducated Estonian we knew and worse, this was my last day in school and I had only minutes ago learned about public libraries.

Where to find a public library? Mrs. Brown had disappeared. The girls in the assembly hall were jumping up and down in excitement, clapping and cheering. The loudspeaker sprang back to life again, followed by shouts of "Anita Lowther, Anita Lowther!" The headmistress was still on stage, prepared to receive the new Children's Day Queen. Anita climbed the steps. She covered her face with her hands, overwhelmed by her good luck and the congratulations being pressed upon her from all sides. Then everyone drifted back to their classrooms for final good-byes. I remained at my desk, too stunned to move. I had honestly thought that my life had changed for the better. I had not braced myself sufficiently for this new disaster.

When I got up, the hall was silent. I crossed the bare space between the classroom and the front entrance. No one stopped me. No one challenged me. The prefects had more important things to do. Woodhouse Lane was a busy road at any time and especially at midday. I stopped at the curb, opposite Leeds University, a building I had faced for weeks with only a vague idea of its profound function.

Trucks and buses belched past, hot exhaust fumes breathing on my legs. Chrome fenders reflected the heat, and the air shimmered and wavered because I was fighting tears. The test aside, I should have known about libraries. It had never occurred to me to ask Mother where she got her books. Had there been libraries during the war? My only reading matter at the orphanage had been forbidden books and comics from the outside toilets. We had a bundle full of books from Grandpa's library in Estonia; I had not made the connection. I had to find a library, but first I needed to go home and put my head in Mämmä's lap. I was too old and too big for that now, but I suspected she would understand. This latest nightmare was not mine alone. Mother and Grandmother suffered from the same ignorance, a common affliction that beset foreigners in other people's countries. My schooling had ended, just as I realized how much more I had to learn.

The document that identified me as "Austrian" also mentioned that I had been registered with Quarry Mount Girls School on 24 May 1948 and attended Blenheim Secondary Modern from 24 April 1952 until 25 July 1952. That is the only proof I have of any formal education other than night school classes at Pitman's College, Leeds College of Commerce, and Leeds College of Music, classes for which I received no credits.

Chapter 14

DARK SATANIC MILLS
1953

When William Blake coined the expression 'dark satanic mills' he was talking about Halifax and maybe Birmingham, but all the mill towns in Northern England were equally blackened by soot and smoke and further blighted by the slums that had been created around them to house the workers. In an effort to keep England's reputation as a "green and pleasant land," Michael Ellison, the chief executive of the Calderdale County Council, bought up and destroyed all postcards that had been on sale showing a smoke-blighted Halifax. Thanks to Michael Ellison few, if any, people outside the United Kingdom knew about the coal-blackened cities or the dangerous and primitive conditions imposed upon the people who worked in the mills and factories in the Industrial North.

In March 1953, Stalin suffered a brain hemorrhage and died.

Grandmother woke me up at half-past four in the morning. It was still dark and although I had prepared myself to rise early, it seemed like the middle of the night. Mother was still sleeping. I dressed in my own little room, just large enough for the bed amid the peacetime purchases we had accumulated over time. The most important being the gramophone and Mother's sewing machine.

The toilet was one floor down. To get there I had to pass the closed door of the room next to ours. Every time I passed it I held my breath. The woman living there had gassed herself and you could still smell the gas. It was as though it had mixed with her spirit and together they were rotting in the woodwork. I did not see them take out the body, but had often passed her on the stairs when she was still alive. She had pressed herself against the wall, already a grey, unhappy ghost. She had had a gas ring same as ours, but we had never smelled her cooking.

When I came back up I went into our main room to sit on the couch while Grandmother bustled around our gas ring. Our room always smelled of cooking. There was a faint glow of streetlights through the window, adding to the blue flame under the kettle, and the two provided enough light to move about and see each other's faces. Grandmother had risen even earlier and made porridge, the English word for oatmeal.

When the kettle began to boil Grandmother snatched it up quickly before it could whistle. Out of the corner of my eye I saw Mother stir and pull the covers over her head. The important thing was to let her sleep on. She did not have to be at the office until nine. I was jealous of the extra sleep she was getting, but reminded myself that I was earning more money than she was. I had almost collected enough to buy a used piano. Mother was still "the breadwinner," supplying our food. Grandmother's pension saw to our other needs, and I was buying the furniture. The man at the Education Board had been right to say I did not need an education because I would be earning good "muni." Plenty of muck, too, and the money was piling up nicely in a cigar box under Mother's bed.

Grandmother made the sandwiches while I ate. The couch was her bed, but we had acquired another chair and side tables. The back of the market continued to be our main source of supplies, and hire purchase our line of credit.

While I ate, I watched the clock. The bus for the mill left at five minutes to six. It passed through the villages of Stanningley, Farsley, and Pudsey on its way to Bradford, the biggest of the mill towns in the area.

I had been on the job for three months. At least I was not scrubbing hospital floors and I had not become a servant or domestic. I was a textile weaver.

When I had finished eating I gathered my things together into a shopping bag. It was Grandmother's old marketing bag from Estonia. One quick glance out of the window confirmed that it was raining again, not heavily, but adding to the cold. It was going to be a miserable walk to the bus station. I decided to wear my work shoes and my overalls under my coat for warmth. My good shoes and clean clothes were in the bag to change into after work, for two hours of night school.

Grandmother handed me the sandwiches wrapped in greaseproof paper. "Cheese and tomato," she whispered. Later she would also make sandwiches for Mother, who called them "doorstops."

Grandmother came downstairs with me to dump the night's ashes into the dustbin and bring up another bucket of coal for the small fireplace, an unexpected luxury, which kept our room warm and cozy. We stood together in the small back yard for a minute to share a breath of fresh air, and then parted. I slipped out through the back gate. She went down to the coal cellar.

The vacant lots extended across Springfield Place and Caledonian Road to Leeds Infirmary, a maze of ruins, concrete rubble and knee-high weeds that looking like a war zone, especially in the dark. I averted my eyes, keeping them on the ground so as not to trip on the chipped pavement. The few shops still in business were closed at that time in the morning. They had grilles across dark doorways and the windows were so grimy you could barely see inside. They, too, would be gone soon. Bundles of newspapers on the newsagent's steps had not yet been taken in. Empty milk bottles were waiting for the milkman. Stray dogs and cats that might have lived around here before now followed their own agendas.

I passed the hospital and Town Hall on the way to The Headrow.[28] Dark eerie shapes were hurrying in front of me and behind me, green ghosts under the new street lighting, all heading for the two bus terminals. The bus terminals served the towns around Leeds City and the rest of Yorkshire. There

---

[28] The Headrow is the main thoroughfare through Leeds City Center.

was a smattering of umbrellas, but most people, like me, could not be bothered. It was not as though rain would spoil anybody's factory-oiled hairdo. The overalls added to the lumpy look. Occasionally I caught a glimpse of myself in a darkened shop window and marveled at how I had become Mrs. Boller. I had my shopping bag and handbag over my arm, my coat and overall tails flapping, and my stockings sagging over my work shoes. Fifteen years old, going on fifty.

The two large department stores on The Headrow were named Lewis's and Schofields. I liked to linger a minute to look at the window displays. Their windows were lit all night and become more elaborate every day; crowded with the things peacetime housewives used in their homes. I thought I had seen it all at the orphanage (and cleaned it all), but not so! One morning, I saw an astonishing thing—a washing machine! It washed the clothes, rinsed them, and even wrung the water out of them. No washboards, no changes of water, no wringers needed! Next to it was a dryer, no more dripping clotheslines over the beds or the back yard, never mind the street. What next?

The bus stood darkly silent in its usual stall. It appeared to be empty, but it was not. I climbed the step and sat in my usual seat between the lolling cloth caps, headscarves, and mops of greasy hair that lay slumped between dirty flannel collars. A sour smell of old sweat and machine oil hung in the air. The oily clothing acted as wadding into which to sink and continue whatever dreams had been interrupted by the alarm clock.

The young Polish woman I sat next to acknowledged my arrival by pulling her coattails aside to make room, and then dropped her head back against the window. Her name was Johanna. I called her Nina. She was twenty-five years old and also worked at Woodhouses, in the same mill as me, in mending. We did not speak in the mornings, but in the evening, on the way back to Leeds, we conversed in German. The Polish community was well established. They had their own shops and Saturday night dances to which Nina invited me, but Mother had already limited my weekends to Estonians only. She said I was becoming too involved with English people of a certain "class," which would hinder my future social development. She was not speaking about Nina, but the weavers who said "you what?" and dropped their h's.

The earliest arrivals were already slumped in sleep, wrapped in silence. The bus seating habits had become set. People were too tired to do anything, but sit where they always sat. The English sat near the front, leaving the back of the bus to the foreigners.

Women, like women everywhere, took things in stride. They adapted more easily to new situations. There were many women whose coats had once been stylish, but had long ago lost their shape. They did not care. They wore headscarves, something Grandmother still would not do. She had always worn hats, not as a fashion statement, but as a declaration of the artistic spirit over the relentless oppression of conformity. "Conformity clogs the spirit," she would tell Mother, wagging her pencil in warning. The five years at the hospital and the many disasters since coming to England had left Mother shaken and unsure of herself. Until England she had never done anything more domestic than pour herself a glass of water. She had never cooked and still did not know how to cook, but she had started dusting. We stared at her in amazement.

"She'll get over it," said Grandmother.

The women were doing all right, but the foreign men were disoriented. They were all highly educated, still "gentlemen" (former teachers, doctors, city officials, even cabinet ministers, or they would not have had to flee Communism). Their identities remained in their ethnic communities and what we saw of them was their form of silent nightmares to which they had become inured. That did not mean they had succumbed—not in the factories, in the steel mills, or the textile mills. They did not mingle with the "low class" culture of the workplace. Some had become the butt of jokes among their English co-workers. If they knew what was being said about them they did not care, and a few might have even taken it as a badge of resistance. There were several such men on our bus. They dressed in shabby, stained, but well-cut overcoats, wide trousers, and Homburgs.[29] In the early morning light they looked like city officials after a hard night on the town. Their English counterparts wore bib overalls, greasy leather jackets, and flat caps. The caricature effect was exacerbated by the battered briefcases they clung to, which doubled as lunch pails. Around the sheds they were known as "the overcoats." The English winked, smirked, and asked each other, "What's in't briefcase, then?"

The answer was, "The official sandwich," it was no joke when an "overcoat's" loom broke down and the tuners did not exactly hurry to "his Lordship's" side, reducing the man's output and wage for the week.

When the bus conductor arrived he switched on the lights, with the cruel humor of someone already awake, while everybody else was groggy.

"Ee-up! Let's 'ave you then!" he joked, and hoisted his satchel around his neck, adjusted the ticket machine and plopped down in the front seat to read the morning newspaper. Time enough to punch the tickets. He knew where everyone got on and got off.

The driver came last, throwing away his cigarette butt. He pulled himself into the cab and a few minutes later we were on our way, through the dark pre-dawn city, picking up additional passengers as we went along. The same faces, the

"Satanic Mill," Farsley, England, 1950s.

---

[29] A man's soft felt hat with a dented crown.

266

same banter at each stop. The unintelligible "Yorkshire" with its flat -a's and -u's was a familiar tune to the sleepy ear.

"Morning luv!"

"Cold innit!"

"Aye, that it is!"

"Summat awful!"

At Stanningley bottom, the first of the "overcoats" got off. Nina had told me he had been a Latvian bigwig. His briefcase was impressive. The next to get off was a former Polish wartime pilot, wearing his leather helmet. The helmet and long leather coat were familiar from camp newsreels.

Nina was partly dozing, mouth open, scarf pulled down over her forehead. She was not interested in learning English. Her favorite expression was "I don't want to be bothered!" I could see her point. My English orphanage "advantage" had done nothing for me and I was busy unlearning Matron's accent to adapt to the Yorkshire dialect of the people at the mill. I wanted to make friends. The foreigners worked in a separate shed from the English and isolated themselves on purpose. Poles dominated, followed by Latvians and Lithuanians with a sprinkling of Italians. I was the only Estonian. Mother's friend Friida had left. She had lost her hearing, but had found herself an English husband whom everybody admired because he really did do the dishes and change diapers.

Farsley had once been a typical Daleside village geared to the sheep and wool trade that had thrived in the valleys between the bare hills and moors of North Yorkshire. You can still see old weavers' cottages running diagonally across hillsides. The Industrial Revolution mechanized the weaving industry. The Wool Barons built mills and the weavers went to work in them. The villages remained pretty isolated until the war brought Americans to the military bases. Soon after the war DPs came with their strange ways and strange clothes.

Woodhouses Mill was at the bottom of a deep valley. Its tall chimney poked out of the sloping hillside like the neck of a prehistoric monster proclaiming its dominance over the empty sheep shelters and stone-littered fields that no longer had a function. The wool was shipped in and half the weavers came by bus from Leeds and Bradford. The other half lived in the old cottages, in newer houses or in the old brick terraces that had been built for the workers along with the mill itself.

As a foreigner, I was assigned to the foreign shed. I was the youngest weaver in the entire mill. Friida had tried to prepare me for the noise, but it still overwhelmed me on my first day. It was like an explosion that did not stop no matter how hard I clamped my hands over my ears. I had been thrown into the jaws of a roaring monster whose moving parts crashed and filled the shed from floor to ceiling, thumping, twirling, spinning and leaping. Most of the machinery was made from steel on leather, all crashing together. The only parts that were not leaping or crashing together were the people who walked on raised wooden platforms between the hot metal parts. Their job was to watch a piece of cloth that kept growing with each thump and twitch, bang and leap. They had to make sure that nothing went wrong—that no warp or weft thread had broken and that there were no visible flaws that could not be combed out quickly.

Some of the Polish men oversaw as many as ten looms while the women had two or four. The oily heat that issued from each machine, mixed with wool dust, filled my eyes and nostrils.

On my first day the foreman who had clocked me in took me into the shed. He guided me between the looms to a corner where a single wooden platform awaited me. It had not yet been turned on. He could not speak to me because of the noise, but motioned for an elderly woman at the next loom to come over. They nodded to each other in agreement. Previous agreements had been made. I understood the woman was going to teach me the job.

While they communicated with hand gestures, I stared in horror at the steel tipped shuttles flying back and forth across the looms like bullets in a crossfire. These were the "hot shots" Mother's friends had joked about, dents in the steel door nearby proved that some of the shuttles occasionally misfired. It was not hard to imagine getting your hair tangled in the shafts and rollers. The shafts leaped like puppets, prompted by wooden pegged scrolls, powered by moving leather pulleys that stretched from the floor to a central ceiling shaft that engaged all the wheels and cogs on the ground so that the whole thing could move together.

The shuttles caused most of the noise and the pulleys were the source of the heat. The shafts caused the dust. A mixture of oil and wool dust covered the concrete floor in a gooey, slippery mess. Falling and slipping against the pulleys was a real danger. Wire cages enclosed the main machinery, but the tops were open. There were no windows, only slanted, grimy skylights that allowed just enough light so you could tell when it was daylight. It was dark when I arrived at work and dark when I left. The main light source was supplied by light bulbs dangling over each loom. Large fans designed to bring in fresh air only stirred the dust and raised it to cover everything like candy floss.

The woman assigned to teach me was an elderly Latvian named Erika Ramins. Because of the noise we could not speak. I did not know her name until later that day. Erika became my teacher. She became my friend for life, also Grandmother's friend. She was one of us. When Erika saw me standing by the wall, holding my ears, she beckoned me forward and put her plump hand on my cheek. Her smile of encouragement reminded me immediately of Grandmother and all the foreigners I had known who did not shrink from physical contact.

"Come. I show," the woman mouthed, gently pulling my hands from my ears. The noise was so terrible I began to cry.

She shook her head sympathetically, then firmly nudged me over to the loom and put my hands on the bar. Thus we began the simple task of turning the loom on and off. She stood behind me, keeping her hand over mine on the loom bar, letting me feel the rhythm of the machine with my body. The English never touched each other. I held myself rigid at first, but there was a definite timing to the shuttles, to the entire circus of leaping wood, wool,

268

and leather. You had to feel it in the body. Once you had grasped the rhythm, everything worked. It was all timing. If you got the timing right, you could operate the loom bar and slide the machine to a safe halt, but the shuttles still frightened me, even though Erika was behind me. The steel tips were flying at more than a hundred miles an hour into constantly moving metal containers designed to catch them. At the same time a line of moving shafts raised the warp. The threads of the warp were fed from a large roller at the back of the loom. Any mistiming on any of those moving parts meant disaster.

Before you could stop the loom you had to catch the last shuttle at exactly the second it entered the slot or it would become a lethal weapon.

Erika was patient. She tapped her temple, her heart, and her lips. "Sooo!"

"*Gut!*" she shouted into my ear.

She taught me how to oil the loom's wheels and metal parts, how to watch for breaks in the warp. We had to constantly check the cloth for broken ends. Erika also taught me the most important task a weaver had to master—how to tie a weaver's knot.[30]

When the hooter[31] sounded for my first midday break Erika told me to get my coat.

"Today, work *gut*. Today, must be afraid" She shook her head and tied her scarf under her chin. "*Morgen* better!" Tomorrow better. She motioned for me to follow her out of the shed and up the village street. I followed her automatically, my ears ringing so badly that I was still hearing the looms outside and nothing else, not even passing cars.

Erika took me to her home, a small brick house on a side street. We entered a dark room where a man was already sitting at the table with his head in his hands. He looked very old. Until he lifted his head and jerked himself back from wherever he had been in his mind. He was not old at all, maybe a bit older than Mother. He did not look well.

A gentleman, he stood up to shake my hand when Erika introduced us.

"*Mein* husband, Vilis. Vilis play concert *violin*, Riga, now play night shift." Erika chuckled at her own joke and began to slice a loaf of bread already on the table. Her husband sat down again.

I was surprised to see that they had an entire house to themselves, one room up and one down, but only limited furniture in the room. There was the essential table, chairs and an old couch. A staircase led upstairs.

Seeing that I was still standing, the husband pulled out a chair.

Erika was watching me from the corner of her eye while she smeared something on the bread. The husband, I could see, did not have enough English to continue a conversation and did not want to speak German. It happened a lot. I knew a few words in Latvian. "*Kutu prauks?*"

"Ah!" Vilis came alive and continued in rapid Latvian.

"No. No!" I protested. "Speak English."

---

[30] A smooth knot that will not slip.

[31] A hooter is a siren, used in English mills much as a whistle is in the US.

"No English." It was his turn to shrug his shoulders.

Erika put the bread on a plate and shoved it in front of me.

"Bread *mit* fats," she explained.

Pork dripping. She must have an oven. You had to have an oven to cook pork. To have an oven you had to have a kitchen, not just a gas ring. She gave her husband a slice and munched on one herself, not bothering with the plate. Now both were watching me strangely, their eyes misted. I must have looked like a child to them with my long braids. I hated my braids, but Mother would not let me cut my hair.

"Not until you're eighteen," she told me.

My head ached, I felt nauseous. I could not think of what more to say, so I just munched on the bread. Erika brought me a glass of milk and sat down also. We ate in silence. They could see I was upset, although I tried not to show it.

Suddenly the husband pushed his chair back and went upstairs. A few seconds later he came down carrying a violin. He brushed it lovingly with knotty fingers, and then sat down again. Nodding to Erika he began to play for me. He played a tune I remembered from Haapsalu, played on the piano instead of the violin. It had never occurred to me to ask the names of the pieces I knew by heart.

Elin at the loom, Woodhouses Mill, Farsley, 1954.

"What is it called?" I asked.

"Is *hoom*", home, said Vilis, in broken English. He placed the instrument on his knees and lowered his head again. He appeared to have fallen asleep.

"Come, must back vork," said Erika quickly. "Vilis he is stay home now. Heart not good."

The first months at the mill felt like years.

The hour-long bus ride became routine, the noise a physical discomfort that lasted through the evening. The constant ringing in my ears varied from the roar of the sea to the sizzle of water on a hot iron. Occasional bouts of dizziness and stabs of earache made me suddenly clutch my head. I had such strong headaches on Saturday mornings that Grandmother had to apply a cold compress before Mother and I could go to the library. I also had to shade my eyes from bright daylight. Mother bought me a pair of sunglasses. Friida assured Mother the symptoms would pass and that her own deafness had nothing to do with the job.

The symptoms changed. Soon I could hear one loom normally, but nothing when they were all turned on—solid silence pressing down against my head. When that first happened I had been listening to a woman talking nearby; suddenly only her mouth moved, but there was no more sound. I panicked, thinking I had already gone deaf. I soon learned to lip-read like everyone else.

When I was able to work my own loom, Erika no longer helped me, but she continued to watch me. I watched for her, the way as a child I had watched Grandmother moving around our kitchen, knowing she would be the first to reach me if I were hit by a shuttle or caught my hair in the rollers. When I looked particularly distressed, she smiled encouragement and tapped her watch. Not long before the tea break. Not long before the dinner break. Not long before it was time to go home.

Although I relied on Erika while I was at the loom, I did not want to become a burden on her during breaks and the dinner hour. I did not want her to feel obligated to take me home with her, because then Vilis would feel obligated to stay awake for me. The foreigners continued to observe European manners, another thing the English weavers laughed at. Men lifted their hats; women shook hands. At home Mother was teaching me etiquette beyond the proper introductions I had already learned as a child. I was not to put my coat on before saying good-bye. I was to always inquire about a person's health and to make polite conversation before getting to why I had come, no matter how urgent. I needed to wait for older people to rise from the table first. At fifteen I was still considered a child; when visitors came I had to sit quietly and answer their questions politely until I was dismissed. I would become an adult when I turned eighteen and was confirmed in the church. That was our way.

The English weaver nearest my age was Daisy. Hetty's girls had taught me how to start a friendship without formal introductions, no etiquette at the mill. When tea break came around I drifted off into the English shed and saw a girl sitting on one of the rollers and straining tea through her teeth. You had to do that so as not to choke on tea leaves.

I sauntered over. "Hallo! So what's up?"

"Nowt," she answered.

After two or three such approaches we began to talk.

Daisy lived in the village. Her parents also worked at the mill. "Always have," she said. "So did my grands." I guessed "grands" meant grand-parents. Her father was a tuner and her mother worked in spinning. Her boyfriend, Kevin, was also a tuner, she informed me with pride.

As soon as the hooter sounded for the tea break, I hurried over to the boiling water tap, mashed my tea leaves with the already added sugar, and carried my mug to the dye pool between the mill outbuildings. Daisy usually got there first because her shed was closest. We never arranged a time, just turned up, and it worked.

The dye pool was a filthy, scummy pond that drained off the dye vats and was referred to as the "dead pool." The water was black with an oily rainbow-colored sheen that made you feel nauseous just looking at it. Nothing lived in it or around it, but it was the only place open enough to catch those rare rays of sunshine we all craved, and it was the only bit of daylight not filtered through dirty glass. The rest of the yard was an uneven mess of mud puddles and tracks left by trucks and forklifts. Piles of wooden pallets and rusting machinery shored up the many outbuildings that surrounded a tall square chimney in the middle of the complex.

"I didn't think you'd speak English an' all!" Daisy confessed. "They don't, you know." She cocked her head towards the foreign shed. "So why don't that lot go back to where they comes from?"

I flushed with guilty pleasure of not being lumped in with "that lot."

"It's the war," I told Daisy. "A lot of bad things happened."

"Not 'ar fault innit! Strange lot, them! Who they think they are, anyroad!"

"I don't think they know," I answered truthfully.

"Might be right at that." Daisy gave me a long look sideways. There was a lot more to Daisy than the greasy hair, the dirty overalls, the oil-soaked shoes, and almost blue complexion of sunless skin. Not that I looked any different. The only daylight we saw during the week was by that pool.

The tea break was short. There was barely enough time to sift a few mouthfuls of tea before the hooter sounded again and it was back to the loom. Daisy and I were not always alone. Daisy's boyfriend, Kevin, interrupted us and injected himself into our conversations, as if they were already married. Kevin was an apprentice tuner and gave himself airs. He hung about during the tea break, swinging his spanner and glaring at me. He even pulled Daisy aside once and whispered something urgently, while looking at me. Daisy listened and pushed him away. "Don't be daft," she said. I could tell he did not want Daisy mixing with that "foreign lot." Feelings were especially heated between the men.

Getting to know Daisy was important to me. Erika was part of my foreign life and old people. Erika had no children and encouraged my friendship with Daisy because she could see I was starting to have fun. Daisy was seventeen, two years older than I was. Even if she did drop her h's and spoke a heavy dialect, she was the English world that I recognized as the "real world," no matter that it was not Mother's ideal. Examples Mother pointed out to me as people I should emulate were "in University" and probably forty-five-year-old midgets. It did not seem disloyal to want to live in the here and now. What good were table manners when we barely had a table and only two chairs? We sat on the beds.

Since getting to know Daisy and Kevin, I was seeing a boyfriend, girl-friend relationship for the first time without anybody pretending that marriage was romance without sex, or worse, that it was sex without romance. Nobody even breathed about this in my Estonian world. Daisy and Kevin were "doin' it," as Daisy put it. She added, "We're in luv," in case I had missed her meaning.

Love and sex were two subjects I had not yet seen in the same context. This was my opportunity to understand why people got married, except to immigrate to Canada.

Sex was still a vague subject, which Pauline's medical books had made even more confusing. I still did not know how the baby was actually put inside the woman. If the baby was at the end of the man's penis, in this sperm jelly, it had to be very, very small indeed. At least the size of a pea, maybe even smaller. What if the man dropped it accidentally while transferring it into the womb and, what if they didn't want babies? What if the man dumped the sperm with the baby inside it on the ground? A horrible thought! A woman definitely had to love a man a lot to let him put babies into her. I could not think of anything nastier. No wonder marriages broke up.

Grandmother shied away from such questions. Mother's replies to anything to do with men was a snort. In Estonian books, which Mother insisted I read, people got married, bore children, and worked from dawn to dark, until some calamity befell them. Not a word about how the children came about. Nothing about romantic love. The grim priorities in fact demanded that a man should love his country first, then the flag, then the children. If the wife was mentioned at all, she was left weeping after her husband and sons went off to war. When it came to choosing between his wife and his horse, the hero always chose his horse.

After finishing *Ivanhoe* I was also left disappointed. The relationships there were equally passionless and lacked common sense.

I wanted to know about love. There had to be love. I understood love for one's parents and relatives. I loved Grandmother. My love for God and God's love for us had turned problematic after my introduction to religion, but I still loved God and Jesus. I also loved goodness and mercy. I understood "cat love" as unfair judging and heartless betrayal. It was what everyone feared, but fell into anyway. Cat love was a terrible risk; it ended friendships, ruined reputations, produced children parents could not cope with, and made normal people hate each other. I had decided a long time ago that I would never get married except to a poet who would die young, but that was then.

Now all I wanted to know was how a girl got a boy to like her. Daisy and Kevin's relationship, what I could see of it, did not look too promising. We could all see them kissing and cuddling behind the shed, but it was usually Kevin pushing Daisy about. I could not see any real love, just Kevin showing signs of becoming a possessive husband. The kind that women eventually wished they had never met.

So how did a girl find the right words to start a romance?

Daisy talked a lot about dancing "at't' Mecca." She called it "bopping." She liked music. When I told Daisy I, too, liked music, she reeled off the names of Bands.

"I like Chopin," I ventured.

Daisy looked at me blankly.

I never mentioned Chopin again.

Daisy continued to invite me to join her and Kevin at this Mecca. "Give it a butchers.[32] We'll 'ave a right blast! An'a bit'o' make-up won't 'urt you neither!" She observed critically. "Wi'a bit'a'color, you won't look like a rabbit." She offered to color my eyebrows and eyelashes.

"No, thanks," I responded in alarm. "But *ta* anyway." Mother would have a fit, but here was my chance to not just talk and behave like English girls (not the kind Mother had in mind), but like the ones I knew. I did not want to become a "painted woman", just not be treated like a child. In Daisy's

---

[32] Yorkshire slang for "have a look."

world I was an adult. The gap between my life at the mill and my life at home had become an open grid. Every step was a hazard, and I had to tread carefully not to fall through to reach either end.

When I had told Daisy that the foreigners did not know who they were, it was the truth. I hardly knew who I was anymore. Constantly changing life-styles, languages, even accents. The English I spoke at night school was not the English I spoke at the mill. Mother thought I was adapting too well to the wrong influences, yet all she could offer me were the schizophrenic lives of people like the "overcoats," the janitor/doctors, carpet weaving/professors, and opera singing/factory hands who lived in the past. I had no past. All I had was the present.

Night school had added to the complexity of my life. I could not tell Daisy that I was studying shorthand and typing. Neither could I tell anyone in night school that I was a weaver. The two worlds did not mix. Even the mill office was barred to me. I had to knock and wait outside the door for one of the office girls to acknowledge my presence. When they did it was with distaste. I had to state my business and remain outside. I knew I looked a fright in my dirty overalls and oily shoes and probably smelled worse.

My workday ended at six. I caught the half-past-six bus back to Leeds, got there at half-past-seven and dashed straight into the women's lavatories. There the transformation from filthy weaver to fairly clean student was ac-complished. I also had a towel and soap, a washrag and hairbrush. Luckily there was hot water and the transformation did not take long. It became a habit. The only thing that troubled me was the smell of oil in my hair. As I was usually late for classes, I sat in the back and endured my reputation as a dawdler.

In addition to Pitman's and Leeds College of Commerce, I caught another bus on Friday nights to the Leeds College of Music for an elocution course to keep the Yorkshire accent at bay. I was not getting any credits for those courses, but the posh atmosphere gave me yet another glimpse of English life.

When I got home in the evenings around ten o'clock Mother was already asleep. Grandmother kept my dinner warm by wrapping the casserole into tea towels and tucking it into my bed. That way I also had a warm bed to slip into.

My Estonian life began on Saturday morning.

We slept until at least seven. Grandmother cooked an "English breakfast" of eggs, bacon, and tomato. I had introduced her to fried tomatoes and fried bread, English style. Mother told us not to eat raw bacon in lieu of smoked ham. "You'll get worms," she warned.

After breakfast Mother and I went to the library. The library was the highlight of my week. Reading had become my passion as it was Mother's, but for different reasons. Mother read to pass the time. I read because I wanted to know more about everything. Mother's "Hardy country" was real. She had also been right about English institutions—I just wished we had not spent so much time in them.

In addition to night school I had an hour of Estonian "school" on Saturdays and an hour on Sundays conjugating French verbs with an old lady up the street, an *émigré* in dire straits and freezing to death. Wearing gloves, we sat beside her one-bar electric heater. I suspected she only turned on the heater because of me. It did not seem right, but Grandmother said the lady would not take the money any other way, so we conjugated verbs and spoke as much French as I had time to memorize between my other homework assignments from the different schools. I still read half a book on Saturday night, before bedtime. I could read English quickly by glancing at the whole page rather than mouthing each word. It took longer to read Estonian. Nothing yet about love or sex, but lots of suffering.

One morning, I arrived at the dye pool and could barely see Daisy. She was surrounded by a circle of young twisters, pattern weavers, tuners and other people who usually gathered by the pool. Menders and women from spinning hovering around the edges, going "ooh!" and "aah!" and crinkling their noses. Daisy had found a mouse under her loom, inside the fluff. It was newly born, still naked, more like a skinned rabbit than a rodent. She was trying to feed it some tea. Its mouth opened, but it didn't know what to do with the tea. The liquid trickled past its mouth into Daisy's cupped hand. I could see its little heart pulsing through the thin skin of the ribcage, rapid frantic beats seemingly detached even from the half-dead body that enclosed it. It does not want to be here, I thought. It does not want to be enclosed in that filthy skin and bones. It was just born for heaven's sake, it was life. I was looking at "life." I had not thought or realized that life could be so completely wasted that it could become trash. How could life be meaningless?

"Throw it in't bin," someone advised.

However not Daisy, she lowered her dark greasy head so that her hair fell forward over her cheeks and tried to blow warm breath into the naked creature's nostrils. The mouse closed its eyes, its head lolled. It looked dead, yet its heart continued beating. Life, life, life! I was mesmerized. That life had been lit less than an hour ago, so how could it fail?

"Into't pool w'it! You're daft if you think it'll live. And what if it do, what for? For't cat to get at?" One of the older women weavers tried to take charge.

"'Ere, let me at it," said Kevin, wielding his spanner so he could bat it to death.

"Oh shut up," said Daisy. Then she did something I would not have been able to do. She gave the mouse a tender kiss, dropped it on the ground, and stomped on it.

"There! That's that!" She wiped away a tear with the back of her hand and stalked off. All that was left of that pulsing heart was a bloody smear of dirt alongside the scummy crust left by the poisonous dyes that had already killed the grass and everything else around there.

"What was that?" a latecomer to the scene asked.

"Daisy just killed a mouse," said Kevin in disgust.

"You cruel thing!"

They all walked back to the shed together, Kevin trailing the women. He was upset, but I wondered why. He had been ready to kill it himself only Daisy got ahead of him. She had acted independently of him and he was jealous of that, too. Their "luv" was already becoming a scary "romance" from what I could see.

Yet what Daisy had done was even scarier. She had done the right thing for the mouse, but not for the life it had contained. The mouse received a merciful escape, but what if it had wanted more for itself than mercy? A life, even if born under a loom in the mucky fibers of wool and dust should at least have had a chance to know more than fear and pain and death. I had always thought death should be more dignified than being run over by a tank. Well, this was worse!

I put my hand over my own heart. It was beating just as furiously as that of the mouse. I was almost choking on the knowledge of my heart's independent existence in my chest cavity. A heart had no choice in whose chest it ended up, but I wanted my heart to be glad it was in me. I wanted my life to have more meaning than it had so far. If I continued the way I was living, there was nothing to look forward to, nothing to make my heart happy, and in the end it might not even get a decent burial.

On the way back to the shed I noticed that the sun had come out again, but because of yellow smoke and haze around the chimney, the sky was the color of piss.

When I got back to my loom the foreman had already noted my lateness. He stood by my loom and pointed to his watch. "Sod you!" I thought helplessly. I had no idea how I could change my life even though I was beginning to see above the pit, beyond the brick walls and unyielding authorities who had put us where we were.

On Friday nights the Leeds College of Music showed me another England that made me understand what had drawn Mother and her friends and how they had been betrayed.

My teacher, Miss Hayes, was a little grey-haired lady, very upper crust, but without the snobbery and putdowns I was used to. I was her private pupil, paying my way with the money I earned at the mill. She was also very artistic. She wore long flowered dresses that looked hand painted. Her glasses hung on a golden chain around her neck and her pale blue eyes had the look of water in a closed bottle. Her eyes moved with the cadences, higher and lower. I had become trapped by Yorkshire vowels and she was teaching me to pronounce the vowels correctly. I could not understand all the words, but as with Italian opera, it was only the sounds that mattered.

"Go and catch a falling star, ah...ah"
Get with child a mandrake root...mah...man...mand...rake.
Tell me, where all past years are...pahst...pahst years a...aar.
Or who cleft the Devil's foot...fut...a shallow '-u-', as in to, not the broad '-u-' of the Yorkshire bus'."

I had a good ear for sounds I copied the teacher exactly.

276

"Good! Good!" She beamed and reminded me of Grandmother reciting "dear Erni's" poems, pressing his books to her chest. Had I not been determined to keep my English and Estonian lives separate, I might have told Miss Hayes that my grandfather had been a poet, but I feared she would ask, "Where was that?" I would have to tell her it was in a country that no longer existed, where foreigners who had come to England after the war had left their dreams. I did not want her to think I was making things up. "Don't tell them anything," Grandmother had told Mother at the hospital.

The elocution lessons were a beautiful ending to a harrowing week. I always went home in a daze.

While we ate breakfast together on Saturday mornings, I showed Grandmother my elocution homework and read her the poems assigned by Miss Hayes. Grandmother closed her eyes to listen and, although she could not understand any of the words, her expression convinced me that the language of poetry really was universal music.

Famous Quarry Hill Flats.
England's first attempt at congregate living.

Our name finally came up on the Council housing list. We were given a two-bedroom flat in a massive block of government housing known as Quarry Hill Flats. It was an experiment in congregate living and had been called a modern marvel, the largest social housing complex in the United Kingdom. The project measured three miles around with arched gates in the perimeter and interior buildings that included a washhouse and a community hall. In some blocks there were eight floors. In ours there were five. Our flat was on the fifth floor.

Each section of ten to sixteen flats included a lift and stairs. Each flat had a bathroom with a bathtub, a kitchen with a solid-fuel range, a state-of-the-art refuse disposal system, and an interior boiler that was heated

277

Grandmother on the balcony of Quarry Hill Flats, late 1950s. She called it her garden.

from the living room fireplace. There was also a small balcony large enough for a chair and a shelf for plants and herbs.

When we arrived, the garbage chute was already clogged, the lift was broken, the stairwells smelled of urine, and every accessible wall was covered with graffiti. How Grandmother got our coal up the steps I will never know because I was at work all day. Many residents hoarded coal in their bathtubs and bathed in the communal bath house/wash house combination where the sinks had been vandalized, the fixtures had been stolen, and the dressing cubicles were used as toilets. The waterlogged wooden platforms that were supposed to keep you off the scummy floor were rotting away. As the light bulbs were constantly stolen, it was so dark inside that you could either break your neck slipping on old soap or fall through the platforms and break a leg instead. Other hazards were drunks and tramps who lived there, enjoying shelter and all the clothes they could steal off the drying racks.

The flats might have been a good idea in the architect's office in 1938, but in reality Quarry Hill Flats had quickly become a worse slum than anything it had been designed to replace. The police came almost every night to deal with drunks, abusive husbands, domestic disputes, vandalism, and derelicts sleeping and urinating in the stairwells.

For us it was a palace — our first real home since leaving Estonia. We had our own kitchen and bathroom. The living room fireplace/boiler arrangement gave us abundant hot water, and the tiny balcony off the kitchen became Grandmother's "garden" where she liked to sit and say she was "outside." "God has remembered us again," she said, with tears in her eyes.

The next luxury I bought was a floor model radiogram.[33] It was such a handsome piece of furniture that it doubled as a cabinet on which to display our family photographs and the Estonian flag.

---

[33] A combination radio and gramophone.

Chapter 15

A WEAVER'S KNOT
1954

1954: Rationing ends in England.

Now that we had our own flat, there was more room to entertain. When Mother's friends came we were no longer forced to sit on beds or on the floor, although we did anyway. Grandmother, almost eighty, still did all the cooking, baking, cleaning, laundry, and housekeeping, but on a grander scale. She grew herbs and made her own "cheese" by suspending bags of sour milk from the kitchen ceiling. Dishes of salt herring soaked in odd places. The balcony became both her garden and pantry. I suggested she buy utensils and gadgets like those I had cleaned at the orphanage, but she said "no need," except for maybe a grater and colander. My offers were not completely altruistic. I wanted our flat to look less "foreign" in case I wanted to bring English friends home with me. Such a thing had not yet happened, and I could not see it happening, because Mother's friends had already established priority.

Sundays became modified versions of our former Haapsalu summers. Mother was writing plays and sometimes had rehearsals in our flat, but her regular circle was made up of music lovers. We now owned two musical instruments—the radiogram and the piano. Everyone brought their favorite records or sheet music. The Latvian "Valkyrie" still worked in a factory and was taking voice lessons and auditioning for small opera companies and choirs. Two former Estonian opera singers were in our group; the husband had lost his voice working in the steel foundry, but his wife Elena still sang

Grandmother tending our fireplace, Quarry Hill Flats, Leeds, 1961.

beautifully. Another couple was younger. Mother was translating popular English songs for the husband, Elmar Järvik, to sing at Estonian get-togethers. The sixth in the group was a younger man named Ivar, five years older than I. Ivar led our folk dance troupe; his passions were ballet music and operettas.

Grandmother supplied coffee and open-faced sandwiches. Sometimes only cheese and tomato. The men brought bottles. Music filled the flat to the accompaniment of clicking glasses and clattering cups and saucers. Napoleon Brandy and Armagnac went well with coffee, salt herring salad, sandwiches, and pastries. Rachmaninoff, Franz Lehar, Maria Callas, and Nat King Cole all had their turn, but the most important element in these gatherings was the sport of intellectual conversation—a wholly European pastime, practically unappreciated in the English-speaking world. Almost everyone smoked. Everyone drank, but it was rare for anyone to get drunk. The room was soon blue with smoke and heated by excited chatter of people who could finally relax, who had a shared fate. They had been soaked like a garment through many washes, over a long period of time. That garment, their fate, had retained little of its original color, but the fabric no longer scratched.

These *musicales* lasted from early Sunday afternoon until the wee hours of Monday morning. There were usually nine or ten of us in the flat. As in the past, we sat on beds, on chairs, or on cushions on the floor. Every bit of comfort was a luxury.

The mood changed when it got dark outside. Everyone found a comfortable position, layback, and listened to music, no longer as background accompaniment, but for the sheer enjoyment of it. Mother turned off the lights. If the fireplace was lit, it shed a glow across the ceiling. If it was too warm, Mother opened windows and let in the evening breeze. Being on the fifth floor insured us enough air to move the smoke about. The music drowned out unwelcome sounds from the courtyard—the drunks, the domestic fights, the brawling neighbors, and police sirens. For a short while we forgot we lived in the worst slum in Leeds.

I enjoyed the music, which brought back memories of Haapsalu, but I had nothing to add to the conversation. I knew nothing of Estonian politics or world affairs. I was present because I happened to live there. At fifteen, going-on-sixteen, I was not expected to add to the conversation anyway, because to the adults I was still a child. I had no place in their adult world.

Mother had gone berserk when she found out that I was not eligible for grammar school or further education of any kind under the British school system. She had not known about the 11+ examination. What made my situation worse was that I was the granddaughter of the *poet Enno*, the daughter of *the former actress* Liki Toona and my father became an even more famous theatre producer in Soviet Estonia, after we left. The use of former professional titles was part of the etiquette of exile. Even Grandmother was introduced first as the *widow of the poet* before her given name. Nuances of Estonian social behavior had been largely meaningless to me until we got our own flat and began to take part in the Estonian community. I did not belong there either. The only title Mother could still hope to someday give me was *proua*, or Mrs. In keeping with our traditions, this included a ceremony where the bride dons the marriage bonnet as a symbol of abandoning her carefree single life and becoming the careworn, harried heroine of Nordic sagas—a symbolic gesture about as romantic as having a root canal.

Mother stoically bore the disgrace of my uneducated state. I endured the acute embarrassment, especially on weekends when I had nowhere to go except into my room, and that would have been impolite. I stayed, lolling on a corner of Grandmother's bed, watching the adults, nibbling on this and that, and waiting for the lights to go out. Actually, while I knew nothing about politics or the Estonian past, I was becoming well aware of what I was missing. I read books every free minute I could squeeze into my days. I even kept a dictionary and pocket encyclopedia in my overall pocket at work and memorized words and general knowledge while walking the rostrum between my looms. I now had two looms.

I was glad when the lights went out. When they came back on, I was fast asleep. Mother woke me so I could go to my own bed, but seldom without a lecture about my cultural decline and lack of appreciation for the finer things of life. She attributed my decline to unfortunate influences, meaning the mill and Daisy in particular. She had heard about Daisy from Erika. Around midnight on Sundays Mother and I ended up having words. We usually went to bed in a bad mood.

Mother and I had never actually lived together. In Estonia she had lived in the theater; in Germany she had always gone ahead of Grandmother and me and had prepared our way. Her presence at the DP camp had been brief, and our interactions in England could have barely covered a page of notes. We had gone to bed at different times, and, while we enjoyed a few hours together on Saturdays, there had seldom been enough time or space to get into arguments. In Quarry Hill Flats we had more room, more time and different ideas about social life in general. Daisy and "boppin' at the Mecca" were unacceptable to Mother, and even I could not see Daisy sitting with us through an opera evening, or even ten minutes of Maria Callas screaming her head off. Of course Callas sang beautifully, but she represented most clearly the invisible wall between the two worlds that I inhabited daily.

I had become a master juggler in keeping both worlds in the air without dropping one on anyone's foot (except maybe Mother's.) I did not think that Mother realized I fell asleep simply because I was tired. I got up at four-thirty to go to work and did not get home until past ten at night. Maybe her impatience with me was a compliment. She expected me to handle myself as bravely as she had in the past. Of course I could have gone to bed before lights-out and still would have heard the music. In addition I had books to read, homework to study, poems to memorize, and French verbs to conjugate. I, too, had an agenda, like the stray cats around Caledonian Road.

I put up with opera divas trapped in golden cages because I wanted to stay close to Ivar. Ivar the beautiful, Ivar the talented. Ivar was the reason I was draining Daisy's romance for every hint that would help me get Ivar to notice me, not as a pesky half-sister sort of teenage nuisance, but as a vision of loveliness. Well not quite that, but at least as a woman, or, failing that, he might ask me to join his dance troupe. Ivar's nearness was the only thing that brightened my weekends. Daisy would have said I was "in luv!"

There were no boys my age in the Leeds/Bradford community, and the only young men who were not in school or University were the "air force boys." These "boys" were not really boys, but were in their middle and late twenties, technically men. Like everyone who had missed the 11+ examination, they were barred from higher education and worked in steel mills, carpet mills, and textile mills.

Just as the Russians had conscripted young Estonian men into the Soviet army, the Germans, when it was their turn, did the same. When the Germans were in Estonia fighting the Soviets, they were desperate for flyers. Some Estonian boys joined the Luftwaffe voluntarily while others were abducted from wherever the Germans could find them—on their way to school, off the fields, or just off the streets. Once picked up, the boys were not even allowed to say good-bye to their families. A great number of them were killed in the last months of the war. Those who survived were rounded up by the Allies and brought into DP camps in the British and American Zones. From DP camps they were shipped to England, America, and other countries within the UNRRA network.

All of the other countries allowed them to continue their education except Great Britain. Even if they had previously attended gümnasium in Estonia or Germany or had demonstrated artistic or academic talents, they could no longer pursue them formally. It was tragic, and the worst was when their former schoolmates and contemporaries who had been taken to other countries were able to return as exchange students to study at English schools—from which those who had remained in England were barred for life. These schools included Leeds University.

The *musicales* in our flat on Sundays were pleasant enough, but our weekend social calendar was seldom complete without the Sunday morning bus ride to Bradford, to the Estonian Club. Mother had theater rehearsals and Ivar folk dance rehearsals. Mother insisted that I accompany them. (How else would she find me an Estonian husband?) Grandmother stayed home to read and sketch. I, too, would have liked to stay at home and read, but I also wanted to be near Ivar. Mother eventually persuaded him to let me join the dance troupe where I was again the youngest, and not the best dancer. I had hoped to be partnered with Ivar, but instead he put me with an older man who kept jumping up and down, out of rhythm. It made my dancing even worse.

"So why can't I be Ivar's partner?" I complained to Mother.

"He thinks you're too fat. Not graceful enough."

That angered me, but in truth, I had come to accept that I was the failure everybody said I was. It was a fact. I even asked Mother whether I was pretty. She hesitated too long, and then said I had beautiful hands.

Ivar had no such failings. Ivar was a special case, thus recognized by the entire community. He was twelve when his family fled Estonia and seventeen when they arrived in England, also too old for the 11+ examination. Like the rest of us, he worked in a textile mill, but unlike me, his lack of education was not a stigma; it was a great tragedy. He had attended school in Estonia and *Gümasium* in Germany and had proved himself to be an extraordinarily talented dancer. He was also beautiful, with golden curls, a chiseled profile, a perfect nose, perfect teeth, a wonderful smile, and the figure of a Greek god. Everyone said he would have had a great career as a ballet dancer, but it was not to be. I wanted to console him. I had enough disappointments of my own, but even so I recognized that Ivar and I were leagues apart. The

284

only thing Ivar and I had in common was that we both winced when Grandmother put on our old record of Handel's *Largo*; he also clamped his fine long
fingers over his pearly-shell ears.

Ivar's father had been a tailor
in Estonia. In Leeds he worked in a
coat factory. He had been known
to bang his fist on the table when
he talked about his son's dancing.
He called it "prancing."

Ivar

Ivar's mother was a quiet
woman who lived in the shadows of
her husband. Our home was the
closest Ivar came to the *artistic
mileu* he craved, and thus he had
become the fourth member of our
household. When he was with us he could play his music, talk ballet, art,
literature, and poetry. Grandmother fed his spirit, and Mother was the only
person in his present world who could support his intellectual cravings.

When we traveled to Bradford Ivar always sat with Mother while I sat
behind them. Mother read a book, Ivar read *Paris Match*. He was also learning French and was far ahead of me. When they talked, they talked about...
Actually I had no idea what they talked about, I tuned them out and did my
crossword puzzles.

I had started writing poetry. My poems were being published in the Estonian newspaper in London. The editor, a well-known Estonian writer, said
I had talent, but alas, it was not the kind of talent that drew people's attention, like singing and dancing would have. Mother described me as "phlegmatic."

When we arrived at the Estonian Club, Ivar and Mother went straight to
their respective rehearsals. We were usually early. This gave me ample time
to go across the street to a private house where the air force boys boarded.
The couple who owned the house were surrogate parents and landlords.
Room and board paid their mortgage. The couple had made their home a
gathering place for anyone who wanted to drop in and feel at home in an
atmosphere less formal than the Club. The front door was unlocked all weekend, and there was always someone in the large living room. The men came
to relax, read newspapers, talk, and drink, play cards, and eat in the dining
room along with the boarders.

*Balts, Poles, "White" Russians, and other World War II exiles in England
shared a common experience in the early 1950's. Interaction with the English
was rare because of English class barriers. As time went by and exiles in
England prospered individually, that social isolation decreased. Ethnic clubs
such as the Estonian Club, Latvian Club, and Lithuanian Club served about
three generations of exiles, until the collapse of the Soviet Union.*

At the Estonian Club, women were generally in the kitchen, preparing
Estonian foods and of course gossiping. One day, while going past the kitchen

285

door, I heard my name. The women were talking about me as they were chopping gherkins for *rosolje*. "Elin won't have any difficulty finding herself an Estonian husband," said one of them. "Of course Ivar would be the natural choice, but we know how that is!" The remark was met by laughter and an undertone I did not understand.

The next comment was just as bad. "There isn't much to be desired all around. None of them is properly weaned, more like kittens removed from their mothers while wet behind the ears. Not a clue about life, especially marriage." More laughter.

I hoped to hear more, but dared not be discovered. Grandmother used to tell me that when you listen at doors you never hear anything good. It served me right. I should not have eavesdropped, but could not forget what I had heard. They had been talking about Ivar and the air force boys, but had lumped me in as well; I despaired. Another time a woman pinched my cheeks and said they were like a baby's bottom.

Mother was just as critical of me. With narrowed eyes, she measured my chubby hips.

"She has no fashion sense," she told Grandmother. My hair was a mess. In a fit of rebellion I had taken the scissors and cut my braids off; I was tired of being treated like a child. I was becoming less and less "phlegmatic." A hairdresser evened out the ragged edges, but I looked awful. Mother was so furious with me that we barely talked for a week.

"What she needs are friends her own age," Grandmother suggested from her bed or her "Eastern divan" as she liked to call it. To save paper she had taken to sketching on meat wrappers with bits of meat still clinging to them. Mother was upset with Grandmother, too. Neither of us was shaping up the way she wanted us to be.

"Estonian friends her own age," Mother corrected.

"Well, we don't have any of those."

"Ten years age difference isn't so bad," Mother pointed out, adjusting her stocking seams and brushing her hat. I knew which way the wind was blowing.

"Don't you think it's a bit premature?" Grandmother murmured, giving me the "don't get alarmed" look over her pencil. She said I was a *backfisch*, the German word for teenagers who are not quite ready to be adults yet, but Mother was not interested in whether or not I was ready for marriage. The important thing was that it would be an Estonian union. The pressure was on.

Mother had several suitors in mind. What no one knew and had not yet noticed was my hopeless infatuation with Ivar, a situation getting worse by the week because Ivar barely acknowledged me personally. Of course we talked, went to the cinema together with another Estonian named Emil, and visited my Polish friend Nina and her husband. We walked back together late at night, but it was always laughter and banter. Yet I remained optimistic. I was still too young and Mother was no help. She should have recognized a suitable match and left us alone together. He was the natural choice. He was closest to my age, and we spent so much time together that we were

286

practically married already. I guessed that was why she had not noticed him and instead encouraged other men, all much older than me.

Daisy and Kevin's romance, rocky as it was, was an example in the right direction. I had to learn how to convey my interest and feelings for a boy without throwing myself at him.

For the time being Mother's choices prevailed. One was a merchant marine, one of the air force boys. His name was Richard. He came on his motorbike, a dazzling huge chrome machine, which he parked downstairs. He was immediately surrounded by men and boys who might have felt tempted to have more than a butchers, except that Richard looked too dangerous to be messed with in his leather jacket and hobnailed boots.

Mother and Grandmother adored Richard. He brought gifts. For me a dozen red roses, for Mother *Crēpe de Chine* perfume from Paris, for Grandmother chocolates, the likes of which they had never known. In return Mother expected me to ride on his bike.

Richard's other hobby was flying planes out of Yeadon airport.

"You're not flying with him," said Grandmother. "Absolutely not!"

I did not mind the motorbike rides. They gave me a chance to see more of the wild North Yorkshire moors that stretched to the Scottish border. Some areas were so barren that it was like riding on the moon.

For the evening meal Grandmother prepared a banquet, and when we were so full we could barely move Richard and I went ballroom dancing. Not "boppin to't Mecca" like Daisy and Kevin, but to a posh ballroom. Richard was always polite and respectful, but I did not like it when he held me close. I told Mother I did not want to dance with him anymore. Mother ignored my protests.

"Richard wants to marry you," Mother told me one day, while she was helping me dress. "How do you feel about it?"

I was horrified.

"So I'll tell him, no?"

"Absolutely!"

At least Mother was giving me a choice.

Another young man Mother encouraged was a Canadian-Estonian exchange student studying at Leeds University. He stopped by regularly. He was good-looking, intelligent, and interesting. We dubbed him "The Nuclear" because his subject was nuclear physics.

"Now there's a catch for you," said Mother.

I was not looking for a "catch." I was waiting for Ivar to notice me.

One Sunday morning when Ivar and I arrived at the Bradford "family house" the atmosphere was awfully quiet. Several men were sitting around a table drinking. Ivar went to find his friend Emil. Richard was among the drinkers, wearing an undershirt, sprawled into a chair, his eyes bloodshot, and a cigarette dangling out of his mouth. I did not know he smoked and had never seen him this sloppy. I was glad I was not marrying him.

He barely acknowledged me.

"Ivar won't find Emil in his room," he said bitterly. "Emil dropped dead Tuesday evening coming home from work. The funeral was yesterday." Richard sank lower into his chair, swirled his drink around the glass, and added morosely, "Two down, five to go." He was speaking about another of the "boys" who had died in his sleep a few months earlier. When Richard spoke, it sent chills down my spine.

"What a stupid thing to say." I scolded him and left the room. It was true. Emil had collapsed in the street of a massive stroke, the second of the young men to die suddenly.

When I visited Bradford in the 1980's, there was only one of the air force boys left. There is no explanation for the premature deaths or the fact that none of them married. Richard was killed when he flew his plane into a hillside near Yeadon. For a good pilot, it was an extraordinary death.

Chapter 16

IN A DIFFERENT LIGHT
1954

Our dance troupe performed on weekends, in English social clubs, church halls, and at the Eisteddfods in Wales. It was there we caught the attention of international folk dance organizers and were invited to dance at a folk festival in Markelo, Holland. We were going to meet Queen Juliana of the Netherlands. It had become obvious to me that Mother now wished she had followed Hilda to Eindhoven.

We were given enough advance notice to coordinate our summer holidays at our respective mills and factories for the week in question. Ivar agreed to take care of his and my passports. Neither of us had had passports, just our Aliens Orders.[34] He got us Estonian passports from the Estonian Embassy in London. When my passport arrived I barely looked at it, except to wish the picture were better. I looked like a convict.

The day we set off for Holland was especially beautiful. England summers were inclined to be wet, so we were lucky. My memories of Europe were not the best, but neither were anyone else's. We were looking forward to making better ones.

---

[34] Aliens Orders were issued by the British government to displaced persons in order to keep track of them. Here is Grandmother's Aliens Order:

The boat train to The Hague was crowded. As we gathered around the rail, I tried to remain close to Ivar. Here was an opportunity to be alone with him at last. If he loved me he would want to be alone with me, too. I had learned that from watching Kevin. When Kevin was near Daisy, he always touched her. He took her hand, he put his arm around her waist, and he only had eyes for her. That had to be love. I tried to hold Ivar's hand once when we crossed the street, but he disengaged it so quickly that I thought he found me repugnant.

Kalev Dance Troupe, Bradford, 1950s.

Rather than accept his rejection, I began to imagine that he loved me secretly, but could not show it until I was confirmed. Comforted by that thought, I further imagined him to be the brave, beautiful hero of Estonian folklore, fighting his heart, restrained by the cultural demands in which we had been raised. I attributed to him every virtue I could think of. He certainly had brains, was an extraordinary dancer, and could keep up an intellectual conversation with Mother and her friends like no one else. When he danced he could leap into the air like a fawn, coming down lightly and gracefully. When his golden curls became damp with the exertions of the dance, he looked like he had been cast in molten bronze, especially in the summer when he sunbathed at every opportunity to get a light tan.

Here he was, but feet away from me during the entire trip, but no matter how hard I tried to catch him alone, he always melted away, and when I next saw him, he was back in the group, laughing and talking normally again.

We arrived in Markelo and spent a wonderful week dancing and mingling with other nationalities from all over Europe. We met Queen Juliana, who admired our folk costumes and said a few words to Ivar, which turned his face bright red with pleasure. It occurred to me that England was the only country that did not have a folk costume.

290

When the week was over, we returned to The Hague to board the boat train back to England. The passengers ahead of me went through passport control quickly. I presented my passport, but instead of receiving a quick stamp and a thank you, the man on the stool got up and left the booth. He came back with another official and then another who spoke English. I was told to step aside. The others in the dance group realized something was wrong and came back. A few minutes later Ivar was also pulled aside. We were being arrested. A man in uniform put Ivar's hands behind his back and handcuffed him. I had never seen Ivar so upset. His face was white, and he was trembling so badly that his handcuffs rattled. The man was going to put them on me, too, but someone stopped him. There was a low-toned, heated discussion between the Dutch officials and our dancers, who wanted to know what was going on.

At the folk festival in Markelo, Holland, 1954.

Expressions were at first anxious, then horrified. Ivar was led away. The official kept his hand on my shoulder. The ship's whistle blew. More confusion as the other dancers wanted to remain with us, but everyone was on restricted visas and would also be in trouble if they missed the boat.

Ivar and I were taken to an office where a uniformed official explained to us in English that we were Soviet citizens entering England illegally and that we were going to be deported to the Soviet Union. The Estonian passports were meaningless. We had not even brought our Aliens Orders, which would have identified us as legal residents of the United Kingdom. An Estonian embassy official was coming from Rotterdam to try to help us. Meanwhile we were under arrest. "Do not fear," the man told me. "You are underage and will be sent back to mother, but young man, could problem be." Ivar was over twenty-one.

I was scared, but not as scared as Ivar. Ivar was sweating and trembling and out of his mind with fear. I thought to lift him a bit with humor.

"At least the Russians do right by their dancers. You'll get out of the mill." I meant it as a joke.

"Just shut up!" he hissed at me.

"Look, we danced for the Queen. She even talked to you. They've obviously got to sort this out. We're not criminals." I tried again to comfort him, but he would have none of it.

"Will you shut your mouth!" he snapped. No sense of humor.

The English-speaking official heard us arguing, so I said no more. I still could not believe our situation was as bad as Ivar thought. I had definitely not expected him to become hysterical.

Queen Juliana of the Netherlands with Princess Beatrix,
thanking the Kalev Dance Troupe for participating at the
Gouden Aren Folk Festival in Markelo, Holland,
August 1954.

The official left us alone. A few minutes later a woman came and placed two bottles of mineral water and a plate of biscuits on the table. "If they are going to send us to Russia, would they be this nice?" I asked Ivar.

"My God, will you shut up!" This time I thought he was going to slap me, except the handcuffs restricted his movements.

"It was you who got us the useless passports," I said nastily and turned away. I wanted to ask the woman why she would bring us biscuits, but not remove Ivar's cuffs. It was obvious he could not reach them. The logical thing would have been for me to feed Ivar and help him with the water, but my feelings for Ivar were undergoing a change that confused and alarmed me. This was a situation where we should have pulled together and Ivar was acting like he hated me. It's true I should not have joked about Russia, but as he cringed, I was reminded of other times when he had avoided physical contact with me. I was too embarrassed to help him. The biscuits and water remained untouched.

About an hour later a plump, middle-aged Estonian woman in a summer dress and straw hat bustled into the office, followed by two harbor officials and a policeman. She was speaking rapid Dutch and had put herself in charge of whatever was going on. The men nodded. They carried papers and looked tired. It was late. The last boat train had left, and the cleaners were emptying the waste bins.

The woman nodded to Ivar and me, and then continued in the same vein. The first official sat down at his desk and began to write. The policeman removed Ivar's handcuffs, then picked up the telephone, dialed and began speaking to someone at the other end, still throwing Ivar swift glances. Ivar looked inconsolate.

Finally the woman stopped talking and addressed us in Estonian. She introduced herself as Mrs. Belinfante, the Estonian representative in the Netherlands. She looked at our passports and shook her head.

"I know who you are, your family," she said to me. Then to us both, "You're in serious trouble, but there is enough evidence to prove it's an innocent mistake. I can't imagine who advised you to travel to Holland on Estonian passports. Yours is now an international matter to be worked out between the Dutch government and the British Foreign Office. Personally I don't think you need to worry." She cast an extra glance at Ivar, who had moved to a corner of the couch and was hugging his knees.

When the official finished writing, he ran his fingers through his blonde hair and handed Mrs. Belinfante a folder. More rapid Dutch followed, which Mrs. Belinfante interpreted briefly. We were being released into her custody. She was going to take us home with her to Rotterdam and would vouch for us. We would have to report to the police station every morning, but were otherwise free until the problem was resolved.

Mrs. Belinfante drove the car. I wanted Ivar to sit in front with her and take care of the polite conversation. After all, she had rescued us, but Ivar climbed into the back seat and I followed him. Again he sat in the corner as far away from me as he could and continued to be a nervous wreck. His hands were shaking and sweat was running down his temples. His damp curls no longer like molten gold, but a tangled mat. I did not know what to say to this new Ivar, so I just listened to the motor and watched my reflection in the car window. What had started out as a wonderful adventure, not to mention an opportunity to be alone with Ivar, had turned into a disaster. I was devastated. My great Estonian hero *Kalev* hated the sight of me. My future husband, whom I had designated to be the head of our family into which I had included his parents, as well as Mother and Grandmother, and had added a big old house on the Yorkshire moors, was falling apart in the car seat next to me.

We remained silent. Mrs. Belinfante concentrated on driving. She said she had spoken to the Takks. Hilda was using her position at Philips to further pressure the authorities to send us back to England. Mrs. Belinfante looked like she knew what she was talking about, I relaxed. Ivar did not.

We arrived at the Belinfantes' home in the middle of the night. They had a huge house full of wonderful furniture. Mrs. Belinfante went to prepare our rooms. I would sleep in her daughter's bedroom, Ivar in her son's. When Ivar and I were alone, I tried to speak to him again, but he put his hands over his ears. He did not even say goodnight.

I was reassured, but not comfortable enough to get undressed. I stretched out on the bed. It was the most marvelous bed I had lain on since my bed at the Bollers. Our situation aside, I was shocked by the new Ivar, but more amazed by the comfortable surroundings this former refugee family were living in. I had only caught a glimpse of other houses in the street, but they all appeared similar. In Markelo, too, no soot-stained chimneys or blocks of back-to-back terraces. The bedcover was of ruffled satin. I dared not look into the wardrobe, but the dressing table and chest of drawers were highly polished and of solid wood. No back-of-the-market rubbish here.

293

Just as the woman in the private hospital wing had reminded me of Mother's dressing gowns and silver foxes, the Belinfante house brought back memories of our Blue Room in Haapsalu—Aunt Alma's piano, and the living room furniture, not as highly polished, but matching. These discoveries disturbed me. I began to suspect that what I thought of as luxuries, were probably just normal in the normal world.

It had not taken me long to discover that our life in England was not normal and to begin to plan a way out, not necessarily from England, but the kind of England we had been forced into. Ivar and I would do it together. We would both leave the mills and get cleaner jobs. I was already halfway there with my shorthand and typing courses. This moment would have been an ideal opportunity for Ivar and me to start discussing our future, except that my future partner did not love me. He would not even talk to me.

In the morning we were taken to the police station. We signed in and were free to go. Mrs. Belinfante lived within walking distance of the town center. It was a beautiful sunny day. The sky was blue, the grass was green, and the air was fresh. Rotterdam was sparkling. I could smell the sea. The houses looked alike, obviously built since the war with brightly painted trim and matching doors. The streets thronged with bicycles. Most of the cyclers were women wearing folk costume skirts and starched caps. The bicycle baskets overflowed with shopping. I guessed the men were at work, but if they worked in factories, the factories were well hidden.

Outside the police station, Mrs. Belinfante asked us if we would like to see the town. We were standing at the end of a pedestrians-only street with shops and cafés. I could smell coffee.

Ivar said „No", he wanted to go back home.

I said, "Yes!"

Torn between the two of us, Mrs. Belinfante did not know what to do until I said I would not mind exploring by myself. I would not go far and knew my way back.

"So why don't you do that?" She seemed relieved. In addition to her pleasant manner, she had very shrewd eyes. She knew my family. She was in touch with Hilda. She seemed to be leading the official proceedings. There was nothing to worry about.

"Please be back by two o'clock. Remember I'm responsible for you." That said, she opened her handbag and handed me some Dutch money. "Buy yourself an ice cream. We'll see you at two."

She looked from me to Ivar. Seeing he had not changed his mind, she took him by the elbow and steered him away. Ivar's expression suggested he hated both of us.

Watching them go, I, too, hated myself for not remaining loyal to Ivar, but his unexpected rejection of me and open hostility intimidated me further. Anger gave me the strength to leave him alone. It was a beautiful day in the middle of the week, a day I would normally not have been able to enjoy in England. I was not in the mill, but instead surrounded by light and by children's laughter from a nearby playground. The air was perfumed by the smell of coffee from outdoor cafés where people sat at tables, drank

294

coffee, and read newspapers. I had never seen anything like that in my whole life.

The sun was hot, the breeze refreshing. When I reached the ice cream stall, I bought a strawberry ice cream cone. No problem with language any more, I spoke English. The vendor was proud to be able to respond.

There was a cinema a few feet away showing a Rock Hudson film. Rock Hudson was an American star. Ivar, Emil, and I had gone only to French films, because Ivar and I wanted to hear French language being spoken. It would be a new experience to see an American film.

When I passed one of the cafés a young waiter was clearing tables. He had straw-colored hair under a white cap, blue eyes, and shaggy yellow eyebrows. He had Ivar's coloring, but was more rugged. Ivar was more like a delicate china vase, about to crack.

The waiter said something to me in Dutch.

"I'm sorry, I don't understand. I'm English," I told him, remembering to speak "posh."

"Oh, England! Ja! I speak English. London. Buckingham Palace." He wanted to talk about England, but not the England I knew.

"I'm sorry, I have to go," I apologized.

"I know, I also working." He stepped back disappointed. "Be good to meet you English. Wonderful country." He twirled into the café, waving his white dishcloth at me as though we were on a train platform, saying good-bye.

After he had gone I looked at my watch. It was ten to eleven. The ice cream vendor and the waiter had both accepted me as English, exactly the way Mother had promised. It had been an enjoyable experience. A wonderful illusion. In a few days I would be back in Farsley, back at the loom, and then this sunny Wednesday morning would become a fading memory. I was trying to remember when I had last been outside on a sunny Wednesday morning, around eleven o'clock, and could not remember. Not for years.

"Blooming heck!" As Daisy would have put it.

The tinkle of music from the cinema drifted toward me and through me with the shrieking and joyous laughter from the park. The coffee aroma lingered. Mother would have loved the coffee. The delicious smells, the sun, the blue sky, all filled me with a terrible longing for something I could not name, but could still remember from somewhere. It might have been Aunt Alma's piano music, Mother's furs, her friends, then and now and their great expectations, which I had not understood. I perceived them now in the narrow prism of my own frustrations. That last day at Blenheim, realizing I had been living the life of a spastic. Now I could see it was even worse. I was living the life of a hairless mill mouse, waiting for someone to stomp on me. If Ivar was not going to join me in stepping out of our self-imposed restrictions, I was going to have to do it alone. It would not be easy.

Unki had told me a story. Once upon a time there was this elephant that had been tied to a tree since it was born. It had never been free. One day somebody untied the rope, but the elephant remained by the tree, only going as far as the rope would have allowed, when it could have gone back into the jungle at any time. I then thought about the tortoise at Cliff Road. It was the same everywhere—all about the food dish.

Mother could find work in some other office. She did not have to stay with Philips if the boss continued to harass her. He resented her contact with Eindhoven. As for me? I, too, could have walked away a long time ago and knew why I had not. It was time for me too to face my fears. Could I break away from mother, grandmother and the Estonian community? It would be difficult. Could I walk away from the mill without regrets? Yes! Yes, if it happened on a bright sunny Rotterdam day, but not on a dark, dismal Farsley morning. Could I do it without Ivar, without assurance that anyone would hire me and that my decision would not break anyone's heart.

How to get such assurance? I looked at my watch, two minutes to eleven. I could hear clocks already striking in the distance. To remember this moment and not have it slip away required some kind of prompt. In the old days I would have prayed for guidance, confident that my expectations would be considered by God in due course. However, since going to church and learning about religion, I was no longer sure of His presence, and I did not want to speak to any more of His agents or representatives. I wanted to speak to Him directly, as we had done in Hausberge. On the off chance that He still remembered us, I stood my ground.

"Dear God," I looked up at the sky, so blue, peaceful, and smokeless. The concept of peacetime was another subject I needed to discuss with Him, but at another time. "Lord, I know you're in charge of the universe. You saved us and brought us to England. I'm grateful. Don't think I'm not, but I'm going to leave the mill as soon as my shorthand and typing speeds are sixty and one hundred. It'll be a sunny Wednesday morning," I checked my watch again, "at exactly eleven o'clock. If it's all right with you, it should not be another disaster. Amen."

I did not specify the year because I had not yet been confirmed. Mother was already sewing my confirmation dress. I was not going to tell anyone about my vow. Mother would have another fit. I was the main breadwinner. Would Grandmother bless me? If God blessed me, she would, too.

Two hours before I had to return to the Belinfantes, I decided to enter the cinema. The Rock Hudson film was in English; I could ignore the Dutch subtitles and forget myself and my new fears of displeasing God and my old fears of displeasing the world. My worst fear was of upsetting Mother and Grandmother.

The cinema was small. It was the middle of the day. There were a few people scattered around the stalls, their foreheads deflecting the light from the screen. I sat in the middle of an empty row. The seats were hard, not the plush velvet of the Leeds Odeon.

Through the flickering beams and dust motes from the screen, Rock Hudson's face loomed large. His American accent filled the dark void around me. I slumped down and drew my knees up the way Ivar had done in the car and on the Belinfante's couch. How to keep my vow from draining out of me like sand in the egg timer I had given Grandmother for Christmas? She had not needed an egg timer, but had liked its shape. "It reminds me of my mortality," she had said.

296

Safe in my aloneness, with no one to tell me to shut up or to pull myself together and keep going, I pressed my knees against the back of the seat in front, lowered my head on my knees, and sobbed my heart out.

It was a quarter to two when I returned. Mrs. Belinfante opened the door before I could knock. "Good girl!" I detected a sigh of relief. Ivar was sitting on the edge of the couch. He gave me a troubled frown, but had calmed down. "We're going to England tonight," he said. "You might at least have been here when the Police came to inform us. They asked where you were. So where were you?"

"At the cinema," I told him. "It was a good film—with Rock Hudson."

"I'm not surprised. Nothing you do surprises me anymore," said Ivar in a strained voice, shaking his head and pursing his lips like a woman scolding a child.

This pain, too, will end, I promised myself darkly.

The Estonian community in Holland went to great lengths on our behalf, with Mrs. Belinfante and Hilda using their influence in what could have been a serious international crisis involving post-war agreements regarding refugees from the Soviet Union. The United States did not recognize the Soviet occupation of Estonia, but Holland did. It helped that we had been invited by the dance festival organizers and, I hope, because we had danced for the Queen.

In England, Mother and Grandmother had been beside themselves. Ivar's parents had come over immediately, and the Estonian community had been upset all the way to London. How could the Embassy have issued the passports? The explanation was simple. Many Estonians still liked to carry Estonian passports as symbols—they knew better than to travel on them. The ignorance remained ours alone.

My Latvian friend from the mill, Erika, had rushed to Leeds to be with Mother and Grandmother on the day I arrived back. She hugged me hard with tears in her eyes and had been so upset she had come to Leeds in mismatched shoes. She had not noticed until she was already on the bus.

My confirmation classes began shortly after our detainment in Holland. The classes were on Sunday evenings. The pastor, who lived in Leeds, was a strict no-nonsense man who barely gave me time to remove my coat before he began to grill me. As in the English church, I did not expect the presence of the Holy Spirit, but I did pray that I would remember the books and prophets in the proper order and that I could memorize psalms and Bible verses to his satisfaction.

One evening I arrived in confirmation class feeling dizzy. I had wakened that morning feeling dizzy, not enough to fall down, but I had to be careful when I moved my head. The dizziness was accompanied by a buzzing in the ears and a feeling of fullness in my head that had started on my first day at the mill. I guessed it had to do with the noise. I wanted to skip class, but the pastor already suspected my heart was not in the lessons. He half-expected me to drop out and I wanted to prove him wrong.

When I arrived in class I could not concentrate. The room was jerking around, the pastor's voice kept fading in and out, and I was afraid I was going to vomit.

The pastor thought I was not paying attention. "Sit up straight!" he kept saying. I told him that I was sitting up straight.

In the middle of reading a psalm, I told him that I was going to throw up. He must have seen my face change color, because he snapped the Bible shut and reached for the wastebasket.

"You'd better go home," he suggested.

I staggered as far as the front door when suddenly the hall began to spin. I fell down on the mat and began to vomit. The pastor was saying, "Get up! Get up!" He was helpless and called the ambulance.

The ambulance arrived quickly. I was lifted and carried because I was unable to sit up or even lift my head because of the spinning. Someone put a pill into my mouth and told me to swallow. In the emergency room a doctor commanded me to focus my eyes on the far wall. "Focus! Focus!" he ordered. "Don't move your head, don't move your eyes!"

Amazingly, it worked. While I kept my eyes fixed on a speck of something on the white wall, I was even able to sit up, but could not lie down again. I must have fallen asleep eventually, because the next thing I knew it was daylight. I was in a hospital bed and Mother and Grandmother were beside me. The pastor himself had gone to our flat to tell them I was in St. James's Hospital.

"They think it's Ménière's Syndrome," said Mother. "They'll take tests to confirm it, but the doctor thinks it's a straightforward case."

"Am I going to die?"

"No, but you could lose your hearing."

"Like Friida?"

Great! Even Mother hated to talk to her friend Friida because you had to shout and repeat yourself constantly. Sometimes conversations became so comical that people had to leave the room or else become hysterical with laughter. One time Mother asked Friida if she would be able to do something, and Friida asked what was on the table.

I remained in the hospital for a few more days, drowsy on medication, but I did not get dizzy again. Tests confirmed that I had Ménière's Syndrome, a disturbance of the inner ear. The good news was that deafness might hold off until later in life. I was given motion sickness pills to carry around with me in case I had another attack.

The first day back at work felt like someone had slapped me across the head. Even with cotton wool in my ears, it was several days before I could stand the noise again. Secretly I wondered if the noise had brought on the illness, but I dared not mention that to Mother, who already accused me of not wanting to work.

The hospital gave me my very first comprehensive medical examination since Estonia. Apparently the soldier in Hausberge had damaged me. The damage was repaired. I heard Mother and the doctor joking about what to

298

tell my future husband, should he question my virginity. The doctor suggested I get in touch with him; he offered to vouch for me.

My confirmation ceremony took place on 21 August of 1955. It was an important event, the great transition from youth to adult. Mother had worked on the dress for a long time. She was sewing all our clothes in order to save money. My dress was made of white satin. I looked in the mirror and got a shock: I looked fifty years old. Grandmother and Mother presented me with the traditional confirmation gift, a small ivory-colored Bible. They, too, were wearing new clothes. Grandmother was again bound into her elastics, and Mother wore her corset, which she called her "Rose Tattoo," after seeing Anna Magnani in a film struggling into a similar contraption.

Confirmation, St. John's Church, Bradford, 21 August 1955.

The ceremony took place in St. John's church in Bradford. My confirmation sister was Ede, the daughter of the couple who worked in a private school so that she could take the 11+ exam. Ede was soon to enter medical school; she was the pride of the community.

The church was beautifully decorated with altar flowers, candles, and in accordance with protocol, the Estonian flag and the Union Jack, placed on either side of the altar. The Union Jack was on Ede's side, and the Estonian flag was on my side.

The front pew was reserved for family and prominent leaders of the North Yorkshire Estonian community. The former opera singer Elena was going to sing *Ave Maria*.

It was an unusually hot day; people fanned themselves with the programs. Grandmother sat with a look of spiritual contentment on her face, ready to witness my transition from *backfisch* to adult. Mother was less relaxed, looking at my dress, making sure the seam that had bunched on the bias was not as obvious to everyone as it was to her. She had done my hair in a roll, but it did not look neat. I should not have cut it. The dark chestnut rinse she had insisted on, to make me less "mousy," did not match my fair eyebrows and eyelashes.

Although Ede was a year older than I was, she seldom came to social functions because she was busy with her studies. We had barely exchanged two words. With Mother's critical eyes on my back, I knew I did not match up to Ede in any way. She was tall, slim, elegant, and cool, while I clutched a bouquet of wilted white flowers in my gloved hands and worried about the sweat in my armpits. What Mother admired above all else was aesthetics—grace and beauty, the arts, music, theater, intellectual friends, and brilliant conversation. What she did not admire was a lumpy adolescent with spots, who could not hold a tune and was constantly steaming with resentment.

Ivar and his parents were sitting farther back. I hoped Ivar would think me beautiful and regret his attitude, but he already knew about the crooked

299

seam and had commented on the hair. "Makes her face look fat," he had told Mother.

The pastor began the liturgy prescribed for the occasion. Suitable music played in the background. He talked about our future, encouraged our faith, and so on. He had chosen a Bible verse for each of us and read it aloud in a solemn tone. Ede's verse went well.

The verse picked for me was about the "olive tree."

John 15:4 Take care to live in me, and let me live in you. For a branch can't produce fruit when severed from the vine. Nor can you be fruitful apart from me.

I guessed it had to do with remaining Estonian.

He was drawing breath for a follow-up when there was a loud crack. Then, like a tree hit by lightning and falling in slow motion, the Estonian flag shuddered, left the wall, plunged forward, and fell on top of me. Luckily it rolled off my shoulder, giving me only a glancing blow before it clattered to the marble floor. People gasped; some jumped to their feet. Amid shocked voices, I heard Mother's shriek. The shriek was piercing and suddenly I knew why. For Mother that was not just a flag falling, but also a terrible omen. She had moved from cards, tea leaves, and horoscopes to serious mysticism in search of an encouraging sign about our future. She had even started going to séances and visiting mediums. Her main contact was a seer in Hunslet called Madam Sybil. In addition she was translating the Kabbala, a system of fortunetelling that had fascinated "dear Erni," her father. Lastly she had become a Rosicrucian. I often heard her chanting in frustration: "O love that knoweth of no fear. A love that sheds a joyous tear; O love that makes me whole and free. Such love shall keep and hallow me." The Estonian flag falling on me during my confirmation might as well have been the guillotine.

I, too, was stunned, but not by the falling flag. I was stunned by another revelation that hit me with equal force, stronger even than a bolt of lightning. Mother's shriek of horror had been for me. It had been her love and fear for me through the years—a love she had not been able to express any other way except through constant worry that the world would notice in me the same problems that had disappointed her and my father. Mother's constant picking on me, correcting me, criticizing me, trying to make me cleverer, more talented, better looking, another Shirley Temple, had worn her out. The Matron at the orphanage had also tried and failed.

My making noises to music and weeping over dead flowers can't have helped either. What does one do with a disappointing child except to shield her and protect her from the horrors that an unaccepting world would inflict on her. I wanted to go and tell Mother she need not worry; her perfect world had already crashed when we fled Estonia.

However this was not the time, the flag was picked up and put back. The ceremony continued. Elena sang *Ave Maria* beautifully. I knew now why Mother had beaten me after that soldier incident. She had been overcome by relief that he had not killed me.

300

Dreams were a major part of our lives together. We spent the first part of every Sunday morning drinking tea or coffee and unraveling each other's dreams. Grandmother even called her dressing gown her "multi-colored dream coat," alluding to one of our favorite Bible stories. Grandmother did not believe in cards or horoscopes, but found great joy in dreams and considered them biblical.

On this particular Sunday morning Mother had had a dream that she found disturbing. As usual she lit her first cigarette before she began to speak.

"There were two candles burning on the table right here, in front of the fireplace." She motioned towards the table. "One candle was an old stub. It was fluttering feebly in the draft blowing down the chimney. The other candle was new, burning brightly, but I was not paying attention to the new candle. I was desperately trying to keep the old one lit, running around the table, shielding it this way and that way until the flame became steady again. When it looked like it would last, I took my hands away and only then did I remember the other candle, the new one that I had almost knocked over. In my preoccupation with the old one, I had neglected the new one. I was aghast and shouted in anguish, 'How stupid! Here I've been guarding and fussing over this old stub ... "Mother stopped abruptly. A strange look came over her face. She usually interpreted the dreams right away, but not this one.

"It's a good thing you saw the new candle in time," said Grandmother, breaking the silence. She continued sipping her coffee, but her glances that slipped over Mother and me spoke volumes. I wondered whether she was thinking about the row Mother and I had recently had about the technical college I said I wanted to attend, to learn dress design. The technical college did not require the 11+ test. I hated sewing, but I liked drawing.

"Dress design?" Mother had looked aghast. "You a dress designer?" Despite my revelation about Mother's need to protect me, we were still at odds.

Chapter 17

COMING OF AGE
1955

The confirmation was over. Mother and I still had two weeks of vacation owed to us. She wanted to go back to Europe, to see what was left of it, visit the Takks in Eindhoven and her friends in Munich, the ones sending Grandmother the Asthmolisin. Ivar was coming with us, of course. He was going to have his twenty-third birthday in Munich, and Mother was planning a birthday celebration at the hotel.

I welcomed getting away from the mill for two weeks, but the prospect of the three of us together for a fortnight did not thrill me. I could only solve so many crossword puzzles and write so much poetry. Ivar's strange behavior in Holland prompted me to remain at a distance. He knew he had hurt me and was friendlier now, but he had made clear he had no romantic interest in me. This time Mother got the passports—British passports!

Our troubles started in Calais when I lost a shoe getting off the boat train. No, I take that back. Our troubles started even before we left Leeds. In the early morning, dark and steady rain, we were crossing the muddy forecourt of Quarry Hill Flats and heading towards the front entrance arch when a black cat darted across our path. The worst possible omen. There was no time to double back to another gate. Ivar was meeting us at the train station; changing course would make us late.

After Mother spat three times and evoked her guardian for "instantaneous control" over the forces that regulated her life and put her mind "under control of a higher power," we continued glumly. Mother was already in the dumps.

In the train Mother and Ivar sat together while I sat opposite them. That pattern would repeat itself on every train thereafter. I concentrated on my crossword puzzles, too much on edge to write poetry. Ivar had his *Paris Match* again, and Mother was reading a book she called light fiction to take her mind off things.

Our first stop was Paris. We became separated in the Louvre. My fault. Further discord when I pronounced Versailles "ver-sails" and then ordered a boiled "eye" instead of a boiled egg. My French was still not as good as Ivar's. I knew that Mother had brought me along because I was her daughter, but I might as well have stayed at home. All I was to them was an extra suitcase they would have gladly left in lost luggage. I was definitely not an asset to their holiday mood as I trailed along behind them in my plimsolls, brought along for climbing only. They were too big and caused me to waddle. In contrast, Mother looked elegant in high heels, and Ivar looked as though he had stepped out of a film magazine.

They expected me to "hurry" or "come along" when they had seen their fill. Never mind me. Every time I injected a comment they turned to me with exasperation, and Mother said, "Not now." She said it kindly, but firmly, afraid I would embarrass myself by my lack of knowledge.

Glowering and with my fists burning holes in my pockets, I endured three days of being nothing more than an apostrophe to their brilliant conversation about French art and literature, which, as it happened, I knew quite a bit about. I had read my way through the entire catalog of French writers and was currently finishing Émile Zola. I was not, however, going to spout my knowledge like some schoolgirl during a test. I had hoped to inject it into a real conversation, the kind from which I had been excluded. I understood that Mother loved me, but still did not like me.

All the same I was thrilled to be in France—to be in Paris. I found it everything I had expected as we tramped down the Champs Élysées, sat on benches in the Bois de Boulogne, climbed to the top of the Eiffel Tower, and craned our necks under the bells in Notre Dame Cathedral. The trip confirmed for me that knowledge was the power I lacked, the power that freed one from other people's opinions. I also understood the shame of ignorance. I was not yet ready to challenge Mother or Ivar on subjects they knew more about, but I was gathering confidence.

Germany was another surprise—not a ruin in sight. Cities were bristling with scaffolding and road works. Steel and glass offices were rising next to department stores bigger even than Lewis's; neon signs blinked constantly, and lifts went up and down on the outsides of buildings. Mother kept stopping for coffee *mit Sahne* (with whipped cream) unknown in England. We ate ourselves silly in restaurants serving foods Grandmother had cooked at home; some were featured in our Danish cookbook. I still spoke German fluently and felt confident enough to chip in.

"Let's go to Bernau. Let's find that Frau who put us out of the house because I smelled bad," I said to Mother.

"Bernau is in East Germany," said Ivar.

"So?"

"You don't understand. East Germany is part of the Soviet Union."

"So let's go to Berlin and find that old cemetery we stayed in," I persisted.

"That part of Berlin is also cut off." Mother spoke with infinite patience. "It's too complicated to explain."

"Oh." There it was again, darn it! I had been put in my place. Ignorance again. I focused on the telegraph lines leaping outside the window to keep at bay the "external forces" that had attached themselves to us at the outset of the trip. It was hopeless. Even Mother's evocations could not hold back the resentment that was building up in me and coming to a head. They had started talking about the Berlin Airlift.

"What's the Berlin Airlift?" I asked deliberately.

"You won't know about that. It happened years ago." Mother's response was automatic.

"I know I don't know, that's why I'm asking," I replied grimly, aware that I had raised my voice.

304

"It happened after the war. I'll explain later." Mother frowned, calculating the consequences of an argument with me versus a terse reply that usually shut me up. I saw Ivar roll his eyes.

I let it go for the moment because I was even surprising myself. Mother's observation that I was "phlegmatic" was not without grounds. Except for that one flash of my bare backside when I was four, I had avoided confrontations. I had always gone to Grandmother who usually defused the situation in her own way, and Mother had never been around long enough for a proper row.

Bavaria was straight out of Grimm's fairy tales. I had never seen anything so beautiful—glorious mountains, thick forests, little villages with gingerbread houses, meadows ablaze with wildflowers. In England and France it had rained, but Germany and Bavaria were sweltering hot. The smell of fir trees, warm soil, barnyard sounds, the clanking of buckets, gurgling streams, and the sight of endless valleys and snowcapped mountains brought tears to my eyes and a lump to my throat. I had never, never expected the world to be so beautiful.

We visited Mother's friends in Munich. The Estonian couple that had been rejected for England because the man had had "a spot on the lung" now lived in a beautiful house with a big garden. They were both school teachers. Their son, Juku, was Ivar's age and was taking his master's degree in ancient languages at the University of Heidelberg.

To dispel the gloom of new discoveries in which our situation in England compared badly, we took the train to Garmisch-Partenkirchen and rode the cable car up the Zugspitze to the snowline. The experience of winter in summer, hot and cold at the same time, had us shrieking and laughing like children. We threw snowballs at each other; I fear I might have put more force into mine than I meant to. I noticed that Ivar threw with his hand under instead of over, more like a girl than a boy. After that we hiked down the forested trail, stopping now and then to rest and sunbathe. Ivar took off his shirt. Mother removed her glasses. I watched them out of the corner of my eye. It was strange that I could still love these two people so deeply. They and Grandmother were all I had in this world, yet we could barely exchange a few words without getting into a row.

Sitting on the bank of the Starnbergersee, at an outdoor café, drinking coffee and eating strudel, Mother mentioned that one of the Austrian Maximilians had become the ruler of Mexico. "Do you know which one?" she asked suddenly, turning to me.

The question caught me by surprise. I was four years old again, Mother barking at me to recite the multiplication tables, and I waiting for her slap because she thought my silence was defiance.

I was eighteen now, officially an adult. Not defiant, just ignorant. I did not know the answer. There were three Maximilians, that much I did recall. One I believed had gone to Mexico, but I had no idea which one. I did not know the answer to the question, so I froze.

Ivar pursed his lips. He was dying to tell, but Mother held up her hand to give me time. I did not know and was not going to guess wrong.

"Well?" Mother raised an eyebrow.

"I don't care!" I choked, humiliated. Rather than burst into tears, I ran from the table.

In the toilet I discovered I had started my period. Great! I returned to the table and told Mother I wanted to go back to the hotel. She insisted on coming with me which meant forgoing the next item on the itinerary, a tour of a castle. Ivar went alone on the castle tour, while Mother and I returned to the *Gasthaus*.

After I had taken care of my problem, Mother said she was going to use the opportunity to buy Ivar's cake and birthday present. I would not have known what to pick for him anyway, something musical, of course. She was also going to send Aunt Alma a postcard. I said fine and went to lie down in our room. I felt even more out of sorts than usual and wondered what was wrong with me.

The *Gasthaus* was perched on the side of a mountain with a breathtaking view of distant peaks, forests, and meadows sloping down to a river. The house was built of brown wood, with balconies and edelweiss trimmings. It looked like a large cuckoo clock.

The window was open. I could hear hotel noises and cowbells tinkling below. Cows were coming down from the high pastures for the night. The smell of warm hay, pine resin, and cowsheds wafted in on the occasional breeze, dispelling heat from the room and cooling my skin. I was still affected by too much beauty. I tried not to weep, but the holiday was turning into an out-of-control roller coaster, taking me to incredible highs and despairing lows. The smell of clean air, warm grass and wildflowers had me walking like a zombie, eyes closed, not wanting to exhale. Then I looked at Ivar and Mother, heads together, laughing at some adult joke, and wanted to throw up.

There was no doubt in my mind any more. I was going to leave them and head out on my own. I would not go far, but they did not need me and I would have to do without them. The exile communities were breaking up anyway, caught in the same struggle between the generations. Beside love, loyalty, and Estonian food, we also needed the past. That past only existed in our loved ones. Which was stronger, the past or the future? I had no idea, because until five years ago I barely recalled having my own bed, but I had seen, was seeing cities that were not in ruins, blues skies that were clear of smoke. I saw people who wore clean clothes, who owned their own houses, who could come and go as they pleased, behaving like summer visitors along Haapsalu Promenade, but without servants. Ordinary people acting normal. Maybe this then was the peacetime I had missed, and was still missing. Whatever that meant, it's what I wanted, and more. I wanted things I had not yet seen, did not yet know about. I wanted a future.

Mother returned with her purchases—a Linzer torte and a record of Mazurkas. I would not have known to buy either the Linzer torte or the Mazurkas.

We met Ivar again in the dining room. While Mother scanned the menu, Ivar slipped me a brochure about the castle he had visited. There was some history about the Austrian Maximilians. At times like these I felt like running out the door screaming "cat love!" Of course it was not like that at all. It was even more complicated.

For dinner we had *Schnitzel* and Black Forest cake *mit Sahne*, again. Clouds of it.

When we were back in our room Mother removed her outer clothing to her slip and threw herself on the bed to read aloud from a book of poems by Rainer Maria Rilke, in German—beautiful poems about love. I was not in the mood for other people's love or poetry. I had worked myself into a lather all day, all week, maybe for years, on that very subject.

"Where is this heart of red stone?" (A rough translation). Mother was reciting in her marvelous actress voice, with correct emphasis on each syllable. The secret of reading poetry, Miss Hayes had taught me, was in the pauses. Mother was in one of the pauses when I jumped up on the mountainous eiderdown and shouted, "Stop!"

Thus it began, our Waterloo. At first Mother blinked, the way she usually did when I interrupted her, expecting me to get her signal to shut up, but I ignored the signal and continued.

"Enough!" I repeated. "We need to talk!"

"What's this?" Mother looked up as though seeing me for the first time, maybe since I was born. She became angry. No, she became furious! "I have tried my best with you," she began, throwing down the book and jumping to her feet.

"I know, I've had your best for eighteen years, and it's going to stop right here." I shouted recklessly, not caring if she hit me or killed me. I was not myself anymore, but someone I had watched from afar, a terrible fat and ugly creature, twisted by anger and hurt.

Mother had always managed to control me by telling me not to upset Grandmother, but Grandmother was not here. I let loose until we were both shouting at the top of our lungs. I was standing on the bed, yelling down at her. She had her hands on her hips and was leaning forward, her glasses askew. Neither of us could hear what the other was saying.

Suddenly Mother's mouth snapped shut. She sat down in the chair. "Just what exactly has upset you?" she asked evenly.

"Everything," I answered truthfully. "And it has gone on for far too long!"

"Maybe we should discuss this like two rational adults. You said you wanted to talk. We can't keep yelling at each other, if we want to solve problems."

"Then let's start at the beginning."

"Yes, let's." Mother composed her face into the usual expression of patience that suggested she knew what she was going to hear, but not this time, I ignored the expression and watched it change as I spilled out my hurts, perceived or real, the result of misunderstandings or just plain wrongs.

"Didn't you even think before you brought me to England that you should have had a place for me?" I challenged.

"I didn't want us to remain in Germany. I know going to Ida Hospital was a mistake. But I didn't know that when I accepted the move."

"Then we should have gone back to the DP camp. I saw Ivar's face when your friends told us their son was at Heidelberg University. Hilda is a Director at Philips. When we were in Eindhoven you asked Hilda to intervene for you again. The Leeds branch manager hates you. If we had gone to Holland you, too, would be working at the real Philips and I would be in art school, maybe university instead of the mill."

"What makes you think you would have got into university?" said Mother coldly. She prided herself on being objective even with those she loved.

"If you're so clever, why didn't you know about the eleven-plus?" I shouted back. "It's your fault, all of it." I accused.

That set us off again.

Mother began pacing the floor, slapping the bed, the walls. I could hear hotel windows opening and slamming. I could hear knocking on our floor, our ceiling, and on our door, but we did not pay attention to any of it. Mother had more years to recount than I had and more disappointments, not just in me, but in her entire life that had gone down the drain. She had made mistakes, she admitted, but everyone had to adjust.

"There was a war on," she pointed out.

"Of course there was a war on." To heck with the war! I was digressing, digging deep into the bottom of the barrel for the child in me who still needed answers. Why had she not let me bring at least one decent toy when we left Estonia? She had brought her doll Maria, but Maria had never been mine, always too valuable to play with, and those awful pants she had sewn for me when I was eight, one leg longer than the other. She had slapped my face for refusing to wear them. What did that have to do with the war? I brought up the soldier, now that I knew what had happened. I had been raped. "I was seven years old! How could you have blamed me?"

"I was distraught. It could have been worse."

"Your reaction was worse! What about me? How do you think I felt? I heard you joking with the doctor at St. James's about my lack of virginity." That was good for another round.

By the time dawn grayed the sky, and the cows were tinkling back to the higher pastures, Mother and I lay on the bed, side by side, exhausted. Mother had blamed, progressively, Stalin, Hitler, Father, even Grandmother, for what the years had done to us.

The breeze through the window had picked up, bringing in colder mountain air.

"I'm leaving the mill," I told Mother. "I'm going deaf. Leena's parents are dying of asbestos poisoning; Ivar is dying of a broken spirit. We're living in a nightmare and I can't go on like this."

"Do what you think is right. I can't stop you. I don't know what more I can do for you when I don't even know what to do for myself." Mother threw her arm across her eyes. We continued to lie on the bed. Nothing had been solved, but our anger had drained us.

Suddenly Mother began to speak again.

"You know me and my dreams. Do you remember that dream I had about the two candles? After I had told it I knew what it meant. We had just had an argument about the technical college. I think this is as good a time as any

308

to try to explain my side, even though it's too late." Mother pulled herself up on the pillow and searched for a cigarette. She found the packet on the side table and began to light up. I waited for the first long inhale, the deep puff before she could speak. I hoped it would not be the usual lecture.

"After I told you the dream," she began, "it all came together. I thought about it all day and over the months, but couldn't bring myself to approach you. You were so angry. Our worlds have turned out so differently. Estonia was a small country and until 1939 we lived well. I had a good career; so did your father, but then I wanted a baby. Your father didn't want a child. He didn't want the responsibilities that would have affected his career. When I became pregnant I told him I was keeping you and hoped for the best, but it didn't work out. I can't blame you for your birth, but it did end my marriage and my career. The career wasn't important, but my marriage …," she broke off for a few seconds as her voice cracked, then rallied. "I had given up medical school, I had even given up my child, you, but all he could think of was his art." She inhaled again, deeply. "Even the war was secondary—another production. I should have known better than to demand his attention."

"By having me?"

"I don't know, but I did have you, and became crushed by the same responsibilities he had rejected. I wanted to do the right thing by you, by Mämmä but too much was happening. Mämmä was all I had left of my life as I had known it. She was the old candle I was trying to save. You were the bright new one that I had neglected by my misplaced sense of duty. I wanted to put things right but I couldn't. England placed too many obstacles in our path. All I could do was try to help you over them, but I failed there because we are so different. You are Mämmä's child. I resented that, too. Now you know. My little love. I am sorry."

Mother stubbed out her cigarette. The room became silent except for hotel noises and sounds below the window—pails clanking, a woman clucking to chickens, a car starting, a dog barking in the village.

Mother's "I am sorry" meant everything to me even though it would not smooth the scars—at least not in one long night, but it was a beginning. Grandmother had told me a long time ago that pain could never be compared. It was so personal that no one could determine who hurt more, who hurt less on the scale of individual suffering. I took a peek at Mother lying back on the pillow, eyes closed, probably wondering if anything would ever go right again. I had observed many war heroes becoming ordinary cripples, confined to beds and walkers. Peacetime had also dethroned Mother. Brave hearts withered into unending insignificance. *Artistes* could not stand boring lives, even though they loved the wife and kiddies. There were few "finest hours" as Churchill had put it—in peacetime.

Suddenly Mother sat up and said, "Good God, look at the time!"

We had forgotten Ivar's birthday. He was expecting us with the cake and presents.

"Let's go home now," I told Mother. There was nothing joyful about this holiday any more.

"So what will we tell Ivar?" asked Mother.

"Why don't we tell him to jump in the lake? The lake, I think that at least one Maximilian drowned himself in, but I'm not sure about that either. And I don't care."

Liki and Elin in Munich, 1955.

Mother began to laugh. I stared at her in amazement. I could not remember the last time I had heard Mother laugh. Really laugh! She looked like heck, lying on the bed in her under slip, totally exhausted, with her hair a mess, and panda eyes where her makeup had smudged. My last hero had come down to earth and had stopped pretending that everything was wonderful. "So what's wrong with you, Elin?"

Mother was inspecting me also and had not changed much in her basic thinking. I could read her mind. "Let her hair grow again, put her on a diet, see a doctor about the acne, and thank God, at least her eye is straight."

What she did say was, "We'd better get dressed and take Ivar his cake and present."

That terrible row with Mother completely changed our relationship from that day on, until she died.

As soon as we got back to Leeds, Grandmother noticed the difference in us. When she had a chance to speak to me alone, she had tears in her eyes. "I have been praying for this to happen ever since you were born."

That scene with Mother gave me the final push I needed to leave the mill exactly as I had promised myself and God. I waited for a sunny Wednesday morning. At exactly eleven o'clock, I shut down my looms, picked up my bag of personal possessions, including my tea mug. I grabbed my coat, and with a kiss for Erika, who knew what I was doing, I walked out of the mill into the sunshine and out of that phase of my life forever.

There was just one more coincidence. I signed up with a temporary office agency. My first assignment was to report to the office of Woodhouses, the textile mill in Farsley that I had just left. I could have refused, but there was something so fateful about it that I could not let the opportunity pass. Maybe it was a sign from God, that He had approved my decision.

Nobody recognized me. When it was lunch time I said I would stay in and eat my sandwich at my desk. The other girls went home. As soon as they had gone, I rushed to the filing cabinet to look up my old file. There was not much in it, but on the last page was this: "Reason for leaving: FED UP!"

310

"So what do you expect to accomplish?" asked Ivar.

We were sitting on the top deck of the bus, going to Bradford. It was pouring rain. Mother had stayed home with a cold. Ivar had his *Paris Match*, and I was memorizing a piece from Shakespeare's *Richard III*. *"This royal throne of Kings, this sceptered isle...."* I remembered how I had mispronounced "sceptered" in Mrs. Brown's English class, seemingly a hundred years ago.

Ivar had not been overly surprised when I left the mill. He had looked amused when I announced that I had joined Leeds Art Centre. However, when I told him I was thinking of going to London for an audition at the Royal Academy of Dramatic Art, he put down his magazine, slowly, very much like Mother might have done.

"How are you going to pay for it?"

"I'll have to try for a scholarship."

"So what do you expect to accomplish?" He was not happy with what he was hearing. His voice had an edge to it.

"So what do *you* expect to accomplish by learning French?" I countered.

"To be able to read *Paris Match*. French is a beautiful language."

"So is English," I replied.

"You could have fooled me."

"You know as well as I do that the 'ee by gums' and 'owt for nowts' is not the English we came here to learn."

"It's what people speak. Elocution lessons are fine, but what will they do for you?" Ivar curled his lip derisively, reminding me of Daisy.

"They'll help me with the auditions. I can't believe Mother hasn't beaten you about the head on the advantages of speaking the King's English? World language and all that."

"Oh, you and your dreams." Ivar turned his head to the window where the rain was streaking rivulets through the grime. "They're laughing at you. Your Mother says you're thinking of becoming an actress. She thinks that's funny. You can't act."

"I can't dance either, but I'm in your dance troupe."

Ivar turned and grimaced. *"Touché!* But seriously, you're heading for a fall and we don't want to see you hurt. You're so ignorant of reality. I mean you went to the cinema while we were under arrest. I couldn't believe it. When I told your mother, she couldn't believe it either. She says it's impossible to prop up an empty sack, but she won't discourage you because you'll blame her if you fail. The only thing you can do well is write."

"Yes, I won that Estonian essay contest."

"So what's it going to be—art, acting, or writing?" Ivar pursed his lips, the way he always did when he wanted to put me down.

"It doesn't matter. The arts are the only way to get out of this shit," I said crudely, trying not to raise my voice. "Don't you want to get out?"

"But you are out, working in offices. There's the Art Centre, too, your English friends. Isn't that enough?"

"Don't you have any ambition?"

"Of course I do, but I'm not going to risk everything for it."

"Ivar," I turned to him fully. "What 'everything' are you risking? We don't have anything."

"I think you're mad." Ivar turned back to the window.

"All right, I'm mad. After I've tried and failed I'll still be mad. But at least I'll have tried."

"You're serious, aren't you?" He turned to me again, his light gray eyes like an English sky on a hazy day.

"I am. And I'm not going to blame Mother if I fail. You can tell her that yourself."

"Your mother really respects your writing and is proud of your poems in the London newspaper. Why can't you continue as you are?"

"I don't know. Office work is only a way to earn a living. I want more for myself."

"So do I, but I don't take myself so seriously."

"Then maybe you should," I said angrily. I was not angry at Ivar, but I was afraid he might be right about my dreams being futile. They were certainly too fragile to argue over. In the world we lived in, good people were powerless and love was never enough.

Ivar and I had our last battle on the day I told him I was going to London. He had not expected me to actually do it. The Royal Academy of Dramatic Art had put me on their shortlist for a scholarship. Apparently my Chekhov monologue and Ruth's speech to Naomi had gone down quite well, but had not been good enough for me to gain a grant. There was no chance that I could become a paying student.

When no one dropped out, I auditioned at a smaller drama school, the Rosselli Academy, and got the scholarship I needed. It was not university, but it was not the mill either. I thought Ivar would be impressed. He was not. He was hurt.

"So you really are leaving."

"Come with me," I pleaded. "There are good dancing schools in London. Even though you're too old for ballet, you could do modern dance."

"You mean be a male stripper," Ivar spat out and began to pace the floor.

Mother and Grandmother left the room quickly so we could be alone.

Ivar's outburst took us right back to our quarrel in Holland. I was surprised at how easily I had forgotten. He said cruel things to me, that I was fat, uneducated, not talented, couldn't act, and that no amount of book learning would make me acceptable among the English. He sounded like Mother, before we had had our heart-to-heart in Munich.

I wanted to fight back. Everything he said was true, had always been true, but I was hanging on to my foolish dreams the way a dog hangs on to a bone. Before long we were both in tears.

"Your family, your friends are all here," Ivar pleaded.

"I have to find a life for myself."

"You have a life here. Besides, you're only doing this to please your mother or to spite her, I wish I knew which."

"What if I am?"

"Then please her by staying here and getting a proper job. Leena is happy at the Gas Works."

312

Bringing Leena into it renewed my resolve. Leena and I had no interests in common anymore. She had an English boyfriend and could barely speak Estonian. I intended to keep up my Estonian. I was determined to stay in both worlds, but at my own pace.

"I'm going, Ivar, no matter what happens." I took his arm. My feelings for him returned in a rush. "You could come, too. There's nothing for you here." I was sobbing, making more of a fool of myself, but he already thought me a fool. "Please, Ivar," I begged.

"Then go to hell!" Ivar tore loose and stormed out of the room, out of the flat, slamming the front door behind him.

I was still crying when Mother and Grandmother came into the room. Mother said Ivar, too, had been crying so hard when he passed her in the hall that she was worried about his mental health. "You know he's not strong." I caught the mild reproof. Mother was on Ivar's side. She was bracing herself for another of my failures. Grandmother took me into her arms and said, "Leave it to God," who, in both our opinions, had already blessed my departure from the mill by that extraordinary coincidental assignment into the mill office. She was ready to let me go. Mother was still adjusting.

"Even the greatest ideals can have dire consequences," Mother said sagely. "Communism is a prime example."

Aunt Alma was our last link to Estonia. Her letters had kept us informed of her struggles with ill health and her efforts to hide Enno's books from the inspectors who had ordered her to destroy them. She had tried to keep the house for us, until she could no longer do repairs and pay taxes, even with our help and the sale of her piano. The chain was breaking. She wrote to Grandmother:

Dear sister!
As I told you in my last letter, I no longer have my musical instrument. It's too bad, but the music in me fell silent a long time ago, especially the Beethoven sonatas that I love.

Alma Saul died on 28 December 1960. Mother's friend Lydia told us of her death.

You have no idea what your aunt suffered. How poor she was and how hard it was for her until I arrived back from Siberia. After you got in touch her situation improved. She never complained. I returned in 1956. There was nothing but hunger. The sensible thing would have been for her to sell the house, but she wouldn't hear of it. She was keeping it for you. Everything you sent her she sold and spent on the house. The sale of the piano was her last personal sacrifice.

Lydia

Ivar died in June of 1988 at age 55. I had not heard of homosexuality when we knew each other and did not fully comprehend it even after it was explained to me. After Ivar's death his mother wrote to me.

> *I knew about your feelings for each other. You were the only one whom Ivar truly loved in this cruel world, but that love had to be recorded differently in the Book of Life by the Highest Authority. He did not get in touch with you because he didn't want to disturb your life, but he kept up with you through Nina and the Polish church. He was not suited for the social life of the church and dropped out. People can be so cruel, especially in churches. The house is still full of his music.*

Uncle Paul died in June 1961 in San Paulo, Brazil.

The hardest part of moving forward, for me, was the guilt of not having taken the past as seriously as I should have, when it was still the present.

My story is typical of the end of an era in Europe, about exiles who survived the war and were then defeated by the ordinary requirements of peacetime, especially in England.

Estonia is still the country of my heart, but it was my grandmother who was my "paradise lost." I did not truly become an exile until after her death in 1974. For my generation exile was never a condition, but more a legacy of dreams and disappointments, bequeathed by loved ones about a past we hardly remembered and a place we barely knew.

Chapter 18

FREEDOM OF INFORMATION
1966

FREEDOM OF INFORMATION AND PRIVACY ACTS: Subject: Elin Toona Gottschalk, File No. 105-154020. Federal Bureau of Investigation. 2/28/69...requesting a check of State Department, Central Intelligence Agency records to determine subject's location...

The first phone call came to our London flat on Finborough Road in the autumn of 1966.

Though I need to digress. The laws of cause and effect are pretty reliable, but not always based on reality. As I had recognized a long time ago, ignorance can cause more damage than the well-laid plans of true schemers. When assumptions and perceptions are taken for truth, things do happen, though not always as intended.

What happened next was no one's fault or everyone's fault—mine for being overenthusiastically liberated from the mill life, the naysayers, and the authorities. I had behaved no better toward my "little people" under the horseradish patch than England had dealt with me. England had impressed me with its might, scared me with its power, shown me mercy and good will, but ultimately it had abandoned me by denying me an education in a world that demands a disciplined mind.

Mother also recovered from England's famous institutions and continued to have faith in them, but she should have realized that the Soviets also had famous institutions. The KGB was no joke.

Mother's greatest pleasure was corresponding with her friends worldwide, especially friends in Estonia. Her school friend Lydia was back from Siberia, and her actress friend Ellen was still in the theater in Tallinn and kept her informed of Father's career. He had divorced Mother in 1946 and married the mother of his son, who was born in 1942, soon after his last dramatic visit to Haapsalu. That was the visit when I put a handful of grass into his pocket to remind him that he also had a daughter.

Mother's letters were long, cheery, and chatty, full of details—as though she had never heard of censors. Grandmother was also writing regularly to Lydia. Between the two of them they informed everyone whom they knew of our life in England. Why would they not? They were living in the normal world where such correspondence was taken for granted.

Mother was telling Ellen about my career as an actress (not much of a career), but more importantly, about my successful venture into writing in both English and Estonian. She told them of my brief and ill-conceived marriage in 1962, which led me to Singapore and back in 1963, and how, on the return journey, as a hitchhiker on an overland English bus, I met an American University student whose name was Don. Don was on an American tour bus. The two buses traveled together through the deserts and mountains bordering Baluchistan, Pakistan, and Afghanistan. Don and I fell in love, and this incredible journey led to my second marriage in 1967, in America.

Liki at her desk in Finborough Road apartment, 1966.

Between 1964 and 1967, I made two trips to America and stayed on Long Island with Mother's Polish friends, the couple from Hausberge. Don visited me there as often as he could. He lived in Philadelphia.

When I was in America in 1964 a strange thing happened.

Don received a phone call. The caller was a woman we had met in India. Her name was Florence. She and her husband Walter were artists, and as Don was also an artist, they had kept in touch. Florence was calling to tell Don that Walter had died. She thought Don might want to come to the wake. Walter's ashes were going to be ceremoniously buried on their property, in a remote part of the Catskill Mountains, near Woodstock.

Don could not get away from work, but he told Florence that I had recently arrived in America and might be interested. I knew Florence only vaguely, but Don was going to drop me off and pick me up again in a day or two. I saw no reason why I shouldn't go.

318

Don dropped me off on Friday night, at a house deep in the woods, and drove away with a honk on his horn and a cheery wave "good-bye," until the following Sunday.

The only person I told about what happened to me in Woodstock in 1964 was my friend Jackie with whom I had visited Hausberge in 1961. I told a vague story to the Polish couple and to Don, letting them know that I did not have a particularly pleasant visit. I did not expect Don to believe me. I definitely did not tell Mother and Grandmother because it would have plunged them back into the nightmares of the past. I put the incident behind me the way I had learned to do as a child, but I had not forgotten.

In 1999 I decided to purchase my FBI file under the *Freedom of Information Act*. That was when I read about what had happened to me in 1964, in a way that I would never have believed possible.

TOP SECRET

To: Director, FBI
From: Legat, London (105-2490) (RUC)
SUBJECT: ELIN KAI GOTTSCHALK nee TOONA
CIA recorded for available background.
3 – Bureau (Encs.4)
1 – Liaison (direct)
1 - London

She and her mother, LIKI TOONA, left Estonia during World War II at the time the Soviets were overrunning her country, approximately 1944. They proceeded to Germany and remained there after the defeat of Germany living in a displaced persons camp for several years before taking up residence in England. She came from a well-known literary family in Estonia, her grandfather ERNEST ENNO, being a national poet of Estonia. In the early 1950's she also began writing Estonian articles and stories and subsequently also had several books published in the Estonian language. She became a somewhat well-known writer in exile of Estonian literature. Her writings concerned cultural aspects of Estonia and avoided political ramifications. In view of the non-political aspect of her writings some have been used currently in Soviet Estonia. Many of her short stories and books are published in Sweden. On occasion her short stories and books are commented about in the Estonian language newspapers ...

In 1964 she visited the United States from approximately April to October at which time an acquaintance (name deleted) was re-established. She had met (deleted) prior to this time while touring (sic) India by bus. In the United States she was staying with friends on Long Island.

(Deleted) called to tell her about the recent death of (deleted) invited her to a party which commemorated her husband's death at a residence in a remote section of Woodstock, N.Y. She attended this party to which (deleted) had invited several other friends of her deceased husband. When it became known that she was of Estonian background, several of the guests became enraged and called her a Nazi. One man who was a refugee from the Nazis tried to strike her. She became very frightened and

"The phone rang again today," said Grandmother, as soon as Mother walked through the door. "I didn't answer it." The telephone had become a menace. It was now 1967.

When Mother was finally home, she picked up the receiver. The caller was a man, speaking Estonian. He gave his name as Toomaru. Mother knew every Estonian in London and immediately became suspicious.

Our resident Communists (there was one in every exile community) were an elderly couple named Einer. They ran a Russian bookshop in the Edgeware Road. You could smell the Russian print ink all the way to Marble Arch, but they also sold Estonian souvenirs such as folk costume dolls, handicrafts, and similarly useful gifts to give to our English friends.

This caller was not Einer. Mother asked him outright if he was "from the Bayswater Road area," meaning the Russian Embassy. The man did not deny it. He said he had an important message to convey, but would only speak to me. Mother told him I did not live there and hung up on him. It was true. I had a separate bed-sitting room in Earl's Court.

Mother was in a panic. That the KGB would be calling our flat, asking for me by name, went beyond the accepted nuisance calls these people attempted from time to time. Everybody ignored them.

Toomaru called again and kept calling. He called at the same time every evening; now it was Mother's turn to dread the telephone. She had explained to Grandmother that the calls were from "Elin's friends." Grandmother knew I had no Estonian friends in London at the time.

After Mother got over her initial panic she decided to find out what the man wanted. Being the actress she was, she engaged him in a reasonable conversation and ascertained that the KGB agent wanted me to meet a special visitor from Estonia. He assured Mother that it was someone I would definitely not want to miss. Only then did Mother tell me about the calls. We conferred about it in the bathroom while Mother was supposed to be coloring my hair.

"It could mean that your father is in London with a theater group," she whispered excitedly. "I think you should consider the opportunity to meet him. Mämma need not know."

320

My last memories of Father were of his dramatic departure from Haapsalu, but yes, I would not mind meeting him, I told Mother.

The next time Toomaru called, Mother agreed to a meeting, but she would not allow me to go alone. Despite living in London and the free world, there was enough going on around the Russian Embassy in Bayswater to strike fear in anyone with an ounce of common sense. She emphasized that we would not be coming to the embassy and that Toomaru was not welcome in our flat.

The meeting was arranged to take place at the Einers' apartment in Notting Hill Gate. An Estonian writer friend, Gert Helbemäe, also lived at Campden Hill Mansions, an old Victorian structure off Church Street, on the same floor as the Einers, and was willing to keep an eye on us. He would leave his door ajar. If he heard anything unusual he would call the police. The invitation was for dinner.

The prospect of Mother meeting her husband again after twenty-three years put two spots of red on each of her cheekbones—ritual kisses marking an ultimate betrayal, unless it was rouge, something she rarely used. I was less nervous. I wondered whether Father had kept the grass.

Helbemäe was waiting for us. He heard us on the stairs and opened his door to let us know he was watching.

Mother rang the Einers' doorbell. There too, the watchers and listeners had been alert. The door was opened immediately by Mr. Einer. He ushered us into the flat. No sign of any visitors, just Mrs. Einer bustling about at a fully decked dinner table. She, too, sported rosy cheeks. Always did! In her case it was definitely rouge.

Ah! Male voices behind a Japanese screen. The screen divided the living room. The only light came from an adjoining doorway. Quiet music. We were about to be entertained by a theater production. Had Mother not befriended Mrs. Takk, who had birthed me and took us in after I was born, I would probably have been born in Mother's dressing room. Either way, it seemed we had never left the theater. In the bedroom the actors were awaiting their cue, murmuring "rhubarb, rhubarb." The production was not unexpected because Soviet agents who were sent abroad were trained in English dialogue from old films and sounded like actors from the 1940's.

We were led to a couch and offered drinks. Mother waived the drinks aside. Einer disappeared and his wife was given an imperceptible signal to make herself scarce—check the roast or something. I could smell the roast, also Mother's perfume or maybe her sweat. She was perched on the edge of the couch, like an Aztec sacrifice, ready to run or leap off the cliff. Her emotions were so high that she had not even reached for a cigarette.

When the moment arrived, we heard a commotion. Three men appeared from behind the screen, discreetly backlit by a tall *torchère*.[35] I did not expect to recognize Father, but Mother had already reacted to the voices. She jumped to her feet. Toomaru and Einer's voices she knew, and the third man's voice was not Fathers. She gave a snort and took the offensive.

---

[35] A bowl-shaped floor lamp that projects light to the ceiling.

"I see. The usual bunch." She grabbed my arm. "They're wasting our time."

"We're not interested in you," said the stranger smoothly. "We're only interested in your daughter." He introduced himself, but his name was meaningless.

Seeing resistance, the man became aggressive enough to step forward and try to separate Mother and me. He even made a joke of it. "It looks like we have to remove the wooden angel from her guardian angel," he laughed, referring to the title of my recent Estonian book.

So it was the book! I had written a book in Estonian in which the hero had no interest in his horse or his sword, but took quite a bit of interest in real life and sex.

Since coming to London, in addition to my acting studies and office jobs, I was also writing for the BBC, short stories, radio plays, monologue and short pieces for "Northern Drift". The BBC had named me an up-and-coming young writer on a program called "World of the Young". "Girl Writer" is how The Yorkshire Post" put it. My English language successes went unnoticed, but my Estonian articles for exile magazines in Sweden and Canada, critical of the Estonian émigré community in England, had already drawn criticism and my novel "Puuingel" was the last straw. They did not know that the book had originally been written in English, titled "Wooden Angel". I had submitted the manuscript to Heinemann's publishers, but was "regretfully" informed, that their reader had left it on the bus. Unable to re-write from illegible carbons the Estonian writer Helbemäe persuaded me to write it again in Estonian and make it my first Estoian novel. English literary tastes were undergoing the same changes as the other arts. „The L-Shaped Room" by Lynne Reid Bans had recently been published and was a best seller.

When my book appeared, Mother's friends were horrified. "How could you allow your daughter to write such a book?" It now appeared that the KGB thought the same and that Mother and I were still at odds. They did not know that we had settled our differences in Munich.

Mother still had my arm. "Come," she yanked at it painfully and pushed me past the man to the front door.

"Have you nothing to say for yourself?" the man asked me. "Have you no voice of your own? Are you their puppet?"

A scene was on the horizon. I did not resist Mother's grip or determined stride as she pulled me with her into the corridor and down the steps. When we passed Helbemäe's door, Mother waved to him to say we were all right, but not happy.

The FBI version runs as follows:

In 1966 she and her mother were invited to a dinner in London, England, which was attended by several publishers of Estonian literature. To her surprise, a couple also attended this function who were identified as (deleted) Estonian by background.

Mother continued to believe Father should have been there. That bit of intuition was later confirmed in a letter from her friend Ellen. "Tom was offered an opportunity to visit London, but he had declined."

"Good for him," said Mother. "At least he had not allowed himself to be thus used."

Although I was writing freelance and doing small parts on TV, I needed a regular income and had a part-time job as a secretary, shorthand typist in an animal health organization funded by prominent members of the English aristocracy. The Animal Health Trust was actually headed by the Queen and included the Duke of Norfolk, Lady Stanley, and many titled personages who supported veterinary medicine and equine research. The director of the trust was one of the founders and a former president of the Royal College of Veterinary Surgeons, Dr. W. R. Wooldridge.

Dr. Wooldridge referred to me as his "Icelandic secretary" although he knew very well that I was Estonian. He was a formidable intellect with a great sense of humor. Like most people whose minds brimmed over with too many thoughts, he often left his notes on the train and cued his speeches from his shirt cuffs, literally! The trust office was small, in a side street near Victoria Station, not far from Westminster Abbey and Westminster Cathedral. I enjoyed my job and I enjoyed London, as did Mother. The war, DP camps, and even our miserable post-war conditions were a distant memory.

For me, Estonia had become a mythical country and my muse. It was my inner voice, speaking to me in a secret language. No one in my everyday life could understand it except Mother, Grandmother, and the Estonian community.

I need to explain why the KGB had singled me out as a person of interest. It had a lot to do with my writing, but also with the lifestyle I was living in my "English life", that did not conform to the tastes and values of the ultra conservative refugees, still living in the past. They were still in the mindset of the 1940's but the world was moving on. England had had enough of gloom and doom. They could not comprehend 'The Swinging Sixties' London of mini-skirts, Elvis Presley, rock music and men with long hair. England was undergoing a social revolution that would eventually go global but in their eyes it was pure anarchy – young people misbehaving. Musicians who could not even read music were becoming famous. Paintings created by throwing

---

[36] The dinner actually never took place, in that we never made it to the table.

323

paint on a canvas, and riding over it with a bicycle were appearing in respectable Art Galleries. They called it 'modern art'. London had become a town for Bohemians and Beatniks and Ernst Enno's grand-daughter was one of them

Unlike the DP's who had come to Northern England to hospitals and factories, the London Estonians arrived under the aegis of the Estonian Embassy, the Lutheran Church and private sponsors. Many were placed into well-paying jobs. The writer Gert Helbemäe is just one example (seeing I had already used his name). He got a job at the BBC, his wife was hired by a big shipping firm and they were able to educate their daugher at the Lycée Francaise. The 11+ eligible children of DP parents in Southern England all ended up in Grammar School and went on to University. My drama school did not qualify as 'higher education'. I was excluded from the Academic Youth groups. Then there were my writings! I had started writing for the refugee newspapers after winning an Essay contest right after leaving the orphanage. First just poetry, to get the language back, then observations of what I saw as the "the refugee mentality". But basically I was 'acting-up', as mother would have said, for being snubbed as 'uneducated' and because my English writings were being completely ignored. I was writing for the BBC and doing small parts on TV, which no one was interested in either. Looking back I should be ashamed because I was no longer a teenager but all of twenty-two. Mother and grandmother had not yet moved to London.

I was also living the "English life". Drama classes until noon, part time as a secretary in an office, and in the evenings working back-stage at two of London's famous theatres. The Royal Court and The Prince of Wales. I was an ASM (Assistant Stage Manager) which sounded grand but all I was doing was running errands for the actors and knocking on Vivien Leigh's dressing room door shouting "five minutes Miss Leigh". Vivien Leigh was in "Look After Lulu" (Noel Coward's adaptation of the French farce "Occupetoi d'Amélie" by Feydeau) and Joan Plowright was in Arnold Wesker's "Roots" at the Prince of Wales. The Olivier's were in the throes of their divorce and Sir Olivier was already courting his new love at the Prince of Wales. It was an exciting time for me, a thousand years from the past; the war, the orphanage, the mill. I was still Estonian but relishing my English life to the hilt. No longer a Verfluchter Ausländer or bloody foreigner! I was accepted as 'just another drama student', spoke perfect English and behaved 'English' the way mother had promised me would change my life. It had! To the conservative Estonians, however, I was a Beatnik and a member of the 'great unwashed'.

The Estonians were not the only ones who were keeping an eye on me and disapproving. Everything written above had direct bearing on why I ended up in the KGB/FBI/CIA files.

In the 1960's, the Soviets had agents assigned to all the exile communities and were constantly trolling for people they could lure back "home" and brainwash for propaganda purposes. They looked for dissent, disruption, name recognition and I was an ideal candidate. I fit the KGB recruitment criteria perfectly: uneducated, undisciplined, unconventional, with a *chip-on-the shoulder and liberal views already expressed in my writings. When my first novel "Puuingel" (Wooden Angel) received the H. Visnapuu award from the World Association of Estonians, the prestigious notification was slipped under our doormat. Grandmother thought it was a bill from the milkman when she first spotted it.*

After receiving the boot from Mother, Toomaru began to call me at work. Getting the telephone number had been easy for him, but he underestimated the kind of people I was employed by the British aristocracy had vast experience in dealing with foreign agents during the war. Their covert operations had included deciphering the Enigma code at Bletchley Park.

Dr. Wooldridge soon noticed that I was getting unwelcome phone calls, slamming down the phone, and acting peculiar. Raised eyebrows and questioning looks over his half-moon reading glasses suggested that he might be thinking I had an unwelcome boyfriend. I asked the switchboard not to put the calls through, but the girl could not do that without Dr.Wooldridge's permission. It was my turn to dread the telephone.

Finally after two calls in one day I broke down and told Dr. Wooldridge that the calls were not from a boyfriend, but from a Soviet agent who had been bothering us for weeks. Dr. Wooldridge did not laugh or accuse me of having a vivid imagination; he sat back in his chair and asked me to tell him everything, from the beginning. My story included the incident with the Communists in America in 1964, and the dinner at the Einers. I confessed to have written a book that had upset the Estonian community. How the sudden reappearance of the KGB in our lives had brought back old fears. Mother was a nervous wreck. Grandmother was already sitting by the window, expecting closed black cars to draw up to the curb to whisk us off to Siberia. When I finished I was in tears.

Dr. Wooldridge nodded throughout, passed me his handkerchief, and not until I had composed myself, did he speak.

"Hmm! We'll have to do something about that then, won't we?"

"I don't know what to do."

"Would you like me to help you?"

I assured him I did. Grandmother was so fearful that Mother dreaded leaving her alone all day.

Dr. Wooldridge reached for his own telephone and dialed.

"You'll have to do exactly as you're told," he warned, fixing me over his glasses. I promised I would.

The conversation he had with someone at the other end of the line was short. He said he was sending a young woman over with a problem and scribbled an address for me, in Whitehall.

"The reception desk will be expecting you." He handed me the slip of paper.

Half an hour later I entered an impressive white building near the Cenotaph. So this is MI5, I was thinking. Reception was ready for me. A grey-suited gentleman escorted me down a long corridor to an office with an opaque glass door. The man who greeted me also wore a grey suit. He was middle-aged and polite. Here was another facet of that „other England", not

325

yet „demi-paradise", but certainly a better part of existence. How different were my experiences of England since leaving the mill!

The MI5 official let me repeat my story without interruption. He took notes. When I had finished, he steepled his forearms and fingers and looked pleased.

"So! Our friend Toomaru is up to his old tricks."

"You know him?"

"Oh yes, and we've been trying to catch him for ages, but can't get anyone to cooperate with us. We need evidence to expel him. Your older generation is afraid of becoming involved."

Then he asked me a strange question.

"Are you in correspondence with your father?"

I assured him I was not.

"Not from the Estonian Club?"

"Why would I write from the Estonian Club? I have my own address." I told him I had barely thought of my father since the dinner at the Einers.

He nodded and began to give me instructions. "Now this is serious," he warned me. "You may not understand why we tell you to do things, but be assured there is a reason. Just do what you are told, even if it makes no sense. Understand?"

I said I did, but deep down I was getting scared. This was no drama class assignment. There were a hundred ways I could mess up.

"And don't sound too eager all of a sudden. Grumble a bit. Have him pick the location, then call me." He gave me a telepone number. Before he let me leave he told me that I was to go to Westminster Cathedral at noon the next day. „Stand five pews down from the altar. Stay there for at least ten minutes" he emphasized.

Westminster Cathedral was on the same street as the Trust Office. I walked there at lunch-time, counted out the pews, and took my stand. It was a hot day. Inside was cool and smelled of incense. A few old people knelt in the pews — dark shapes, headscarves or swatches of grey hair. A few others were lighting candles by the altar. I felt a bit foolish standing there waiting for one of the people that I could see join me. Ten minutes passed. No one even came near.

When my lunch time was up, I went back to work and told Dr. Wooldridge that no one had approached me. I feared I had got the instructions wrong. Dr. Wooldridge did not appear concerned. In fact he looked quite pleased and changed the subject. He asked me to take dictation for an upcoming speech at Cambridge University on vivisection. I feared I had messed up.

A few days later Toomaru called. The ringing telephone made me almost jump out of my skin. My desk was right next to Dr. Wooldridge's office. The door was kept open unless he had a meeting. He was motioning for me to answer.

Bearing in mind not to sound too different, I was quite rude. "So what do you want ?" I asked in Estonian. "You've got to stop calling me. You are jeopardizing my job."

Toomaru said he would stop calling if I would meet him. He had something important to tell me.

I grumbled some, as per instructions, but remained on the line and heard him out.

"All right, just this once. And then get out of my life," I told him.

After that I phoned Whitehall. The man did not want details.

My new instructions were to go to Victoria Station and sit on a bench outside the coffee bar at noon. A gentleman wearing a bowler hat, carrying an umbrella, sporting a red carnation in his buttonhole, and reading *The Times* would sit next to me. I was to tell him the time and place for my meeting with the KGB agent. It was surreal. I had done small parts and walk-ons in English B-Films at Pinewood Studios and had to pinch myself that this was not another episode of "The Net" or some such series.

There were several benches outside the station café or "caff," as we liked to call it, and hundreds of people milling about the station concourse. How would the man know me? And then I remembered the seemingly mindless wait at the cathedral. No one had approached me because all they had needed was to see what I looked like. Very clever.

The loudspeaker was announcing platforms, completely unintelligibly. Trains were arriving, trains were departing. The benches outside the coffee bar were occupied. I managed to squeeze myself onto one directly by the door and began to do my crossword puzzle, but I worried. There was no room on the bench for anyone else. As soon as one person got up, another one grabbed the spot. After several such changes, the person sitting next to me suddenly got up, and a city gent in a bowler hat, with exactly the other described accessories, took his place. He opened *The Times* and without turning his head said, "So?"

"I'm meeting Mr. Toomaru on Saturday at 3:00 PM at the Sombrero Restaurant in Kensington High Street," I told him, also not turning, but staring ahead at the station clock. Definitely the stuff of spy films. The gentleman folded his newspaper and walked away. I had no idea whether he had even heard me.

Saturday arrived. I decided to be late. Somehow it seemed appropriate to be late rather than early. Toomaru saw me at once and I recognized him too, sitting in a booth. He was a chubby fellow, perhaps in his fifties, with thinning hair and nervous fingers. He was fiddling with a packet of sugar. His tea already had scum on top and was getting cold. He had come early.

He got up to greet me, not easy for a man with a rotund stomach. He signalled to the waiter to get me a cup of tea. Did I want anything else?

Hardly. The seriousness of the meeting was finally sinking in. I had spent the night on the spare mattress in our Finborough Road flat and had barely closed my eyes. Only Mother knew what was happening. The way her bed had creaked, I knew she had not slept either.

It was difficult not to cast glances at the other customers, knowing someone was not who they appeared to be. Was it the derelict with his elbows on the table, hugging his cuppa or the young hippie covered in peace signs, slouching in another booth? Or was the MI5 agent the mother yelling at her children at one of the tables? Two old women were gossiping across from each other, leaning forward. One had a big hearing aid in her ear, but no, they left almost as soon as my tea arrived.

Toomaru skipped preliminaries. He was impatient and kept looking over my shoulder, probably expecting Mother to turn up any minute and yank me out of there by my hair. Actually, I had left Mother at Marks & Spencers across the street, frozen next to a rack of cashmere cardigans. She was even more of a nervous wreck than she had been at that bogus dinner.

"You know you'll not get anywhere if you stay in England," Toomaru began. "You're wasting your time and talent here. In Estonia everybody has heard of you. You can become a famous writer. You will be recognized, you'll live well, you'll be able to travel to your heart's content," he warbled on, as though I really were the moron he took me for.

"I didn't know people in the Soviet Union were free to travel," I replied innocently.

"What nonsense!" He made a dismissive gesture at my ignorance. "You can travel as much as you like."

"You mean I could come to London at any time, to vist my mother and grandmother? Go to Paris?"

He ignored the first. "You've already been to Paris," he said impatiently. "I'm talking about places very few people have ever been to."

"Such as?" I wanted to say "Siberia", but held my tongue.

"Baku, Sochi, the Caucasus. Imagine it—Samerkand. You've probably not even heard of Samerkand." A curl of the lip, a slurp of cold tea.

"Very interesting, but you're only talking about the Soviet Bloc."

He dismissed that, too. "It's obvious you know nothing except what you've been told by your elders. They're all living in the past. Their lives are ruined and they want to ruin yours also. Estonia is looking to the future. Estonia is where you belong, where you have a family."

"I have no family in Estonia."

"Ah, you're wrong! You have a father in Estonia." He said this with a flourish, as though presenting his ace.

"I know, but he already has a new wife and son."

Toomaru frowned and let it go. He had not known that I knew about Father's wife and my half-brother.

"Nevertheless." The dismissive gesture again. "If you are determined to stay in England I can at least further your career. I can introduce you to famous writers."

"Such as?" I realized that by naming names he was going to reveal writers in a way they might not have wished to be revealed.

He did name names, famous writers, and he surprised me no end. It was none of my business, but one of the writers was C.P. Snow, whose political views were no secret to anyone.

Again I told him I wasn't interested. I told him I was already writing stories and radio plays for the BBC and had been named an "up-and-coming young writer" in the English press. My Estonian writings were being distributed to exile communities worldwide.

"Hah!" A topic, at last, that he could sink his teeth into. "*Puuingel*" You know very well what they are saying about that. Even your mother's friends are shocked." His voice was rising and the conversation was getting strappy. It was time to end it with a final "no thank you," then add the requisite words "I don't want to return to Estonia," and leave. The Whitehall man had said to keep him talking for at least fifteen minutes. I had not looked at my watch.

"You are a stupid girl," hissed Toomaru. "You don't even recognize the opportunities I'm offering you. Most people would be thrilled at the chance of becoming famous. You are not just a disappointment to your family, your community, but also to your country. Your book is trash." He pounded his fist on the table so that the cups and saucers rattled.

People stopped talking and looked around. "You're a stupid, stupid girl!" he repeated. "All you've been told is lies. All lies! You've been brainwashed by your mother and grandmother and their kind and will never amount to anything. Not anything!" I saw that he was about to pound the table again and thought it best to leave at once. His contempt for my book had rattled me. I wanted to argue that the book had won Estonia's highest literary award, but already wondered about that, too. Even the Estonian Embassy had snubbed me, which was why the KGB had seen me as an easy mark.

"I'd better go now," I told him. "Thank you for the tea." I grabbed my handbag and coat, slid out of the booth, and left so fast that it was not until I was on the other side of Kensington High Street that I again remembered my obligation to MI5. I had probably left too early.

No one contacted me again. Dr. Wooldridge never mentioned it either. I was sure I had failed until one day Mother came from work and pulled a newspaper out of her handbag. An article mentioned that an Estonian diplomat attached to the Russian Embassy had been recalled.

The FBI version of my meeting with Toomaru was as follows:

> *Later she was in contact with him (deleted) at a café in London at which time she very strongly told (deleted) that she did not desire to be contacted any more by him. The latter incident was the last time (deleted) contacted her. Subsequently (name blacked out) received considerable publicity in the English newspapers conerning his efforts to encourage Estonian immigrants to return to their homeland. As a result of this unfavorable publicity, (name blacked out) had to leave England in July 1966.*

Yet incredibly that was still not the end of it.

In 1967 I returned to America. In October I became Mrs. Donald F. Gottschalk. I had married on a Visitor's Visa and had to return to England for the immigration process to begin. It would take some time I was warned.

This time there was no phone call, but a letter, written in flowing cursive from a Finnish student studying at London University. She said she was a tour guide on the Helsinki-Tallinn ferry, visited Estonia regularly, had heard of me, and would like to meet me. She hoped to find a friend in London.

Mother immediately suspected it was another attempt by our old friends down Bayswater Road. MI5 had told me to call Whitehall the moment anyone else involved with the Soviet Embassy got in touch with me, but Mother had another idea. "Let's see what she has to say, then decide." Since the previous incident Mother had had time to think and suggested we should take advantage of the KGB's interest in me and play along. Perhaps I really could be reunited with Father, if only by post. The opportunity might not come again.

I agreed.

Of course we had reason to be cautious. We had questions. Was the Finnish student following instructions or was she genuinely interested in meeting me? Another possibility was that the KGB was using her without her knowing it, suggesting an innocent contact to further their own hidden agenda.

I will call my new friend "Linda," which is not her real name.

Linda's letter gave an address and telephone number, which I called. A few days later I was looking up at a block of flats on High Holborn. From the general look of the foyer, it was typical student lodging, much like my previous residence in Notting Hill Gate.

The student who answered the door was about my age, fair, tall, and slender. She was very pleasantly spoken in both English and Estonian with a slight Finnish accent. She asked me to sit down while she left the room to make coffee.

The central table was of polished wood, bare except for an Estonian/Soviet newspaper, *Sirp ja Vasar* (Hammer and Sickle) folded on a corner of it. There was nothing else on the table. I took a closer look and saw a picture of my father on the front page. I had last seen him when I was five and would not have recognized him had he not been named. The man I was looking at had aged and put on weight, but certain features were familiar. The article praised him for some successful theater production. I decided not to mention it to Linda when she came back with the coffee. She did not mention the newspaper either.

We conversed in Estonia. She told me about her studies and her duties as a tour guide. I told her I had never lived in Tallinn, but that my father lived in Tallinn, that he was a well-known theatrical producer. "Do you know of him?" I asked casually.

She said she did not.

We talked for over an hour. I really liked her. When it was time for me to leave, I asked whether I could borrow the Estonian newspaper as I had never seen one before. I did not mention the article on the front page. Linda gave me the paper, also without comment.

We agreed to meet again. It was almost Christmas 1967.

As we neared the door Linda remembered a student party for Saturday night, near Russell Square. She invited me. I said I would be delighted. She

330

jotted down the address and time. I thanked her and did not look at the note until I was on the Tube headed home.

When I stepped into our flat, Grandmother was in the kitchen and Mother was sitting on her bed reading. I signalled to her urgently to join me downstairs in the hall. I had taken the introductory letter with me to High Holborn. When Mother and I were alone in the foyer, I produced Linda's note from my handbag and put it next to the letter. We compared them and Mother immediately saw the problem. The introductory letter and the note had not been written by the same person. The letter was in large cursive, but the note was written in a small cramped hand that was barely legible. I then showed Mother the newspaper article.

"Oh dear!" Mother looked long at the picture of her husband of twenty-some years ago. "He's aged, as I have," she said at last. "But eating well by the look of it. Ellen told me he was a great success. The article confirms it. That's good." Her eyes had become misty behind her glasses.

"Mother, what do you think we should do?" I had to get her back into the present. "Linda said she knows nothing of Father, but he's famous."

"I know," she patted my arm. "We have to think."

We agreed to invite Linda to our flat. If she was innocent, I had gained an interesting new friend. If she was a plant, she was a possible conduit to Father. The conflicting handwriting was hard evidence that someone was pulling our strings. Until we knew more, we would have to keep our eyes open and be wary.

We decided to refer to Linda as "our friend from Smersh," alluding to the James Bond stories we both enjoyed. Mother and I hugged and giggled like schoolgirls. I could understand why Mother had always had so many friends. She gave as much friendship as she got in return. I wished I had grown up sooner.

The party was in a basement near Russell Square. Many foreign students were there. They all spoke good English. I spent most of the evening sitting on the floor, talking to a Bulgarian student named Krishna. He showed me his red Soviet passport. I had never seen a Soviet passport before.

Linda came to our apartment the following weekend, and Mother and Grandmother were immediately impressed. She was not only highly intelligent, with two doctorates and working on her third, but was also open to our questions about Soviet Estonia. Grandmother made coffee, Mother passed the Drambuie. Linda knew of my grandfather. It was a conversation we could never have had with anyone English. Mother had not lost her focus. When least expected, she asked the crucial question: "When you take your tour groups to Estonia, do you take them to the theaters?"

"Sometimes," Linda admitted.

"Then perhaps you have met my husband, the theater producer, Enn Toona?"

"Not personally, but I have heard of him."

I almost gasped. She had denied that knowledge to me. It was hard not to accuse her.

"I think he is mostly in Pärnu," she added, speaking naturally.

331

Mother's glass did a little wobble. She corrected it. "That is wonderful. Do you think you might be seeing him this Christmas?" Mother continued. "I expect you'll be going home for the holidays."

"Yes, I am going home for Christmas, but I probably won't be going to Estonia until the new year."

"In that case, perhaps you could do us a favor." Mother! Five curtain calls!

"I'll be happy to," said Linda, sitting comfortably on Mother's bed, completely relaxed, sipping Drambuie and nibbling on German *Spitskuchen*.

"I would like to send Tom," Mother used father's nickname, "an English briar pipe. The very best. Even if he doesn't smoke, he can use it as a prop."

Linda agreed to take it and deliver it personally.

Mother and I went to a famous tobacconist on Bond Street and picked out the most expensive English pipe in the display case. Mother was in her element, her eyes were shining behind her glasses, while she selected a Christmas gift for her husband after their twenty-three years apart. The act of giving the gift far surpassed any gift she herself had ever received. I was struck again by my lack of knowledge of some of the simplest things in life that most people took for granted.

Linda visited us a few more times. We gave her the package containing the pipe and a Christmas card signed by the three of us.

Linda was a problem because we did not know who we were dealing with. We wanted to ask her outright, but decided against it. If she were an agent, our knowledge of her activities could put her in danger. If she thought we were accusing her unjustly, she might not deliver the pipe. If she was innocent, she would become alarmed and begin to examine her own friends and contacts who might have led her down this path. We decided to say nothing and let the situation disentangle itself in time.

Then something else happened that aroused my suspicions anew. A few days before Christmas and before Linda went back to Finland, she suggested we do a bit of Christmas shopping together on Oxford Street. She asked me to pick her up at an office building near Russell Square, where she said she was doing part-time bookkeeping. "Five'ish," she said.

It was a miserable evening, already dark and raining buckets. Oxford Street and Regent Street were festooned with Christmas lights, the department store windows festive, their revolving doors blasting Christmas carols into the street. The pavements were so crowded you had to step into traffic to make any progress at all, while making sure you did not get run over. This was the London that Mother and I had come to love. When I would go to live in America, I would miss this.

I walked to Russell Square. The office building, a converted Georgian residence like most houses in London, was in a row of similar facades, but dark. The front door was open. I stepped into what I can only describe as an unoccupied building. There was a musty smell in the hall with an underlying dampness of exposed plaster and mildewed wallpaper. A light at the top of the stairs showed that a back office was occupied.

332

Unsure of myself, I called, "Hello?"

A man's voice answered in English. "Come on up!"

The second floor landing was also dark. The light came from an open door directly opposite the stairs. The room I entered was bare except for a desk, a filing cabinet, and two people. A youngish woman was sitting at the desk with an open ledger in front of her and a man was standing by the filing cabinet, leaning against it, holding a file. Another low-budget B-Film with a minimum of props. There was not even a picture on the wall or a chair for the man to sit on. No sign of Linda. To retreat quickly or take the initiative? I chose the latter and asked for Linda by name.

"She is not quite ready to leave yet," the woman informed me.

There was nowhere to sit, so I reached out my hand to the woman at the desk. Speaking Estonian I told her my name and asked for hers.

She said her name was Silvi. I mentioned that I knew every Estonian in London, but had not seen her at our gatherings. "Have you been here long?" I asked.

"Not very long," she replied.

The man holding the file did not speak, but remained by the cabinet. He did not introduce himself, and I ignored him.

When the woman spoke again she mentioned that the weather was foul. The upcoming holidays were welcome. And that they were going to a Christmas party after work. "We would like to invite you to join us." She said. I did not know whether Linda was part of the "we."

She glanced at the man.

"Yes, do come," he said heartily, in English. "We've got a car, so you won't get wet." A slight Cockney inflection. He was English.

"Where is this party?" I asked, trying to sound normal. Soviet Estonians with a car nearby?

"Bayswater way." Silvi waved her hand in an unspecified direction.

"You mean the Russian Embassy?" I asked, pleasantly, in English.

"Near there. Why does that matter?" Her voice became aggressive. "Are you one of those ridiculous people who believe all the stories you hear about the Russian Embassy? Underground tunnels? Secret basements? What nonsense! Complete rubbish!" Her English was strongly accented. She threw back her head and began to laugh harshly. Not a good actress. Toomaru had been better.

Fortunately, Linda appeared in the doorway at that same moment and announced brightly. "I'm ready! Let's go."

God bless her, I thought! Whatever her mission, she was on my side on this.

Silvi closed the ledger and got to her feet. "Let us take you. It is raining heavily. Even if you don't want to come to the party, we can drop you off on Oxford Street."

The man put aside the file and took a set of keys from his pocket. "I'll bring the car around." He strode to the door. "The car is just around the corner. I'll get it."

"No! No! I panicked. Car, Russian Embassy! I should have left as soon as I recognized the setup. It was my first time to be truly afraid since the entire KGB thing had started.

Then Linda surprised me again. "No, really! We'll walk." She spoke normally and gave me a little shove towards the door. "There's too much traffic. It will be faster to walk."

"Thanks anyway," I managed quickly, and almost fell downstairs in the dark. Linda was behind me. When we got to the street, the car had not yet appeared. Silvi was looking disconcerted, trying to delay us. I did not pause, but brushed past her and almost ran to get to a well-lighted street. Linda stayed with me.

Linda and I never spoke of the incident then or later. It was well after Estonian independence when I finally broached the subject. I hoped we could discuss what had really happened, compare notes, maybe have a good laugh. I believed we had both been hoodwinked. Alas, Linda took offense and broke off our friendship.

Father got the pipe. He thanked us in the first letter I had ever received from him, dated 27 February 1967. His letter actually arrived in January 1968 to my new home address in America. I had barely arrived there myself.

I was overjoyed to receive the letter and thanked Linda in my mind. All the same it was the strangest letter I had ever read. It mentioned things that had happened in 1967 alongside what was happening in 1968, referring to things that had never happened and things he could not have known about. He knew about my first marriage. He knew about my second marriage and that I was expecting a child, the last about two weeks after I myself had learned I was pregnant.

*****Apparently MI5 was already aware of something I did not know. That was why the Whitehall man asked me if I was writing to my father. *****

In 1966 or thereabouts the KGB had initiated a bogus correspondence between "me" (KGB agent, probably Toomaru) and my Father, through the Estonian Club in London. The letters were probably sent in a cover envelope, picked up by the Einers from the Estonian Club's letter rack. Toomaru fabricated the replies based on information gleaned from mother's and grandmother's letters to their friends in Estonia. The information was then threaded into "my" letters to my father. Father thought he was replying to me. The KGB were hoping to establish a bonafide correspondence that would prompt me to return to Estonia where I would be welcomed with open arms etc.

Father's first letter, arrived to my new address in America.

My dear daughter!

334

Finally I've found you! Eureka! Blessed day! Though actually it was you who found me. It gives me joy to think that you were searching for me and needed me or you wouldn't have looked for me after almost a quarter of a century. I need you, too, and have also been searching - *(He thought I had been searching for him. I would of course have searched had I known how to search!)* - and have found you at last, my lost daughter! We must not lose each other again! But now enough of the sentimentalities! They are not necessary.

I will try to answer some of your obvious questions. *(What questions? I had never written to him, ever!)* But before that let me congratulate you on your second marriage! I hope this time you will be happy! And I will be crossing my fingers for the happy event expected in September! As I said, this letter will be short, to the point, an introduction to someone you don't know, who has done nothing for you but whom you can address with the world's most moving words: Dear father! I hope I will earn the full meaning of those words.

Now to the facts. Who am I? I am an old man. I will be 60 years old next January. Strange, I don't feel old. I am very involved in my work. I love my work, although there was a time when I wanted to become a writer. It was not to be. Right now I'm the Chief Producer at the Lydia Koidula Theater in Pärnu. I had that job from 1958 - 1960. Before that I was Chief Producer of Estonian Radio and Secretary of the Estonian Theater Union. Back to Pärnu in 1964. I was an actor from 1948 onwards. *(Not so, he was an actor already in 1934 when he married Mother and a producer in 1944 when we fled Estonia and he promised to "look us up.")* That would be my short biography. I would add that I have directed plays in all the Estonian theaters and television, written plays and stories for radio, television and open-air theater, worked as theater critic for newspapers and dramatized many books and stories for the stage. That will do for now. My family lives in Tallinn. The rail connection with Pärnu is very good. My wife is a violinist with the National Conservatory and also teaches violin at the Music Academy. We have one child, a son named Toomas. That gives you a half-brother not half-sister, as you mentioned in your letter. *(What letter? Hardly! I already knew I had a half-brother, not half-sister as Mrs. Takk also delivered Toomas at the same clinic. That was how Mother first heard about Father's other child.)* He (Toomas) will be 25 years old this autumn. He is interested in sports, is married, but has no children so far.

I received your letters and photos a few years ago and replied to you at the Estonian Club address you gave me. *(Incredible!)* There was no reply. I made some inquiries and was told my letters had left our country. What happened to them in London—I don't know? *(Communism is what happened!)* I will reply to your question on whether you should choose acting or writing as your lifelong career. I replied then, very firmly, that you should stick to writing! Which you have done. Whether on my advice or perhaps you did not get that letter—I don't know. But your choice makes me happy. Your book *Puuingel* is a fine novel. The award is well deserved. Congratulations! If you want to make me happy, continue with your writing. I see in it my own failed dreams being realized. (...) We simply have to meet. *(This is a significant*

*line because, the object of this exercise, to get me to return to Estonia. I
don't believe Father thought of it that way. I think he genuinely wanted to
see me, and I him. It was what the KGB banked on.)*

Your letter arrived in my mailbox at the beginning of February. I was on
an assignment and only got it when I returned. I don't know how you got my
address. I will be looking forward to your next letter with great anticipation
and hopefully with some photos. I will send some also. Best wishes also to
your husband, Mr. Gottschalk. By the way—some excerpts from your novel
were read at the Writer's Union last year, at the "Literary Wednesday" meeting. You are known in our literary circles.

With best wishes,

Your happy father.

The conflicting information, however puzzling, the mixture of time frames,
the mention of letters "lost", and others never written, photos I had never
sent, and the lack of proper replies, did not diminish the fact that this was
a great moment in my life.

This was the first contact with Father since he had walked away from our
Haapsalu house in a temper, and I ran after him with a handful of grass. He
had not forgotten that incident either and mentioned it in another letter.

I remember many things from Haapsalu and Tambu. But there is one
incident that has haunted me, which I have wanted to talk to you about and
cannot put out of my mind. It happened the last time we were together. I
had taken a day off from work and had decided to come to Haapsalu for a
quick visit between trains. I brought your grandmother some food. It was
wartime.

You were playing in the garden. You were wearing a green dress with
white polka dots and were barefoot. You always ran to greet me, but this
time you were too involved in your game. I didn't want to disturb you. I
watched you from a distance. I was in a hurry. Thus we were both involved
in our own worlds. When I left the house to go back to the station, I saw you
next to the kitchen steps stuffing grass into a hole in the wall, absorbed in
some game. I lifted you up, gave you a kiss, and told you to be a good girl.
You continued your game and I left.

When I was on the street, I heard you calling to me. "Taat! . Taadu!" And
you ran after me. You were holding a handful of grass with some soil still
clinging to it and gave it to me. "This to remember me by," you said. I was
overwhelmed and slightly stunned by the gesture and your strange mood.
You were not yourself. I accepted the grass, but before I could thank you,
you had turned on your heels and were running back towards the house, your
green dress and bare legs rounded the corner and you were gone. I called

after you. You didn't respond. It was time to catch my train. I put the grass bouquet into my pocket. Something strange, inexplicable had happened. I could not shake the mood. Sitting in the train I decided I had to return to Haapsalu as soon as possible, in a few day's time if I could get away. Why, I don't know. It was a feeling.

When I got back to Tallinn I returned to my usual tempo of work and responsibilities and eventually I calmed. I decided to go back to Haapsalu at the very next opportunity, but that next opportunity never materialized. Instead, new worries followed. Was it an event of circumstance, brought on by a particular mood, or a child's uncanny intuition that you managed to convey to me?

Time does distort, changes moods, takes away or adds, but the fingerprint of a happy moment usually remains on anything it touches, if only briefly. Even the least and smallest memory it is left behind. There were no kisses or embraces at that last meeting except in best intentions. Reading between the lines, I could see we had both been preoccupied by what had actually happened moments earlier—the row in the kitchen, the words I had over-heard. That argument also had left an indelible fingerprint. At our parting, it had dominated the mood.

Father also remembered my one visit to Tallinn. He did not mention my failed singing audition, but he remembered my staying over and sleeping on the couch.

The divan was wide, but high, hard, and curved. You were very light and restless. I thought it best to sleep close by, as my stomach would have been softer than the floor.

Father died 22 March 1973. His new wife Marta wrote me a beautiful letter, informing me of the passing of her "love of thirty years." It was a touching dose of reality for me from a world that had ceased to be real.

The last page of my FBI file, over 30 pages long, was written on 22 August 1968:

A pretext telephone call to subject, at her residence, 256, Iven Avenue, St.Davids, Pa, on 8-20-68, ascertained that she was expecting the birth of a child momentarily. In view of the subject's condition, no recommendation is being made at this time to interview the subject. However, another communication will be directed to the Bureau in October 1968, with a recommendation to interview the subject if no changes develop in the meantime.
FBI Bureau (105-154020), SAC Philadelphia (105-15281)

Mother had been having strange dreams. She had always dreaded certain dates. The latest dread was 1ST June 1981.

In the last week of May Mother was having pain in her side and went to see her doctor. A substitute doctor looked her over and thought she had gas. He told her to go home and take an antacid. It was Friday. On Monday the pain was worse, but it was a bank holiday. National Health rules were that you had to have a doctor's note to go to a hospital. Mother had become a stickler for rules and was waiting for the doctor to return from his holiday. She was found on Monday night, unconscious on the hall floor, and taken to the emergency room. Her appendix had burst.

She suffered a massive stroke at exactly five minutes after midnight into 1st June 1981. She was placed into the geriatric ward of St. Mary Abbot's Hospital, and stayed there for the next four years. She was paralyzed down her right side, unable to speak, but could convey some of her thoughts through facial expressions. Rather ruefully she let me know that having always been proud of her power of speech; she had suffered the ultimate loss.

The other ominous date for Mother had always been New Year's Eve. "Someone will die," she had maintained as long as we had known her. That was why we had never celebrated or even stayed up past midnight.

It was already 1st January 1985 in England, but still New Year's Eve 1984 in America, when I received the call from St. Mary Abbot. Mother had died. Another prediction had come true.

No one was left to console me except my son, whom I had left in sunny Florida when I arrived, inadequately dressed, in snow-bound London.

Mother's Estonian friends in England had mostly deserted her after the stroke. Their excuse was, "We want to remember her as she was." The only friends who had visited regularly had been the "monocle" from Sweden and Marga Takk from Holland.

Mother's wishes had been clear. She wanted her ashes scattered from the top of the "Cow and Calf," a well-known crag formation on the edge of the Yorkshire Moors. It was where she had been meeting her friend and the last love of her life, until he died.

My Polish friend Nina, still mending worsteds at Woodhouses Mill, drove me to Ilkley. It had stopped snowing when I began the climb up the steep slope. The cardboard box I carried was surprisingly heavy. Mother had been a small woman. The sky was a dramatic Blake canvas of teals and turquoises, pewters and pinks, rimmed by brilliant sunlight from open gashes in the clouds. It was here that Blake had received his inspirations.

Streamers of light occasionally fanned across the snowy fields, like the searchlights of war, picking out bombers. Shafts of sunlight moved over the fieldstone walls and Yorkshire cottages that I had once looked at impassively from bus windows. There was much I had not understood about England, which Mother had tried so hard to impart to me at the wrong time.

I carried the box gently, mindful of last good-byes and closing doors. A major part of me was now going with her. I had lost loved ones and countries

338

the way people lose car keys. In the English language, when someone dies you say, "I lost him or her."

"How careless," you might reply, to "lose" a loved one. You lose umbrellas and cameras, not people. My loved ones had constantly been somewhere else—around the corner, in Estonia, in England, on duty—their absences felt and reunions constantly anticipated.

It was a hard climb. I could hear Nina's car down below, the engine running, and the heater going full blast. Panting and out of breath from my exertion, I finally reached the summit and lifted my head. One of those strange rifts in the clouds had opened above me. I had to hurry. Mother would have been delighted by this rare opportunity to be on center stage again. No arc lights could rival the special effects of that winter sky and the sun streaming down onto the snow. Blinded and dazzled by the brilliance under heaven, I tore into the box. The wind was strong. Soon the clouds would shift again. Taking large handfuls, I cast the ashes out in a wide arc, symbolic of the way Vikings had once launched lighted candles into a fast-flowing stream. Never mind that the wind was blowing the ashes back into my face. They were a part of me anyway.

It was evening "Taps" for Mother, at the end of her long battle to survive peacetime. It had served her even less honorably than it had served Grandmother and me.

It was done. Just as dramatically the sky closed again. The Snow Queen had received her final curtain call. I slid down the slope a lot faster than I had climbed up. It started snowing again on the drive back to Leeds. The road was a salted slushy ribbon of black tarmac between dirty snow banks. Nina's profile had not changed much in twenty years.

It was not over. I still had to get rid of the London flat. I did not have the money to buy it. The Council offered it to me for £8,000. It was a pittance considering the Chelsea-Kensington location, but I had no way to raise even that small a sum.

My English friends helped me pack. What I had dreaded in 1970 had come to pass. All I could send to America had to fit into a cabin trunk. The rest had to be left behind. The outside storage unit had been crammed full of papers—my school certificates, letters, books, old greeting cards, all melded together with a white shiny scum of mildew, too damp to even pick through. I threw everything into the overflowing rubbish skip in the back yard. The desk and rocking chair I carried out into the street and sat in the chair to wait for Jackie to bring the van around. She and I had been friends since the Leeds Arts Centre.

Traffic on Finborough Road was horrendous. Huge juggernauts from France and Holland hurtled past, articulated Lorries with eighteen wheels belched diesel fumes only inches apart from the buses and the smaller traffic that moved between them. I sat in the chair, on the pavement, buffeted by hot exhausts and icy gusts that leaped off the building and skimmed across the top of the rubbish container. Suddenly a strong downdraft tore into the yard, lifted a handful of the papers from the top of the bin and deposited a small scrap of cardboard into my lap. I picked it up and turned it over. It was the corner of a birthday card from long ago, with the words, "*Sinu* Mämmä!" Your Mämmä!

When I entered our house in Florida, my son Timothy-Rein was watching television.

"Hi, Mom!" He jumped up to greet me.

"Why aren't you in bed?" I asked automatically, the way a mother does when her mind is on something else.

"I know," he admitted sheepishly, staring at the floor.

"Then what's the problem?"

"I was waiting for you," he mumbled. "Happy New Year, Mom." He hugged me.

He was all I had left. He was my new world for which I was going to have to prepare and learn not to look back, so as not to break his or my own heart. It was a promise I have struggled with all my life. I did not want to burden him with unfulfilled legacies or anything that could not be translated into English.

Chapter 19

RETURNING THE MISSING PIECES
1990

In August 1991, during a failed military coup in Moscow by communist hardliners, Mikhail Gorbachev was ousted and the Soviet Union was no more. Estonia regained its independence on 20 August 1991.

It was still 1990 when I received a telegram from the Estonian Writers' Union with an invitation to visit Tallinn. I was going to be an official guest with the use of an apartment. They also promised to organize a trip to Haapsalu under the guise of a short interview with the local newspaper on the occasion of "Ernst Enno's granddaughter returning to Haapsalu after forty-six years in exile." I folded the invitation, tucked it into my address book and forgot about it. I had other things to attend to like renewing my passport, and obtaining a Soviet visa.

The Russians were still in the country, but the Soviet regime was falling apart. I wanted to be among the first to return. I was nervous. The days of being bundled into a car and whisked back to the airport, or worse were past, but what about the KGB agent Toomaru? He was probably still working at the Foreign Ministry. Would he know I was coming and what if he was not forgiving?

I chose early April as the best time to return and the worst time of year for making memorable journeys. I wanted to shake off romantic notions of odysseys as depicted in literature, I need not have worried. The ferry ride from Helsinki to Tallinn dispelled all spiritual reflection. There was not even time to think between the pushing; shoving and shin splintering jostling that filled the passageways and corridors. The ferry was overcrowded with what appeared to be a male sports team of drunken Finns. There was no mistaking the language, the neon bright Western-style track suits, and chunky trainers—harbingers of what the free world was about to dump on the Soviet Union. There was going to be a major culture shock all around, but until the collapse was final the adjustment would have to be mine alone

To avoid the unpleasant, red-faced louts lurching about the ship in groups and knocking everyone ahead of them into the walls, I ducked under the first set of stairs and stayed there. I sat on my suitcase and straining my ears for the sound of the Estonian language. All I could hear around me was Russian and Finnish.

The weather was awful. Once the corridors were clearer I went up to the lounge. All the tables and chairs were taken. I sat on the windowsill and looked out of the window. There was nothing to see, but heaving, pewter-colored water. It brought back unpleasant memories of the freighter journey to Danzig. The same high waves against the glass, recreating the heaving troughs of water, mercifully without the inert bundles of clothing held together by cork vests, but it was the same sea.

I returned to my suitcase.

When the ship's motors changed rhythm I knew we were getting close to land. This was going to be the epic moment. Despite the drunks and my resolve to keep emotions in check I did not want to miss my first glimpse of Tallinn's famous skyline. I had seen pictures of it, but the country had become so much myth and fantasy that I was not sure what I would see. Many older people had decided not to return because they were afraid they would have a heart attack caused by an overload of emotions. My fear was not of having a heart attack, but of losing my muse to the harsh reality of which I was already getting an initial dose. I shoved my suitcase further into the niche and took two stairs at a time to the main deck. When I passed the snack bar I noticed a bowl brimming with bananas, but I was too agitated to be hungry. Food was the last thing on my mind. *(I was going to remember those bananas later!)*

Tallinn's skyline coming home, on the ferry from Helsinki

The rain was coming down in sheets. The wind was so brutal that it took me and a gentleman behind me to push the heavy door open. The lifeboats provided some shelter until I reached the open deck, where it became a fight between the elements and my desire not to miss the skyline. A thick mist enclosed the ship. I could barely even see the rail. The man who had helped me open the door became a hooded figurehead in the bow. He was not the only one. Huddled together and separately were plastic-wrapped individuals, clutching the rail, straining towards the mist. I identified them as Westerners, like myself, by their windblown ponchos and raincoats recognizable as London Fog and Lord and Taylor, of the global shopping malls. Everyone looked like Americans, but I was sure most of them were Estonians returning to a land that time had forgotten, but we had not. Sentimental or not, it was a special moment.

344

The hooded figure with whom I had come on deck took off his shapeless Totes rain hat as a sign of respect, and stuffed it into his coat pocket. His gray hair was plastered to his balding scalp and his profile had the look of granite. I knew he was an Estonian simply by that "look." It had shaped itself through endless Independence Day speeches and promises about the "one day," and the "someday." There were couples holding on to each other, their faces hidden under plastic hoods. I envied them their ability to share, what the single figures could not. One elderly man was clutching the rail so tightly he appeared to be keeping himself from jumping overboard. Perhaps to join the thousands of refugees who had in fact sunk and drowned in these waters. No one would ever know how many small boats such as ours had set out for Sweden and never arrived. All one had to do was to close one's eyes to imagine the desperate cries of the drowning, mimicked by the screams of seagulls escorting the ferry into the harbor. In another world we might have spoken to each other with the ease of Americans on a cruise ship. English trippers going to the Costa Brava, but Estonian history had inured its people to solitary suffering. They had suffered under Danes, Swedes, Poles, Germans and Russians. The only freedom Estonians had known in modern times was from 1918 until June 1940.

When the skyline did appear through the rain and mist, we were too close to see anything. All that loomed ahead were hulking cranes, rusting warehouses, a cobbled quay, and Soviet soldiers with rifles patrolling the wharf. The sight of the soldiers completely unnerved me.

In the downpour a knot of workers were putting their backs into a set of tall, steep, metal stairs. That would be our gangplank. We would have to climb down it with our luggage. The rain was bouncing off the puddles, the tin roofs, people's backs and the chipped cobblestones of a country that had been frozen in time. The ferry had brought me onto a 1940's film set about the Second World War. Another production! Only now the costumes and props were authentic, the real thing. I had come to Estonia, but had arrived in Russia.

I was glad I had only brought one suitcase.

Once the exit door opened the disembarkation process began. The Finns gave themselves priority. One by one they threw their bags down the ladder, then followed, some sliding down the rails, some on their backs or backsides. They all landed in a heap on the quay to shouts of encouragement and merriment from their companions. I was witnessing the breaking of something priceless, but could not stop it. I looked away.

I learned later that the ferry between Helsinki and Tallinn was a regular "ship of fools" for drunken Finnish men seeking cheap liquor and prostitutes.

The rest of the passengers followed more cautiously. The idea was to have the travel bag in one hand and to hold the rail with the other. I could see why the luggage of choice was soft-sided duffel bags.

When it was my turn, I stepped onto the platform, but could see immediately that my suitcase was too big for the steps and the wheels were going to be dangerous. Turning it sideways made it too wide to fit between the

345

rails. In desperation I hoisted the damned thing over my head, but only managed to hold it for a couple of seconds before I had to let go. My suitcase rattled down the steps on its own and landed with a crash. I followed gingerly, feet sideways. At least the rain was easing off. The sky was getting lighter. I held on to the handrail, but did not feel safe.

While I was making the slippery descent it occurred to me that I had not seen my compatriots from the ship's deck, the "London Fogs" and "Aquascutums" and guessed they had rented cabins. A cabin had been an option I could not afford.

The rain stopped, but the gangplank was still wet and the cobblestones on the wharf were awash with puddles. Determined to reach the bottom without falling, I gritted my teeth and made it to the last step before my foot slipped—and thus I arrived in Estonia on my hands and knees, not much better than the drunken Finns did.

One of the dockworkers retrieved my suitcase; another helped me to my feet and pointed the way to the customs shed. When I looked up I saw one of the young Soviet border guards standing nearby, leaning on his rifle and grinning from ear to ear. "A mother's son, far from home", Grandmother would have said. We were all extras in a grainy black and white war documentary, until the producer yelled, "Cut!"

The customs shed was packed, the lines long, and customs procedures universal, until I saw that all the signs and the declaration forms were in Cyrillic. I turned to the nearest person and asked for help, first in Estonian, then in English. All I got in return were blank stares and nudges to keep moving. No one let me through to ask a question so I called out loudly, in English "Excuse me!" Heads turned. The official ignored me.

While shuffling along I happened to glance over my shoulder. The door to the dockside was open and I saw the gentleman with whom I had struggled against the weather and forged a symbolic link making his way down the same metal stairs, just as carefully as I, but unburdened by his suitcase. One of the uniformed stewards was carrying it for him. When they reached the bottom the steward received a tip before he passed the suitcase on to one of the dockworkers who motioned for the gentleman to follow him. The new porter with the same suitcase and the gentleman with his hands free proceeded to another part of the building and disappeared from view. I had learned a valuable lesson. In order not to appear like an American tourist I had left my London Fog coat at home, but here was a world where looking like an American tourist was not such a bad thing.

The nudges eventually landed me in front of the surly customs official who took the declaration form automatically, saw it was blank and only then came to life. He slapped it and snarled at me in Russian. Lines from the same script in the same vintage war film.

"I can't read Russian!" I shouted loudly, hoping someone in the glassed-in office nearby would hear me and come to see what the commotion was. A face appeared in the window, a hand waved and the official pulled me out of line. He handed my papers to a young woman who spoke English. "This way, please come."

346

I had done this before in Holland, with Ivar. Since Helsinki I had been going backwards in time.

The customs woman was pleasant enough. She motioned for me to sit at a table and with her standing over me we began to fill the customs form together. We did well until she asked me if I had any gold. I told her I had no gold except my wedding ring, my Mother's watch and a gold cross on a gold chain, a gift from my late husband. Surely she did not mean those? But she did. Then she really alarmed me. "Must have *resept*," she said.

"Receipt?" I told her no-one in the West keeps those kinds of receipts. She shook her head sternly. "*Resept*," she repeated, tapping the paper.

Now what? Mother had parted with her wedding ring in order to pay passage to Sweden, but this was absurd. The wedding ring I was wearing was not mine, but Grandmothers. The name engraved inside was "Ernst Enno." I had worn it symbolically for Grandmother.

The woman's English was limited to trained phrases.

"*Resept*," the woman repeated lamely and tapped the form. She recognized the impasse and went to find someone who would be able to speak to me. She returned with an older gentleman whose lapel markings showed a higher rank. The man looked at my passport, and then asked in English. "Do you have an invitation?"

"Yes." I had an invitation.

He wanted to see it.

That was when I remembered the telegram from the Writers' Union which I had carelessly tucked into my address book. I produced it.

"Do you have anyone meeting you?" he asked.

"Yes," I had people meeting me.

"Names please?"

I named names and a miracle happened. The "Russian" interrogator and the young woman turned into Estonians. They helped me complete the form, which I signed. While signing it I asked the woman to explain why I needed a receipt. She looked puzzled for a moment then almost smiled. (I had noticed that the only smiles I had seen since boarding the ferry had been the Finns and theirs had been drunken laughter). The stern look returned and she explained that the customs form was the receipt. I had to have it to show when I left the country so they could check off the gold to prove I had not sold it.

The Kafkaesque ordeal was over. The man grabbed my suitcase and with the woman following, we hurried back outside and walked along the quay to another door, the one that my fate-mate had availed himself of earlier. The rain clouds were breaking up, letting through a white light that reflected off the rain puddles. It might become a good day yet, I thought.

The other door led to a comfortably furnished waiting room, some kind of V.I.P. lounge. It was empty. We crossed to another door. At the door the gentleman handed me my suitcase and I stepped through into a large departure and arrivals hall. I had been brought through a side entrance reserved for people who had official invitations and could name names. The regular exit was further along, surrounded by a milling crowd, craning their necks on tiptoe, clutching bouquets of flowers, trying to spot friends and loved ones.

The couple under whose aegis I had arrived spotted me at once and came forward with flowers, the customary Estonian welcome. Viiu Härm and Paul-Eerik Rummo were well known poets and had attracted a small circle of onlookers. The gawkers stepped aside in deference to them or in order see this person who had just received preferential treatment—me? Sour glances at my plastic raincoat, jeans and sneakers suggested I did not deserve it.

We elbowed our way out of the main hall into a cobbled square. My friends had brought their youngest daughter with them, a girl about seven or eight. She was skipping around purposefully scanning the ground, sometimes running back and forth, and then squatting down to examine each crevice carefully. Now and then she turned to her mother and said, "Look, here's one!"

"One what? What is she looking for," I asked.

"Banana peels" her Mother laughed. "It's all the children can think about. Bananas! They've seen pictures of bananas on Finnish television, but few have tasted them. Passengers getting off the ferry sometimes drop banana peels on the ground and if there's still a small piece left inside they scrape it out."

Too late I remembered the plates of bananas at the snack bar. Forty-six years ago I had run around the Promenade in Haapsalu checking the grass for chocolate wrappers, when I had known chocolate only by its smell.

Tallinn's Old Town is really the inside courtyard of a 13th century fortress built by the Danes. At one time it had forty-six tower-gates of which many were intact. Amazingly the mediaeval architecture and cobbled streets had also survived half a century of Soviet neglect. There were iron gates worked into fine filigree, massive studded doors carved into scenes usually seen in old paintings, some shops still bore the original signs of their trade—a pair of boots, eyeglasses, a needle and thread. An apothecary dating from 1422 was still in business. Narrow passages, hidden courtyards, a portcullis jutting out of an overhead arch made it a magical place. These were the treasures left behind by all the conquerors who had ever flown their flags above Tall Hermann, the fortress's main tower. The conquerors had all been deposed. Only the Soviets had left nothing behind, but misery and crumbling concrete.

The oldest churches had been the burial places for the Baltic nobility. The stunningly ornate Guild Halls were the legacy of the Hanseatic League of merchants in the Middle Ages, who had also built Lübeck in Germany and Visby on the island of Gotland, Sweden. There were exquisite horse troughs, covered wells, warehouses with pulleys hanging from loft doors, for hauling salt, one of the main commercial commodities. Wrought iron had been worked into every structure as locks or hinges, and the most sinister were the iron grilles everywhere, especially across dungeon-like, half-exposed cellar windows, at pavement level. They exuded the age-old smell of hopelessness and misery. The KGB had used many of those basements to extract agony from ordinary citizens whose crimes might only have been the owning of a forbidden book. Aunt Alma's letters about hiding grandfather's library books took on a grim reality.

I regretted not having taken more interest in Mother and Grandmother's descriptions of Tallinn and (to be frank) I had become a bit bored by the superlatives. How could it compare to London? To Paris? Yet it did! Old Tallinn was like a museum and art gallery rolled into one. I was rubbernecking the corner of a building that had been carved into a regency gentleman gazing down scornfully through his lorgnette[37] at a smaller house next door, and caught my toe in a pothole. I would have fallen to my knees if Viiu had not caught my elbow in time.

For all its splendor, Old Tallinn was tragically neglected. The ancient masonry was crumbling, the original cobblestones were chipped, the pastel walls were stained by rusting pipes, and the mullioned windows were so dirty they looked like solid lead. Many windows had been bricked in or boarded up. Yet amazingly, though the lintels were porous and termite-infested, they still held the massive doors in place. The doors themselves were unpainted, girded by wrought metal and closed with rusting locks, but they continued to be portals that appeared not to have been opened since 1154 AD when the famous Arabian geographer Abu Abdullah Muhammad al-Idrisi first came here and named the town Kolovan. Although Soviet occupation was visible in every pothole, in every gaping front door that lacked a lock, in every filthy hall stinking of urine, nothing was as awful as what might have happened if the Russians had razed everything to the ground and replaced it with Soviet-style concrete cities that loomed outside the Old Town walls.

My apartment in the Writers' Union was on the second floor of a building with a central courtyard accessible through two archways. A strong urine smell permeated the archway. It reminded me of the lifts in Quarry Hill Flats. Toilets seemed to be the defining line between the civilized and the uncivilized everywhere on the planet.

When we entered the courtyard we encountered a group of Soviet soldiers sitting on the grass, passing a bottle between them. They watched us go by, taking note of my Western clothes and pull-along suitcase. They made me nervous, and more so when I saw that the front door to the apartment building had a round hole where the lock should have been.

My apartment was on the second floor and comfortable by 1940s standards, in fact luxurious compared to the closets and corners we had called home in the real 1940s. There was a bedroom with a Finnish bed, a kitchen off the living room and a bathroom with a large deep Victorian bathtub. I even had a telephone. (I had been warned not to speak too freely on the phone). My hosts handed me the apartment key and left me to settle in.

Left alone, I indulged myself in some major emotional reflection as the enormity of the moment set in. It was only two o'clock, but the day seemed endless, lengthened by the overnight flight from America, long stopovers in England and Belgium, and the grueling ferry ride. I could hardly think straight. The weak sun did not reach my windows. It was especially somber

---

[37] Eyeglasses held up with a long handle.

in the bedroom. I was exhausted. The bed was right there. I only meant to sit, but because it was a narrow Finnish bed with a thin mattress in a shallow box with wooden edges, it was impossible to sit, so I stretched out, thinking I should take off my raincoat and shoes, but when I woke, I was still fully dressed.

The room had darkened and it was freezing cold. My mouth was dry and my bones ached. I had no idea where I was. Fingering the wooden sides I guessed I was lying in a coffin. Amazingly this did not alarm me. For the first time in my life I did not feel a need to panic. No one was missing me. I continued to lie there, drained of all priorities until I realized why I was cold. I had left the window open. The need to close the window was the impetus that got me up. I was just about to pull it shut when I looked down at the narrow street below me. A couple were strolling past; I could only see the top of their heads. The woman was wearing a brownish scarf, the man a dark cap. Their footsteps created a canyon effect and their voices reverberated off the stonewalls. It took a moment to realize they were speaking Estonian. I remained by the window long after they had gone. For three generations of exiles, Mother and Grandmother included, that couple represented the impossible dream—hearing your own language spoken in the street. It was finally coming together, as in Heine's poem: *ein Märchen aus Alten Zeiten!* A fairy tale from the past and not just for Estonians, but everyone who had been robbed of half their lives both here and in exile. My eyes welled over and the dam burst at last. I fell back on the bed and sobbed until my lungs could no longer draw air and I was afraid I was going to strangle myself on my own breath. Still I continued to lie on the bed, shivering, and thinking of the grief I had inherited. The last time I had cried like this had been in the cinema in Rotterdam.

I continued to lie there until I noticed a shaft of sunlight in the far corner of the room and jumped up in alarm. That was the afternoon sun already! What time was it? My sponsors would arrive any minute and I had not even unpacked my suitcase.

What I needed was an English *cuppa,* the remedy for every mood. When Mother and I had gone out together in London we had always stopped at Joe Lyons. Alas, I did not have any milk. Drinking tea without milk was like Mother smoking cigarettes without tobacco. I made do and saluted her presence. I felt it keenly. Tied by birth, we had fought our bonds until we had joined forces and here we were, together again, back to back, one in reality, the other in spirit. It occurred to me that I had spent a lifetime adapting to adversity because she had forbidden me to do otherwise.

There were no plugs to either the bathtub or the sink so I had to improvise. I mixed boiling water in a cooking pot with cold water from the sink and thought of all the times we had had less and still believed that we had everything anyone would ever need.

I was "home,"—but not yet—not quite. This was Mother's town and Father's town. My true return would not be complete until I was in Haapsalu and saw whatever awaited me there. The thought caused me to tense up and I could easily have burst into tears again, feeling the loneliness of a solitary runner coming in last.

350

Viiu and her husband picked me up at the appointed time and we went to eat at a restaurant.

A huge crowd was clamoring to get past a beefy doorman outside the restaurant, but he only allowed a select few, including us, over the threshold. The food was good, but the meat was mostly fat. There were cucumbers in cream, sliced tomatoes and boiled potatoes followed by incredibly rich pastries and coffee. I realized these were luxuries and felt a bit humbled by what I had come to take for granted in the West.

The concert was in one of the towers leading to the Danish King's Garden, renovated into a delicate (if you can imagine such with six foot thick walls) concert venue. The steps were built for one and the right side left open (for the sword arm) to prevent the enemy getting past. The keep had only arrow slit windows and the chairs were placed on the original bare floorboards.

There we sat, surrounded by candles in sconces, listening to Mozart and Vivaldi stirring up ancient dust and the lost souls of long departed court musicians.

My first night was disturbed by a girl crying, drunken shouting and scuffling along the cobbled street below. I went to the window and keeping my light off saw two men dragging a beautiful young girl in white between them. They were kicking her shins to make her move faster. She was pleading with them in Russian. In the morning I looked out of the window again and saw a long line of derelicts sitting on the ground and leaning against the wall of a perfumery. I could not imagine why anyone would be queuing up for perfume at that time in the morning.

It was explained to me later that the drunks were drinking perfume and cologne.

The world beyond the Writers' Union apartment, without privileged escorts who had whisked me through unofficial entrances and past doormen, was totally hostile. I was so helpless I could not even buy a loaf of bread, cheese or even a bottle of milk. In the milk shop I needed my own bottle. When I asked the clerk if I could borrow an empty bottle and bring it back later she turned to look at me as though I had gone mad. In the cheese shop I asked for the price of cheese. The hefty serving woman in a white cap and apron yelled at me in Russian. When I did not understand she turned her back on me and refused to serve anyone until I stepped away. I had been speaking Estonian.

In the bread shop things were even worse. The line passed a cake counter with a display of cakes. I had been invited to dinner at Viiu's house that evening and thought to take a cake. Two women, behind the counter, chatting animatedly completely ignored my attempts to address them. When I persisted they turned abruptly and left through an inside door. The other shoppers in the queue saw my problem, heard me and continued to look through me. Many of the customers appeared to be Estonians, elegantly dressed in 1940's coats and hats. They reminded me of Mother in old photographs and as in photographs they remained inanimate. Finally I made a general plea for someone to help me buy a cake. No response. Even the well-dressed woman ahead of me in line lifted her chin and looked away.

I returned to the Writers' Union and asked for someone to come with me so I could buy necessities. One of the men in the office looked amused by my request and obliged. He came with me and on the way he initiated me into the mysteries of Soviet-style shopping.

In the food shops you did not ask questions. You were expected to know what you wanted. Foreign tourists did not shop there. In other stores you stood in three queues. In the first queue you gave your chosen purchase to a clerk who handed you a price ticket. She held the purchase for you while you stood in a second line to pay. You then returned to the first line, queued again, showed your receipt and only then did you receive your purchase. If the shop was busy the process could take a long time.

We first went to the dairy. When the Russian woman saw me again she turned a bright red and I thought she was going to explode. My escort spoke to her in soothing, rapid Russian. From the tone of voice, he was apologizing for me. I got the milk, eggs, butter and cheese. He also had an empty wine bottle tucked into his coat pocket for the milk. In the cake shop I found out that you had to order the cakes ahead.

I also learned that it was not a good idea to engage strangers in conversation, even store clerks, or to speak to anyone in public. My guide also suggested I should smile less. Smiling was a sign of untrustworthiness.

Most jobs were held by Russians who did not speak Estonian. You had to address them in Russian. Foreigners did not wander about without interpreters. I wanted to respond by asking why I should need an interpreter if I was speaking Estonian in Estonia, but that argument was precisely the kind of reactionary thinking that separated the Western *naif* from the brainwashed true believer. I consoled myself that once the free-market economy arrived it would bring devastating revelations to the sullen, snarling clerks, now supremely confident in their rudeness. I almost felt sorry for them. You do not know what you don't know. I had been there.

On the way back to the Writers' Union my escort thought I should visit yet another shop, this one was for tourists only. He called it a "dollar store", but not as we know them in America. There was no sign outside the building to even indicate that it was a shop. There were iron bars across the door and windows. My escort rang the doorbell. The door was unlocked by a uniformed doorman whose gleaming smile made me take a step backwards. After my recent encounters with unhelpful sales people he reminded me of rug sellers in Morocco. The man even executed a small bow while a woman clerk scurried forward, arms outstretched: "Hello! *Velcom!*" She too was smiling. They were both bad actors. I could see why smiling in the Soviet Union was discouraged.

Alas, we were not let in. I did not have my passport with me. I had purposely hidden it in the electric meter in my apartment. After some of the things I had seen from my window I worried about my passport and return ticket to America and had put them inside the fuse box. I had the Alan wrench to the box in my money belt. That way, I reasoned, if I were mugged I would still have my passport and ticket home.

Another problem was finding toilets. It became easy to understand why every dark stairwell smelled of urine. Russians seemed to have no interest in the toilet culture of the West. They had made no provisions for repairing the existing water closets in the almost fifty years they had been in Estonia. Even in government buildings the toilets leaked or ran water constantly. In private homes the best that could be offered was a stained porcelain bowl with a wooden lid and a bucket of water on the side. I had seen men urinating in the streets all through the war, but women had usually sought a bush or a wall. I was, therefore, totally shocked to see a well-dressed woman squatting in plain sight of passers-by with her handbag around their neck and her skirts aloft. When she saw me looking she started screaming at me in Russian as though I were the one offending her.

Instructional sign in Soviet toilet.

There was only one public toilet in the Old Town, built into the Viru Gate. The attendant glared at me suspiciously every time I came in. She had good reason to. The first time I had gone in there I had noticed an illustrated plaque tacked to the inside of the stalls showing in graphic detail how to use a water closet. Crossed out was the man standing with his feet on the toilet bowl. Meeting with approval was the smiling gent sitting down with his trousers around his ankles. The photo opportunity was irresistible. The stall doors were only from chin to mid-calf. I had to take the picture quickly.

The flash brought the hefty rubber-booted attendant out of her cubbyhole like a bear shot in the foot. Screaming and shaking her fist she chased me into the street. When I returned I always showed her that I no longer had the camera. It was hidden in my shopping bag. I had moved through many cultures, but had not yet encountered so much public screaming and yelling as was common among Russians—shop assistants, clerks, officials, washroom attendants, and even ordinary people when a normal tone of voice would have been... well, normal.

A few days after my arrival I was given a tour of the venues associated with my family—starting with everything having to do with theater I was taken to the Theater Museum where I was shown Mother's and Father's memorabilia. There were only three pictures of Mother. Father, however, had done well. There were many files tied with string and I spent about an hour going through them. What he had written to me was true—his "official career" had begun in 1948. We had been wiped off his slate.

At the Drama Theater the new seats were plush velvet. The original theater had burned to the ground and this was a replica. It felt familiar, but small and cozy, not the vast threatening auditorium where I had flunked my first opportunity to please my parents. It was unsettling when I realized that the people I was speaking to knew more about my family than I did. A few older actresses remembered Mother, vaguely, but seemed nervous about saying so. One actress remembered me sitting on her knee when I was two. I caught a few exchanged glances and lifted eyebrows. What was all this about if Father did not start his career until 1948? I should have braced myself better for this kind of magical mystery tour.

A visit to the Academic Library was much more pleasant. It was a bit of an ego booster so see my books on the shelves mainly because it was so unexpected. I had not even imagined such a thing could happen in the real world and not in a dream.

It was April. Mornings were lighter than in Florida and I woke early. There was still snow on the ground under the bushes in the courtyard, around two big dumpsters that backed onto what appeared to be a canteen. I liked to stand at the kitchen window in the predawn hours and put myself into the center of this unreal universe that I had once belonged to and had lost. I could not leave the kitchen light on because I did not want to be seen by a group of people who gathered outside the back door of the canteen at dawn and stood there, waiting for the door to open. These people were not drunks, but well-dressed citizens in overcoats, boots, jackets and mufflers. I knew it was a canteen by the canteen sounds I remembered from Ida Hospital, trays falling, dishes breaking, cutlery rattling. When the door was finally opened, the people moved forward, lit by the light from within the building. A few minutes' later kitchen workers appeared wearing white caps, aprons, and carrying buckets full of, not scraps for the bins, but neatly wrapped

parcels. The parcels were quickly distributed among the waiting crowd. The transactions continued for about fifteen minutes until the door closed and everyone dispersed, just as the sun appeared behind the trees. There was no need to question what I saw in this unreal universe, because it was only unreal to me.

When the permit arrived, giving me permission to go to Haapsalu, I was both excited and nervous. This was going to be the true homecoming for which I had braced myself, but could never have prepared for adequately.

We set off in a small van with three escorts from the Writers' Union—two officials, also writers, and my poetess friend Viiu. I was glad to have them with me, but deep in my heart I wished I could have gone alone. The moment I was going to face was going to be too painful and personal to be witnessed by strangers, however well meant. On the other hand, I had seen the

Elin at the Ernst Enno monument in Haapsalu, 1990.

dangers of traveling alone under an American millionaire persona and knew that it was safer to be escorted and spoken for.

There was an agenda—a little welcome speech, a tour of the Haapsalu Museum. A meeting with town officials in the Ernst Enno Reading Room, pictures taken beside Grandfather's memorial, a newspaper interview, and so forth. It was reasonable, but all I wanted was to run, run, run until I could run no more and find the Quiet Lagoon or Evening Lagoon, Back Bay, Tchaikovsky's allée or Chocolate Promenade—whatever they now called it—to the only home I had ever known.

As we neared town and I saw the road sign for Haapsalu, the need to run became a need to flee. The recurring nightmares of returning to exploding attics and strangers at the front door had not been dispelled despite my determination to tear out that page for good. My stomach churned and my heart pounded. I whispered to Viiu that I could not face the official reception before seeing what was left of our house. The escorts were not allowed to leave me alone, but the men agreed to give Viiu and me an hour to ourselves. We promised to turn up at the museum reception on time.

Viiu and I set off on foot. I had an address, but we were told the addresses had changed. Viiu did not know the town. We had to find the right bay, but Haapsalu is a peninsula surrounded by bays and inlets. I had no idea which one was ours. Many things change in fifty years, but the sea and sky remain the same, so instead of an address I started looking for a view that would correspond with the view through our kitchen window. I kept my eyes on the horizon, how it angled and blended together into a familiar frame—like a mother's face to a child.

When we found Tchaikovsky's Bench I knew we were at the right lagoon. The bench had been to the left of our back gate. It now fronted a big multi-storey building. The Promenade was really an unpaved path that skirted the curve of the lagoon. I followed the path to the only section that directly faced the water, closed my eyes, and then opened them again. Our house had disappeared. There was no woodshed, no garden. There was nothing familiar. Even our tall trees had gone. I had prepared myself for strangers and rejection, but not for the absence of anything familiar in the one and only homecoming of my life. So there it was, a death-in-the-family moment, an ironic, symbolic confirmation of the disloyalty of time. Just what had I expected?

I might have walked away, but there was something worse to deal with than a vacant lot. A hideous imposter had been placed upon our property. It was not even a house, but a grotesquely ugly brick structure that seemed to have no visible utility. Its windows were covered with corrugated tin and the wall facing the water was crumbling into orange-colored dust. Broken bricks were scattered around the base of the building. It looked as though some angry giant had torn them out by the fistful to hurl at everything in the area that had once represented life and beauty. Plastic and broken glass further littered the ground. A few weeds and clumps of grass had survived next to the neighbor's chicken wire fence, but even that was yellow instead of green. I had not seen ugly grass since Leeds. My idyllic home beside the lagoon and

Promenade had become a rubbish dump. On closer inspection of Tchaikovsky's bench I saw that it, too, was crumbling. The seat and back were cracked and discolored. The copper notes had been gouged out, so only the grooves remained. Viiu could see I was distressed and walked on to give me space.

Standing there, stunned by the brutal and unexpected blow to my senses, I noticed a small stunted fir tree near what would have been our horseradish patch. The tree was listing, clearly ailing, but nevertheless still clinging to the ground for support. I guessed it must have been a Christmas tree someone had planted and tried to preserve from a forbidden celebration. It looked like I felt, and it gave me the courage to square my shoulders and move on to the front of the house to see if there was anything I could recognize on the street side. The gateposts were gone. Our five trees had been newly hewn, leaving five flat table-sized stumps naked, obscenely and rudely exposed, amid a pile of fresh sawdust. The roots must have been embedded too deeply to allow them to be completely removed. The windows on the street side of the building were also covered with corrugated tin. A padlocked metal door showed that the building had, at one time, served a purpose.

I called Viiu back. We took photos. I felt nauseous, but self-discipline kept me from vomiting.

I learned in due course that a storm in 1967 had toppled some of our trees and one of them had fallen through the roof of our house. The house was razed in 1976 and the land annexed by the Workers' Sanatorium complex next-door, all part of the Mud Spa that had expanded across our property as Aunt Alma had feared it would.

Haapsalu cemetery was on the main aptly named Post Road leading out of town. There had been a light, late snowfall prior to my arrival. Snow still clung to the crevices between the grave borders, trees, and plot markers. Grandpa's cherry tree had little lumps of ice on the branches. The marble tombstone was as I remembered it; his birth date was still incorrect, but what I wanted to see was the new inscription and I was not disappointed. Grandmother's name had been added: "Ella Enno." Next to it, on a small headstone, was written: "Alma Saul." Clumps of snowdrops were peeping through the black, crusty soil, proof that the grave was being tended. Grandmother had always planted lilies-of-the-valley, but for me snowdrops had always been the flowers of choice. I lit a candle. Grandmother would have approved. She herself had taught me how important it was to have candles handy to dispel darkness.

Viiu and I rejoined our escorts for the official program. When we were by Grandfather's monument I looked up at him, but he looked beyond me. He loomed over the petty scrambling's at the base, the photographing, the inevitable posing, the brief speeches spoken into the wind and time's invisible gulf between everyone and no one. During the official reception and a tour through the Haapsalu Museum I recognized our Blue Room cabinet. The one where Mother had kept her bisque doll Maria. I did not expect to see our piano. Aunt Alma had already sold it in order to keep up the property. She had made every possible effort to keep it for us, believing that one of us would surely come back. And here I was!

It was not the loss of the house or the land that was upsetting me, but the loss of something far more valuable—a real home. I did not know the exact measurements of that land. An acre, half acre? In my family no one except Aunt Alma had ever measured anything more solid than a thought, an idea or an inspiration. Even that house had been an *apropos*, a kind of *impromptu in C minor*, in readiness for our old age. Yet it was the only home I had ever had.

I was fifty-three, far from old age. I had never been one for possessions either. I had never needed bigger rooms or worldly goods. Growing up among exiles, I had learned to dismiss worldly goods, but had finally understood the value of identity, in a world where people called you a *bloody foreigner* and could barely pronounce your name. I had fought the orphanage to keep my foreign self-intact. It had been my flag of protest, but never my true identity. Unlike the adults, I had never had a past or the kind of identity that had sustained doctors while cleaning toilets and opera singers in steel and textile mills. I had been a mere piece of paper, a form incorrectly and carelessly filled out by people who had never taken a moment to think what they were writing or rubber stamping, then calling "next". Since I was seven I had taken full advantage of their preoccupation and had cut and shaped that paper to fit my own needs. To them one foreigner was just like any other and I didn't really care because I had an identity; I had a real home and a country (even if it wasn't on the map) and did belong somewhere as surely as every bird has a nest and every ant an anthill. All I had personally brought from Estonia had been a celluloid doll. All I had inherited was Marie. Marie I still had and I had come back to Haapsalu to claim the rest of my inheritance, namely my identity.

Haapsalu owned me. It was here where I had learned of my existence, in the absence of loved ones and in the presence of ghosts, whether in the cemetery, in another room, or in Tallinn. I could now understand why so many other exiles were afraid to return. It had nothing to do with heart attacks, muses or shattered myths, but with the stark reality and shock of a missing self. Tallinn had lulled me with its fabled images. It had carried me on memories bequeathed from my parents. Not my own. I had looked and admired, but Haapsalu had been the starting point of my life. I had been displaced, but never homeless. Supeluse Street 6, in a small town called Haapsalu, in a tiny country on the Baltic, called Estonia, had always existed, with me or without me. I had never expected to return, to see it again, but I had always been satisfied that it was safe in the care of "our own"; promise keepers. Aunt Alma had kept her promise, obviously not knowing that promises and promise keepers had no place in war or peace. I felt like that mill mouse beside the dye pool in Farsley before Daisy had conferred upon it a merciful death. All I had inherited here was the view from our kitchen window.

Back to Tallinn where there was still one place I needed to go.

The Soviet-style building was so decrepit on the outside that I feared it would collapse before I could get up the stairs. However, I had discovered that the decrepitude associated with those concrete eyesores was part of the system that endorsed the proletariat ideal that everyone was living in equal squalor. Far from it. The interior of Father's flat was small, but beautifully furnished.

Father's widow, Marta, was not the wicked stepmother of my imagination. She was an elegant and gracious lady who drew the necessary boundaries at our very first introduction. Firmly but politely, she asked me to address her with the formal "thou" and not the familiar "you," and to call her *proua* (Mrs.).

Marta led me into the living room. The windows were open. I could smell pine trees from a nearby copse and freshly brewed coffee from the kitchen. The contrast between the outside world of crumbling plaster and leather-jacketed louts lolling around the entrance and the cozy apartment was startling. There were modern bookshelves across one wall, curio cabinets, a sofa, easy chairs, and a coffee table of Finnish design. Crisp white curtains blew in the breeze. The parquet floor was highly polished, and the pictures on the walls were all original Estonian artworks by painters we had also heard about in the West. Father had lived well and had perhaps made the right decision not to leave. It was a hard thought, but even harder to picture him as a hospital porter or carpet weaver, which would have happened had he come with us.

Marta excused herself towards the kitchen. The coffee table was piled with photo albums, neatly arranged to one side. I walked over to the bookshelf and saw my books. My mind was in turmoil. After a lifetime of thinking one way, seeing only one perspective, my brain was turning impressions like stones, exposing new realities and trying to be both objective (the way Mother had taught me) and loyal at the same time.

Marta returned with the coffee. We sipped and made enough polite conversation to lay the groundwork. She had read my letters to Father and asked about my son. She was sorry my husband had died—that sort of thing. She mentioned Mother and dropped a little reference that implied Mother had run off with the Germans. She even suggested there had been a man involved. I told her just as politely that, if there had been a man, he would have been most welcome to help carry our bundles. She did not believe me, but concurred nevertheless, smiled, and nodded.

We sipped more coffee. I actually knew everything about her relationship with Father from Mother herself and Mother's friends, but there was no point in hashing it over. Marta had been a young girl, a budding violinist, traveling with the theater troupe. It spoke well for Father that he had remained with her and helped raise their child. She apologized for her son, who had not been able to get off work to meet me. Her granddaughter, my niece, Stella, was in school. We mentioned the correspondence with Father without the KGB's role in bringing it about.

Nothing was said about those final weeks in 1944. I had Father's last letter in my handbag. I had meant to produce it, but with all I had seen since coming to Estonia, and from what I had learned, it had become redundant. The moment to put things right had passed a long time ago.

When Marta went back into the kitchen to make more coffee, I turned to the albums, placed on the low table for just such a moment. I did not expect her to return too soon.

There were pictures of Father alone, with Marta, with their son, and the three of them. Happy family photos, the kind I had always daydreamed about. A mother and father with their child. Yet it must have been as difficult for Marta, as it had been for Mother, maybe even worse.

As I turned the pages, I filled in the blanks behind the toasts to each other, the loving looks, the domestic scenes. Father had actually maintained a separate apartment in Pärnu, near his theater. Mother's friend Ellen had kept us posted. I mistook a photo of my niece for one of me, which Mother had sent to Ellen when I was eighteen. I turned it over and sure enough, mother had written a humorous blurb on the back: "Heir to Tambu Farm."

Before I left, Marta wanted to show me something. She took me to the study.

"This was your father's desk," she said and opened the middle drawer. It was empty. "I want you to know there was a small square of plastic film in here, filled with dried grass." She touched her fingers to the wood. "Had I known you would come here I would have kept it. I'm sorry I threw it away when I cleaned out the desk."

Over the years I'm sure Father must have often wondered how he had gone from not wanting any dependents to having two families and two children. I think he just let fate write the script for him as he went along, in much the same way as my own had been written.

After leaving Marta's apartment I went to the Central library, where I read newspaper articles that had to do with my family. More of the same! The magical mystery tour was still on. I read that Unki had been a French Army Officer who had rescued us from the DP camp and taken us to London. Wonderful!

More serious, however, was a story about how Father had been mobilized into the infamous Yaroslavl Ensemble, in deepest Russia, where many prominent artists and musicians had been sent during the 1940s. That could not have been true!

From the library to the Theater Museum to check the Yaroslavl dates against his biography and his productions. The Yaroslavl story was not true. Father had been in Estonia the whole time. I noted the name of the journalist who had written the piece and arranged to meet with him.

Oskar Kuningas, the journalist, was in his eighties. He was an old man bent and crumpled like a much-thumbed manuscript, living in a house held up by books. The piled books, from floor to ceiling, began at the front door and continued through the hall into the living room. A passage to the kitchen was also lined with books, as were the stairs to the second floor. I guessed the rest of the house was similarly insulated by the written word.

Mr. Kuningas welcomed me with a cheerful twinkle in his eyes and threaded me through the dusty canyons of precariously balanced volumes to a central island of light where he had his desk. Even the windowsills were filled with books, leaving just enough light at the top to tell if it was night or day. It was a sunny day. Scattered rays of sunlight revealed the dust motes that floated in the air, opaque as falling snow. The overall effect was that of an ancient tomb, but there was nothing mummy-like about the man or his wife. She was sitting in a wheelchair beside the desk, one useless hand across some files and the other hand outstretched and welcoming. A table lamp illuminated this oasis of action. We made introductions, but they already knew whom I was. They had been expecting me. In a way this was an occasion for them—meeting Ernst Enno's granddaughter.

After the polite preambles, we got down to business. I had come to ask about my father's years in the Yaroslavl ensemble. What was that all about?

Kuningas dismissed the question with an impatient gesture, but his eyes were kindly and he condensed his reply suitably. He had been a young newspaper reporter at the time. "If you want to spread misinformation, who better to approach than a journalist?"

"But why would he lie?"

Kuningas gave me a pitying look, the kind you would confer upon a child who asks why the sky is blue. It would take too long to explain. He had no time to unscramble for me the mental arithmetic of communism. Instead he reached across the desk and tapped the files upon which his wife's withered hand was firmly planted.

"Here is something far more important. I have kept these files for you, knowing that one day in the future you would turn up and would need them to write your grandfather's biography."

"I hadn't thought ...."

"But you will." He gave me a satisfied smile, revealing a mouth full of teeth stumps that would have made an American dentist blanch in horror.

"Let me tell you how I got these files." He leaned back and proceeded to tell me the story at length. His wife kept nodding to me. She had obviously had a stroke, but there was abundant life still behind the paralyzed extremities. Her eyes and ears were following every word.

In 1960, when he had heard that Aunt Alma had died, he had dropped everything and hurried to Haapsalu—along with every other journalist and reporter in the country.

The "Dear Erni" shawl (Enno's *suurrätt*) now on display at the Ernst Enno Reading Room Museum in Haapsalu.

Everybody had known about Enno's library of esoteric books and manuscripts that Alma had been trying to sell. Few had dared to possess them. Kuningas did not know how much of the collection was left, but he hoped to find something of interest. When he got there the house had already been ransacked, stripped of everything, but the wallpaper. Disappointed but not giving up, he had climbed the ladder to the empty attic where he had noticed how in some places the wallpaper had not looked quite right. He had stripped it back and uncovered pages and pages of Enno's original poems and writings. On a hunch he had also dug through the sand between the floor beams and had found folders filled with Grandmother's artwork, Mother's theater memorabilia and Grandfather's correspondence with other poets of his era. He also found some of Enno's as yet unpublished poems. It was all in the folders under his wife's useless hand. He now reached over, took them from her and presented them to me with a flourish.

I was stunned. I had come to Estonia hoping to have a good look around, dust off a few memories, shed a few tears, and then return to my real life. That monstrosity on my property had made it clear that I did not belong here. Instead quite the opposite had happened. Estonia had come to me, luring me with stories that should have been mine, with people I should have known, places where I should have been. It was showing me a life that could have been mine, but was not. Was God being deliberately cruel in showing me the full jigsaw puzzle picture in which I was the missing piece? Was He being kind, letting me see what might have been, but with a warning to leave well enough alone.

Kuningas was looking at me as though he knew exactly what was going on in my mind.

"I'll think about the biography," I told him.

He nodded and walked me to the door.

When I was on the bus I thought about what I had seen and been told about the life, the one I had missed. I had just received a course in citizenship among people who spoke my language and shared my roots, but that did not mean I could even claim kinship with my own flesh and blood. I had been removed and replaced. There was no doubt that lies had been a political necessity and a major part of survival under the Soviets. Still I felt betrayed. To put it more bluntly, I was reacting with English/American naiveté and was deeply hurt. Father had written us out of his life. He had denied the years he had been my Taat. Father's brother Rick was dead, but his wife still lived. She had told Marta she did not want to meet me. Grandmother Tomson, my Tambu Mamma had been told I was dead. Father's family had disowned us yet I had corresponded with him for five years, thanks to the KGB, and I was grateful for that – as ironic as that might seem. Otherwise no one here and nothing here had ever belonged to me.

It was time to re-hash, re-shuffle. From the photos in the albums Father's relationship with Marta seemed to have been a good one, maybe even better than when he had been with us. That my half-brother did not wish to know me made sense. That they had told grandmother Tomson, that I was dead was a blow as was the loss of our farm, mother's beloved Tambu. Despite her joking comment to Ellen, I was heir to nothing. I had been wiped out of my past and out of the lives of everyone we had left behind. The joke was on me. I had brought back all the missing pieces, thinking to fit them into place again, not suspecting that the place itself would no longer be there. With that thought I began to experience a final unraveling of Mother's and Grandmother's carefully hand-woven quilt, put together for me, of family and homeland, so I would have something to return to and people I could belong to; more than just the two of them and the little we had brought with us.

On the plane back to America I tried to pull together the remnants of what I had always thought of as my foundation and concluded that all I had ever possessed in Estonia had been that view from our kitchen window.

The cabin lights were off and the drone of the engines should have helped me sleep, but every time I closed my eyes I saw the brick monster that had robbed me of my horizon and the only home I had ever had. I was crossing an ocean of emptiness back to the British me, with the English accent and the American me who lacked a public culture of music and poetry. Yet I appreciated America's diversity and freedom of opportunity. To the familiar sounds of soda cans popping, and voices twanging the music of the Malls, I tried to inch away from the timeless absurdity of communism and decided to watch the in-flight movie. Estonia had managed without me. I would have to manage without it, but *if* Estonia regained independence ... IF ... the thought popped into my head at the sound of the cabin attendant yanking the tab off a can of Seven-up. IF such a thing were to happen then everything would change. The surly clerks and shop assistants would lose their jobs, of course, and all Soviet confiscated property would have to be returned to rightful owners. Property deeds and wills would be honored. I might still get my land back. From the mists of the 1940s, my thoughts made a quantum leap into the 1990s as though Grandmother had lit one of her candles or Mother had sat on the piano stool to play a short scherzo to change the mood. Amazing how quickly hope could be revived.

The next time I returned to Estonia was in the spring of 1992. Estonia had indeed regained its independence. I had filled out claim forms and sent them, along with relevant documents, to the Haapsalu authorities, asking that the plot at Supeluse Street 6, be returned to me because I was the legal owner of that land. I had registered the package and mailed it in December

362

1991, but had received no reply. I assumed my claim was not going to be honored.

I was in Haapsalu because Estonian television was doing documentaries about exiles returning home. My story was going to be produced under the title "The Mist on Two Shores."

The weather was still wintry, the kind when Grandmother would have kept me indoors, but it was dry and sunny. I hurried straight to Tchaikovsky's Bench on the former Evening Lagoon, now the Back Bay. The crumbling mud reservoir was even uglier than before because all the windows had been bricked in. This left a patched wall of many colors that the local graffiti artists had seen as an irresistibly blank page on which to express themselves with the obscene outpourings of the young and newly disenfranchised. The surroundings were the same as they had been in 1990, except that it was colder. The sanatorium's heating vents were spewing forth white and black vapor, and the hospital looked like a huge dragon breathing steam and smoke from its mouth and nostrils.

The fir tree had recovered. It had straightened its spine. Amazingly, also, the bare tree boles in the front garden had healed and were sprouting new shoots. New grass covered the worst of the litter, and little yellow flowers brought hope of better springs and summers in the future.

The promise of new life bothered me because this time I had come to say farewell and to accept the loss of my land. I had become helpless in a situation that needed lawyers in a country that had had no proper laws for nearly fifty years. Besides, American lawyers would demand big money, if they could even manage such a case. I had no money, only documents. I was relying on justice and fair play, the chinless euphemism on which the British had gained an Empire and lost its servants. The newspapers were full of articles about lawlessness and corruption that were turning the former Soviet Union into a modern day Wild West.

My mission to reclaim the past was proving fruitless. I had already accepted Estonia for what it was and had been willing to make new memories, determined to stop pining for something that was beyond my ability to reach; this time realistically. I had actually come to Haapsalu to place a wreath upon a long endured heartache suffered by Mother and Grandmother and close this painful wound for good.

As I walked around the monster I was glad of its decline, but at the same time, I was noting all the positive changes, the new tree shoots, the sleepy buds peeping out of the soil, clear changes that Estonia was coming back to life. Estonia had a future and was still intact, but I was not. I was seeing the revival and re-blossoming of a country, from which I had departed. The vigor of its determination seemed to even taunt my mood of dismay, reminding me that I had been the one who had left, and that the new republic was going to have a future that would not include me. I was still in exile—a temporary visitor, who would never again have a home here to come home to.

I was truly sorry I had never met Grandfather in real life. Only he could have advised me on how to overcome the crumbling of childhood memories

363

and the loss of lifelong dreams. Only he could have dissuaded me from seeking meaning in things that no longer existed—and perhaps had never existed.

It was in the summer of 1995, when I received a surprise letter from the Haapsalu authorities informing me of the court's decision Nr. 114, dated 7 July that I had indeed proved ownership of Supeluse Street 6, and my file would be forwarded to the town council, which would rule on the claim. A letter dated 8 February 1996, however, informed me that although I had been declared the rightful heir to the land it could not be returned to me because it was occupied by a structure (the monster) belonging to the owner of Supeluse 12, (the mud spa/workers' sanatorium), but that I would be compensated. A further letter dated 3 May 1996 reinforcing the decision. In July 1996, I received a further document which informed me that 14,873 EVP's (Government Notes) (about $200) had been put into a bank account in my name. Would I please sign that I had accepted the money?

It seemed a paltry sum for waterfront property. The legal description, 181 *ruutsülda* had no meaning for me, but the property was in the center of the bay, and in the real world was definitely worth more than $200. I wrote and appealed, but the appeal was turned down. Apparently they had sent me a letter on the 5 May, with limited response time. The letter had been returned to them marked "Post Box Closed." My protest had come too late.

The next time I was in Haapsalu I was shown the envelope in which the alleged letter had been sent and returned. Indeed the envelope was marked "Post Box Closed" yet correctly addressed to my house, not a Post Box. I had never had a Post Box in my life.

Admitting defeat I signed the receipt for the $200 in November 1996 and fired off another letter of formal protest, to the Haapsalu authorities, just for the record, pointing out that I had now been stripped of my property twice, first by the communists and the second time by the new Haapsalu government. I also cited that a house at number 4 Supeluse Street was on the market for $22,000. I was mad and even more upset when I read in the town's newspaper that the same person who owned the mud spa/workers' sanatorium and my land was a town official. Then I perked up when I read further along that the town was planning to develop the area around the Promenade and sell shares. The development would be called the Haapsalu Resort.

Believing that the properties had gone public, I wrote again, on 10 November 1997, and told them I wanted to buy shares.

Their reply this time was—yes indeed, a resort was planned, but shares had not yet been issued. They added that EVP notes could not be used to buy them. A later newspaper article suggested that the emission had lasted only a short time and the bulk of the shares had been bought by town leaders.

I was too far away and too ignorant of the laws in the country I had come to love all over again. It was time to step away and give up.

Though not yet! In August 1998 I saw an article in the Haapsalu newspaper "*Lääne Elu*" (*Western Life*), informing its readers that the same authorities

364

who had confiscated my land for peanuts were seeking a buyer for a totally crumbling wooden house a few lots down from mine. The town was hoping to sell it to a "creative member of the arts," who would develop it as an art gallery or similar venue to enhance the cultural tone of the Haapsalu Resort Complex. It mentioned that the house was at a wonderful location, in fact in "one of Haapsalu's three best areas," and was on sale for 550,000-600,000 Estonian kroons, (about $37,000). The article quoted someone making the comment that there was little chance of finding an artist in Estonia who could come up with almost a million kroons.

I read the article several times and thought I would have a bit of fun. I wrote to the same authorities with whom I had been playing bureaucratic chess since 1990, and applied for that house in the "best area of town." I noted that I qualified under the "arty type" specification and told them I would be happy to open the house to the public. I did not have the million kroons, but because the house was on the same street as the land that had been taken from me, we could do a simple swap. They could use the money they owed me to renovate the building and I would be glad to take up residence as a live-in docent.

Of course I did not receive a reply, but it was gratifying to know that the letter would end up in my file, representing a mill mouse that roared at the vicissitudes of changing fortunes.

In June 2010 I brought my son Tim with me to Haapsalu to his great-grandfather's 135th jubilee. We were given guest beds at the library. After speeches at the usual historic sites, we repaired back to the library for a small reception attended by council members. I said my few words, vaguely alluding to my repeated visits to Haapsalu, wearing out my friends' couches. My son wished his *vana-vana* great-grandfather a happy 135th, in Estonian, (with the help of his BlackBerry). The mayor of Haapsalu then got up and addressed the gathering. He said he was going to make every effort to try to solve my property problems. Everyone knew what we were actually talking about, I accepted the offer in the spirit of similar offers and promises, of the "one day" and "someday", but he impressed my son. "He promised," said Tim, and began typing into his BlackBerry with the solemnity of a scribe at the Final Judgment.

EPILOGUE

The difference between an exile and an emigrant is that the exile does not leave voluntarily, arrives with foreboding and exists in a country that will never become "home"; the original homeland becomes paradise lost. The emigrant cannot wait to get away, retains almost nothing of the past and has only hopes and dreams for the future.

The Baltic exiles maintained a unique identity and even though their numbers are dwindling (due to old age) they are still a cityful, a citadel of psychological resistance against worldwide apathy and unfair publicity. Their descendants are still trying to raise a universal conscience to a missing part of European history that equals the Holocaust, but because at that time the Russians were Allies, a confusion of context has been carried forward into the modern media and the free world does not yet fully understand or appreciate the suffering of the one hundred million victims of Communism worldwide.

The arrival of the Germans in 1941 interrupted the deportations to Siberia, but with a population of a little over one million people the Estonians were just as helpless to resist the Germans as they were the Russians. Overall Estonia lost a fifth of its population — killed, deported or fled. A similar situation occurred in Latvia and Lithuania. Then in 1945 the tragedy was compounded at Yalta. With another stroke of the pen, thousands more were written off.

At the beginning of the Cold War the Estonians who had escaped stopped calling themselves "refugees" and opted instead for the term "exiles" in line with the Oxford Dictionary definition: "long absence from one's country." They were never banished, but left of their own free will, fearing the returning Soviets would continue the killing and deporting, which they did.

In this memoir I have attempted to narrate an eidetic childhood in which the larger war is almost secondary to the smaller battles around personal relationships and the unexplained cruelties a child has no capacity to judge. A memoir is not a document about who did what and when, on a specific date, but who did what and when in a specific situation. A memoir is a passing caravan of events and characters creating an indelible impression on eyewitnesses, whether age seven or seventy, who write it down. One person's memoir becomes a book. A hundred similar books become history. While my story is based upon real events and real places, my knowledge of those places and events was limited. I was only seven years old when I left Estonia and only eight when the war ended. There are incidents that I cannot frame with words and frames that I cannot fill adequately with facts, but the scenes are as vivid now as they were at the time they happened. For that reason alone, I must dub this book a work of "faction"—a blending of fact and fiction; what my eyes saw and my mind perceived, without conception of time or space.

I'm not without possessions. Possessions await me all over the world. Some left there on purpose, others lost, stolen or given away. In Haapsalu, the few remnants of our refugee journey will be waiting for my son and his descendants in the Enno Reading Room/Museum at the Haapsalu City Annex. In Ranna, on Lake Peipsi, I have a pair of red boots. In Tallinn, several Union Jack tea mugs. I left a pair of sneakers in Nõmme and a pair of jeans in Tartu. In England I still visit my grandmother's rocking chair and bury my face in our kitchen towels, smelling of fried onions. I sit at my mother's writing desk and although I don't tell fortunes, I still have the cards she used to shuffle and I see her there forever, cigarette dangling from the corner her mouth, anxious to know her future.

Estonia is now a popular tourist destination. Many of the 13th and 14th century churches have been restored and hold choral recitals during the white nights of the summer months.

In 1994 I was coming back to my hotel around one o'clock in the morning. Passing a church I heard singing inside. It was Andrew Lloyd Webber's *Requiem*. A shaft of silvery white light was streaming out of a bank of dark clouds and was reflected on the copper roof. The effect was of the sky having opened, just as it did when I was scattering mother's ashes on Ilkley moor, and I was not sure whether the music was rising up from the church or was being beamed down from heaven, but it did remind me that we are always under the same sky no matter what country we're in and the view from our kitchen window will never change because the sky will always guide me.

In June 2000 I finished the Enno biography, for his 125th Jubilee. Standing on the Promenade, gazing over the quiet lagoon, I was beset by the unreliability of existence. I was wondering whether I would ever come back. Then it hit me — I had never left!

I am grateful that Great Britain offered us a refuge, grateful for the English orphanage experience which taught me excellent language skills and fostered in me a fighting spirit to keep going against all odds, but also to surrender useless pride, and move on. I am just as grateful to be in America, a citizen of the free world, yet deep down, in my innermost being a certain amount of isolation remains unappeased. I can still close my eyes at night, before going to sleep, and recall that other place, for which I yearned, which still represents the loss of something I cannot explain, cannot remember and will never forget.

Had England been the "Promised Land?" Would England become "The Kingdom?" Will we be speaking English in heaven or will we have to learn yet another language? Mämmä gave me a little black book of her own poems to take to London. She had written on the flyleaf, "I touched your heart once, and the light from that touch remained on my fingertips."

It is only now that I realize the light she attributed to me was a reflection of her own.

About the Author

Elin was born in Tallinn, Estonia, in July 1937. Her parents were well-known actors who lived in the theatre dressing room during the 'season'. After Elin was born she was given to her grandmother and great-aunt Alma Saul in Haapsalu, Estonia. Her grandmother, "Mämmä" was a trained artist and widow of the respected Estonian poet Ernst Enno. Alma Saul was a music teacher. Elin was raised by the two old ladies in a house dedicated to art, poetry, literature and music. Her parents came to visit during the theatre's "off-season".

After the war broke out in 1939 the Russians began to move into the Baltic States. Elin and her family escaped the mass deportations to Siberia on June 14th, 1941. The deportations were interrupted when the battlefront shifted toward Russia, but then it shifted again, and in 1944 the Russians were returning. Knowing that the deportations would resume 70-80,000 Estonians fled to the West. Elin, her mother and grandmother set off in September 1944 on a journey of survival that took them through the war, the DP Camps and eventually to Northern England. Elin grew up in post-war Great Britain, where she acquired a fighting spirit under difficult circumstances. She began to write and was published at an early age in Estonian and English. She later attended Drama school in London and got parts on TV and B-Films. She wrote for the BBC and was published in English by Penguin/Kestrel, Thomas Nelson and Dell. She has written for magazines, newspapers and received numerous prizes in both languages and the White Star V Class Medal from the President of Estonia in 2004. Her current mission is to preserve the true history of the Baltic States during WWII, in the ideological battle between Hitler and Stalin that continues to haunt world opinion and will do, for generations to come.

elingottschalk@gmail.com
www.linkedin.com/pub/elin-toona-gottschalk
www.facebook.com/pages/Author-Elin-Toona-Gottschalk/335097749975065